HANGŬL

Simple Vowels		Diphthongs							
아	a (*father*)	야	ya (*yard*)						
어	ŏ (*hut*)	여	yŏ. (*yearn*)						
오	o (*home*)	요	yo (*yoke*)	와	wa (*wan*)	왜	wae (*wag*)		
우	u (*do*)	유	yu (*you*)	위	wi (*wield*)	워	wo (*won*)	웨	we (*wet*)
으	ŭ (*taken*)	의	ŭi (*taken + we*)						
이	i (*ink*)								
애	ae (*hat*)	얘	yae (*yam*)						
에	e (*met*)	예	ye (*yes*)						
외	oe (*Köln*)								

The "o" written with each vowel is an unvoiced consonant which functions to indicate where an initial consonant maybe affixed to the vowel when writing a syllable. See the inside back cover for information on forming syllables.

Standard
KOREAN-ENGLISH
DICTIONARY

For Foreigners

Edited by
Gene S. Rhie (이 시진) & B. J. Jones

HOLLYM

First published in 1986
Reprinted in 1989
by Hollym International Corp.
18 Donald Place
Elizabeth, New Jersey 07208 U.S.A.

Published simultaneously in Korea
by Hollym Corporation; Publishers
14-5 Kwanchol-dong, Chongno-gu, Seoul, Korea
Phone: (02)735-7554   FAX: (02)730-5149

ISBN: 0-930878-49-3
Library of Congress Catalog Card Number: 85-80494

Printed in Korea

Preface

Since the "Standard English-Korean Dictionary for Foreigners" was first published in 1982, many of its users and book reviewers expressed a strong desire to see a Korean-English version as its companion volume. The number of people who are interested in learning Korean has grown tremendously in recent years throughout the world.

This dictionary, as a companion to the "Standard English-Korean Dictionary for Foreigners", was designed as a convenient reference tool for those who want to find necessary words easily and quickly. Therefore, a special effort was made to select the most useful and essential words, basing their romanization upon Ministry of Education system which accommodates McCune-Reischauer system. This would be especially helpful for those travelling to Korea.

To illustrate the entries which do not transfer the concepts in a single English word, this dictionary provides appropriate synonyms and contexts while maintaining its simplicity.

The editors are grateful to the editorial staff members whose commitment and enthusiasm made it possible to complete this dictionary after many years of endurance. They also wish to solicit further suggestions and advice to make this publication more useful and accurate.

Gene S. Rhie
B. J. Jones

Korean Alphabet I

	ㄱ k(g)	ㄴ n	ㄷ t(d)	ㄹ r(l)	ㅁ m	ㅂ p(b)	ㅅ s(sh)
ㅏ a	가 k(g)a	나 na	다 t(d)a	라 r(l)a	마 ma	바 p(b)a	사 sa
ㅑ ya	갸 k(g)ya	냐 nya	댜 t(d)ya	랴 r(l)ya	먀 mya	뱌 p(b)ya	샤 sya
ㅓ ŏ	거 k(g)ŏ	너 nŏ	더 t(d)ŏ	러 r(l)ŏ	머 mŏ	버 p(b)ŏ	서 sŏ
ㅕ yŏ	겨 k(g)yŏ	녀 nyŏ	뎌 t(d)yŏ	려 r(l)yŏ	며 myŏ	벼 p(b)yŏ	셔 syŏ
ㅗ o	고 k(g)o	노 no	도 t(d)o	로 r(l)o	모 mo	보 p(b)o	소 so
ㅛ yo	교 k(g)yo	뇨 nyo	됴 t(d)yo	료 r(l)yo	묘 myo	뵤 p(b)yo	쇼 syo
ㅜ u	구 k(g)u	누 nu	두 t(d)u	루 r(l)u	무 mu	부 p(b)u	수 su
ㅠ yu	규 k(g)yu	뉴 nyu	듀 t(d)yu	류 r(l)yu	뮤 myu	뷰 p(b)yu	슈 syu
ㅡ ŭ	그 k(g)ŭ	느 nŭ	드 t(d)ŭ	르 r(l)ŭ	므 mŭ	브 p(b)ŭ	스 sŭ
ㅣ i	기 k(g)i	니 ni	디 t(d)i	리 r(l)i	미 mi	비 p(b)i	시 shi

Korean Alphabet II

○ ng	ㅈ ch(j)	ㅊ ch'	ㅋ k'	ㅌ t'	ㅍ p'	ㅎ h
아 a	자 ch(j)a	차 ch'a	카 k'a	타 t'a	파 p'a	하 ha
야 ya	쟈 ch(j)ya	챠 ch'ya	캬 k'ya	탸 t'ya	퍄 p'ya	햐 hya
어 ŏ	저 ch(j)ŏ	쳐 ch'ŏ	커 k'ŏ	터 t'ŏ	퍼 p'ŏ	허 hŏ
여 yŏ	져 ch(j)yŏ	쳐 ch'yŏ	켜 k'yŏ	텨 t'yŏ	펴 p'yŏ	혀 hyŏ
오 o	조 ch(j)o	초 ch'o	코 k'o	토 t'o	포 p'o	호 ho
요 yo	죠 ch(j)yo	쵸 ch'yo	쿄 k'yo	툐 t'yo	표 p'yo	효 hyo
우 u	주 ch(j)u	추 ch'u	쿠 k'u	투 t'u	푸 p'u	후 hu
유 yu	쥬 ch(j)yu	츄 ch'yu	큐 k'yu	튜 t'yu	퓨 p'yu	휴 hyu
으 ŭ	즈 ch(j)ŭ	츠 ch'ŭ	크 k'ŭ	트 t'ŭ	프 p'ŭ	흐 hŭ
이 i	지 ch(j)i	치 ch'i	키 k'i	티 t'i	피 p'i	히 hi

The Korean Alphabet and Their Sounds

(1) Vowels

1) Simple:

Korean Letter		Romanization	English sound
ㅏ	아	a	as *ah*
ㅓ	어	ŏ	as h*u*t
ㅗ	오	o	as *oh*
ㅜ	우	u	as d*o*
ㅡ	으	ŭ	as t*a*ken
ㅣ	이	i	as *i*nk
ㅐ	애	ae	as h*a*nd
ㅔ	에	e	as m*e*t
ㅚ	외	oe	as K*ö*ln

2) Compound:

Korean Letter		Romanization	English sound
ㅑ	야	ya	as *ya*rd
ㅕ	여	yŏ	as *yea*rn
ㅛ	요	yo	as *yo*ke
ㅠ	유	yu	as *you*
ㅒ	얘	yae	as *ya*m
ㅖ	예	ye	as *ye*s
ㅟ	위	wi	as *wi*eld
ㅢ	의	ŭi	as taken+we
ㅘ	와	wa	as *wa*n
ㅙ	왜	wae	as *wa*g
ㅝ	워	wo	as *wo*n
ㅞ	웨	we	as *we*t

(2) Consonants

1) Simple:

Korean Letter	Romanization	English sound
ㄱ	k (g)	as *k*ing or *g*rocer
ㄴ	n	as *n*ame
ㄷ	t (d)	as *t*oy or *d*epend
ㄹ	r (l)	as *r*ain or *l*ily
ㅁ	m	as *m*other
ㅂ	p (b)	as *p*in or *b*ook
ㅅ	s (sh)	as *s*peech
ㅇ	ng	as *ah* or ki*ng*
ㅈ	ch (j)	as *J*ohn
ㅊ	ch'	as *ch*ur*ch*
ㅋ	k'	as *k*ite
ㅌ	t'	as *t*ank
ㅍ	p'	as *p*um*p*
ㅎ	h	as *h*igh

2) Double:

Korean Letter	Romanization	English sound
ㄲ	kk	as *sk*y or Ja*ck*
ㄸ	tt	as *st*ay
ㅃ	pp	as *sp*y
ㅆ	ss	as e*ss*ential
ㅉ	tch	as *j*oy

A Comprehensive Chart for the Romanization of the Korean Language

I Consonants (Showing euphonic changes in consonant sequences within words.)

Final \ Initial	ㄱ K	ㄴ N	ㄷ T	ㄹ (R)	ㅁ M	ㅂ P	ㅅ S	ㅈ CH	ㅊ CH'	ㅋ K'	ㅌ T'	ㅍ P'	ㅎ H	ㄲ KK	ㄸ TT	ㅃ PP	ㅆ SS	ㅉ TCH
ㄱ,ㅋ,ㄲ,ㄳ,ㅌ	K	ng-		ngn- ng-	ng-								-k'	kk				
ㄴ	N	n-g		-d	ll		-b	s-	-j									
ㄷ,ㅅ,ㅈ,ㅊ,ㅌ,ㅆ,ㄸ	N	-k'	n-			(nn) n-	(p')	s-		-ch'								ss	tch
ㅂ	P		m-			mn m-		ms-									pp		
ㅎ	H	k'	n-	t'		(nn) n-	-p'	s-	ch'		k'				k' kk				
ㄹ (verb) ㄼ, ㄾ	L		ll											r-					
ㄹ, ㅄ (noun)	L	-g		-l	-l		-b	ls-		ls-ch'				r-					
ㄾ	L	-k'		-l			-b		-ch'					r-					
ㅁ (noun)	M	-g		-d	-n		-b		-j										
ㅁ, ㄻ (verb)	M	-g		-d	-n		-b		-j										
ㅂ, ㄼ, ㄿ, ㅄ	P	-b						ms-											
ㅇ	NG	-g			-n		-b		-j										
ㅇ (+ㅅ)	NG				-n												(tt)		(tch)
ㅎ	H	k'	n-	t'		(nn) n-		s-	ch'								pp		

II Vowels

ㅏ	ㅑ	ㅓ	ㅕ	ㅗ	ㅛ	ㅜ	ㅠ	ㅡ	ㅣ	ㅘ	ㅝ	ㅐ	ㅔ	ㅚ	ㅟ	ㅢ	ㅙ	ㅞ	ㅒ	ㅖ
a	ya	ŏ	yŏ	o	yo	u	yu	ŭ	i	wa	wo	ae	e	oe	wi	ŭi	wae	we	yae	ye

Simplified Chart for the Romanization

Initial \ Final		ㄱ	ㄴ	ㄹ	ㅁ	ㅂ	ㅇ
		K	N	L	M	P	NG
ㅇ		g	n	r	m	b	ng
ㄱ	K	kk	n-g(k)	lg(k)	mg(k)	pk	ngg(k)
ㄴ	N	ngn	nn	ll	mn	mn	ngn
ㄷ	T	kt	nd(t)	lt(d)	md(t)	pt	ngd(t)
ㄹ	(R)	ngn	ll	ll	mn	mn	ngn
ㅁ	M	ngm	nm	lm	mm	mm	ngm
ㅂ	P	kp	nb(p)	lb(p)	mb(p)	pp	ngb(p)
ㅅ	S	ks	ns	ls	ms	ps	ngs
ㅈ	CH	kch	nj(ch)	lj(ch)	mj(ch)	pch	ngj(ch)
ㅊ	CH'	kch'	nch'	lch'	mch'	pch'	ngch'
ㅋ	K'	kk'	nk'	lk'	mk'	pk'	ngk'
ㅌ	T'	kt'	nt'	lt'	mt'	pt'	ngt'
ㅍ	P'	kp'	np'	lp'	mp'	pp'	ngp'
ㅎ	H	k'	nh	rh	mh	p'	ngh

Guidelines for the Romanization of Korean

(1) Basic Principles for Transcription

1) Romanization is based on standard Korean pronunciation.
2) No symbols except Roman letters are used, so far as possible.
3) Romanization follows the principle of 'one letter (or set of letters) per phoneme.'

(2) Summary of the Transcription System

1) Vowels are transcribed as follows:

simple vowels ㅏ ㅓ ㅗ ㅜ ㅡ ㅣ ㅐ ㅔ ㅚ
         a ŏ o u ŭ i ae e oe

diphthongs ㅑ ㅕ ㅛ ㅠ ㅒ ㅖ ㅢ ㅘ ㅝ ㅙ ㅞ ㅟ
        ya yŏ yo yu yae ye ŭi wa wo wae we wi

[Note] Long vowels are not marked in transcription.

2) Consonants are transcribed as follows:

plosives (stops)	ㄱ	ㄲ	ㅋ
	k, g	kk	k'
	ㄷ	ㄸ	ㅌ
	t, d	tt	t'
	ㅂ	ㅃ	ㅍ
	p, b	pp	p'
affricates	ㅈ	ㅉ	ㅊ
	ch, j	tch	ch'
fricatives	ㅅ	ㅆ	ㅎ
	s, sh	ss	h

nasals	ㅁ	ㄴ	ㅇ
	m	n	ng
liquids	ㄹ		
	r, l		

[Note 1] ㄱ, ㄷ, ㅂ and ㅈ are transcribed respectively as *g*, *d*, *b* and *j*, between vowels, or between ㄴ, ㄹ, ㅁ, or ㅇ and a vowel; otherwise they are transcribed as *k, t, p,* and *ch*.

e.g.　가구 kagu　바둑 paduk　갈비 kalbi 제주 Cheju 담배 tambae 받침 patch'im

[Note 2] ㅅ is transcribed as *s* except in the case of 시, when it is transcribed as *sh*.

e.g.　시루 shiru 신안 Shinan 신촌 Shinch'on 부산 Pusan 상표 sangp'yo 황소 hwangso

[Note 3] ㄹ is transcribed as *r* before a vowel, and as *l* before a consonant or at the end of a word: ㄹㄹ is transcribed as *ll*.

e.g.　사랑 sarang 물건 mulgŏn 발 pal 진달래 chindallae

(3) Special Provisions for Transcription

1) When Korean sound values change as in the following cases, the results of those changes are transcribed as follows:

1. The case of assimilation of adjacent consonants

e.g.　냇 물 naenmul　　부엌문 puŏngmun 낚는다 nangnŭnda 닫는다 tannŭnda 갚는다 kamnŭnda 진 리 chilli 심 리 shimni　　압 력 amnyŏk

독 립 tongnip

2. The case of the epenthetic ㄴ and ㄹ

e.g. 가랑잎 karangnip　낯 일 nannil
담 요 tamnyo　홑이불 honnibul
풀 잎 p'ullip　물 약 mullyak

3. The case of palatalization

e.g. 굳 이 kuji　해돋이 haedoji
같 이 kach'i

4. The case when ㄱ, ㄷ, ㅂ and ㅈ are adjacent to ㅎ

e.g. 국 화 kuk'wa　낳 다 nat'a
밟히다 palp'ida　맞히다 mach'ida

[Note] The tense (or glottalized) sounds, which occur in cases when morphemes are compounded as in the examples below, are transcribed by voiceless consonants.

e.g. 장기 (長技) changki　사 건 sakŏn
냇 가 naetka　작 두 chaktu
신 다 shinta　산 불 sanpul

2) When there is a possibility of confusion in pronunciation, or a need for segmentation, a hyphen '-' may be used.

e.g. 연 구 yŏn-gu　잔기 (殘期) chan-gi
물가에 mulka-e　종로에 Chongno-e

[Note] In the transcription of personal names and names of administrative units, assimilated sound changes before or after a hyphen are not transcribed.

e.g. 김 복남 Kim Pok-nam
사북면 Sabuk-myŏn

3) The first letter is capitalized in proper names.

e.g. 인 천 Inch'ŏn　대 구 Taegu

세 종 Sejong

4) Personal names are written by family name first, followed by a space and then the given name. A hyphen will separate given names, except that non-Sino-Korean given names may be joined without a hyphen.

  e.g. 김정호 Kim Chŏng-ho
        남궁 동자 Namgung Tong-cha
        손 미희자 Son Mi-hŭi-cha
        정 마리아 Chŏng Maria

5) In spite of the Note to 2) above, administrative units such as 도, 시, 군, 구, 읍, 면, 리, 동 and 가 are transcribed respectively as *do, shi, gun, gu, ŭp, myŏn, ri, dong*, and *ga* and are preceded by a hyphen.

  e.g. 충청북도 Ch'ungch'ŏngbuk-do
        제 주 도 Chĕju-do
        의정부시 Ŭijŏngbu-shi
        파 주 군 P'aju-gun
        도 봉 구 Tobong-gu
        신 창 읍 Shinch'ang-ŭp
        주 내 면 Chunae-myŏn
        인 왕 리 Inwang-ri
        당 산 동 Tangsan-dong
        봉천 2 동 Pongch'ŏn 2-dong
        종로 2 가 Chongno 2-ga
        퇴계로 5 가 T'oegyero 5-ga

  [Note] Terms for administrative units such as 특별시, 직할시, 시, 군, 읍 and so on may be omitted.

  e.g. 부산직할시 Pusan   신창읍 Shinch'ang

6) Names of geographic features, cultural prop-

erties, and man-made structures may be written without hyphens.

e.g.
남 산　Namsan
속 리 산　Songnisan
금 　강　Kŭmgang
독 　도　Tokto
해 운 대　Haeundae
경 복 궁　Kyŏngbokkung
도산서원　Tosansŏwon
불 국 사　Pulguksa
현 충 사　Hyŏnch'ungsa
독 립 문　Tongnimmun

[Note] Hyphens may be inserted in words of five syllables or more.

e.g. 금동 미륵보살 반가상　Kŭmdong-mirŭk-posal-pan-gasang

7) Some proper names, which cannot be abruptly changed in view of international practices and common longstanding transcriptions, may be written as follows:

e.g.
서 울　Seoul　　이순신　Yi Sun-shin
연 세　Yonsei　　이 화　Ewha
이승만　Syngman Rhee

8) When they are difficult to print or to type-write, the breve '˘' in ŏ, ŭ, yŏ, and ŭi, and the apostrophe ' ' ' in k', t', p', and ch', may be omitted as long as there is no confusion in meaning.

A

a 아 Ah!; Oh!; O dear; O!; Dear me!

abŏji 아버지 father; papa; daddy; dad.

abu 아부 flattery. *abuhada* 아부하다 flatter; fawn.

ach'im 아침 morning. *ach'ime* 아침에 in the morning.

ach'im chŏnyŏk 아침 저녁 morning and evening.

ach'ŏm 아첨 →**abu** 아부.

adamhada 아담하다 (be) refined; elegant; tidy; neat; cozy.

adong 아동 child; juvenile. *adongŭi* 아동의 juvenile.

adŭk'ada 아득하다 (be) far; distant; remote; dim. *adŭk'an yennal* 아득한 옛날 dim past.

adŭl 아들 son; boy. *adŭlttal* 아들딸 son(s) and daughter(s).

aech'ak 애착 attachment; affection; love.

aech'o 애초. *aech'o-e* 애초에 at first; at the start.

aech'ŏ 애처 one's (beloved) wife. *aech'ŏga* 애처가 devoted husband.

aech'ŏropta 애처롭다 (be) pitiful; pitiable; touching.

aedangch'o 애당초 →**aech'o** 애초.

aedo 애도 condolence; grief; mourning. *aedohada* 애도하다 mourn; lament; grieve.

aedok 애독. *aedok'ada* 애독하다 read with pleasure. *aedokcha* 애독자 (regular) reader; subscriber.

aeguk 애국 love of one's country; patriotism. *aeguk-chŏk* 애국적 patriotic. *aegukcha* 애국자 patriot.

aegukka 애국가 national anthem.

aegyo 애교 charms. *aegyo innŭn* 애교 있는 attractive; charming.

aeho 애호 love; liking. *aehohada* 애호하다 love;

be fond (of).

aein 애인 (her) lover; (his) lover; sweetheart.

aejijungjihada 애지중지하다 prize; cherish; treasure; think[make] much of; set high value(upon).

aejŏng 애정 love; affection. *aejŏngi innŭn* 애정이 있는 affectionate.

aeju 애주. *aejuhada* 애주하다 be fond of liquor.

aek 액 amount; sum. *saengsan[sobi]aek* 생산[소비]액 amount of production[consumption].

aekch'e 액체 liquid; fluid. *aekch'e yŏllyo* 액체 연료 liquid fuel.

aekku 애꾸 one-eyed person; blind of an[one] eye.

aeksu 액수 sum; amount.

aemae 애매. *aemaehan* 애매한 vague; ambiguous.

aemŏgida 애먹이다 harass; annoy; bewilder; embarrass.

aemŏkta 애먹다 have a hard time (with); have bitter experience.

aengmusae 앵무새 parrot.

aengmyŏn 액면 face-value; par value; denomination.

aero 애로 narrow path; bottleneck.

aesŏk 애석. *aesŏk'ada* 애석하다 sad; sorrowful; mournful; regrettable.

aessŭda 애쓰다 exert[strain] oneself; make effort.

aet'ada 애타다 be anxious (about); be nervous[much worried] (about).

aewŏn 애원 supplication; entreaty. *aewŏnhada* 애원하다 entreat; implore; supplicate.

agassi 아가씨 ① young lady; girl; maid(en) ② Miss; young lady!

agi 아기 ① baby; infant ② (daughter; daughter-in-law) dear; darling.

agin 악인 bad[wicked] man; villain.

agŭi 악의 evil intention; ill will; malice.

agun 악운 ill luck; bad fortune; evil fate.

agungi 아궁이 fuel hole; furnace.

agyo 아교 glue.

ahop 아홉 nine. *ahoptchae* 아홉째 the ninth.

ahŭn 아흔 ninety. *ahŭntchae* 아흔째 the ninetieth.

ahŭre 아흐레 nine days; the ninth day (of a month).

ai 아이 child; kid; boy-child; boy; girl-child; girl.

ajanggŏrida 아장거리다 toddle; totter; shamble.

ajik 아직 yet; as yet; still.

ajikkaji 아직까지 so[thus] far; up to now; till now; up to the present.

aju 아주 very; quite; utterly; exceedingly.

ajumoni 아주머니 aunt; auntie.

ak 악 badness; evil; wrong; vice; wickedness.

akchil 악질. *akchirŭi* 악질의 vicious; ill-natured; evil. *akchil punja* 악질 분자 bad elements.

akch'wi 악취 bad[nasty] smell; offensive odo(u)r; stink; stench.

akkapta 아깝다 ① (be) pitiful; regrettable ② (be) dear; precious. *akkapkedo* 아깝게도 regrettably; lamentably.

akki 악기 musical instrument.

akkida 아끼다 ① grudge; spare; be stingy ② value; prize; hold (a thing) dear.

akkimŏpshi 아낌없이 unsparingly; ungrudgingly; without stint.

akpo 악보 musical note; sheet music; score. *akpojip* 악보집 music book.

akp'yŏng 악평 bad reputation; ill repute. *akp'yŏng hada* 악평하다 speak ill of.

aksa 악사 band(s) man; musician.

aksu 악수 handshake. *aksuhada* 악수하다 shake hand (with).

aktae 악대 (musical) band; brass band.

aktan 악단 orchestra. *kyohyangaktan* 교향악단 symphony orchestra.

aktŏk 악덕 vice; immorality. *aktŏk sangin* 악덕 상인 wicked dealers.

al 알 egg; spawn; roe. *arŭl nat'a* 알을 낳다 lay an egg; spawn.

alda 알다 know; be informed of; be aware of.

allak 안락 ease; comfort. *allak'ada* 안락하다 (be) easy; comfortable.

allida 알리다 let (a person) know; inform; notify.

allŭnsori 앓는소리 moaning; groaning, *allŭnsori-hada* 앓는소리하다 moan; groan.

allyak 알약 tablet; tabloid.

allyŏjida 알려지다 be[become] known (to); come to light. *chal allyŏjin* 잘 알려진 well-known; famous.

allyŏk 알력 friction; discord; strife.

almatta 알맞다 (be) fit; becoming; suitable.

alt'a 앓다 be ill (with); be sick; suffer from.

altcha 알짜 cream; essence; choice.

alttŭrhada 알뜰하다 (be) thrifty; frugal; economical. *alttŭrhi* 알뜰히 frugally; thriftily.

am 암 cancer. *wi*[*p'ye, chagung*]*am* 위[폐, 자궁] 암 stomach[lung, uterine] cancer.

ama 아마 probably; perhaps; maybe; possibly; presumably.

amch'o 암초 reef; (sunken) rock.

amgi 암기. *amgihada* 암기하다 learn[get] by heart;

memorize (*Am.*).

amho 암호 code; cipher; password.

amk'ae 암캐 she-dog; bitch.

ammŏri 앞머리 forehead; forefront.

amu ttae 아무 때 any time; any day; whenever; always; all the time.

amnal 앞날 future; days ahead[to come].

amnyŏk 압력 pressure; stress. *amnyŏgŭl kahada* 압력을 가하다 give[apply] pressure (to). *amnyŏk-sot* 압력솥 pressure cooker.

amp'yosang 암표상 ticket broker; speculator(*Am.*).

amsal 암살 assassination. *amsarhada* 암살하다 assassinate; murder. *amsalcha* 암살자 assassin.

amsan 암산 mental arithmetic. *amsanhada* 암산하다 do (a sum) in mental arithmetic.

amshi 암시 hint; suggestion. *amshihada* 암시하다 hint (at); suggest.

amshijang 암시장 black market.

amt'ak 암탉 hen; pullet.

amtallŏ 암달러 black-market dollar.

amugae 아무개 Mr. [Mrs., Miss] So and so; certain person. *Kim amugae* 김 아무개 certain Mr. Kim; one Kim.

amulda 아물다 heal (up); be healed (of a wound).

amuraedo 아무래도 anyhow; anyway; for anything; come what may.

amuri 아무리 however much; no matter how.

amutchorok 아무쪼록 by all means; as much as one can; in any case; at any cost.

an 안 ① inside; interior ② in; within; less than. *ane* 안에 within; inside; in. *anŭrobut'ŏ* 안으로 부터 from the inside; from within.

anae 아내 wife; better-half; spouse.

anangne 아낙네 woman; wife.

anchuin 안주인 lady of the house; hostess.

andoeda 안되다 ① must not; shall not ② be sorry; ⌐be a pity.

an-gae 안개 fog; mist.

anggap'ŭm 앙갚음 revenge; retaliation. *anggap'ŭmhada* 앙갚음하다 revenge oneself; get revenge.

an-gida 안기다 (be) embraced; be in (a person's) arms[bosom].

angma 악마 evil spirit; devil; demon.

angmong 악몽 bad[evil] dream; nightmare.

angshim 앙심 grudge; enmity. *angshimŭl p'umta* 앙심을 품다 bear[nurse] a grudge against.

an-gyŏng 안경 spectacles; glasses.

anikkopta 아니꼽다 ① (be) sickening; disgusting ② be nauseated; be sick.

anjŏlbujŏl mot'ada 안절부절 못하다 be restless [nervous]; flutter; be irritated.

anjŏn 안전 safety; security. *anjŏnhan* 안전한 safe; secure. *anjŏnhi* 안전히 safely; securely.

anjŏng 안정 stability; steadiness.

annyŏng 안녕 public peace. *Annyŏnghashimnikka?* 안녕하십니까? ① How are you? ② Good morning [afternoon, evening]. *Annyonghi ka[kye]shipshio.* 안녕히 가[계]십시오. Good-bye.

anju 안주 appetizer dishes; side dish.

anma 안마 massage. *anmahada* 안마하다 massage.

annae 안내 guidance; leading. *annaehada* 안내하다 guide; conduct. *annaeyang* 안내양 conductress.

anp'ak 안팎 ① interior and exterior; inside and outside. ② about; some; around(*Am.*).

ansaek 안색 complexion; countenance.

anshikku 안식구 female members of a family.

anshim 안심 relief; peace[ease] of mind. *anshim-hada* 안심하다 feel at rest; feel easy (about).

ansonnim 안손님 lady visitor; woman caller.

anta 안다 ① hold[carry] in one's arm(s); embrace; hug. ② answer for; take charge of.

anta 앉다 sit down; take a seat; be seated.

ant'akkapta 안타깝다 ① (be) impatient; irritated ② (be) pitiful; pitiable.

anŭk'ada 아늑하다 (be) cozy; snug; comfortable.

anyak 안약 eye-water[lotion]; eye drops.

ap 앞 front; fore. *ap'ŭi* 앞의 front; preceding. *ap'e* 앞에 in front of; ahead.

apchabi 앞잡이 agent; tool; cat's-paw.

apchi 압지 blotting paper; (paper) blotter.

apch'ima 앞치마 apron. *apch'imarŭl turŭda* 앞치마를 두르다 put on[wear] an apron.

apchip 앞집 house in front.

apch'uk 압축 compression; condensation. *apch'uk'ada* 압축하다 compress; condense.

apkasŭm 앞가슴 breast; chest (part).

appa 아빠 papa; daddy; dad; pop(*Am.*).

appak 압박 pressure; oppression. *appak'ada* 압박하다 oppress; suppress.

appak'wi 앞바퀴 fore wheel; front wheel.

appal 앞발 paw; forefoot; foreleg.

apsŏ 앞서 before; previously; already.

apsu 압수 confiscation; seizure. *apsuhada* 압수하다 seize; confiscate.

aptanggida 앞당기다 move[carry] up; advance.

apto 압도. *aptohada* 압도하다 overwhelm; overcome; overpower. *aptojŏk[ŭro]* 압도적[으로]

overwhelming[ly]; sweeping[ly].

aptwi 앞뒤 before and behind; front and rear.

ap'ŭda 아프다 (be) painful; sore; have[feel] a pain.

ap'yŏn 아편 opium; opiate.

arae 아래 low part; foot; bottom; base. *araeŭi* 아래의 lower; under. *araee* 아래에 down; under; beneath; below.

araech'ŭng 아래충 downstairs. *araech'ŭngesŏ[ŭro]* 아래충에서[으로] downstairs.

araessaram 아랫사람 one's junior; one's inferior; subordinate.

araewi 아래위 up and down; above and below; high and low.

arajuda 알아주다 acknowledge; recognize; appreciate.

aramach'ida 알아맞히다 guess right; make a good guess.

aranaeda 알아내다 find out; make out; detect.

arida 아리다 ① (be) smarting; tingling ② (be) pungent; acrid.

arisonghada 아리송하다 (be) ambiguous; vague; obscure; indistinct. ⌈side job.

arŭbait'ŭ 아르바이트 Arbeit (*Ger.*); part-time job;

arŭmdapta 아름답다 ① (be) beautiful; pretty; lovely; fair ② (be) handsome; good-looking. *arŭmdapke* 아름답게 beautifully; prettily.

arŭn-gŏrida 아른거리다 flicker; flit; glimmer.

asa 아사 death from hunger[by starvation] *asahada* 아사하다 die of[from] hunger.

ashwipta 아쉽다 miss; feel the lack of; (be) inconvenient; (feel) regret.

at 앗 Oh!; O dear!; O my!; Heaven!

au 아우 man's younger brother; woman's younger sister.

ausŏng 아우성 shouting a clamor; scream. *ausŏng-ch'ida* 아우성치다 clamor; scream.

ayang 아양 coquetry. *ayang ttŏlda* 아양 떨다 play the coquette.

⚓ C ⚓ 【ch】

cha 자 foot rule; rule; measure.

chabadanggida 잡아당기다 pull; draw; tug; jerk.

chabaek 자백 confession; profession. *chabaek'ada* 자백하다 confess; make a clean breast.

chabamaeda 잡아매다 tie up; bind; fasten.

chabamŏkta 잡아먹다 slaughter; butcher; prey on.

chabi 자비 mercy; charity; benevolence. *chabiroun* 자비로운 merciful; compassionate; tenderhearted.

chabi 자비. *chabiro* 자비로 at one's own expense.

chabon 자본 capital; funds. *chabon-ga* 자본가 capitalist *chabonjuŭi* 자본주의 capitalism.

chabŭm 잡음 noise; dissenting voices.

chach'i 자치 self-government; autonomy. *chach'i-hada* 자치하다 govern oneself.

chach'o 자초. *chach'ohada* 자초하다 bring on oneself.

chach'wi 자취. *chach'wihada* 자취하다 do one's own cooking; cook for oneself.

chach'wi 자취 traces; vestiges; marks.

chada 자다 sleep; go to bed; go to sleep; be in bed.

chadong 자동. *chadongjŏgin* 자동적인 automatic. *chadongjŏguro* 자동적으로 automatically. *chadong-*

mun 자동문 automatic door.

chadongch'a 자동차 motorcar; automobile(*Am.*).

chae 재 ashes. *tambaetchae* 담뱃재 cigarette ash.

chaebae 재배 cultivation; culture. *chaebaehada* 재배하다 cultivate; grow.

chaebal 재발 recurrence. *chaebarhada* 재발하다 recur; return; have a relapse.

chaebŏl 재벌 financial clique[combine]; plutocracy.

chaebong 재봉 sewing; needlework. *chaebonghada* 재봉하다 sew; do needlework.

chaebongt'ŭl 재봉틀 sewing machine.

chaech'a 재차 twice; again; a second time.

chaech'i 재치 wit; cleverness; resources. *chaech'i innŭn* 재치 있는 quick-witted; smart.

chaech'ok 재촉 pressing; urging. *chaech'ok'ada* 재촉하다 press; urge.

chaeda 재다 measure; weigh; gauge.

chaedan 재단 foundation. *chaedan pŏbin* 재단 법인 juridical foundation.

chaegae 재개 reopening; resumption. *chaegaehada* 재개하다 open again; reopen.

chaegŏn 재건 reconstruction. *chaegŏnhada* 재건하다 rebuild; reconstruct.

chaehae 재해 calamity; disaster.

chaehyang kunin 재향 군인 exsoldier; veteran(*Am.*).

chaeil 재일. *chaeirŭi* 재일의 in Japan. *chaeil kyop'o* 재일 교포 Korean residents in Japan.

chaejangnyŏn 재작년 the year before last.

chaejik 재직. *chaejik'ada* 재직하다 hold office; be in office[service].

chaejŏng 재정 finance; financial affairs.

chaeju 재주 ability; talent; gifts. *chaeju innŭn* 재

주 있는 talented; able; gifted.

chaemi 재미 interest; amusement; enjoyment; fun. *chaemiitta* 재미있다 be interesting.

chaemi 재미. *chaemi kyop'o* 재미 교포 Korean residents in America. *chaemi yuhaksaeng* 재미 유학생 Korean students studying in America.

chaemok 재목 wood; lumber (*Am.*); timber (*Eng.*) →**mokchae** 목재.

chaemul 재물 property; fortune; means; treasures.

chaenan 재난 misfortune; calamity; disaster.

chaengban 쟁반 tray; salver.

chaenggi 쟁기 plow; plough (*Eng.*).

chaenŭng 재능 → **chaeju** 재주.

chaeoe 재외. *chaeoeŭi* 재외의 abroad; overseas. *chaeoe konggwan* 재외 공관 embassies and legations abroad; diplomatic establishment abroad.

chaep'an 재판 trial; judgement. *chaep'anhada* 재판하다 try; judge; decide on; pass judgment on. *chaep'anil* 재판일 court day.

chaepssada 잽싸다 (be) nimble; quick; agile.

chaerae 재래. *chaeraeŭi* 재래의 conventional. *chaeraeshik* 재래식 conventional type.

chaeryo 재료 material; raw material; stuff; data. *chaeryobi* 재료비 material costs.

chaeryŏk 재력 financial power; means; wealth.

chaesa 재사 man of talent[ability].

chaesan 재산 property; fortune; assets; wealth.

chaesu 재수 luck; fortune.

chaetpit 잿빛 ash color; grey; gray (*Am.*).

chaewon 재원 gifted[talented] young lady.

chagae 자개 mother of pearl; nacre.

chagaek 자객 assassin; assassinator.

chagal 자갈 gravel; pebbles.

chagayong 자가용 private car; one's own car.

chagi 자기 oneself; self; ego. *chagiŭi* 자기의 one's own (self); personal.

chagi 자기 porcelain; china(ware); ceramics.

chagŏp 작업 work; operations. *chagŏp'ada* 작업하다 work; conduct operations.

chaguk 자국 mark; traces; scar; track; stain.

chagŭk 자극 stimulus; impulse. *chagŭk'ada* 자극하다 stimulate; irritate; incite; give an impetus.

chagŭm 자금 funds; capital; fund.

chagŭmahada 자그마하다 (be) smallish; small; short.

chagŭnabŏji 작은아버지 uncle; one's father's younger brother.

chagung 자궁 womb; uterus. *chagungam* 자궁암 uterine cancer.

chagŭnŏmŏni 작은어머니 aunt; wife of one's father's younger brother.

chagwi 작위 peerage; title and rank of nobility.

chagyŏk 자격 qualification; eligibility. *chagyŏgi itta* 자격이 있다. be qualified; be eligible (for).

chagyong 작용 action; operation. *chagyonghada* 작용하다 act; operate on.

chahwasang 자화상 self-portrait.

chajae 자재 materials. *kŏnch'uk chajae* 건축 자재 construction material.

chajak 자작 viscount. *chajak puin* 자작 부인 viscountess.

chajangga 자장가 lullaby; cradlesong.

chaje 자제 self-control[-restraint]. *chajehada* 자제하다 control[restrain] oneself.

chaje 자제 sons; children; young people.

chaji 자지 penis; cock (*Am.*).

chajilgurehada 자질구레하다 (be) small; trifling.

chajŏn 자전 →**sajŏn** 사전.

chajŏng 자정 midnight.

chajŏn-gŏ 자전거 bicycle; bike.

chajonshim 자존심 self-respect; pride.

chaju 자주 often; frequently.

chakchŏn 작전 (military) operations; strategy. *chakchŏnsang* 작전상 strategically; tactically.

chakka 작가 writer; author; artist. *inki chakka* 인기 작가 popular[favorite] writer.

chakkok 작곡 (musical) composition. *chakkok'ada* 작곡하다 compose. *chakkokka* 작곡가 composer.

chakku 자꾸 ① constantly; incessantly; always ② eagerly; strongly.

chakpu 작부 barmaid; waitress.

chakp'um 작품 work. *munhak chakp'um* 문학 작품 literary work.

chakpyŏl 작별 farewell; parting; leave-taking. *chakpyŏrhada* 작별하다 take leave.

chakta 작다 (be) small; little; tiny; young.

chaktonghada 작동하다 operate; move; come into action; start.

chal 잘 well; nicely; skilfully.

challada 잘나다 ① (be) handsome; good-looking ② (be) distinguished; great.

challok'ada 잘록하다 (be) slender; constricted (in the middle).

chalmot 잘못 fault; error; blunder; mistake. *chalmot'ada* 잘못하다 do wrong; make a mistake.

chalsaenggida 잘생기다 → **challada** 잘나다 ①.

cham 잠 sleep; nap; slumber; doze. *chamjada* 잠
자다 sleep; go to sleep.

chamae 자매 sisters. *chamae hakkyo* 자매 학교 sister school.

chaman 자만 self-conceit; vanity; boast. *chamanhada* 자만하다 be conceited; be vain.

chambangi 잠방이 (farmer's) knee-breeches.

chambok 잠복. *chambok'ada* 잠복하다 conceal oneself; lie hidden.

chamdŭlda 잠들다 ① fall[drop] asleep; drop off to sleep ② lie (in the churchyard).

chamgŭda 잠그다 lock (up); fasten; bolt.

chamgyŏl 잠결 while asleep.

chamjada 잠자다 → **cham** 잠.

chamjak'o 잠자코 without a word; silently; without objection.

chamjamhada 잠잠하다 ① silent; mute; tacit ② be hushed; subside; become quiet[still, calm].

chamjari 잠자리 dragonfly. *koch'u jamjari* 고추 잠
자리 red dragonfly.

chamkkan 잠깐 (for) a while; (for) a moment; (for) some time; for a (short) time.

chamkkodae 잠꼬대 sleep talking. *chamkkodaehada* 잠꼬대하다 talk in one's sleep; talk nonsense.

chammok 잡목 miscellaneous wood; scrubs.

chammu 잡무 miscellaneous[add] business[duties].

chamnyŏm 잡념 worldly[earthly] thoughts; idle thoughts.

chamŏn 잠언 aphorism; maxim.

chamot 잠옷 nightclothes; pajamas; nightgown.

chamshi 잠시 short time[while]; (little) while. *chamshi hue* 잠시 후에 after a while.

chamsu 잠수 diving. *chamsuhada* 잠수하다 dive; submerge. *chamsubu* 잠수부 diver.

chamulsoe 자물쇠 lock; padlock.

chamun 자문 consultation. *chamunhada* 자문하다 inquire; consult.

chamyŏl 자멸 self-destruction. *chamyŏrhada* 자멸하다 destroy[ruin] oneself; perish.

chan 잔 (wine) cup; glass. *ch'atchan* 찻잔 teacup.

chanaek 잔액 balance; remainder.

chanakkaena 자나깨나 (whether) awake or asleep; night and day; always.

chanch'i 잔치 feast; banquet; party. *saengil chanch'i* 생일 잔치 birthday party.

chandi 잔디 lawn; sod; turf. *chandibat* 잔디밭 lawn; grassplot.

chane 자네 you.

chang 장 head; chief; chieftain; boss (*Am.*).

chang 장 soy (sauce). *toenjang* 된장 bean paste.

chang 장 intestines; bowels; entrails.

chang 장 wardrobe; chest of drawers; cabinet; bureau (*Am.*).

changae 장애 obstacle; hindrance; impediment. *changaemul* 장애물 obstacle; obstruction.

changbal 장발 long hair. *changbarŭi* 장발의 long-haired. *changbaljok* 장발족 long-hair group.

changbonin 장본인 ringleader; prime mover.

changbu 장부 (account) book; ledger.

changbyŏng 장병 officers and men; soldiers.

changch'i 장치 apparatus; equipment; installation. *changch'ihada* 장치하다 equip; install; fit.

changch'im 장침 →**punch'im** 분침.

changchŏm 장점 merit; strong[good] point; one's

forte. *changdanchŏm* 장단점 strong and weak points.

changch'ong 장총 (long-barreled) rifle.

changdam 장담 assurance; assertion. *changdamhada* 장담하다 assure; vouch (for).

changdori 장도리 hammer; claw hammer.

changga 장가 marriage. *changga kada*[*tŭlda*] 장가가다[들다] marry; get married; take a wife.

changgap 장갑 (a pair of) gloves[mittens].

changgi 장기 (game of) Korean chess. *changgip'an* 장기판 chessboard.

changgi 장기 long time[period, term]. *changgiŭi* 장기의 long(-dated).

changgŏri 장거리 long distance[range]. *changgŏri chŏnhwa* 장거리 전화 long-distance call [telephone] (*Am.*); trunk-call (*Eng.*).

changgu 장구 (Korean) hourglass drum.

changgun 장군 general.

changgwan 장관 grand sight; magnificent view [spectacle].

changgwan 장관 minister (of state); Cabinet member; secretary.

changgyo 장교 officer; commissioned officer.

changhak 장학. *changhakkŭm* 장학금 scholarship. *changhaksaeng* 장학생 scholarship student[holder].

changhwa 장화 top[high] boots; boots (*Am.*).

changja 장자 eldest son.

changji 장지 burial place[ground].

changki 장기 one's forte; special skill [ability]; one's speciality; one's great forte.

changma 장마 long rain; spell of wet weather. *changmach'ŏl* 장마철 the rainy[wet] season.

changman 장만. *changmanhada* 장만하다 prepare; provide oneself.

changmi 장미 rose. *tŭlchangmi* 들장미 wild rose.

changmo 장모 wife's mother; man's mother-in-law.

changmun 작문 composition.

changnae 장래 future. *changnaeŭi* 장래의 future; prospective. *changnaee* 장래에 in the future.

changnam 장남 eldest son.

changnan 장난 game; play; mischief; joke. *changnanhada* 장난하다 do mischief; play a trick.

changnankam 장난감 plaything; toy; sport.

changnim 장님 blind man; the blind.

changnong 장롱 wardrobe; bureau (*Am.*); dresser.

changnye 장례 funeral [burial] service.

changnyŏ 장녀 eldest daughter.

changnyŏ 장려 encouragement. *changnyŏhada* 장려하다 encourage; promote.

changnyŏn 작년 last year; past year.

chan-go 잔고 balance; remainder → **chanaek** 잔액.

changŏ 장어 eel. *changŏ kui* 장어 구이 broiled eels.

changsa 장사 funeral. *changsa chinaeda* 장사 지내다 hold a funeral.

changsa 장사 man of great strength; powerful man.

changsa 장사 trade; business; commerce. *changsahada* 장사하다 do[engage in] business.

changshigan 장시간 for many hours.

changshik 장식 decoration; adornment; ornament. *changshik'ada* 장식하다 ornament; decorate; adorn.

changshin-gu 장신구 accessories; trinkets; furnishings; fancy goods.

changso 장소 place; spot; location; site.

changsŏ 장서 collection of books; one's library.

changtae 장대 (bamboo) pole; rod.

changt'ŏ 장터 market place[site].

changŭi 장의 →**changnye** 장례. *changŭisa* 장의사 undertaker's shop; funeral parlor (*Am*.).

chan-gŭm 잔금 balance; remainder.

chanin 잔인. *chaninhan* 잔인한 cruel; atrocious; brutal; merciless; harsh.

chanjae 잔재 leftovers; dregs; remnants; waste matter.

chanjaeju 잔재주 petty artifice; trick. *chanjaeju purida* 잔재주 부리다 play petty tricks.

chanjurŭm 잔주름 fine wrinkles.

chanshimburŭm 잔심부름 sundry errands[jobs].

chanson 잔손 elaborate care. *chansonjil* 잔손질 small touch; piecework.

chansori 잔소리 scolding; rebuke; complaint. *chansorihada* 잔소리하다 scold; nag; rebuke.

chanyŏ 자녀 children; sons and daughters.

chaoesŏn 자외선 ultraviolet rays.

chapchi 잡지 magazine; journal; periodical.

chapch'ida 잡치다 ① harm; hurt; injure ② fail (to); (make a) mistake[error] ③ spoil; ruin; mar.

chapch'o 잡초 weeds.

chapchong 잡종 hybrid; cross; half[mixed] breed.

chap'ida 잡히다 be caught[arrested; apprehended; seized]; get captured; fall into.

chap'il 자필 one's own handwriting; autograph.

chapkok 잡곡 (miscellaneous) cereals; minor grains.

chappajida 자빠지다 ① fall on one's back; fall backward. ② lie down.

chappi 잡비 sundries.

chappugŭm 잡부금 miscellaneous fees.

chapta 잡다 butcher; kill; slaughter.

chapta 잡다 ① catch; seize; grip; hold; grasp ② capture; arrest.

chapt'ang 잡탕 mixed soup.

chaptongsani 잡동사니 sundries; odds and ends.

chap'wa 잡화 miscellaneous[sundry] goods. *chap'wasang* 잡화상 grocer's.

chara 자라 snapping turtle; terrapin.

charada 자라다 grow (up); be bred; be brought up.

charak 자락 skirt; foot; bottom; train.

charang 자랑 pride; boast. *charanghada* 자랑하다 boast; be proud (of).

charhada 잘하다 ① do well[nicely, skilfully] ② do often; do a lot.

chari 자리 ① seat; one's place ② status.

charijapta 자리잡다 take one's seat; be situated.

charip 자립 independence; self-reliance[-support]. *charip'ada* 자립하다 establish oneself.

charu 자루 sack; bag. *ssalcharu* 쌀자루 rice bag.

charu 자루 handle; haft; hilt; shaft.

charŭda 자르다 cut (off); chop; sever.

charyo 자료 material; data.

charyŏk 자력. *charyŏgŭro* 자력으로 by one's own efforts; for oneself.

chasal 자살 suicide. *chasarhada* 자살하다 kill oneself; commit suicide.

chasan 자산 property; fortune; asset.

chasang 자상. *chasanghada* 자상하다 (be) detailed; thoughtfully kind.

chase 자세. *chasehan* 자세한 detailed; minute. *chasehi* 자세히 in detail; minutely.

chase 자세 posture[pose]; attitude. *ko[chŏ]jase* 고[저]자세 haughty[humble] attitude.

chashik 자식 ① one's children; offspring ② chap; wretch; "bastard".

chashin 자신 self-confidence. *chashin innŭn* 자신 있는 self-confident.

chashin 자신 one's self; oneself. *chashinŭi* 자신의 one's own. *chashini* 자신이 (by) oneself; in person.

chasŏjŏn 자서전 autobiography; life story.

chasŏk 자석 magnet. *chasŏgŭi* 자석의 magnetic.

chason 자손 descendants; posterity; offspring.

chasŏn 자선 charity; benevolence. *chasŏn nambi* 자선 남비 charity pot.

chasu 자수 self-surrender; (voluntary) confession. *chasuhada* 자수하다 deliver oneself to justice.

chasu 자수 embroidery. *chasuhada* 자수하다 embroider. *chasuhan* 자수한 embroidered.

chasujŏng 자수정 amethyst; violet quartz.

chat'aek 자택 one's own house[home].

chatta 잦다 (be) frequent; (be) quick; rapid.

chatta 잣다 ① pump[suck; draw] up ② spin; make yarn.

chaŭm 자음 consonant.

chawon 자원 resources. *inchŏk[mulchŏk] chawon* 인적[물적] 자원 human[material] resources.

chayŏn 자연 nature. *chayŏnŭi* 자연의 natural. *chayŏnhi* 자연히 naturally; of itself.

chayu 자유 freedom; liberty. *chayuŭi[roun]* 자유의[로운] free; liberal. *chayuro(i)* 자유로(이) freely; as one pleases.

chean 제안 proposal; suggestion. *cheanhada* 제안하다 propose.

chebal 제발 kindly; please; pray. *Chebal yong-*

sŏhashio 제발 용서하시오 Excuse me, please.

chebang 제방 bank; embankment; dike.

chebi 제비 swallow.

chebi 제비 lot; lottery; lottery-ticket. *chebi ppopta* 제비 뽑다 draw lots.

chebikkot 제비꽃 violet; pansy.

chebok 제복 uniform. *chebogŭl ibŭn* 제복을 입은 uniformed; in uniform.

chebon 제본 bookbinding. *chebonhada* 제본하다 bind (a book). *chebonso* 제본소 bookbindery.

chebŏp 제법 nicely; quite (good); pretty. *Chebŏp tŏpta* 제법 덥다. It is quite warm.

chech'il 제 7 the seventh; number seven [No. 7].

chech'ul 제출 presentation; submission. *chech'urhada* 제출하다 present; submit; bring forward.

chech'yŏnot'a 제쳐놓다 put[lay] aside; set apart.

chedae 제대 discharge from military service.

chedan 제단 altar.

chedo 제도 system; institution. *chedosangŭi* 제도상의 institutional.

chedo 제도 drafting; drawing; cartography. *chedohada* 제도하다 draw [draft] a plan.

chedok 제독 admiral; commodore (*Am.*).

chedong 제동 braking. *chedongŭl kŏlda* 제동을 걸다 put on[apply] the brake.

chedŭng 제등 paper lantern. *chedŭng haengnyŏl* 제등 행렬 lantern procession[parade].

chegi 제기, **chegiral** 제기랄 Shucks!; Phew; Damn [Hang] it!; Ugh!; Tut!; Pshaw.

chegŏ 제거. *chegŏhada* 제거하다 get rid of; eliminate; exclude; remove.

chegong 제공 offer; supply. *chegonghada* 제공하다

(make an) offer; proffer.

chegop 제곱 square. *chegop'ada* 제곱하다 square [multiply] (a number).

cheguk 제국 empire. *chegugŭi* 제국의 imperial.

chegwa 제과 confectionery. *chegwa hoesa*; 제과 회사 confectionery company.

chehŏn 제헌 establishment of a constitution. *chehŏnjŏl* 제헌절 Constitution Day.

chehan 제한 restriction; limitation. *chehanhada* 제한하다 restrict; limit; restrain. *sana chehan* 산아제한 birthcontrol.

chehyu 제휴 cooperation; concert. *chehyuhada* 제휴하다 cooperate (with); act in concert with. *kisul chehyu* 기술 제휴 technical tie-up.

chei 제2 the second; number two [No. 2].

cheil 제1 the first; number one [No. 1].

cheja 제자 pupil; disciple; follower.

chejae 제재 sawing; lumbering. *chejaeso* 제재소 sawmill; lumbermill.

chejak 제작 manufacture; production. *chejak'ada* 제작하다 manufacture; produce; make.

cheji 제지 restraint; control. *chejihada* 제지하다 control; check; restrain.

chejo 제조 making; manufacture. *chejohada* 제조하다 make; manufacture; turn out.

chejŏn 제전 festival; fete.

chemak 제막. *chemak'ada* 제막하다 unveil. *chemakshik* 제막식 unveiling ceremony.

chemok 제목 subject; theme; title; caption.

chemyŏng 제명 title. ⋯*ŭi chemyŏnguro* ⋯의 제명으로 under the title of ⋯.

chemyŏng 제명 expulsion. *chemyŏnghada* 제명하다

strike a name off; expel.

chenjang 젠장 Hang it!; Damn it!; Hell!

cheo 제5 the fifth; number five[No. 5].

cheoe 제외. *cheoehada* 제외하다 except; exclude; save; exempt; rule out.

chep'um 제품 manufactured goods; product. *oeguk chep'um* 외국 제품 foreign products.

cheryŏn 제련 refining. *cheryŏnhada* 제련하다 refine. *cheryŏnso* 제련소 refinery.

chesa 제사 religious service; sacrificial rite.

cheya 제야 New Year's Eve; watch night.

cheyak 제약 medicine manufacture; pharmacy. *cheyak hoesa* 제약 회사 pharmaceutical company.

chibae 지배 control; rule. *chibaehada* 지배하다 govern; rule. *chibaein* 지배인 manager.

chiban 지반 base; foundation; foothold. *chibanŭl takta* 지반을 닦다 establish one's foothold.

chiban 집안 family; household. *chiban shikku* 집안 식구 (members of) a family.

chibang 지방 district; region; locality. *chibangjŏk* 지방적 local; provincial. *chibang sat'uri* 지방 사투리 local accent.

chibang 지방 fat; grease; lard.

chibu 지부 branch (office); chapter.

chibul 지불 payment; discharge. *chiburhada* 지불하다 pay; discharge.

chibung 지붕 roof; roofing; housetop. *kiwa chibung* 기와 지붕 tiled roof.

chibyŏng 지병 chronic disease; old complaint.

chich'ida 지치다 be[get] tired; be exhausted; be worn out; be done up.

chich'ida 지치다 slide on[over]; skate on.

chich'ul 지출 expense; outgo. *chich'urhada* 지출
하다 expend; pay.

chida 지다 be[get] defeated; lose; yield (to).
kyŏnggie chida 경기에 지다 lose in a contest.

chida 지다 ① bear; carry on the back ② owe; be
indebted.

chida 지다 ① fall; fade and fall ② set; sink; go
down.

chidae 지대 zone; region; belt. *pimujang chidae*
비무장 지대 demilitarized zone[DMZ].

chidaegong 지대공. *chidaegong misail* 지대공 미사
일 ground-to-air missile.

chido 지도 map. *chidoch'aek* 지도책 atlas.

chido 지도 guidance; directions. *chidohada* 지도하
다 guide; lead; coach.

chidok 지독. *chidok'ada* 지독하다 (be) vicious; severe; awful. *chidok'an ch'uwi*[*tŏwi*] 지독한 추위
[더위] severe cold[heat].

chigak 지각. *chigak'ada* 지각하다 be[come] late;
be behind time; be tardy.

chigap 지갑 purse; pocketbook.

chigekkun 지게꾼 A-frame man; burden carrier.

chigŏp 직업 occupation; calling; profession; voca-
tion; business.

chigu 지구 the earth; the globe.

chigu 지구 district; zone; region; area; section.
sangŏp[*chut'aek*] *chigu* 상업〔주택〕지구 business
[residence] zone[area].

chiguk 지국 branch[district] office.

chigŭm 지금 now; the present; this moment. *chi-
gŭmkkaji* 지금까지 till now; up to the present.
chigŭmbut'ŏ 지금부터 from now on; after this.

chigŭp 지급. *chigŭbŭi* 지급의 urgent; pressing; express. *chigŭp chŏnbo* 지급 전보 urgent telegram.

chigwon 직원 personnel; staff-member; employee.

chigyŏpta 지겹다 (be) tedious; tiresome; detestable.

chiha 지하. *chihaŭi[-e, -esŏ]* 지하의[에, 에서] underground.

chihwi 지휘 command; orders; direction. *chihwihada* 지휘하다 command; order; lead.

chihye 지혜 wisdom; sense; intelligence. *chihye innŭn* 지혜 있는 wise; intelligent.

chijang 지장 obstacle; difficulty. *chijangi ŏpsŭmyŏn* 지장이 없으면 if it is convenient to you.

chiji 지지 support; backing. *chijihada* 지지하다 support; back (up); uphold.

chijida 지지다 stew; panfry; frizzle.

chijin 지진 earthquake.

chijŏbunhada 지저분하다 (be) messy; disordered; untidy; dirty(-looking).

chijŏm 지점 branch shop[office, house]. *chijŏmjang* 지점장 branch manager.

chijŏng 지정 appointment; designation. *chijŏnghada* 지정하다 appoint; fix; designate.

chiju 지주 landowner; landlord.

Chijunghae 지중해 Mediterranean Sea.

chik'aeng 직행. *chik'aenghada* 직행하다 go straight [direct, nonstop]; run [go] through *chik'aeng pŏsŭ* 직행 버스 nonstop bus.

chikchang 직장 one's place of work; one's post.

chikchŏp 직접 directly; firsthand; personally. *chikchŏpchŏk* 직접적 direct; personal; firsthand.

chik'ida 지키다 ① protect; defend ② watch; guard ③ keep; observe.

chikkak 직각 right angle.

chikkong 직공 worker; workman; factory hand.

chikkŏrida 지껄이다 chatter; chat; gabble.

chikkyŏng 직경 diameter.

chiksŏn 직선 straight line; beeline. *chiksŏn k'osŭ* 직선 코스 straight course.

chikt'ong 직통. *chikt'onghada* 직통하다 communicate directly. *chikt'ong chŏnhwa* 직통 전화 direct telephone line[service].

chil 질 quality. *chilchŏgin* 질적인 qualitative. *chilchŏguro* 질적으로 qualitatively.

chilgida 질기다 (be) tough; durable; tenacious.

chilgŭrŭt 질그릇 clayware; unglazed earthenware.

chilli 진리 truth. *kwahagŭi chilli* 과학의 진리 the truth of science.

chillida 질리다 ① become disgusted with; get sick of ② turn pale.

chillo 진로 course (to advance); one's path in life.

chillyŏ 질녀 niece.

chilmŏjida 짊어지다 bear; carry on one's back; shoulder.

chilmun 질문 question; inquiry. *chilmunhada* 질문하다 ask a question.

chilshik 질식 suffocation. *chilshik'ada* 질식하다 be suffocated; be choked.

chilsŏ 질서 order; system. *chilsŏ innŭn* 질서 있는 orderly; systematic; methodical.

chilt'u 질투 jealousy. *chilt'uhada* 질투하다 be jealous (of); envy; be envious of.

chim 짐 load; cargo; luggage; baggage (*Am.*).

chimang 지망 wish; desire; choice. *chimanghada* 지망하다 desire; apply for; choose. *chimangja*

지망자 applicant; candidate.

chimch'a 짐차 goods wagon[van]; freight car; truck.

chimjak 짐작 guess; conjecture. *chimjak'ada* 짐작하다 guess; conjecture.

chimkkun 짐꾼 porter; luggage porter.

chimmach'a 짐마차 cart; wagon.

chimsŭng 짐승 beast; brute; animal.

chimtchak 짐짝 package; parcel; piece of baggage.

chimun 지문 fingerprint; finger mark.

chimyŏn 지면 surface; ground.

chimyŏng 지명 nomination. *chimyŏnghada* 지명하다 nominate; name.

chimyŏng 지명 place name; name of a place.

chinach'ida 지나치다 ① go too far; exceed; do too much ② pass through. *chinach'in* 지나친 excessive. *chinach'ige* 지나치게 excessively.

chinada 지나다 ① pass by; go past; pass through ② expire; terminate; be out.

chinaeda 지내다 ① spend[pass] one's time; get along ② hold; observe.

chinanbŏn 지난번 last; last time; the other day. *chinanbŏnŭi* 지난번의 last; previous; recent.

chinbo 진보 progress; advance. *chinbohada* 진보하다 make progress; improve.

chinch'al 진찰 medical examination. *chinch'arhada* 진찰하다 examine. *chinch'alkwŏn* 진찰권 consultation ticket.

chinch'ang 진창 mud; mire. *chinch'angkil* 진창길 muddy road.

chindallae 진달래 azalea.

chindan 진단 diagnosis. *chindanhada* 진단하다 diagnose. *chindansŏ* 진단서 medical certificate.

chindong 진동 vibration; shock. *chindonghada* 진동하다 shake; quake; vibrate.

chindŭgi 진드기 tick; mite.

ching 징 hobnail; clout nail.

ching 징 gong.

chin-gae 진개 dust; dirt; garbage.

chingbyŏng 징병 conscription; military draft (*Am.*). *chingbyŏng kŏmsa* 징병 검사 physical examination for conscription.

chinggŏmdari 징검다리 steppingstone.

chinggŭrŏpta 징그럽다 (be) creepy; crawly; uncanny; disgusting.

chin-gi 진기. *chin-gihan* 진기한 new; novel; rare; uncommon; strange.

chingmu 직무 duties; work; job. *chingmusangŭi* 직무상의 official.

chingmul 직물 cloth; textile fabrics. *chingmul kongjang* 직물 공장 textile factory[mill].

chingmyŏn 직면. *chingmyŏnhada* 직면하다 face; confront; be faced[confronted] (with).

chin-gong 진공 vacuum. *chin-gongŭi* 진공의 vacuous. *chin-gonggwan* 진공관 vacuum tube[bulb].

chin-gŭp 진급 promotion. *chin-gŭp'ada* 진급하다 be [get] promoted (to); win promotion.

chingyŏk 징역 penal servitude. *chingyŏksari* 징역살이 prison life; imprisonment.

chinhaeje 진해제 cough remedy.

chinhŭk 진흙 mud; mire; dirt.

chinhwa 진화 evolution. *chinhwahada* 진화하다 evolve. *chinhwaron* 진화론 evolutionism.

chinjŏlmŏri 진절머리. *chinjŏlmŏrinada* 진절머리나

다 be sick of; be disgusted with.

chinjŏng 진정 petition; appeal. *chinjŏnghada* 진정하다 make a petition; appeal. *chinjŏngsŏ* 진정서 written petition.

chinju 진주 pearl. *chinju mokkŏri* 진주 목걸이 pearl necklace *chinju chjogae* 진주 조개 pearl oyster.

chinka 진가 true[real] value; true worth[merit].

chinmaek 진맥. *chinmaek'ada* 진맥하다 feel[examine] pulse.

chinnunkkaebi 진눈깨비 sleet.

chinsang 진상 truth; actual fact; what's what.

chinshil 진실 fact; truth; reality. *chinshirhan* 진실한 true; real. *chinshillo* 진실로 in fact; really.

chinshim 진심 true heart; sincerity. *chinshimŭro* 진심으로 heartily; sincerely.

chinsul 진술 statement. *chinsurhada* 진술하다 state; give an account of.

chint'ang 진탕 to one's heart's content; to the full. *chint'ang mŏkta[mashida]* 진탕 먹다[마시다] eat[drink] one's fill.

chintcha 진짜 genuine article; real thing; real stuff (*Am.*).

chint'ongje 진통제 pain-killing drug; pain-killer.

chinŭng 지능 intelligence; mental faculties; intellect *chinŭng chisu* 지능 지수 intelligence quotient

chinŭrŏmi 지느러미 fin. ⌐[I. Q.].

chinyŏl 진열 exhibition; show; display. *chinyŏrhada* 진열하다 exhibit; display.

chinyŏng 진영 camp; bloc; quarters. *minju chinyŏng* 민주 진영 democratic camp.

chiok 지옥 hell; inferno; Hades *kyot'ong chiok* 교통 지옥 traffic jam.

chiŏnaeda 지어내다 make up; invent; fabricate.

chip 집 house; home. *kiwa*[*ch'oga*]*jip* 기와[초가] 집 tile[thatch] roofed house. *yangokchip* 양옥집 western style building.

chip 짚 straw. *milchip* 밀짚 wheat straw. *milchip moja* 밀짚 모자 straw hat.

chip'angi 지팡이 (walking) stick; cane.

chipch'ak 집착 attachment. *chipch'ak'a da* 집착하다 be attached; cling[stick] to; be stubbornly bent.

chipchŏkkŏrida 집적거리다 tease; provoke; vex.

chipchuin 집주인 owner of a house; head of a family; landlord; landlady.

chipke 집게 tongs; nippers; tweezers; pincers. *pujipke* 부집게 fire tongs.

chipkesonkarak 집게손가락 index finger; forefinger.

chip'oe 집회 meeting; assembly. *chip'oehada* 집회하다 meet together; gather. *chip'oe changso* 집회 장소 meeting place; assembly hall.

chipp'il 집필 writing. *chipp'irhada* 집필하다 write. *chipp'ilja* 집필자 writer.

chipse 집세 (house) rent; house-rent.

chipshin 짚신 straw sandles[shoes].

chipta 집다 pick up; take up. *chipkero chipta* 집게로 집다 pick up with tongs.

chiptan 집단 group; mass; collective body.

chip'ye 지폐 paper money[currency]; (bank) note (*Eng.*); bill (*Am.*).

chip'yŏngsŏn 지평선 horizon; horizontal line.

chiri 지리 geography; topography.

chiroe 지뢰 (land) mine.

chirŭda 지르다. (*sorirŭl*) *chirŭda* (소리를) 지르다 yell; cry aloud; scream; shout.

chirŭmkil 지름길 shortcut; shorter way.

chiryŏng 지령 order; instruction. *chiryŏnghada* 지령하다 order; direct; give instruction.

chisa 지사 (provincial) governor →**tojisa** 도지사.

chisa 지사 branch (office).

chisang 지상 ground. *chisangŭi* 지상의 earthly; terrestrial. *chisangkwŏn* 지상권 surface rights.

chishi 지시 directions; indication. *chishihada* 지시하다 direct; indicate; point out.

chishik 지식 knowledge; information; learning. *chishik kyegŭp* 지식 계급 the educated classes; the intelligentsia; highbrows. ⌜station.

chisŏ 지서 *kyŏngch'al chisŏ* 경찰 지서 police sub-

chisŏng 지성 intellect; intelligence. *chisŏngin* 지성인 intellectual; highbrow.

chitkutta 짓궂다 (be) annoying; bothersome; harassing; ill-natured; spiteful.

chitta 짖다 bark; bay; howl.

chitta 짙다 (be) dark; deep; thick; dense.

chitta 짓다 ① boil; cook (rice) ② compose (composition) ③ raise; grow (barley) ④ commit (crime) ⑤ wear (smile) ⑥ build; construct (house).

chiuda 지우다 erase; rub[wipe] out; cross out.

chiugae 지우개 eraser.

chiwi 지위 position; status; rank; post; situation.

chiwon 지원 application; volunteering. *chiwonhada* 지원하다 apply for; volunteer for. *chiwonja* 지원자 applicant; candidate.

chiyŏk 지역 area; region; zone. *chiyŏkchŏk* 지역적 local; regional.

cho 조 million million; billion(*Eng.*); trillion(*Am.*).

chŏ 저 (pair of) chopsticks →**chŏtkarak** 젓가락.

chŏ 저 that. *chŏ saram* 저 사람 that man. *chŏgŏt* 저것 that thing[one].

choahada 좋아하다 ① like; love; prefer ② be pleased[delighted, glad].

chŏbŏn 저번 last time; the other day. *chŏbŏnŭi* 저번의 last; recent; previous.

chobu 조부 grandfather. →**harabŏji** 할아버지.

chŏch'uk 저축 saving; savings. *chŏch'uk'ada* 저축하다 save; lay by[aside, up]; store up.

chŏdang 저당 mortgage; security. *chŏdanghada* 저당하다 mortgage.

choe 죄 crime; sin; offense; guilt. *choerŭl pŏmhada* 죄를 범하다 commit a crime[sin].

choeda 죄다 ① tighten; make tight ② feel anxious.

choein 죄인 criminal; convict; offender; sinner.

choga 조가 dirge; elegy.

chogabi 조가비 clam shell; shell.

chogae 조개 shellfish; clam.

chogaek 조객 condoler; caller for condolence.

chogak 조각 piece; bit; fragment; splinter.

chogak 조각 sculpture; carving; engraving. *chogak'ada* 조각하다 sculpture; carve; engrave.

chogamdo 조감도 bird's-eye-view.

chogan 조간. *chogan shinmun* 조간 신문 morning paper.

chogi 조기 mourning flag; flag at half-mast.

chŏgi 저기 that place; there. *chŏgie* 저기에 there; over[up, down] there.

chŏgiap 저기압 low (atmospheric) pressure.

chŏgŏdo 적어도 at (the) least.

chŏgori 저고리 coat; Korean jacket.

chŏgŭi 적의 hostility; enmity. *chŏgŭi innŭn* 적의

있는 hostile; inimical.

choguk 조국 fatherland; one's native land.

chŏgŭm 저금 saving; savings; deposit. *chŏgŭmhada* 저금하다 save; deposit.

chogŭm 조금 ① small quantity; a little ② small number; a few ③ somewhat; a bit.

chŏgŭp 저급 low grade. *chŏgŭp'ada* 저급하다 (be) inferior; vulgar; low(-grade); lowbrow.

chogyo 조교 assistant (teacher, instruction).

chŏgyong 적용 application. *chŏgyonghada* 적용하다 apply (to).

chogyosu 조교수 assistant professor.

chŏhang 저항 resistance; opposition. *chŏhanghada* 저항하다 resist; oppose; fight against.

chohap 조합 association; partnership; union; guild; league. *hyŏptong chohap* 협동 조합 cooperative association[union]; co-op.

chŏhŭidŭl 저희들 we. *chŏhŭidŭrŭi* 저희들의 our. *chŏhŭidŭrŭl* 저희들을 us.

chohwa 조화 harmony. *chohwahada* 조화하다 harmonize (with); be in harmony.

chohwa 조화 artificial flower.

choin 조인 signature; signing. *choinhada* 조인하다 seal; sign; affix one's seal.

chŏja 저자 writer; author; authoress.

chojak 조작 invention; fabrication. *chojak'ada* 조작하다 fabricate; invent.

chŏjang 저장 storage; storing. *chŏjanghada* 저장하다 store; preserve.

chŏji 저지. *chŏjihada* 저지하다 hinder; obstruct; prevent; arrest; check.

chojik 조직 organization; system. *chojik'ada* 조직

하다 organize; form; set up; compose.

chojim 조짐 symptoms; omen; signs.

chojŏl 조절 accommodation; adjustment.

chŏjŏllo 저절로 of itself; naturally; of its own accord; spontaneously; automatically.

chojŏn 조전 telegram of condolence.

chojong 조종 management; operation. *chojonghada* 조종하다 manage; operate.

chojŏng 조정 regulation; adjustment. *chojŏnghada* 조정하다 regulate; adjust.

chŏju 저주 curse; imprecation. *chŏjuhada* 저주하다 curse; imprecate; wish ill of.

chŏk 적 enemy; foe; opponent; rival. *chayuŭi chŏk* 자유의 적 enemy of freedom.

chok'a 조카 nephew. *chok'attal* 조카딸 niece.

chokcha 족자 hanging roll〔scroll〕.

chŏkcha 적자 red figures; deficit; loss.

chokchipke 족집게 (hair) tweezers.

chŏkchŏl 적절. *chŏkchŏrhan* 적절한 fitting; proper; adequate. *chŏkchŏrhi* 적절히 properly; aptly.

chokki 조끼 vest (*Am.*); waistcoat.

chokki 조끼 jug; mug; pitcher. *maekchu han chokki* 맥주 한 조끼 a jug(ful) of beer.

chŏkkuk 적국 enemy country; hostile power.

chŏkkŭk 적극. *chŏkkŭkchŏgin* 적극적인 positive; active; (very) energic. *chŏkkŭkchŏgŭro* 적극적으로 positively; actively.

chokŏn 조건 condition; term; stipulation. *nodong chokŏn* 노동 조건 labor condition.

chokpo 족보 genealogy; pedigree; family tree.

chŏksaek 적색 red (color); crimson *chŏksaek punja* 적색 분자 Red; communist.

chomiryo 조미료 seasonings; spices.

chŏmida 저미다 cut thin; slice.

chŏmjangi 점장이 fortuneteller; diviner.

chŏmjant'a 점잖다 (be) dignified; genteel; decent. *chŏmjanŭn saram* 점잖은 사람 decent man.

chŏmjŏm 점점 by degrees; gradually; more and more; less and less.

chŏmnyŏng 점령 occupation. *chŏmnyŏnghada* 점령하다 occupy; take possession of; capture.

chomo 조모 grandmother. →**halmŏni** 할머니.

chomok 조목 article; clause; item.

chŏmp'o 점포 shop; store.

chŏmshim 점심 lunch(eon). *chŏmshimŭl mŏkta* 점심을 먹다 have[take] lunch.

chŏmsŏn 점선 dotted[perforated] line.

chŏmsu 점수 marks; score; points. →**chŏm** 점.

chŏmta 젊다 (be) young; youthful. *chŏlmŭni* 젊은이 young man; youth.

chŏmulda 저물다 get[grow] dark[dusk].

chomun 조문 call of condolence. *chomunhada* 조문하다 make a call of condolence.

chŏmwŏn 점원 shop-assistant; (shop) clerk. *yŏjŏmwŏn* 여점원 shopgirl.

chomyŏng 조명 lighting; illumination. *chomyŏnghada* 조명하다 light up; illuminate.

chŏn 전 all; whole; entire; total. *chŏn-gungmin* 전국민 whole nation. *chŏnjaesan* 전재산 entire fortune.

chŏn 전. *chŏnŭi* 전의 previous; former; last. *chŏne* 전에 before; previously.

chŏnaek 전액 total[full] amount; sum total.

chonham 존함 your (honorable) name.

chonan 조난 disaster. *chonanhada* 조난하다 meet with a disaster[accident].

chŏnbang 전방 front (line). *chŏnbangŭi* 전방의 front; forward. *chŏnbange* 전방에 ahead.

chŏnbo 전보 telegram; wire. *chŏnbo ch'ida* 전보 치다 telegraph; send a telegram.

chŏnbu 전부 all; whole. *chŏnbuŭi* 전부의 all; whole; total. *chŏnbu hapch'yŏ* 전부 합쳐 in all; altogether; in full.

chŏnch'a 전차 tank. *chŏnch'a pudae* 전차 부대 tank corps. *taejŏnch'ap'o* 대전차포 antitank gun.

chŏnch'a 전차 electric car; tramcar (*Eng.*).

chŏnch'e 전체 the whole; all. *chŏnch'eŭi* 전체의 whole; entire; general. *chŏnch'ejŏgŭro* 전체적으로 generally; as a whole.

chonch'ing 존칭 title of hono(u)r; honorific title.

chŏnch'isa 전치사 preposition.

chŏnch'ŏl 전철 electric railway.

chonchu 전주 last week; preceding week.

chŏnch'uk 전축 record player; electric phonograph.

chondae 존대. *chondaehada* 존대하다 treat with respect. *chondaeŏ* 존대어 term of respect.

chŏndal 전달 delivery; conveyance. *chŏndarhada* 전달하다 deliver; convey; transmit.

chŏndang 전당. *chŏndang chap'ida* 전당 잡히다 pawn; put in pawn. *chŏndangp'o* 전당포 pawnshop.

chŏndo 전도 one's future; prospects. *chŏndo yumanghan* 전도 유망한 promising.

chŏndŭng 전등 electric light[lamp]. *hoejung chŏndŭng* 회중 전등 flashlight.

chong 종 bell. *chongŭl ullida* 종을 울리다 ring [strike, toll] a bell.

chong 종 servant; slave; maid(servant); help.

chŏng 정 tablet; tabloid; pill.

chongalgŏrida 종알거리다 mutter; murmur; prate.

chongari 종아리 calf of the leg; calf.

chŏngbak 정박 anchorage; mooring. *chŏngbak'ada* 정박하다 cast anchor; moor.

chŏngbanghyŏng 정방형 →**chŏngsagak'yŏng** 정사각형.

chŏngbi 정비 adjustment; equipment. *chŏngbihada* 정비하다 fully equip; fix. *chadongch'a chŏngbigong* 자동차 정비공 car mechanic.

chŏngbo 정보 information; report; news. *chungang chŏngbobu* 중앙 정보부 Central Intelligence Agency (C. I. A.).

chŏngbok 정복 conquest. *chŏngbok'ada* 정복하다 conquer; subjugate; master.

chŏngbok 정복 formal dress. *chŏngbok kyŏngch'algwan* 정복 경찰관 policeman in full uniform.

chŏngbu 정부 paramour; (secret) lover; mistress.

chŏngbu 정부 government; administration. *chŏngbuŭi* 정부의 governmental; ministerial. *Han-guk chŏngbu* 한국 정부 Korean government.

chŏngbyŏn 정변 political change; coup d'état (*Fr.*).

chŏngch'a 정차 →**chŏnggŏ** 정거. *chŏngch'a shigan* 정차 시간 stoppage time.

chŏngch'aek 정책 policy.

chŏngch'al 정찰 reconnaissance; scouting. *chŏngch'arhada* 정찰하다 reconnoiter; scout.

chŏngch'al 정찰 price label[mark, tag]. *chŏngch'alje* 정찰제 price tag[fixed price] system.

chongch'angnyŏk 종착역 terminal station; terminus.

chŏngch'i 정치 politics; government. *chŏngch'ijŏ-*

gin 정치적인 political.

chongchŏm 종점 terminal (station); terminus (*Eng.*).

chongdalsae 종달새 skylark; lark.

chŏngdang 정당 political party. *posu*[*hyŏkshin*] *chŏngdang* 보수[혁신] 정당 conservative[progressive] party.

chŏngdang 정당. *chŏngdanghan* 정당한 just; fair; proper; right. *chŏngdanghage* 정당하게 justly; rightly; lawfully.

chŏngdap 정답 correct[right] answer.

chŏngdapta 정답다 (be) affectionate; tender; loving. *chŏngdapke* 정답게 affectionately; warmly.

chŏngdo 정도 grade; degree; standard; extent.

chŏngdon 정돈 order; arrangement. *chŏngdonhada* 정돈하다 arrange; put in order.

chŏnggak 정각 ① fixed time ② exact time. *chŏnggage* ① 정각에 at the appointed time ② just; punctually, sharp.

chŏnggang 정강 political principle; party platform.

chŏnggangi 정강이 shin; shank.

chonggi 종기 swell(ing); boil; tumo(u)r.

chŏnggi 정기. *chŏnggiŭi* 정기의 regular; periodical. *chŏnggijŏguro* 정기적으로 regularly; periodically; at a fixed period. *chŏnggi kanhaengmul* 정기 간행물 periodical publications.

chŏnggŏ 정거 stop; stoppage. *chŏnggŏjang* 정거장 station depot (*Am.*); stand.

chŏnggu 정구 tennis. *chŏngguhada* 정구하다 play tennis. *chŏnggujang* 정구장 tennis court.

chŏngguk 정국 political situation. *chŏnggugŭi puranjŏng*[*wigi*] 정국의 불안정[위기] instability [crisis] of a political situation.

chŏnggye 정계 political circles[world].

chonggyo 종교 religion. *chonggyosangŭi* 종교상의 religious. *chonggyo chaep'an* 종교 재판 the Inquisition.

chŏnggyŏn 정견 one's political view. *chŏnggyŏn palp'yohoe* 정견 발표회 campaign meeting.

chŏnggyu 정규 regularity; formality. *chŏnggyuŭi* 정규의 regular; formal.

chŏnghada 정하다 decide; fix; determine; settle; arrange; appoint.

chŏnghak 정학 suspension from school. *chŏnghaktanghada* 정학당하다 be suspended from school.

chonghap 종합 synthesis. *chonghapchŏk* 종합적 synthetic; composite. *chonghap pyŏngwŏn* 종합 병원 general hospital.

chŏnghwak 정확 correctness; accuracy; precision. *chŏnghwak'an[k'i]* 정확한[히] correct[ly]; exact [ly]; accurate[ly].

chŏnghyŏng 정형. *chŏnghyŏng susul[oekwa]* 정형 수술[외과] orthopedic operation[surgery].

chongi 종이 paper. *chongi han chang* 종이 한 장 a sheet of paper. *saekchongi* 색종이 colored paper.

chŏn-gi 전기 biography; life story.

chŏn-gi 전기 electricity. *chŏn-giŭi* 전기의 electric; electrical. *chŏn-girŭl k'yŏda[kkŭda]* 전기를 켜다 [끄다] turn[switch] on[off] the electrical light.

chongil 종일 all day (long) ; whole day; from morning till night; throughout the day.

chongja 종자 seed. →**ssi** 씨.

chŏngja 정자 pavilion; arbor.

chŏngje 정제 tablet; tabloid; pill.

chŏngji 정지 stop; suspension. *chŏngjihada* 정지 하다 stop; suspend.

chongjibu 종지부 full stop. →mach'imp'yo 마침표.

chŏngjik 정직 honesty. *chŏngjik'an*[*k'age*] 정직한 [하게] honest[ly].

chŏngjo 정조 chastity; virginity.

chŏngjŏk 정적 political opponent[rival, enemy].

chŏngjŏn 정전 stoppage of electric current; power failure.

chŏngjŏn 정전 ceasefire; truce. *chŏngjŏnhada* 정전 하다 have a truce; suspend hostilities. *chŏngjŏn hoedam* 정전 회담 ceasefire conference[order]

chŏngjŏng 정정 correction; *chŏngjŏnghada* 정정하 다 correct; revise; amend.

chŏngjŏngdangdang 정정당당. *chŏngjŏngdangdang han* 정정당당한 fair and square. *chŏngjŏngdang danghi* 정정당당히 fairly (and squarely).

chŏngka 정가 fixed[set, regular, list] price. *chŏng kap'yo* 정가표 price list[tag].

chŏngkwon 정권 political power[regime]. *chŏng kwon kyoch'e* 정권 교체 change of regime.

chŏngmaek 정맥 vein. *chŏngmaek chusa* 정맥 주사 venous injection.

chŏngmal 정말. *chŏngmallo* 정말로 really; quite; indeed; actually; truly.

chŏngmi 정미 net content[weight].

chŏngmil 정밀 minuteness; precision. *chŏngmirhan* [*hi*] 정밀한[히] minute[ly]; accurate[ly].

chongmok 종목 item; lines. *yŏngŏp chongmok* 영업 종목 lines of business.

chŏngmun 정문 front gate; main entrance.

chŏngmyŏn 정면 front; façade(*Fr.*). *chŏngmyŏnŭi* 정면의 front; frontal. *chŏngmyŏn ch'ungdol* 정면 충돌 head-on collision.

chŏngni 정리 arrangement. *chŏngnihada* 정리하다 put in order; adjust; arrange.

chongnyŏ 종려 hemp palm; palm. *chongnyŏnamu* 종려나무 palm tree.

chŏngnyŏk 정력 energy; vigo(u)r; vitality. *chŏngnyŏkchŏgin* 정력적인 energetic; vigorous.

chŏngnyŏl 정열 passion; ardor. *chŏngnyŏlchŏgin* 정열적인 passionate; ardent.

chŏngnyŏn 정년 retirement age; age limit. *chŏngnyŏn t'oejik* 정년 퇴직 retirement under the age limit.

chongnyu 종류 kind; sort. *on-gat chongnyuŭi* 온갖 종류의 all kinds(sorts) of.

chŏngnyu 정류. *chŏngnyujang* 정류장 stop; station.

chŏngo 정오 (high) noon; midday. *chŏngo-e* 정오에 at noon; at midday.

chŏn-gong 전공 special study. *chŏn-gonghada* 전공하다 specialize(major) (in).

chongŏbwon 종업원. employee; worker; operative; hands. 종업원 대표 *chongŏbwòn taep'yo* spokesman of the workingmen.

chŏngŏri 정어리 sardine. *chŏngŏri t'ongjorim* 정어리 통조림 canned sardines.

chongsa 종사. *chongsahada* 종사하다 engage in; pursue; follow; devote; be employed. ⌈affair.

chŏngsa 정사 ① love suicide; double suicide. ② love

chŏngsagak'yŏng 정사각형 regular(perfect) square.

chŏngsang 정상 normalcy; normality. *chŏngsangjŏk* 정상적 normal. *chŏngsanghwa* 정상화 normalization.

chŏngsang 정상 top; summit; peak. *chŏngsang hoedam* 정상 회담 summit meeting(conference).

chŏngse 정세 situation; conditions. *kungnae(kukche)*

chŏngse 국내〔국제〕 정세 domestic〔international〕 situation.

chŏngshik 정식 formality. *chŏngshigŭi* 정식의 formal; due. *chŏngshik susok* 정식 수속 formal process〔procedure〕.

chŏngshik 정식 regular meal; ordinary(*Eng.*).

chongshin 종신 (whole) life. *chongshinŭi* 종신의 life-long; life.

chŏngshin 정신 mind; spirit; soul. *chŏngshinjŏgin* 정신적인 spiritual; mental.

chŏngsuk 정숙 chastity; female virtue. *chŏngsuk'an* 정숙한 chaste; virtuous; faithful.

chŏngt'ong 정통. *chŏngt'onghada* 정통하다 be well versed〔informed〕 (in); have a thorough knowledge.

chŏn-gu 전구 electric bulb; light bulb.

chŏngŭi 정의 definition.

chŏngŭi 정의 justice; righteousness. *chŏngŭigam* 정의감 sense of justice.

chŏn-guk 전국 whole country〔nation〕. *chŏn-gugŭi* 전국의 nation-wide; national.

chŏn-gŭn 전근 transference. *chŏn-gŭnhada* 전근하다 be〔get〕 transferred to (another office).

chŏngwol 정월 January. *chŏngwol ch'oharu* 정월 초하루 New Year's Day.

chŏngwon 정원 garden. *chŏngwonsa* 정원사 (landscape) gardener.

chŏngwon 정원 the full member; regular staff.

chongyang 종양 tumor. *aksŏng chongyang* 악성 종양 malignant tumor.

chŏngyok 정욕 sexual〔sensual, carnal〕 desire; lust.

chon-gyŏng 존경 respect; reverence. *chon-gyŏnghada* 존경하다 respect; esteem. *chon-gyŏnghal man-*

han 존경할 만한 honorable; respectable.

chŏngyuk 정육. *chŏngyukchŏm* 정육점 butcher's (shop); meat market (*Am.*).

chŏnhada 전하다 ① convey[deliver] a message. ② hand down; transmit.

chŏnhak 전학. *chŏnhak'ada* 전학하다 change[transfer] to another school.

chŏnhu 전후 front and rear; before and behind.

chŏnhu 전후. *chŏnhuŭi* 전후의 postwar; after the war. *chŏnhup'a* 전후파 postwar generation.

chŏnhwa 전화 telephone; phone. *chŏnhwahada* 전화하다 (tele)phone; call; call[ring] up.

chŏnhyŏ 전혀 entirely; completely; utterly; quite.

chŏnhyŏng 전형 model; pattern; type. *chŏnhyŏngjŏk* 전형적 typical; model.

chŏnim 전임. *chŏnimŭi* 전임의 former. *chŏnimja* 전임자 predecessor in office.

chŏnim 전임 full-time service[employment]. *chŏnim kangsa* 전임 강사 full-time instructor.

chŏnja 전자 electron. *chŏnja kyesan-gi* 전자 계산기 electronic computer.

chonjae 존재 existence. *chonjaehada* 존재하다 exist.

chŏnjaeng 전쟁 war; warfare; battle; fight.

chŏnji 전지 change of air. *chŏnji yoyang* 전지 요양 change of air for one's health.

chŏnji 전지 electric cell; battery. *kŏnjŏnji* 건전지 dry battery.

chŏnjik 전직 one's former occupation[office]. *chŏnjik changgwan* 전직 장관 ex-minister.

chŏnjik 전직. *chŏnjik'ada* 전직하다 change one's occupation; switch jobs (to).

chŏnjin 전진 advance; progress. *chŏnjinhada* 전진

하다 advance; march forward.

chŏnjo 전조 sign; omen; foreboding; premonition.

chŏnju 전주 electric pole; telegraph[telephone, electric-light] pole.

chŏnju 전주 financier; capitalist.

chŏnjugok 전주곡 prelude; overture.

chonjung 존중 respect; esteem. *chonjunghada* 존중하다 respect; value.

chŏnmang 전망 view; prospect; outlook.

chŏnmun 전문 speciality; major. *chŏnmunŭro* 전문으로 specially; professionally. *chŏnmun-ga* 전문가 specialist; professional; expert.

chŏnmyŏl 전멸 complete[total] destruction; annihilation. *chŏnmyŏrhada* 전멸하다 be completely destroyed.

chŏnnal 전날 the other day; some time[days] ago; previous[preceding] day.

chŏnnap 전납 advance payment. *chŏnnap'ada* 전납하다 pay in advance; prepay.

chŏnnyŏn 전년 the previous year; the year before.

chŏnp'a 전파 electric wave. *chŏnp'a t'amjigi* 전파 탐지기 radar.

chŏnp'a 전파 transmission; propagation. *chŏnp'ahada* 전파하다 be propagated; be disseminated.

chŏnp'yo 전표 chit; ticket; slip. *maech'ul chŏnp'yo* 매출 전표 sales check.

chŏnsa 전사. *chŏnsahada* 전사하다 be killed in action[battle].

chŏnsa 전사 fighter; warrior; combatant.

chŏnse 전세. *chŏnsechip* 전세집 house for rent (*Am.*); house to let (*Eng.*). *chŏnse pŏsŭ* 전세 버스 chartered bus.

chŏnsegye 전세계 whole world. *chŏnsegyee* 전세계에 all over[through] the world.

chŏnshi 전시 exhibition; display. *chŏnshihada* 전시하다 exhibit.

chŏnshi 전시 wartime. *chŏnshi naegak* 전시 내각 war cabinet.

chŏnshi 전시 whole city. *chŏnshimin* 전시민 all the citizens.

chŏnshin 전신 whole body. *chŏnshine* 전신에 all over the body.

chŏnsŏl 전설 legend; tradition. *chŏnsŏlchŏk* 전설적 legendary; traditional.

chŏnsŏn 전선 electric wire[cord]; cable.

chŏnsong 전송 send-off. *chŏnsonghada* 전송하다 see (a person) off; give a send-off.

chŏnsongnyŏk 전속력 full speed. *chŏnsongnyŏgŭro* 전속력으로 at full speed.

chŏnsul 전술 tactics; art of war. *chŏnsulsangŭi* 전술상의 tactical.

chŏnt'ong 전통 tradition. *chŏnt'ongjŏgin[ŭro]* 전통적인[으로] traditional[ly].

chŏnt'u 전투 battle; fight. *chŏnt'uhada* 전투하다 fight; battle. *chŏnt'ugi* 전투기 fighter.

chŏnŭng 저능. *chŏnŭnghan* 저능한 weak-[feeble-]minded. *chŏnŭnga* 저능아 imbecile child.

chŏnwi 전위 advance(d) guard; vanguard.

chŏnwŏn 전원 all (the) members; entire staff. *chŏnwŏn ilch'iro* 전원 일치로 unanimously.

chŏnyŏk 저녁 evening. *chŏnyŏkttaee* 저녁때에 toward evening.

chŏnyŏm 전염 contagion; infection. *chŏnyŏmhada* 전염하다 be contagious[infectious]. *chŏnyŏm-*

pyŏng 전염병 infectious[contagious] disease; epidemic.

chŏnyŏn 전연 →**chŏnhyŏ** 전혀.

chŏnyong 전용 exclusive use. *chŏnyongŭi* 전용의 private; exclusive. *chŏnyongch'a* 전용차 private car.

choŏn 조언 advice; counsel. *choŏnhada* 조언하다 advise; give (a person) advice.

chŏon 저온 low temperature.

chŏpcha'k 접착 adhesion; glueing.

chŏpch'akche 접착제 adhesive (agent); cement.

chŏpch'ok 접촉 contact; touch. *chŏpch'ok'ada* 접촉하다 touch; come into contact[touch] (with).

chŏpchong 접종 inoculation; vaccination. *chŏpchonghada* 접종하다 inoculate; vaccinate.

chŏpkŭn 접근 approach; access. *chŏpkŭnhada* 접근하다 approach; draw[get] near.

chŏp'ada 접하다 touch; adjoin; border (on); be adjacent (to).

chŏpshi 접시 plate; dish; saucer; platter.

chŏpsu 접수 receipt; acceptance. *chŏpsuhada* 접수하다 receive; accept. *chŏpsugu* 접수구 usher's window[desk].

chopta 좁다 (be) narrow; small; limited.

chŏpta 접다 fold (up); furl; double; turn up[down].

chŏptae 접대 reception. *chŏptaehada* 접대하다 receive; entertain.

chorida 졸이다 ① boil down ② feel nervous[anxious]

chŏrida 저리다 be benumbed; become numbed.

chŏrida 절이다 pickle; salt (vegetable).

chorigae 조리개 thin cord; tightening string.

chorim 조림 hard-boiled food. *t'ongjorim* 통조림 canned food.

chorip 조립 assembly; framework. *chorip'ada* 조립하다 assemble; put[fit] together.

chorong 조롱 ridicule; sneer. *choronghada* 조롱하다 ridicule; make fun of; laugh at.

chorŏp 졸업 graduation. *chorŏp'ada* 졸업하다 finish; graduate from. *chorŏpsaeng* 졸업생 graduate.

chorŭda 조르다 ① tighten; strangle ② importune; press.

chŏryak 절약 saving; economy; thrift. *chŏryak'ada* 절약하다 economize; save; spare.

choryŏk 조력 help; aid; assistance. *choryŏk'ada* 조력하다 help; aid; assist.

chosa 조사 investigation; inquiry. *chosahada* 조사하다 inquire; investigate.

chosan 조산 premature birth. *chosanhada* 조산하다 give premature birth to.

chosang 조상 ancestor; forefather.

chosanwŏn 조산원 midwife; maternity nurse.

choshim 조심 caution; heed; care. *choshimhada* 조심하다 take care; be careful[cautious].

chŏsŏ 저서 one's writings; work; book.

chosu 조수 assistant; helper. *unjŏn chosu* 운전 조수 assistant driver.

chŏsuji 저수지 reservoir.

chosuk 조숙 early maturity. *chosuk'an* 조숙한 premature; precocious.

chŏt 젖 milk. *chŏtkkokchi* 젖꼭지 teat; nipple. *chŏsso* 젖소 milch cow.

chŏt 젓 pickled[salted] fish. *saeujŏt* 새우젓 pickled shrimps.

chot'a 좋다 (be) good; fine; nice. *kajang choŭn* 가장 좋은 best.

chŏt'aek 저택 mansion; residence. *chŏt'aekka* 저택 가 residential quarters.

chŏtchok 저쪽 there; over there; the opposite side.

chŏtkarak 젓가락 (pair of) chopsticks.

chŏtta 젓다 ① row ② stir ③ wave.

chŏtta 젖다 get wet; be damp; be soaked[drenched]. *chŏjŭn* 젖은 wet; damp.

chot'oe 조퇴. *chot'oehada* 조퇴하다 leave (school, office) earlier (than usual).

choŭi 조의 condolence. *choŭirŭl p'yohada* 조의를 표 하다 express one's condolence.

chŏul 저울 balance; scales; weighing beam.

choyak 조약 treaty; pact. *p'yŏnghwa choyak* 평화 조약 peace treaty.

choyaktol 조약돌 gravel; pebbles.

choyonghada 조용하다 (be) quiet; silent; still; tranquil; placid.

chu 주 share; stock. *ŭnhaengju* 은행주 bank stocks. →**chushik** 주식.

chubin 주빈 guest of honor; principal guest.

chubu 주부 mistress of a house; housewife.

chubyŏn 주변 circumference; environs; outskirts.

chuch'a 주차 parking. *chuch'ahada* 주차하다 park.

chuch'oe 주최 auspices. *chuch'oehada* 주최하다 sponsor. *chuch'oero* 주최로 under the auspices of.

chuda 주다 give; bestow; award. *kihoerŭl chuda* 기회를 주다 give[afford] a chance.

chudan 주단 silks and satins; silk goods.

chudong 주동 leadership. *chudonghada* 주동하다 take the lead.

chudun 주둔 stationing. *chudunhada* 주둔하다 be stationed. *chudun-gun* 주둔군 stationary troops.

chudungi 주둥이 mouth; beak; mouthpiece.

chugan 주간 week. *toksŏ chugan* 독서 주간 book week. *chugan nonp'yŏng* 주간 논평 weekly review.

chugan 주간 daytime; day; diurnal. *chugan kŭnmu* 주간 근무 day-duty.

chugida 죽이다 kill; slay; murder.

chugŭm 죽음 death. *chugŭmŭl murŭpssŭgo* 죽음을 무릅쓰고 at the risk of one's death.

chugŭp 주급 weekly wages[pay, salary].

chuil 주일 week(day). *ibŏn* [*chinan, taŭm*] *chuil* 이번[지난, 다음] 주일 this [last, next] week.

chuim 주임 person in charge; head; chief.

chuin 주인 master; employer; host.

chuin-gong 주인공 hero; heroine.

chujang 주장 assertion; claim. *chujanghada* 주장하다 assert; claim.

chuje 주제 main subject; theme; motif.

chujenŏmta 주제넘다 (be) forward; cheeky; impudent; pert; saucy.

chuji 주지 chief[head] priest.

chujŏ 주저 hesitation. *chujŏhada* 주저하다 hesitate.

chujŏanta 주저앉다 fall down; sit down plump.

chujŏm 주점 tavern; pub; grogshop; wineshop.

chujŏnja 주전자 (copper, brass) kettle; teakettle.

chuju 주주 shareholder (*Eng.*); stockholder (*Am.*).

chuk 죽 (rice) gruel; porridge.

chŭk 즉 namely; that is; so to speak.

chŭkkak 즉각 on the spot; at once; instantly.

chŭksa 즉사 instantaneous death. *chŭksahada* 즉사하다 die on the spot.

chuksun 죽순 bamboo shoot[sprout].

chukta 죽다 die; pass away; be killed; lose one's life. *chugŭn* 죽은 dead; deceased; the late.

chul 줄 rope; cord; string; line.

chulda 줄다 decrease; diminish; lessen.

chuldarigi 줄다리기 tug of war. *chuldarigihada* 줄다리기하다 play at a tug of war.

chŭlgida 즐기다 enjoy oneself; take pleasure in; amuse oneself.

chŭlgŏpta 즐겁다 (be) pleasant; delightful; glad. *chŭlgŏi* 즐거이 happily; pleasantly; cheerfully.

chulgot 줄곧 all the time[way]; all along[through].

chumak 주막 tavern; inn. *chumak chuin* 주막 주인 innkeeper.

chumal 주말 weekend. *chumare* 주말에 on weekends.

chumi 주미. *chumiŭi* 주미의 stationed[resident] in America. *chumi Han-guk taesa* 주미 한국 대사 Korean Ambassador to[in] the United States.

chumin 주민 inhabitants; residents.

chumok 주목 attention; notice. *chumok'ada* 주목하다 pay attention to.

chumŏk 주먹 (clenched) fist.

chumŏni 주머니 bag; sack; pouch; purse.

chumun 주문 order; request. *chumunhada* 주문하다 order; give an order.

chumurŭda 주무르다 finger; fumble with.

chunbi 준비 preparation; arrangements; provision. *chunbihada* 준비하다 prepare; arrange; provide for; get ready for.

chunjang 준장 brigadier general (*army*); commodore (*navy*).

chung 중 Buddhist priest; monk; bonze.

chungang 중앙 center; middle; heart. *chungangŭi* 중앙의 central; middle.

chŭngbal 증발 evaporation. *chŭngbarhada* 증발하 다 evaporate; vaporize.

chungbok 중복 duplication. *chungbok'ada* 중복하다 overlap; duplicate.

chungbyŏng 중병 serious[severe] illness. *chungbyŏnge kŏllida* 중병에 걸리다 fall[get] seriously ill. *chungbyŏng hwanja* 중병 환자 serious case.

chungdae 중대 company. *chungdaejang* 중대장 company commander.

chungdae 중대 importance. *chungdaehan* 중대한 important; serious; grave.

chungdan 중단 discontinuance. *chungdanhada* 중단 하다 discontinue; suspend; break off.

chungdo 중도. *chungdo-esŏ* 중도에서 halfway; midway; in the middle.

chungdok 중독 poisoning; toxication. *chungdoktoeda* 중독되다 be poisoned. *shikchungdok* 식중독 food-poisoning.

chŭngga 증가 increase; addition. *chŭnggahada* 증 가하다 increase; rise; grow.

chunggan 중간 middle; midway. *chungganŭi* 중간 의 middle; midway; interim; intermediate.

chŭnggi 증기 steam; vapor.

chunggo 중고. *chunggoŭi* 중고의 used; old; second-hand. *chunggop'um* 중고품 second-hand article. *chunggoch'a* 중고차 used car.

chŭnggŏ 증거 evidence; proof; testimony.

Chunggong 중공 Communist[Red] China.

chunggongŏp 중공업 heavy industry.

Chungguk 중국 China.

chunggyŏn 중견 backbone; main body. *chunggyŏn inmul* 중견 인물 leading figures.

chunggyŏngsang 중경상 serious and slight injuries [wounds].

chunghakkyo 중학교 middle school; junior high school (*Am.*).

Chunghwamin-guk 중화민국 (Rep. of) China.

chunghwanja 중환자 serious case.

chŭngin 증인 witness; attestor.

chungjae 중재 arbitration. *chungjaehada* 중재하다 mediate; arbitrate.

chungjang 중장 lieutenant general (*army*); vice admiral (*navy*).

chungji 중지 suspension; discontinuance. *chungjihada* 중지하다 stop; suspend; discontinue.

chungjin-guk 중진국 semi-developed country.

chingjip 징집 enlistment; enrollment; recruiting. *chingjip'ada* 징집하다 levy; enlist; recruit.

chungchŏm 중점 importance; emphasis; stress. *…e chungchŏmŭl tuda* …에 중점을 두다 lay emphasis [stress] on.

chungjŏlmo 중절모 soft hat; felt hat.

chŭngjŏng 증정 presentation. *chŭngjŏnghada* 증정하다 present; make a present.

chŭngkwon 증권 bill; securities. *chŭngkwon hoesa* 증권 회사 stock company; security corporation.

chungmae 중매 matchmaking. *chungmaehada* 중매하다 make a match.

Chungmi 중미 Central America.

chŭngmyŏng 증명 proof; evidence. *chŭngmyŏnghada* 증명하다 prove; show; verify.

chungnip 중립 neutrality. *chungnipchŏk* 중립적

neutral. *chungnipkuk* 중립국 neutral power (state).

chungnyŏng 중령 lieutenant colonel (*army*); commander (*navy*).

chungnyu 중류 middle class. *chungnyu kajŏng* 중류 가정 middle class family.

chŭngnyu 증류 distillation. *chŭngnyuhada* 증류하다 distill. *chŭngnyuju* 증류주 spirituous liquor.

chŭngŏn 증언 testimony; witness; (verbal) evidence. *chŭngŏnsŏ* 증언서 written testimony.

chungp'ung 중풍 palsy; paralysis.

chungsang 중상 slander. *chungsanghada* 중상하다 slander. *chungsangjŏgin* 중상적인 slanderous.

chungsanmo 중산모 derby(*Am.*); bowler (*Eng.*).

chungse 중세 the Middle Ages; medieval times. *chungseŭi* 중세의 medieval.

chŭngse 증세 symptoms; condition of a patient.

chungshi 중시 serious consideration. *chungshihada* 중시하다 attach importance to; take a serious view (of); make much (of).

chungshim 중심 center; focus; core. *kongŏbŭi chungshim* 공업의 중심 industrial center.

chŭngsŏ 증서 deed; bond; certificate; voucher.

chungsun 중순 second[middle] ten days of a month.

chungt'ae 중태 serious[critical] condition.

chungwi 중위 first lieutenant (*Am. army*); lieutenant junior grade (*Am. navy*).

chungyo 중요. *chungyohan* 중요한 important; essential; momentous. *chungyoshihada* 중요시하다 make[think] much of. →chungshi 중시.

chun-gyŏlsŭngjŏn 준결승전 semifinal game[match].

chunusŭng 준우승 coming out second best.

chungyŏk 중역 director. → **isa** 이사.

chungyu 중유 crude[raw] petroleum; heavy oil.

chuŏ 주어 subject.

chŭp 즙 juice; sap. *p'odo[sagwa]jŭp* 포도[사과] 즙 grape[apple] juice.

chupta 줍다 pick up; gather (up); find.

churida 줄이다 reduce; decrease; diminish.

churo 주로 mainly; chiefly; principally.

churŭm 주름 wrinkles; crumples. *churŭmjin ŏlgul* 주름진 얼굴 wrinkled[furrowed] face.

churye 주례 officiator. *churyerŭl sŏda* 주례를 서다 officiate at a marriage.

churyŏk 주력. *churyŏk'ada* 주력하다 exert oneself (for).

churyŏk 주력 main force. *churyŏk pudae* 주력 부대 main force unit.

churyu 주류 main current; mainstream. *churyup'a* 주류파 leading faction.

chusa 주사 injection; shot (*Am.*). *chusahada* 주사 하다 inject. *yebang chusa* 예방 주사 preventive injection.

chusan 주산 abacus calculation.

chusawi 주사위 die.

chushi 주시 steady look; gaze. *chushihada* 주시하 다 gaze at; watch carefully.

chushik 주식 shares (*Eng.*); stock (*Am.*).

chuso 주소 one's residence[abode]; address.

chusŏngbun 주성분 chief[main] ingredient.

chut'aek 주택 house; residence. *hohwa chut'aek* 호화 주택 luxurious house[mansion].

chuŭi 주의 attention; care. *chuŭihada* 주의하다 be careful of; take care of.

chuŭi 주의 principle; doctrine; ism; cause.

chuwi 주위 circumference. *chuwiŭi* 주위의 neighboring.

chuya 주야 day and night.

chuyŏk 주역 leading title[part, role].

chwach'ŏn 좌천 relegation; demotion. *chwach'ŏnhada* 좌천하다 relegate; demote (*Am.*).

chwach'ŭk 좌측 left (side). *chwach'ŭk t'onghaeng* 좌측 통행 "Keep to the left."

chwadam 좌담 table-talk. *chwadamhoe* 좌담회 roundtable talk; symposium.

chwaik 좌익 left wing. *chwaik punja* 좌익 분자 left-wing element.

chwajŏl 좌절 frustration; setback. *chwajŏrhada* 좌절하다 get ruined; be frustrated.

chwasŏk 좌석 seat. *chwasŏksu* 좌석수 seating capacity.

chwau 좌우 right and left. *chwaue* 좌우에 on right and left.

chwaugan 좌우간 anyhow; in any case; at any rate.

chwi 쥐 rat; mouse. *chwiyak* 쥐약 rat poison.

chwida 쥐다 hold; take hold of; grasp; seize.

C 〔ch'〕

ch'a 차 (motor)car; auto(mobile). *ch'arŭl t'ada* 차를 타다 take a car. *ch'asago* 차사고 vehicular accident.

ch'abi 차비 carfare; train[railway, bus] fare.

ch'abyŏl 차별 distinction; discrimination. *ch'abyŏrhada* 차별하다 discriminate.

ch'ada 차다 ① kick; give a kick. ② click(tongue).

ch'ada 차다 carry; wear; put on.

ch'ada 차다 (be) full (of); be filled (with); be jammed[overcrowded].

ch'ada 차다 (be) cold; chilly; icy. *ch'anbaram* 찬 바람 chilly[cold] wind.

ch'ado 차도 roadway; carriageway; track.

ch'aegim 책임 responsibility; liability. *ch'aegimi innŭn* 책임이 있는 responsible.

ch'aejip 채집 collection. *ch'aejip'ada* 채집하다 collect; gather.

ch'aek 책 book; volume. *yŏngŏch'aek* 영어책 English book.

ch'aekcha 책자 book; pamphlet; leaflet.

ch'aekchang 책장 bookcase; bookshelf.

ch'aekchang 책장 leaf of a book; pages.

ch'aekkoji 책꽂이 bookshelf; bookcase.

ch'aekpang 책방 bookstore; bookshop. →**sŏjŏm** 서점.

ch'aeksang 책상 desk; (writing) table[bureau].

ch'aemu 채무 debt; obligation; liabilities. *ch'aemuja* 채무자 debtor.

ch'aeso 채소 vegetables; greens. →**yach'ae** 야채.

ch'aetchik 채쩍 whip; lash; rod.

ch'aeyong 채용 adoption. *ch'aeyonghada* 채용하다 adopt.

ch'ago 차고 car shed; garage; carport.

ch'agwan 차관 loan. *ch'agwanŭl ŏtta* 차관을 얻다 obtain a loan.

ch'ai 차이 difference; disparity. *ŭigyŏnŭi ch'ai* 의견의 차이 difference of opinion.

ch'ail 차일 sunshade; awning; tent.

ch'ajanaeda 찾아내다 find out; discover; detect.

ch'ajang 차장 conductor(*Am.*); guard (*Eng.*). *yŏ-*

ch'ajang 여차장 conductress.

ch'ajihada 차지하다 occupy; hold; take; possess.

ch'ak'ada 착하다 (be) good; nice; kind-hearted. *ch'ak'an saram* 착한 사람 good-natured person.

ch'akch'wi 착취 exploitation. *ch'akch'wihada* 착취하다 exploit; squeeze.

ch'akkak 착각 illusion. *ch'akkak'ada* 착각하다 have [be under] an illusion.

ch'akshil 착실. *ch'akshirhada* 착실하다 (be) steady; trustworthy; faithful; sound. *ch'akshirhi* 착실히 steadily; faithfully.

ch'alssak 찰싹 with a slap →**ch'ŏlssŏk** 철썩.

ch'alttŏk 찰떡 glutinous rice cake.

ch'amhada 참하다 (be) nice and pretty; charming; good-looking. *ch'amhan agassi* 참한 아가씨 pretty girl.

ch'amga 참가 participation. *ch'amgahada* 참가하다 participate[take part] (in); join.

ch'amgo 참고 reference. *ch'amgohada* 참고하다 refer; consult. *ch'amgosŏ* 참고서 reference book.

ch'amhok 참혹. *ch'amhok'an* 참혹한 cruel; brutal. *ch'amhok'age* 참혹하게 cruelly; brutally.

ch'ammal 참말 true remark[story]; truth. *ch'ammallo* 참말로 truly; really; indeed.

ch'amp'ae 참패 crushing defeat. *ch'amp'aehada* 참패하다 suffer a crushing defeat.

ch'amsae 참새 sparrow.

ch'amsŏk 참석 attendance. *ch'amsŏk'ada* 참석하다 attend; be present; take part in.

ch'amta 참다 bear; endure; tolerate; stand.

ch'amŭro 참으로 really; truly; indeed.

ch'anae 차내 inside[interior] of a car.

ch'ang 창 window. *yurich'ang* 유리창 glass window. *ch'angŭl yŏlda* [*tatta*] 창을 열다[닫다] open [close] a window.

ch'ang 창 spear; lance. *ch'angdŏnjigi* 창던지기 javelin throw.

ch'angbu 창부 →**ch'angnyŏ** 창녀.

ch'anggo 창고 warehouse; storehouse.

ch'anggŭk 창극 Korean classical opera.

ch'angja 창자 intestines; bowels; entrails.

ch'angjak 창작 original work; creation. *ch'angjak'ada* 창작하다 create; write (a novel).

ch'angjo 창조 creation. *ch'angjohada* 창조하다 create. *ch'angjojŏk* 창조적 creative.

ch'angmun 창문 →**ch'ang** 창.

ch'angnip 창립 foundation; establishment *ch'angnip'ada* 창립하다 found; establish.

ch'angnyŏ 창녀 prostitute; whore; street girl.

ch'angp'i 창피 shame; dishonor. *ch'angp'ihada* 창피하다 (be) shameful; humiliating.

ch'anjo 찬조 support; patronage. *ch'anjohada* 찬조하다 support; back up.

ch'anmul 찬물 cold water. →**naengsu** 냉수.

ch'ansong 찬송. *ch'ansonghada* 찬송하다 praise; chant. *ch'ansongga* 찬송가 hymn; psalm.

ch'ansŏng 찬성 approval; agreement. *ch'ansŏnghada* 찬성하다 approve of; agree.

ch'ap'yo 차표 ticket. *wangbok ch'ap'yo* 왕복 차표 round-trip ticket (*Am.*); return ticket (*Eng.*).

ch'aryang 차량 vehicles; cars; carriage.

ch'arye 차례 order; turn. *ch'aryero* 차례로 in order; by [in] turns.

ch'assak 찻삯 (car)fare. →**ch'abi** 차비.

ch'atta 찾다 search[hunt, look] (for); seek (for, after); look out.

ch'atchan 찻잔 teacup.

ch'atchip 찻집 tea[coffee] house; tea[coffee] shop; tearoom. →**tabang** 다방.

ch'atkil 찻길 roadway; carriageway; track.

ch'ayong 차용 borrowing; loan. *ch'ayonghada* 차용하다 borrow; have the loan.

ch'e 체 sieve; bolter; riddle. *ch'ero ch'ida* 체로 치다 sieve; screen; sift.

ch'ejung 체중 (body) weight. *ch'ejungŭl talda* 체중을 달다 weigh[measure] oneself.

ch'egye 체계 system. *ch'egyejŏk(ŭro)* 체계적(으로) systematic(ally).

ch'egyŏk 체격 physique; build; constitution.

ch'ejo 체조 gymnastics; gym; physical exercises. *kigye ch'ejo* 기계 체조 heavy gymnastics.

ch'eon 체온 temperature; body heat. *ch'eon-gye* 체온계 clinical thermometer.

ch'ep'o 체포 arrest; capture. *ch'ep'ohada* 체포하다 arrest; capture.

ch'eryŏk 체력 physical strength[stamina]. *ch'eryŏk kŏmsa* 체력 검사 strength test.

ch'eyuk 체육 physical education. *ch'eyuk'oe* 체육회 athletic association.

ch'ian 치안 public peace. *ch'ian-guk* 치안국 Headquarters of National police.

ch'ibun 치분 tooth powder. →**ch'iyak** 치약.

ch'ida 치다 strike; hit; beat.

ch'ida 치다 ① attack; assault ② cut; trim ③ denounce; charge.

ch'ida 치다 send (a telegram).

ch'ida 치다 put (soy) into[in, on].

ch'ida 치다 put up; hang; draw. *k'ŏt'ŭnŭl ch'ida* 커튼을 치다 draw a curtain.

ch'ikwa 치과. *ch'ikwa pyŏngwon* 치과 병원 dental clinic. *ch'ikwa ŭisa* 치과 의사 dentist; dental surgeon.

ch'ilgi 칠기 lacquer(ed) ware.

ch'ilmyŏnjo 칠면조 turkey.

ch'ilp'an 칠판 blackboard.

ch'ilship 칠십 (70) seventy. *che ch'ilshibŭi* 제 칠십의 the seventieth.

ch'im 침 spittle; saliva. *ch'imŭl paetta* 침을 뱉다 spit.

ch'im 침 ① needle; pin ② hand ③ prickle ④ hook.

ch'im 침 acupuncture. *ch'imŭl not'a* 침을 놓다 acupuncture; apply acupuncture.

ch'ima 치마 skirt.

ch'imch'imhada 침침하다 (be) dark; gloomy; dim. *ch'imch'imhan pang* 침침한 방 dimly-lit room.

ch'imdae 침대 bed; berth. *ch'imdaech'a* 침대차 sleeping car.

ch'imgu 침구 bedding; bedclothes.

ch'imip 침입 invasion. *ch'imip'ada* 침입하다 invade.

ch'immuk 침묵 silence. *ch'immuk'ada* 침묵하다 be silent; hold one's tongue.

ch'imnyak 침략 aggression; invasion. *ch'imnyak'ada* 침략하다 invade.

ch'imnye 침례. *ch'imnye kyohoe* 침례 교회 Baptist Church.

chimshil 침실 bedroom; bedchamber.

ch'imt'u 침투 permeation; penetration. *ch'imt'uhada* 침투하다 permeate; penetrate.

ch'imul 침울. *ch'imurhan* 침울한 melancholy; gloomy.

ch'inch'ŏk 친척 relation; relative; kinsman.

ch'ingch'an 칭찬 praise; applause. *ch'ingch'anhada* 칭찬하다 praise; admire; speak highly of.

ch'ingŏlgŏrida 칭얼거리다 whimper; whine; fret.

ch'in-gu 친구 friend; companion; pal. *yŏja ch'in-gu* 여자 친구 girl friend.

ch'inhada 친하다 (be) intimate; friendly. *ch'inhan pŏt* 친한 벗 intimate friend.

ch'inil 친일. *ch'inirŭi* 친일의 pro-Japanese. *ch'inilp'a* 친일파 pro-Japanese (group).

ch'injŏl 친절 kindness. *ch'injŏrhan* 친절한 kind. *ch'injŏrhi* 친절히 kindly.

ch'inmi 친미. *ch'inmiŭi* 친미의 pro-American. *ch'inmip'a* 친미파 pro-Americans.

ch'inmok 친목. *ch'inmok'oe* 친목회 social meeting [gathering]; sociable (*Am.*).

ch'insŏ 친서 autograph letter; personal letter.

ch'insŏn 친선 goodwill; friendship; amity. *ch'insŏn kyŏnggi* 친선 경기 friendly match.

ch'iril 칠일 seventh (of the month); seven days.

chirwol 칠월 July.

ch'iryo 치료 medical treatment. *ch'iryohada* 치료하다 treat; cure.

ch'isol 치솔 toothbrush.

ch'isu 치수 measurement; size; dimensions.

ch'it'ong 치통 toothache.

ch'iuda 치우다 put in order; tidy up; clear away.

ch'iyak 치약 tooth paste.

ch'o 초 candle. *ch'otpul* 촛불 candlelight.

ch'o 초 vinegar. *chorŭl chida* 초를 치다 add vinegar.

ch'ŏ 처 wife; one's better-half. →**anae** 아내.

ch'obo 초보 first steps; rudiment. *ch'oboŭi* 초보의 elementary; rudimentary.

ch'ŏbŏl 처벌 punishment; penalty. *ch'ŏbŏrhada* 처벌하다 punish.

ch'ŏbun 처분 disposal; management. *ch'ŏbunhada* 처분하다 dispose of; do[deal] with.

ch'och'im 초침 second-hand (of a watch).

ch'ochŏm 초점 focus.

ch'och'ŏng 초청 invitation. *ch'och'ŏnghada* 초청하다 invite. *ch'och'ŏngchang* 초청장 letter of invitation.

ch'odae 초대 invitation. *ch'odaehada* 초대하다 invite. *ch'odaekwŏn* 초대권 complimentary ticket. *ch'odaechang* 초대장 invitation card.

ch'ŏdinsang 첫인상 one's first impression.

ch'oeak 최악. *ch'oeagŭi* 최악의 the worst. *ch'oeagŭi kyŏnguenŭn* 최악의 경우에는 in the worst case.

ch'oech'o 최초 first; beginning. *ch'oech'oŭi* 최초의 first. *ch'oech'o-e* 최초에 in the first place.

ch'oego 최고. *ch'oegoŭi* 최고의 highest; maximum.

ch'oeha 최하 lowest. *ch'oeha kagyŏk* 최하 가격 lowest price.

ch'oehu 최후 the last; the end. *ch'oehuŭi* 최후의 the last; final.

ch'oejŏ 최저. *ch'oejŏŭi* 최저의 lowest; minimum. *ch'oejŏ imgŭm* 최저 임금 minimum[floor] wages.

ch'oejong 최종. *ch'oejongŭi* 최종의 last; final.

ch'oegŭn 최근. *ch'oegŭnŭi* 최근의 recent; late; up-to-date. *ch'oegŭne* 최근에 recently; lately.

ch'oemyŏnsul 최면술 hypnotism; mesmerism.

ch'oeshin 최신. *ch'oeshinŭi* 최신의 newest; latest;

up-to-date. *ch'oeshinshik* 최신식 latest fashion; newest style.

ch'ogi 초기 early days; first[early] stage.

ch'ogŭp 초급 beginner's class; junior course. *ch'ogŭp taehak* 초급 대학 junior college.

ch'ogwa 초과 excess; surplus. *ch'ogwahada* 초과하다 exceed.

ch'oharunnal 초하룻날 first day of the month.

ch'ŏji 처지 situation; circumstances; condition.

ch'ŏjida 처지다 hang down; droop; sag.

ch'ojo 초조 fret; impatience. *ch'ojohada* 초조하다 (be) fretful; irritated.

ch'ojŏnyŏk 초저녁 early evening; early hours of evening; toward evening.

ch'ŏkch'u 척추 backbone; spinal column.

ch'ŏl 철 iron; steel. *ch'ŏrŭi changmak* 철의 장막 the Iron Curtain. *ch'ŏlmun* 철문 iron gate.

ch'ŏl 철 season. *sach'ŏl* 사철 four seasons.

ch'ŏlbŏkkŏrida 철벅거리다 splash; dabble in.

chŏlbong 철봉 iron rod[bar]; horizontal[exercise] bar.

ch'ŏlchŏ 철저 thoroughness. *ch'ŏlchŏhan* 철저한 thorough(going). *ch'ŏlchŏhi* 철저히 thoroughly.

ch'ŏlchomang 철조망 (barbed) wire entanglements.

ch'ŏlgŏ 철거 withdrawal. *ch'ŏlgŏhada* 철거하다 withdraw; remove.

ch'ŏlgong 철공 ironworker. *ch'ŏlgongso* 철공소 ironworks. *ch'ŏlgongŏp* 철공업 iron manufacture.

ch'ŏlgwan 철관 iron pipe[tube].

ch'ŏlgyo 철교 iron bridge; railway bridge.

ch'ŏlmang 철망 wire-netting; wire net; wire gauze.

ch'ŏlmo 철모 helmet; steel[iron] cap.

ch'ŏlssa 철사 wire. *ch'ŏlssa kat'ŭn* 철사 같은 wiry.

ch'ŏlto 철도 railway; railroad(*Am.*). *ch'ŏlto sago* 철도 사고 railroad accident.

ch'ŏma 처마 eaves. *ch'ŏma mit'e* 처마 밑에 under the eaves.

ch'ŏmbu 첨부 appending; annexing. *ch'ŏmbuhada* 첨부하다 attach; append. *ch'ŏmbu sŏryu* 첨부 서류 attached[accompanying] papers.

ch'omch'omhada 촘촘하다 (be) close; dense; thick.

ch'ŏn 천 cloth; fabric; (woven) stuff; texture.

ch'ŏn 천 (1,000) a thousand. *such'ŏnŭi* 수천의 thousands of. *ch'ŏllian* 천리안 clairvoyance.

ch'ŏnch'e 천체 heavenly body.

ch'ŏnch'ŏnhi 천천히 slowly; leisurely; without hur- ［ry

ch'ŏndang 천당 Heaven; Paradise. →ch'ŏn-guk 천국.

ch'ŏndung 천둥 thunder. *ch'ŏndungch'ida* 천둥치다 thunder; roll; grumble.

ch'ong 총 gun; rifle. *ch'ongŭl ssoda* 총을 쏘다 shoot[fire] a gun.

ch'ong 총 all; whole; total; general. *ch'ongin-gu* 총인구 total population.

ch'ŏng 청 request; one's wishes. *ch'ŏnghada* 청하다 ask; beg; request.

ch'ongaek 총액 total amount; sum[grand] total.

ch'ongal 총알 bullet; shot. →t'anhwan 탄환.

ch'ŏngbu 청부 contract. *ch'ŏngbuŏp* 청부업 contracting business. *ch'ŏngbuŏpcha* 청부업자 contractor.

ch'ŏngch'ŏpchang 청첩장 letter of invitation; invitation card.

ch'ŏngch'un 청춘 youth; springtime of life. *ch'ŏngch'un-gi* 청춘기 adolescence.

ch'ŏngdong 청동 bronze. *ch'ŏngdong hwaro* 청동 화

로 bronze brazier.

ch'ŏnggu 청구 demand; claim. *ch'ŏngguhada* 청구하다 request; demand. *ch'ŏnggusŏ* 청구서 request; demand bill[draft, note, loan].

ch'ŏnggwa 청과 vegetables and fruits. *ch'ŏnggwa shijang* 청과 시장 vegetable and fruit market.

ch'onggye 총계 total amount; (sum) total. *ch'onggyehada* 총계하다 totalize; sum up.

ch'ŏnggyodo 청교도 Puritan. *ch'ŏnggyodojŏk* 청교도적 puritanical.

ch'ŏnggyŏl 청결 cleanliness; purity. *ch'ŏnggyŏrhada* 청결하다 (be) clean; neat; pure. *ch'ŏnggyŏrhi* 청결히 cleanly.

ch'ŏn-guk 천국 Heaven; Paradise.

ch'onghoe 총회 general meeting; plenary session.

ch'ŏnghon 청혼 propose; proposal of marriage.

ch'ŏngja 청자 celadon porcelain. *Koryŏ ch'ŏngja* 고려 청자 Koryŏ celadon.

ch'ongjae 총재 president; governor. *puch'ongjae* 부총재 vice-president.

ch'ongjang 총장 ① president(*university*) ② secretary general(*business, office work*).

ch'ŏngju 청주 refined rice wine.

ch'ŏngjung 청중 audience; attendance.

ch'ongmyŏng 총명 cleverness. *ch'ongmyŏnghan* 총명한 wise; sagacious; intelligent.

ch'ongni 총리 premier; prime minister.

ch'ŏngnyŏn 청년 young man; youth.

ch'ŏngsaek 청색 blue (color).

ch'ŏngsajin 청사진 blueprint.

ch'ŏngsan 청산 liquidation. *ch'ŏngsanhada* 청산하다 liquidate; pay off.

ch'ŏngso 청소 cleaning. *ch'ŏngsohada* 청소하다 clean; sweep. *ch'ŏngsobu* 청소부 scavenger. *ch'ŏngsoch'a* 청소차 refuse cart; sewage truck.

ch'ongsŏn-gŏ 총선거 general election.

ch'ŏngsonyŏn 청소년 youth; younger generation; teenagers.

ch'ongyŏngsa 총영사 consul general. *ch'ongyŏngsa-gwan* 총영사관 consulate general.

ch'ŏnhada 천하다 ① (be) humble; low(ly) ② (be) vulgar; mean.

ch'ŏnjae 천재 genius. *ch'ŏnjaejŏk* 천재적 gifted; talented.

ch'ŏnjae 천재 (natural) calamity[disaster].

ch'ŏnjang 천장 ceiling.

ch'ŏnji 천지 ① heaven and earth; universe ② world ③ top and bottom.

ch'ŏnju 천주 Lord of Heaven; God; Creator.

ch'ŏnjugyo 천주교 Roman Catholicism. *ch'ŏnju-gyohoe* 천주교회 Roman Catholic Church.

ch'ŏnmak 천막 tent; marquee; awning.

ch'ŏnmin 천민 man of humble[lowly] birth.

ch'ŏnmunhak 천문학 astronomy.

ch'ŏnnal 첫날 first day; opening day.

ch'ŏnnalpam 첫날밤 bridal[wedding] night.

ch'onnom 촌놈 country fellow; rustic.

ch'ŏnnun 첫눈 the first sight[glance]. *ch'ŏnnune* 첫눈에 at first sight; at a glance; on sight.

ch'ŏnnun 첫눈 first snow (of the season). 「gelic.

ch'ŏnsa 천사 angel. *ch'ŏnsa kat'ŭn* 천사 같은 an-

ch'onttŭgi 촌뜨기 →**ch'onnom** 촌놈.

ch'ŏnyŏ 처녀 virgin; maiden. *ch'ŏnyŏŭi* 처녀의 virgin; maiden. *ch'ŏnyŏji* 처녀지 virgin soil.

ch'ŏnyŏn 천연. *ch'ŏnyŏnŭi* 천연의 natural. *ch'ŏnyŏn kasŭ* 천연 가스 natural gas. *ch'ŏnyŏnsaek* 천연색 natural color.

ch'ŏnyŏndu 천연두 smallpox.

ch'ŏp 첩 concubine; (secret, kept) mistress.

ch'orahada 초라하다 (be) shabby; poor-looking.

ch'ŏrhak 철학 philosophy. *ch'ŏrhak paksa* 철학 박사 doctor of philosophy.

ch'ŏrya 철야. *ch'ŏryahada* 철야하다 sit[stay] up all night; keep vigil.

ch'osanghwa 초상화 portrait.

ch'ŏssarang 첫사랑 one's first love; calf love.

ch'osok 초속 velocity[speed] per second.

ch'ŏt'ae 첫해 first year.

ch'ŏtkŏrŭm 첫걸음 first step; start; ABC (of).

ch'ŏtpŏn 첫번 first time. *ch'ŏtpŏnenŭn* 첫번에는 at first; in the beginning.

ch'otpul 촛불 candlelight.

ch'ŏtchae 첫째 first (place); No. 1; top. *ch'ŏtchaeŭi* 첫째의 first; primary. *ch'ŏtchaero* 첫째로 first of all; to begin with.

ch'ŏŭm 처음 beginning; start[outset]; origin. *ch'ŏ-ŭmŭi* 처음의 first; initial; early. *ch'ŏŭme* 처음에 at the beginning; first. *ch'ŏŭmŭn* 처음은 at first. *ch'ŏŭmbut'ŏ* 처음부터 from the first[beginning].

ch'u 추 weight; bob; plummet.

ch'uch'ŏm 추첨 drawing; lottery. *ch'uch'ŏmhada* 추첨하다 draw lots.

ch'uch'ŏn 추천 recommendation. *ch'uch'ŏnhada* 추천하다 recommend

ch'uch'ŭk 추측 guess; conjecture. *ch'uch'ŭk'ada* 추측하다 guess; suppose.

ch'ŭk'u 측후. *ch'ŭk'uso* 측후소 meteorological station.

ch'ulch'urhada 출출하다 feel a bit hungry.

ch'udo 추도 mourning. *ch'udohada* 추도하다 mourn.
. *ch'udoshik* 추도식 memorial service.

ch'uhada 추하다 ① (be) dirty; filthy ② (be) mean;
base; vulgar; coarse.

ch'ujap 추잡. *ch'ujap'ada* 추잡하다 (be) filthy;
foul; indecent.

ch'uk'a 축하 congratulation; celebration. *ch'uk'a-
hada* 축하하다 congratulate; celebrate.

ch'ukcheil 축제일 public holiday; gala day.

ch'ukchŏn 축전 congratulatory telegram.

ch'ukch'uk'ada 축축하다 (be) moist; damp; wet.

ch'ukku 축구 football; soccer. *ch'ukku sŏnsu* 축구
선수 football player.

ch'ukpae 축배 toast. *ch'ukpaerŭl tŭlda* 축배를 들
다 drink a toast.

ch'uksa 축사 congratulatory address; greetings.

ch'ukso 축소 reduction; curtailment. *ch'uksohada*
축소하다 reduce; curtail.

ch'uktae 축대 terrace; embankment.

ch'ugu 추구 pursuit. *ch'uguhada* 추구하다 pursue.

ch'ulbal 출발 departure; start. *ch'ulbarhada* 출발
하다 start; set out; leave.

ch'ulchang 출장 official[business] trip. *ch'ulchang-
gada* 출장가다 go on a business[an official] trip.

ch'ulgu 출구 exit; way out; outlet. *pisang ch'ulgu*
비상 출구 fire escape[exit].

ch'ulguk 출국. *ch'ulguk'ada* 출국하다 depart from
[leave] the country.

ch'ulgŭn 출근 attendance. *ch'ulgŭnhada* 출근하다
attend one's office.

ch'ulma 출마. *ch'ulmahada* 출마하다 run〔stand〕 for; offer oneself as a candidate.

ch'ulp'an 출판 publication. *ch'ulp'anhada* 출판하다 publish; issue.

ch'ulsan 출산 childbirth; delivery. *ch'ulsanhada* 출산하다 give birth to.

ch'ulse 출세 success in life. *ch'ulsehada* 출세하다 rise in the world.

ch'ulshin 출신 ① native ② graduate ③ birth. *ch'ulshinida* 출신이다 come from; be a graduate of. *ch'ulshin-gyo* 출신교 one's Alma Mater.

ch'ulsŏk 출석 attendance; presence. *ch'ulsŏk'ada* 출석하다 attend; be present at.

ch'um 춤 dancing; dance. *ch'umch'uda* 춤추다 dance.

ch'umun 추문 scandal; ill fame.

ch'ŭng 층 story; floor; stairs. *ilch'ŭng* 1층 first floor (*Am.*); ground floor (*Eng.*).

ch'ungbun 충분. *ch'ungbunhan* 충분한 sufficient; enough; full. *ch'ungbunhi* 충분히 enough; sufficiently; fully.

ch'ungch'i 충치 decayed tooth.

ch'ungch'unghada 충충하다 (be) dark; dim; gloomy; dusky.

ch'ungdol 충돌 collision; conflict. *ch'ungdorhada* 충돌하다 collide with.

ch'unggo 충고 advice; counsel. *ch'unggohada* 충고하다 advise; counsel.

ch'ŭnggye 층계 stairs; staircase; stairway. *ch'ŭnggyech'am* 층계참 landing.

ch'ŭngnyang 측량 surveying; measuring. *ch'ŭngnyanghada* 측량하다 survey; measure.

ch'ungshil 충실 faithfulness. *ch'ungshirhan*[*hi*] 충실한[히] faithful[ly].

ch'ungsŏng 충성 loyalty; devotion; allegiance. *ch'ungsŏngsŭrŏun* 충성스러운 loyal; devoted.

ch'unwha 춘화 obscene picture; pornography.

ch'unyŏ 추녀 ugly[unlovely] woman.

ch'unyŏm 추념 *ch'unyŏmsa* 추념사 memorial address.

ch'uŏ 추어 loach. *ch'uŏt'ang* 추어탕 loach soup.

ch'uŏk 추억 remembrance; memory.

ch'ubang 추방 exile; purge. *ch'ubanghada* 추방하다 expel; banish.

ch'upta 춥다 (be) cold; chilly; feel cold.

ch'urak 추락 fall; drop. *ch'urak'ada* 추락하다 fall; crash.

ch'urhang 출항 departure (of a ship from port). *ch'urhanghada* 출항하다 leave port; set sail.

ch'urhyŏn 출현 appearance. *ch'urhyŏnhada* 출현하다 appear; turn[show] up.

ch'uri 추리. *ch'urihada* 추리하다 reason; infer. *ch'uri sosŏl* 추리 소설 mystery[detective] story.

ch'urip 출입. *ch'urip'ada* 출입하다 go[come] in and out. *ch'uripku* 출입구 entrance.

ch'uryŏn 출연 performance. *ch'uryŏnhada* 출연하다 appear on the stage; perform.

ch'usŏk 추석 Harvest Moon Day[Festival].

ch'usu 추수 harvest. *ch'usuhada* 추수하다 harvest.

ch'uwi 추위 cold; coldness *shimhan ch'uwi* 심한 추위 intense[bitter] cold.

ch'waryŏng 촬영 photographing. *ch'waryŏnghada* 촬영하다 take a photo(graph).

ch'wihada 취하다 get drunk; become intoxicated [tipsy]; feel high.

ch'wiim 취임 inauguration. *ch'wiimhada* 취임하다 take[assume] office.

ch'wiip 취입. *ch'wiip'ada* 취입하다 put (a song) on a record; make a record (of).

ch'wijik 취직. *ch'wijik'ada* 취직하다 find[get] employment; get a job[position].

ch'wiju 취주. *ch'wijuak* 취주악 wind-instrument music. *ch'wijuaktae* 취주악대 brass band.

ch'wimi 취미 taste; hobby. *ch'wimi saenghwal* 취미 생활 dilettante life.

ch'wisa 취사 cooking. *ch'wisa tangbŏn* 취사 당번 cook's duty. *ch'wisa togu* 취사 도구 cooking utensils.

ch'wiso 취소 cancellation; withdrawal. *ch'wisohada* 취소하다 cancel; withdraw.

ch'yŏdaboda 쳐다보다 look up; stare[gaze](at).

❦ E ❦

ege 에게 to; for; with; from.

en-ganhada 엔간하다 (be) proper; suitable; be considerable; passable.

enuri 에누리 ① overcharge; two prices ② discount; reduction.

esŏ 에서 ① at; in. ② from; out of.

ewŏssada 에워싸다 surround; enclose; encircle.

❦ H ❦

habok 하복 summer clothes[wear, uniform]; summer suit.

hach'a 하차. *hach'ahada* 하차하다 leave[get off] (the car); alight from.

hada 하다 do; act; try; play; practice.

hadŭng 하등. *hadŭngŭi* 하등의 low; inferior; vulgar. *hadŭngp'um* 하등품 inferior article.

hae 해 sun. *haega ttŭda[chida]* 해가 뜨다[지다] sun rises[sets].

hae 해 year. *chinanhae* 지난해 last year. *haemada* 해마다 every year.

hae 해 injury; harm; damage. *haerŭl chuda* 해를 주다 do harm (to). *haerŭl ipta* 해를 입다 suffer damage.

haean 해안 seashore; coast; seaside.

haebang 해방 liberation; release. *haebanghada* 해방하다 liberate; release.

haebu 해부 anatomy. *haebuhada* 해부하다 dissect.

haebyŏn 해변 beach; seashore; coast.

haebyŏng 해병 marine. *haebyŏngdae* 해병대 marine corps.

haech'o 해초 seaweeds; sea plants; algae.

haego 해고 discharge; dismissal. *haegohada* 해고하다 dismiss; discharge; fire.

haegyŏl 해결 solution. *haegyŏrhada* 해결하다 solve.

haegun 해군 navy. *haegunŭi* 해군의 naval; navy.

haehak 해학 joke; jest; humo(u)r. *haehakchŏgin* 해학적인 humorous; witty.

haehyŏp 해협 straits; channel.

haeje 해제. *haejehada* 해제하다 cancel; release; remove. *mujang haeje* 무장 해제 disarm.

haejŏ 해저 bottom of the sea; sea bottom.

haejŏk 해적 pirate. *haejŏkp'an* 해적판 pirate edition. *hajŏksŏn* 해적선 pirate ship.

haek 핵 nucleus. *haengmugi* 핵무기 nuclear weapons. *haek shirhŏm* 핵실험 nuclear test. *haekchŏnjaeng*

핵전쟁 nuclear war.

haemyŏn 해면 sponge.

haengbang 행방 one's whereabouts. *haengbangŭl kamch'uda* 행방을 감추다 disappear.

haengbok 행복 happiness; welfare. *haengbok'an* 행복한 happy; blessed; fortunate. *haengbok'age* 행복하게 happily.

haengdong 행동 action; conduct; deed. *haengdonghada* 행동하다 act.

haenghada 행하다 act; do; carry out; practice.

haengjin 행진 march; parade. *haengjinhada* 행진하다 march; parade; proceed.

haengjŏng 행정 administration. *haengjŏng kwanch'ŏng* 행정 관청 government office.

haengnyŏl 행렬 procession; parade; queue. *kajang haengnyŏl* 가장 행렬 fancy parade.

haengsang 행상 peddling. *haengsangin* 행상인 peddler.

haengun 행운 good fortune; good luck. *haengunŭi* 행운의 fortunate; lucky.

haengwi 행위 act; action; deed. *pulpŏp haengwi* 불법 행위 illegal[unlawful] act.

haenyŏ 해녀 woman diver.

haeoe 해외. *haeoeŭi* 해외의 oversea(s); foreign. *haeoee* 해외에 abroad; overseas.

haeŏjida 해어지다 wear[be worn] out; get tattered.

haepssal 햅쌀 new rice; the year's new crop of rice.

haeropta 해롭다 (be) injurious; harmful; bad.

haesanmul 해산물 marine products.

haesŏk 해석 interpretation; explanation. *haesŏk'ada* 해석하다 interpret; explain.

haesu 해수 sea[salt] water. *haesuyok* 해수욕 sea-bathing. *haesuyokchang* 해수욕장 bathing resort.

haetpit 햇빛 sunshine; sunlight.

haetpyŏt 햇볕 sunbeams; heat of the sunlight.

haeyak 해약 cancellation of a contract. *haeyak'ada* 해약하다 cancel[break] a contract.

hagi 하기 summer(time). *hagi panghak* 하기 방학 summer vacation. →**hagye** 하계.

hagŭp 하급 lower[low] class. *hagŭpsaeng* 하급생 lower class student.

hajik 하직 leave-taking; a farewell.

hak 학 crane; stork.

hakcha 학자 scholar; learned man.

hakchang 학장 dean; rector; president.

hakchil 학질 malaria. *hakchire kŏllida* 학질에 걸리다 be infected with malaria.

hakki 학기 (school) term; semester (*Am.*).

hakkwa 학과 subject of study. *hakkwa shihŏm* 학과 시험 achievement test.

hakkye 학계 learned circles; academic world.

hakkyo 학교 school; college. *hakkyo-e tanida* 학교에 다니다 attend[go to] school.

hakpŏl 학벌 academic clique.

hakpuhyŏng 학부형 parents of students.

hakpyŏng 학병 student soldier.

haksaeng 학생 student. *haksaeng shijŏl* 학생 시절 school days.

haktae 학대 ill-treatment; maltreatment. *haktaehada* 학대하다 ill-treat; maltreat.

halk'wida 할퀴다 scratch; claw.

hallan-gye 한란계 thermometer; mercury. → **ondogye** 온도계.

halmŏni 할머니 ① grandmother; grandma; granny

② old lady[woman].

halt'a 핥다 lick; lap.

haltang 할당 assignment; allotment. *haltanghada* 할당하다 assign; allot; divide.

hamburo 함부로 at random; indiscriminately; without reason.

hamjŏng 함정 pitfall; pit; trap. *hamjŏnge ppajida* 함정에 빠지다 fall in a pit.

hamkke 함께 together (with, along); in company with.

hamnyang 함량 content. *alk'ol hamnyang* 알콜 함량 alcohol content.

hamsŏk 함석 zinc; galvanized iron.

hamul 하물 luggage (*Eng.*); baggage (*Am.*).

han 한 ① one; a. *han saram* 한 사람 one man. *han madi* 한 마디 one word ② about; nearly; some.

hana 하나 one. *hanaŭi* 하나의 one; a.

hanbamchung 한밤중 midnight; the middle of the night.

hanbok 한복 Korean clothes.

hanbŏn 한번 once; one time. *tan hanbon* 단 한번 only once. *hanbône* 한번에 at a time. *hanbŏn tŏ* 한번 더 once more.

hancha 한자 Chinese character.

hanch'ang 한창 height; peak; bloom. *hanch'ang-ida* 한창이다 be at its height.

handu 한두 one or two; couple. *handu saram* 한두 사람 one or two persons. *handu pŏn* 한두 번 once or twice.

han-gaji 한가지 ① a kind[sort] of ② the same.

hangbok 항복 surrender. *hangbok'ada* 항복하다 surrender; submit.

hanggong 항공 aviation; flight. *hanggong up'yŏn* 항공 우편 airmail.

hanggu 항구 port; harbor.

hanghae 항해 voyage; navigation. *hanghaehada* 항해하다 navigate; sail for.

han-gil 한길 main street[road]; thoroughfare; highway.

hangmun 학문 learning; study. *hangmuni innŭn* 학문이 있는 educated.

hangno 항로 sea route; course; line.

hangnyŏk 학력 school career; academic background.

hangnyŏn 학년 school year; grade (*Am.*); form (*Eng.*).

hangsang 항상 always; at all times; usually.

hangŭi 항의 protest; objection. *hangŭihada* 항의 하다 make a protest; object to.

Han-guk 한국 Korea; Republic of Korea (R. O. K.).

han-gŭl 한글 Korean alphabet; *han-gŭl*.

han-gye 한계 limits; bounds. *han-gyerŭl nŏmta* 한 계를 넘다 pass[exceed] the limit.

hanhwa 한화 Korean money[currency].

hanil 한일. *hanirŭi* 한일의 Korean-Japanese. *hanil hoedam* 한일 회담 Korean-Japanese Conference.

hankkŏbŏne 한꺼번에 at a time; at once; at a clip.

hanmi 한미 Korea and America. *hanmiŭi* 한미의 Korean-American.

han ssang 한 쌍 pair; couple. *han ssangŭi* 한 쌍의 a pair[couple] of.

hansum 한숨 (heavy) sigh. *hansum shwida* 한숨 쉬 다 (heave[draw] a) sigh.

hant'ŏk 한턱 treat; entertainment. *hant'ŏk naeda* 한턱 내다 give a treat.

hanttae 한때 ① a short time[while]; for a time ② once; (at) one time.

hanŭl 하늘 sky; air; heaven.

hanŭnim 하느님 (Lord of) Heaven; God.

hanyak 한약 Chinese[herb] medicine. *hanyakpang* 한약방 herb shop.

hanyŏng 한영. *hanyŏngŭi* 한영의 Korean-English. *hanyŏng sajŏn* 한영 사전 Korean-English dictionary.

hao 하오 afternoon. →**ohu** 오후.

hapch'ang 합창 chorus. *hapch'anghada* 합창하다 sing together[in chorus]. *hapch'angdan[dae]* 합창단[대] chorus.

hapch'ida 합치다 ① put together; joint together; unite; combine ② sum up.

hapchu 합주 concert; ensemble. *i[sam]bu hapchu* 2[3]부 합주 duet[trio].

hapkye 합계 total; sum total. *hapkyehada* 합계하다 sum[add] up.

hapkyŏk 합격. *hapkyŏk'ada* 합격하다 pass; be successful; be accepted.

hapsuk 합숙. *hapsuk'ada* 합숙하다 lodge together. *hapsuk hullyŏn* 합숙 훈련 camp training.

hapsŭng 합승. *hapsŭnghada* 합승하다 ride together. *hapsŭng t'aekshi* 합승 택시 jitney (cab).

hap'um 하품 yawn; gape. *hap'umhada* 하품하다 yawn; gape.

harabŏji 할아버지 ① grandfather; grandpa ② old man.

harin 할인 discount; deduction. *harinhada* 할인하다 discount; reduce.

haru 하루 a[one] day. *haru chongil* 하루 종일

all day long.

haruach'im 하루아침 one morning. *haruach'ime* 하루아침에 in a day; all of a sudden.

harubappi 하루바삐 as soon as possible.

harutpam 하룻밤 one [a] night. *harutpam saie* 하룻밤 사이에 in a single night.

hasagwan 하사관 noncommissioned[petty] officer.

hasoyŏn 하소연 appeal; petition. *hasoyŏnhada* 하소연하다 appeal to; complain of.

hasuk 하숙 lodging; boarding. *hasuk'ada* 하숙하다 lodge; board; room (*Am.*). *hasukchip* 하숙집 lodging[boarding. rooming (*Am.*)] house.

hayat'a 하얗다 (be) pure white; snow white.

hearida 헤아리다 ① fathom; conjecture ② count; calculate.

hech'ida 헤치다 push aside; make one's way (through).

hemaeda 헤매다 wander[roam] about; rove.

heŏjida 헤어지다 part from; separate; part company (with).

heŏm 헤엄 swimming; swim. *heŏmch'ida* 헤엄치다 swim.

him 힘 ① strength; force; might ② power; energy.

himch'ada 힘차다 (be) powerful; forceful. *himch'age* 힘차게 powerfully; strongly.

himchul 힘줄 ① muscle; sinew ② fiber; string.

himdŭlda 힘들다 (be) tough; laborious; toilsome.

himkkŏt 힘껏 with all one's might[strength].

himseda 힘세다 (be) strong; mighty; powerful.

himssŭda 힘쓰다 ① exert oneself; make efforts ② be industrious; be diligent (in).

hobak 호박 pumpkin; squash.

hobak 호박 amber. *hobaksaegŭi* 호박색의 amber-colored.

hodu 호두 walnut.

hoe 회 sliced[slices of] raw fish.

hoebi 회비 (membership) fee; dues.

hoebok 회복 recovery; restoration. *hoebok'ada* 회복하다 restore; recover; get better.

hoech'ori 회초리 switch; whip; lash.

hoedam 회담 talk; conversation. *hoedamhada* 회담하다 have a talk; interview.

hoedap 회답 reply; answer. *hoedap'ada* 회답하다 reply; answer.

hoegap 회갑 one's 60th birthday anniversary.

hoego 회고 reflection; recollection. *hoegohada* 회고하다 look back; recollect.

hoegye 회계 account(ing); finance. *hoegyehada* 회계하다 account; count.

hoehap 회합 meeting; gathering. *hoehap'ada* 회합하다 meet; assemble.

hoehwa 회화 conversation; talk; dialogue. *hoehwahada* 회화하다 converse[talk] (with). *Yŏngŏ hoehwa* 영어 회화 English conversation.

hoehwa 회화 →**kŭrim** 그림.

hoejang 회장 president; chairman.

hoejang 회장 place of meeting.

hoejŏn 회전 revolution; rotation. *hoejŏnhada* 회전하다 revolve; rotate.

hoejung 회중 one's pocket. *hoejung shigye* 회중 시계 watch. *hoejung chŏndŭng* 회중 전등 flashlight.

hoengdan 횡단. *hoengdanhada* 횡단하다 cross; run across. *hoengdan podo* 횡단 보도 pedestrian crossing; crosswalk (*Am.*).

hoeram 회람. *hoeramhada* 회람하다 circulate.

hoesa 회사 company; corporation; firm. *hoesawŏn* 회사원 company employee; office worker.

hoesukwŏn 회수권 commutation ticket(*Am.*); book of tickets (*Eng.*).

hoeŭi 회의 meeting; conference. *hoeŭihada* 회의하 다 confer (with); hold a conference.

hoewŏn 회원 member(of a society). *hoewŏni toeda* 회원이 되다 become a member.

hŏga 허가 permission; approval. *hŏgahada* 허가하 다 permit; allow; approve.

hogak 호각 whistle.

hogishim 호기심 curiosity. *hogishimi kanghan* 호 기심이 강한 curious; inquisitive.

hohŭp 호흡 breath; breathing. *hohŭp'ada* 호흡하 다 breathe.

hohwa 호화. *hohwasŭrŏun* 호화스러운 splendid; luxurious. *hohwap'an* 호화판 de luxe edition.

hojŏk 호적 (census) register. *hojŏk tŭng[ch'o]bon* 호적 등[초]본 copy[abstract] of one's family register.

hojumŏni 호주머니 pocket.

hok 혹 wen; lump; bump.

hoekkijŏk 획기적 epoch-making; epochal.

hŏlda 헐다 destroy; demolish; pull down.

hollan 혼란 confusion; disorder. *hollanhada* 혼란 하다 be confused.

holsu 홀수 odd number.

hom 홈 groove. *homŭl p'ada* 홈을 파다 hollow out [cut] a groove.

homi 호미 weeding hoe.

hŏmurŏjida 허물어지다 collapse; fall[break] down;

crumble.

hon 혼 soul; spirit.

hŏn 헌 old; shabby; worn-out; secondhand. *hŏn ot* 헌 옷 old clothes. *hŏn ch'aek* 헌 책 secondhand book.

honhap 혼합. *honhap'ada* 혼합하다 mix; mingle; compound.

hŏnbyŏng 헌병 military police (M. P.).

hondong 혼동. *hondonghada* 혼동하다 confuse; mix up.

hongbaek 홍백 red and white. *hongbaekchŏn* 홍백전 contest between red and white teams.

hongbo 홍보 public information. *hongbo hwaltong* 홍보 활동 information activities.

hongch'a 홍차 black tea.

hongsaek 홍색 red; red color.

hongsu 홍수 flood. *hongsuga nada* 홍수가 나다 have a flood.

honhyŏl 혼혈 mixed blood[breed]. *honhyŏra* 혼혈아 a half-breed; interracial child.

hŏnhyŏl 헌혈 donation of blood. *hŏnhyŏrhada* 헌혈하다 donate blood.

honja 혼자 alone; by oneself; for oneself. *honja salda* 혼자 살다 live alone.

honjap 혼잡 confusion; disorder. *honjap'an* 혼잡한 confused; congested.

honnada 혼나다 ① get frightened; become startled ② have bitter experiences.

hŏnpŏp 헌법 constitution.

hooe 호외 extra (edition).

hoŏn 호언 big[tall] talk. *hoŏn changdamhada* 호언장담하다 talk big; boast.

horabi 홀아비 widower.

hŏrak 허락 consent; assent; permission. *hŏrak'ada* 허락하다 consent to; permit.

horangi 호랑이 tiger; tigress.

hŏri 허리 waist; loins; hip. *hŏritti* 허리띠 belt; sash; band.

horihorihada 호리호리하다 (be) (tall and) slender; slim.

horŏmi 홀어미 widow. →**kwabu** 과부.

horyŏng 호령 command; order. *horyŏnghada* 호령하다 order; command.

hŏse 허세 bluff; (false) show of power[influence].

hoso 호소 appeal; petition; complaint. *hosohada* 호소하다 appeal (to).

hŏssori 헛소리. *hŏssorihada* 헛소리하다 talk in delirium; talk nonsense.

hŏssugo 헛수고 vain effort; lost labor. *hŏssugohada* 헛수고하다 make vain efforts.

hŏsuabi 허수아비 ① scarecrow ② dummy; puppet.

hŏtkan 헛간 barn; open shed.

hoŭi 호의 goodwill; good wishes. *hoŭijŏgin* 호의적인 kind; warm-hearted.

howi 호위 guard; escort. *howihada* 호위하다 guard; escort. *howibyŏng* 호위병 (body)guard.

hoyŏlcha 호열자 cholera.

hŏyŏng 허영 vanity. *hŏyŏngshim* 허영심 (sense of) vanity.

hu 후 after; afterward(s); later. *kŭ hu* 그 후 after that; since then.

hubae 후배 one's junior. *hakkyo hubae* 학교 후배 one's junior in school.

huban 후반 latter[second] half. *hubanjŏn* 후반전

second half of the game

hubang 후방 rear. *hubangŭi* 후방 backward. *hubange* in〔at〕 *bangŭro* 후방으로 rearward; bac

hubida 후비다 scoop〔scrape, dig〕 out; pick

hubo 후보 candidate. *hubo sŏnsu* 후보 선수 substitute.

huch'u 후추 black pepper. *huch'urŭl ch'ida* 후추를 치다 sprinkle pepper.

hudŭlgŏrida 후들거리다 tremble; shake; shiver.

hŭgin 흑인 Negro; colored person; nigger. *hŭginjong* 흑인종 black race.

huhoe 후회 repentance; regret. *huhoehada* 후회하다 repent of; regret.

hŭida 희다 (be) white; fair.

hŭigok 희곡 drama; play.

hŭigŭk 희극 comedy. *hŭigŭkchŏk* 희극적 comic(al).

huil 후일 later days; some (other) day; (the) future.

hŭimang 희망 hope; wish; desire. *hŭimanghada* 희망하다 hope (for); wish; desire.

hŭimi 희미. *hŭimihan* 희미한 faint; dim; vague. *hŭimihage* 희미하게 faintly; dimly.

hŭinjawi 흰자위 ① white of the eye ② white of an egg.

hŭisaeng 희생 sacrifice; victim. *hŭisaenghada* 희생하다 sacrifice. *hŭisaengjŏgin* 희생적인 sacrificial.

huja 후자 the latter; the other one.

hujin 후진. *hujinŭi* 후진의 backward; underdeveloped. *hujin-guk* 후진국 backward〔underdeveloped〕 nation.

흙 earth; soil; ground.

kp'an 흑판 blackboard.

hŭkt'usŏngi 흙투성이. *hŭkt'usŏngiga toeda* 흙투성이가 되다 be covered with mud.

hŭlgida 흘기다 look askance; glare fiercely at.

hŭllida 흘리다 ① spill; drop; shed ② lose ③ take no notice (of).

hullyŏn 훈련 training; exercise. *hullyŏnhada* 훈련하다 train. *hullyŏnso* 훈련소 training school[center].

hullyunghada 훌륭하다 (be) fine; splendid. *hullyunghi* 훌륭히 nicely; splendidly.

hult'a 훑다 thresh; strip; hackle.

hŭm 흠 ① scar ② flaw; crack. *hŭmi innŭn* 흠이 있는 flawed; bruised.

humch'ida 훔치다 ① steal ② wipe (off).

hŭmut'ada 흐뭇하다 (be) pleasing; satisfied.

hŭndŭlda 흔들다 shake; wave; swing; rock.

hŭngbun 흥분 excitement. *hŭngbunhada* 흥분하다 be excited; become warm.

hŭngmi 흥미 interest; zest. *hŭngmi innŭn* 흥미 있는 (be) interesting.

hŭngŏlgŏrida 흥얼거리다 hum; croon; sing to oneself.

hŭngshinso 흥신소 inquiry agency; credit bureau.

hunjang 훈장 decoration; order; medal.

hunnal 훗날 later days; some (other) day. *hunnare* 훗날에 some (other) day; in (the) future.

hŭnŭkkida 흐느끼다 sob; whimper; weep softly.

hŭpsa 흡사. *hŭpsahada* 흡사하다 resemble closely; (be) exactly alike.

hŭpsu 흡수 absorption. *hŭpsuhada* 흡수하다 absorb; suck in.

hŭrida 흐리다 ① (be) cloudy; overcast ② (be) vague; dim; faint.

hŭrŭda 흐르다 flow; stream; run (down).

huryŏnhada 후련하다 feel refreshed[unburdened].

husaeng 후생 public[social] welfare. *husaeng saŏp* 후생 사업 welfare work.

huson 후손 descendants; posterity; offspring.

hut'oe 후퇴 retreat. *hut'oehada* 후퇴하다 retrograde; recede; retreat.

hŭt'ŏjida 흩어지다 be scattered; be dispersed.

huwi 후위 back player; rear guard.

huwŏn 후원 support; backing; patronage. *huwŏnhada* 후원하다 support; back (up).

hwa 화 disaster; calamity. *hwarŭl ipta* 화를 입다 meet with a calamity.

hwabo 화보 pictorial; graphic; illustrated magazine [news].

hwabun 화분 flowerpot.

hwabyŏng 화병 (flower) vase.

hwach'o 화초 flower; flowering plant. *hwach'o chaebae* 화초 재배 floriculture.

hwadan 화단 flower bed; flower garden.

hwae 홰 perch.

hwaetpul 횃불 torchlight; torch.

hwaga 화가 painter; artist.

hwagin 확인 confirmation; affirmation. *hwaginhada* 확인하다 confirm; affirm.

hwagyo 화교 Chinese residents abroad.

hwahae 화해 reconciliation; compromise. *hwahaehada* 화해하다 compromise with; make peace with.

hwahak 화학 chemistry. *hwahagŭi* 화학의 chemical. *hwahak yakp'um* 화학 약품 chemicals.

hwahwan 화환 wreath; garland; lei.

hwajae 화재 fire; conflagration. *hwajae kyŏngbogi* 화재 경보기 fire alarm.

hwajang 화장 toilet; make up. *hwajanghada* 화장하다 make one's toilet; make up one's face.

hwajang 화장 cremation. *hwajanghada* 화장하다 cremate; burn to ashes.

hwaje 화제 subject[topic, theme] of conversation.

hwakchang 확장 extension; expansion. *hwakchanghada* 확장하다 extend; enlarge; widen.

hwakchŏng 확정 decision; settlement. *hwakchŏnghada* 확정하다 decide; confirm; fix.

hwaktae 확대 magnification; enlargement. *hwaktaehada* 확대하다 magnify; expand; spread.

hwakshil 확실. *hwakshirhan* 확실한 sure; certain. *hwakshirhi* 확실히 certainly; surely.

hwakshin 확신 conviction; firm belief. *hwakshinhada* 확신하다 be convinced of; be sure of.

hwaksŏnggi 확성기 loudspeaker; megaphone.

hwal 활 bow. *hwarŭl ssoda* 활을 쏘다 shoot an arrow.

hwalbal 활발. *hwalbarhan* 활발한 active; brisk; vigorous ; lively. *hwalbarhi* 활발히 briskly; actively.

hwalcha 활자 type; printing type.

hwalch'ok 활촉 arrowhead.

hwalchuro 활주로 runway; landing strip.

hwalgi 활기 vigor; life; activity. *hwalgi innŭn* 활기 있는 active; lively.

hwaltong 활동 activity; action. *hwaltongjŏgin* 활동적인 active; dynamic. *hwaltongga* 활동가 man of action.

hwamul 화물 goods; freight (*Am.*) ; cargo. *hwamulsŏn* 화물선 cargo boat. *hwamul chadongch'a* 화물자동차 truck.

hwan 환 (note of) exchange; check; money order.

hwanaeda 화내다 get angry (at, with) ; loose one's temper.

hwandŭng 환등 film slide; magic lantern.

hwanggŭm 황금 gold. *hwanggŭmŭi* 황금의 gold; golden.

hwan-gi 환기 ventilation. *hwan-gihada* 환기하다 ventilate. *hwan-git'ong* 환기통 ventilator.

hwangje 황제 emperor.

hwangnip 확립 establishment. *hwangnip'ada* 확립하다 establish.

hwangsaek 황색 yellow; yellow color. *hwangsaek injong* 황색 인종 yellow race.

hwangt'aeja 황태자 Crown Prince.

hwangya 황야 wilderness; desert land.

hwan-gyŏng 환경 environment; circumstance. *hwangyŏng oyŏm* 환경 오염 environmental pollution.

hwanhada 환하다 (be) bright; light. *hwanhan pang* 환한 방 well-lighted room.

hwanja 환자 patient; case. *k'ollera hwanja* 콜레라 환자 cholera patient[case].

hwanmyŏl 환멸 disillusion. *hwanmyŏrŭl nŭkkida* 환멸을 느끼다 be disillusioned.

hwansang 환상 illusion; vision. *hwansanggok* 환상곡 fantasy; fantasia.

hwansong 환송 farewell; send-off. *hwansonghada* 환송하다 give (a person) a hearty send-off. *hwansonghoe* 환송회 farewell party.

hwanyak 환약 pill; globule.

hwanyŏng 환영 welcome. *hwanyŏnghada* 환영하다 welcome; receive warmly. *hwanyŏnghoe* 환영회 reception.

hwanyul 환율 exchange rate. *hwanyul insang* 환율 인상 raise in exchange rates.

hwap'ye 화폐 money; currency; coinage.

hwaro 화로 brazier; fire pot.

hwasal 화살 arrow. *hwasalt'ong* 화살통 quiver. *hwasalp'yo* 화살표 arrow.

hwasan 화산 volcano.

hwasang 화상 burn; scald. *hwasangŭl ipta* 화상을 입다 get burned[scalded].

hwashil 화실 studio; *atelier*.

hwasŏng 화성 Mars. *hwasŏngin* 화성인 Martian.

hwassi 화씨 Fahrenheit. *hwassi hallan-gye* 화씨 한 란계 Fahrenheit thermometer.

hwat'u 화투 Korean playing cards; "flower cards".

hwawon 화원 flower garden.

hwayak 화약 (gun) powder. *hwayakko* 화약고 powder magazine.

hwayoil 화요일 Tuesday (Tues.).

hwibal 휘발. *hwiballyu* 휘발유 gasoline; volatile oil.

hwida 휘다 bend; curve; warp; be bent.

hwidurŭda 휘두르다 brandish; flourish; throw about. *p'arŭl hwidurŭda* 팔을 휘두르다 flourish one's arms.

hwigamta 휘감다 wind around; tie[fasten] round.

hwijang 휘장 badge; insignia.

hwijŏtta 휘젓다 stir (up); churn; beat up.

hwinallida 휘날리다 flap; fly; flutter; wave.

hwip'aram 휘파람 whistle. *hwip'aram pulda* 휘파

람 불다 (give a) whistle.

hwipssŭlda 휩쓸다 ① sweep (away, up, off) ② overrun.

hwŏlssin 훨씬 by far; very much; greatly.

hyanggi 향기 fragrance; perfume; scent; sweet odor. *hyanggiropta* 향기롭다 (be) fragrant; sweet-smelling.

hyangnak 향락 enjoyment; pleasure. *hyangnak saenghwal* 향락 생활 gay life.

hyangno 향로 incense burner.

hyangnyo 향료 ① spice; spicery ② perfume; aromatic.

hyangsang 향상 elevation; improvement. *hyangsanghada* 향상하다 rise; be elevated; improve.

hyangsu 향수 perfume; scent.

hyangt'o 향토 one's native place. *hyangt'osaek* 향토색 local colo(u)r.

hyet'aek 혜택 favo(u)r; benefit; benevolence. *munmyŏngŭi hyet'aek* 문명의 혜택 benefit of civilization.

hyŏ 혀 tongue. *hyŏrŭl naemilda* 혀를 내밀다 put out one's tongue.

hyokwa 효과 effect; efficacy. *hyokwa innŭn* 효과 있는 effective.

hyŏlgwan 혈관 blood vessel.

hyŏlsŏ 혈서. *hyŏlsŏrŭl ssŭda* 혈서를 쓰다 write in blood.

hyŏlt'ong 혈통 blood; lineage; pedigree.

hyŏmnyŏk 협력 cooperation. *hyŏmnyŏk'ada* 협력하다 cooperate with; work together.

hyŏmŭi 혐의 suspicion; charge. *hyŏmŭiro* 혐의로 on the suspicion of. *hyŏmŭija* 혐의자 suspect.

hyŏnak 현악 string music. *hyŏnakki* 현악기 stringed instrument.

hyŏnch'ungil 현충일 the Memorial Day.

hyŏndae 현대 present age[day]; modern times; today. *hyŏndaeŭi* 현대의 current; modern. *hyŏndaehwa* 현대화 modernization.

hyŏngbŏl 형벌 punishment; penalty.

hyŏngbu 형부 brother-in-law; husband of one's[a girl's] elder sister.

hyŏnggwang 형광. *hyŏnggwangdŭng*[*p'an*] 형광등 [판] fluorescent lamp[plate].

hyŏngje 형제 brothers; sisters. *hyŏngje chamae* 형제 자매 brothers and sisters.

hyŏngmuso 형무소 prison; jail. →**kyodoso** 교도소.

hyŏngmyŏng 혁명 revolution. *hyŏngmyŏngjŏgin* 혁명적인 revolutionary.

hyŏngp'yŏn 형편 situation; condition; circumstance.

hyŏngsa 형사 (police) detective.

hyŏngshik 형식 form; formality; mode. *hyŏngshikchŏgin* 형식적인 formal. *hyŏngshikchŏgŭro* 형식적으로 formally.

hyŏngsu 형수 sister-in law; elder brother's wife.

hyŏngt'ae 형태 form; shape.

hyŏn-gŭm 현금 cash; ready money. *hyŏn-gŭmŭro* 현금으로 in cash. *hyŏn-gum chibul* 현금 지불 cash payment.

hyŏn-gwan 현관 porch; entryway; entrance hall.

hyŏngyong 형용 description. *hyŏngyonghada* 형용 하다 describe; modify.

hyŏnjae 현재 the present time; now; at present. *hyŏnjaekkaji* 현재까지 up to now. *hyŏnjaeŭi* 현재 의 present.

hyŏnjang 현장 spot; scene (of action). *hyŏnjang-esŏ* 현장에서 on the spot.

hyŏnmigyŏng 현미경 microscope.

hyŏnmyŏng 현명. *hyŏnmyŏnghan* 현명한 wise; sagacious; advisable.

hyŏnsang 현상 the present state[situation].

hyŏnsang 현상. *hyŏnsang mojip* 현상 모집 prize contest. *hyŏnsanggŭm* 현상금 prize money.

hyŏnshil 현실 actuality. *hyŏnshirŭi* 현실의 actual; real. *hyŏnshilchŏgŭro* 현실적으로 actually; really. *hyŏnshiljuŭi* 현실주의 realism.

hyŏnyŏk 현역 active service. *hyŏnyŏk kunin* 현역 군인 soldier on service.

hyŏpchugok 협주곡 concerto.

hyŏp'oe 협회 society; association. *kŏnch'uk hyŏp'oe* 건축 협회 building society.

hyŏppak 협박 threat; menace. *hyŏppak'ada* 협박하다 threaten; intimidate.

hyŏraek 혈액 blood. *hyŏraek kŏmsa* 혈액 검사 blood test. *hyŏraek ŭnhaeng* 혈액 은행 blood bank. *hyŏraek'yŏng* 혈액형 blood type.

hyŏrap 혈압 blood pressure. *ko[chŏ]hyŏrap* 고[저] 혈압 high[low] blood pressure.

hyudae 휴대. *hyudaehada* 휴대하다 carry; take with. *hyudaeyongŭi* 휴대용의 portable.

hyuga 휴가 holidays; vacation. *yŏrŭm hyuga* 여름 휴가 summer vacation.

hyuge 휴게 rest; recess. *hyuge shigan* 휴게 시간 recess. *hyugeshil* 휴게실 rest room; lounge.

hyuji 휴지 toilet paper; waste paper. *hyujit'ong* 휴지통 waste(paper) basket.

hyujŏn 휴전 truce; armistice. *hyujŏnsŏn* 휴전선

truce line. *hyujŏn hoedam* 휴전 회담 truce[armistice] talks.

hyung 흉 scar. *hyungi innŭn ŏlgul* 흉이 있는 얼굴 scarred face.

hyungak 흉악. *hyungak'an* 흉악한 wicked; atrocious.

hyungboda 흉보다 speak ill of; disparage.

hyungnae 흉내 imitation; mimicry. *hyungnaenaeda* 흉내내다 imitate; mimic.

hyuŏp 휴업 closing; suspension of business[trading]. *hyuŏp'ada* 휴업하다 close (office, factory).

hyushik 휴식 rest; repose; recess. *hyushik'ada* 휴식하다 (take a) rest.

◆◀━ I ━▶◆

i 이 this; present; current. *idal* 이달 this month. *i ch'aek* 이 책 this book.

i 이, 2 two; the second.

i 이 tooth. *iŭi* 이의 dental. *iga ap'ŭda* 이가 아프다 have a toothache.

ibal 이발 haircut(ting); hairdressing. *ibarhada* 이발하다 have one's hair cut. *ibalso* 이발소 barbershop.

ibŏn 이번 this time; now. *ibŏnŭi* 이번의 new; present. *ibŏn iryoil* 이번 일요일 this coming Sunday.

ibu 이부 two parts; second part. *ibuje* 이부제 two shift system.

ibul 이불 overquilt; quilt; coverlet.

ibwon 입원. *ibwŏnhada* 입원하다 enter[be sent to] hospital.

ibyang 입양 adoption. *ibyanghada* 입양하다 adopt

(a son); affiliate.

ibyŏl 이별 parting; separation. *ibyŏrhada* 이별하다 part; separate.

ich'a 이차 second; secondary. *ich'a taejŏn* 이차 대전 Second World War; World War Ⅱ.

ich'i 이치 reason; principle. *ich'ie matta* 이치에 맞다 be reasonable.

ichŏm 이점 advantage; vantage point. .

ich'ŏrŏm 이처럼 thus; like this; in this way.

ich'ŭng 이층 second floor[story] (*Am.*); first floor [storey] (*Eng.*).

idal 이달 this month; the current month. *idal shiboire* 이달 15일에 on the 15th of this month.

idong 이동 transfer; movement. *idonghada* 이동하다 move; transfer.

idŭng 2등 second; second class [grade, prize, place].

idŭn(ji) 이든(지) whether ...or; either...or.

igach'i 이같이 like this; thus; in this way[manner].

igi 이기. *igijŏk* 이기적 selfish; egoistic. *igijuŭi* 이기주의 egoism.

igida 이기다 win; gain a victory; defeat.

igong 이공 science and engineering. *igong taehak* 이공 대학 science and engineering college.

igot 이곳 this place; here. *igose* 이곳에 here; in this place.

igŏt 이것 this; this one. *igŏsŭro* 이것으로 with this; now. *igŏt chom pwa* 이것 좀 봐 I say; Look here.

iha 이하. *ihaŭi* 이하의 less than; under; below.

ihae 이해 understanding; comprehension. *ihaehada* 이해하다 understand; comprehend.

ihae 이해 interests; advantages and disadvantages.

ihon 이혼 divorce. *ihonhada* 이혼하다 divorce.

ihu 이후 after this; from now on; hereafter. *kŭ ihu* 그 이후 since then; thereafter.

iik 이익 profit; gain. *iigi innŭn* 이익이 있는 profitable; paying.

iin 이인 two persons[men]. *iinsŭng* 2인승 two-seater. *iinjo* 이인조 duo.

ija 이자 interest. *ijaga putta* 이자가 붙다 yield interest.

iji 이지 intellect; intelligence. *ijijŏk* 이지적 intellectual.

ijŏn 이전. *ijŏnŭi* 이전의 previous; former. *ijŏne* 이전에 before; formerly; once.

ijŏn 이전 removal; moving (*Am.*); transfer. *ijŏnhada* 이전하다 remove; transfer.

iju 이주 removal; migration. *ijuhada* 이주하다. move(*Am.*); remove(*Eng.*); migrate.

ijung 이중. *ijungŭi* 이중의 double; twofold; dual. *ijung kukchŏk* 이중 국적 dual nationality. *ijungju[ch'ang]* 이중주[창] duet.

ikki 이끼 moss. *ikki kkin* 이끼 낀 mossy; moss-grown.

ikkŭlda 이끌다 guide; conduct; lead; show[usher] in.

iksa 익사 drowning. *iksahada* 익사하다 be drowned (to death).

iksal 익살 joke; jest; humor. *iksal purida* 익살 부리다 crack jokes; jest; be funny.

iksuk'ada 익숙하다 (be) familiar; be skilled in; be at home in.

ikta 읽다 read; peruse. *chalmot ikta* 잘못 읽다

misread; read wrong. *ta ikta* 다 읽다 read
through.

ikta 익다 ripen; mature; become[get] ripe. *igŭn*
익은 ripe; mellow.

il 일, 1 one, *cheil* 제일 the first.

il 일 work; task; labo(u)r. *irhada* 일하다 work.

ilban 일반. *ilbanŭi* 일반의 general; universal. *ilban-
jŏgŭro* 일반적으로 generally; in general.

ilbang 일방 one side; one hand; one way. *ilbang
t'onghaeng* 일방 통행 one-way traffic.

Ilbon 일본 Japan. *Ilbonŭi* 일본의 Japanese. *Ilbon-
mal* 일본말 Japanese (language). *Ilbonin* 일본인
Japanese.

ilbŏn 일번 first; No. 1. *ilbŏnŭi* 1번의 first; top.

ilbu 일부 part; portion. *ilbuŭi* 일부의 partial;
divisional.

ilburŏ 일부러 on purpose; intentionally; purposely.

ilcha 일자 →**naltcha** 날짜.

ilchari 일자리 job; position. *ilcharirŭl ŏtta* 일자리
를 얻다 take[get] a job.

ilche 일제. *ilcheŭi* 일제의 of Japanese manufacture;
made in Japan.

ilche 일제. *ilchehi* 일제히 altogether; in a chorus.

ilch'e 일체. ① all; everything. *ilch'eŭi* 일체의 all;
every; whole. ② entirely; wholly; altogether.
ilch'e chungsaeng 일체 중생 all living beings.

ilchi 일지 diary; journal →**ilgi** 일기.

ilch'i 일치 coincidence; agreement; consent. cooperation. *ilch'ihada* 일치하다 agree (with); accord
(with); coincide(with); consent to; cooperate(with).

ilchik 일직 day duty; day watch. *ilchik'ada* 일직
하다 be on day duty.

ilchŏn 일전 the other day; some time ago.

ilchong 일종 kind; sort; species. *ilchongŭi* 일종의 a kind[sort] of.

ilchŏng 일정 day's program(me)[schedule].

ilchŏng 일정. *ilchŏnghan* 일정한 fixed; definite; regular; settled.

ilchu 일주 round; tour. *ilchuhada* 일주하다 go [travel] round.

ilch'ŭng 일층 ① first floor (*Am.*); ground floor (*Eng.*) ② more; still more.

ilgan 일간 daily publication[issue].

ilgi 일기 weather. *ilgi yebo* 일기 예보 weather forecast[report].

ilgi 일기 diary; journal. *ilgijang* 일기장 diary.

ilgop 일곱 seven. *ilgoptchae* 일곱째 the seventh.

ilgŭp 일급 daily wages; day's wage.

ilgŭp 일급 first class. *ilgŭbŭi* 일급의 first-class.

ilgwa 일과 daily lesson[work]; (daily) routine.

ilgwang 일광 sunlight; sunshine. *ilgwangnyok* 일광욕 sun bath(ing).

ilkŏri 일거리 piece of work; task; things to do.

ilkun 일군 workman; worker; laborer; coolie.

illiri 일일이 one by one; in detail; everything.

illŏjuda 일러주다 let know; tell; notify; advise.

illu 일루 first base.

illyŏk 인력 gravitation; magnetism.

illyŏkkŏ 인력거 ricksha(w).

illyŏl 일렬 line; row; file. *illyŏllo* 일렬로 in a row [line]; in a file.

illyŏn 일년 a[one] year. *illyŏnŭi* 일년의 yearly; annual.

illyu 일류. *illyuŭi* 일류의 first-class[rate]; top-ranking; leading.

illyu 인류 human race; mankind; human beings. *illyuŭi* 인류의 human; racial.

ilmak 일막 one act. *ilmakkŭk* 일막극 one-act play.

ilp'a 일파 school; party; sect.

ilp'um 일품. *ilp'um yori* 일품 요리 one-course dinner. *ch'ŏnha ilp'um* 천하 일품 article of peerless quality.

ilsaeng 일생 lifetime; one's(whole) life. *ilsaengŭi* 일생의 lifelong.

ilsang 일상 every day; daily; usually. *ilsangŭi* 일상의 daily; everyday.

ilsapyŏng 일사병 sunstroke; heatstroke.

ilshi 일시 at one time; for a time[while]. *ilshijŏk* 일시적 momentary; temporary.

ilshik 일식 solar eclipse; eclipse of the sun.

ilsŏn 일선 fighting line; front.

ilsu 일수 daily installment; day-to-day loan.

ilt'a 잃다 lose; miss; be deprived [bereft] of.

iltae 일대 whole area[district]; neighborhood (of).

iltae 일대 a[one] generation; one's lifetime. *iltaegi* 일대기 life story; biography.

iltan 일단 once (at least); for the moment; first.

iltang 일당 daily allowance[pay, wages]; day's wage; per diem (*Am.*). →**ilgŭp** 일급.

iltchigi 일찌기 early; once; formerly; one time.

iltŭng 일등 first class; first rank[grade]. *iltŭngsang* 일등상 first prize.

ima 이마 forehead; brow.

imamttae 이맘때 about[around] this time; at this time[moment, point] of day[night, year].

imank'ŭm 이만큼 this[so] much[many, big, long];

to this extent.

imbu 임부 pregnant woman; woman with child.

imdae 임대. *imdaehada* 임대하다 lease[rent] out; hire out. *imdaeryo* 임대료 rent.

imgi 임기 term of service[office].

imgŏm 임검 official inspection. *imgŏmhada* 임검하다 visit and inspect.

imgŭm 임금 wages; pay. *imgŭm insang* 임금 인상 wage increase[raise].

imgŭm 임금 king; sovereign.

imi 이미 already; now; yet.

imin 이민 emigration; immigration. *iminhada* 이민하다 emigrate (to); immigrate (from).

imja 임자 owner; possessor; proprietor.

imji 임지 one's post; place of one's appointment.

imjil 임질 gonorrhea.

imjong 임종 hour of death; dying hour; one's deathbed.

immat 입맛 appetite; taste.

immatch'uda 입맞추다 kiss; give (a person) a kiss.

immu 임무 duty; task; mission. *chungdae immu* 중대 임무 important duty.

immun 입문 introduction; guide; primer.

immyŏng 임명 appointment; nomination. *immyŏnghada* 임명하다 appoint to; nominate.

imshi 임시. *imshiŭi* 임시의 temporary; provisional. *imshiro* 임시로 specially; temporarily.

imshin 임신 pregnancy; conception. *imshinhada* 임신하다 become[be] pregnant; conceive.

imŭi 임의. *imŭiŭi* 임의의 free; optional; voluntary. *imŭiro* 임의로 at will; as one pleases.

imyŏn 이면 the back; the reverse; the inside.

inbu 인부 labo(u)rer; coolie; hand.

inch'e 인체 human body; (human) flesh.

indo 인도. *indohada* 인도하다 deliver; turn[hand] over; transfer.

in-ga 인가 approval; authorization. *in-gahada* 인가하다 approve; authorize.

in-gam 인감 seal impression. *in-gam tojang* 인감 도장 one's registered seal.

in-gan 인간 human being; man. *in-ganŭi* 인간의 human; mortal.

ingŏ 잉어 carp.

in-gong 인공. *in-gongŭi*[*jŏk*] 인공의[적] artificial; unnatural. *in-gong wisŏng* 인공 위성 artificial satellite.

ingt'ae 잉태 conception; pregnancy. *ingt'aehada* 잉태하다 conceive. →**imshin** 임신.

in-gu 인구 population. *in-gu chosa* 인구 조사 census.

in-gye 인계. *in-gyehada* 인계하다 hand over; transfer.

inha 인하. *inhahada* 인하하다 pull[draw] down; lower. *imgŭm inha* 임금 인하 wage cut.

inhada 인하다 be due (to); be caused (by); be attributable (to).

inhyŏng 인형 doll. *inhyŏng kat'ŭn* 인형 같은 doll-like.

injang 인장 seal. →**tojang** 도장.

inji 인지 (paper) stamp. *suip inji* 수입 인지 revenue stamp.

injong 인종 (human) race. *injong ch'abyŏl* 인종 차별 racial discrimination.

injŏng 인정 recognition; acknowledgement. *injŏng-hada* 인정하다 recognize; acknowledge; approve.

injŏng 인정 humanness; sympathy; humanity.

inju 인주 red stamping ink.

inki 인기 popularity. *inki innŭn* 인기 있는 popular; favorite.

inkwon 인권 human rights; rights of man.

inkyŏk 인격 personality; character. *inkyŏkcha* 인 격자 man of character.

inmul 인물 man; person. *k'ŭn inmul* 큰 인물 great man[figure].

ingmyŏng 익명 anonymity. *ingmyŏngŭi* 익명의 anonymous. *ingmyŏngŭro* 익명으로 anonymously.

innae 인내 patience; endurance. *innaehada* 인내하 다 endure; be patient with.

inal 이날 ① today; this day ② that day; the (very) day.

inp'um 인품 personality; character.

insa 인사 greeting; salution; bow. *insahada* 인사 하다 greet; salute; (make a) bow.

insaeng 인생 life; human[man's] life. *insaenggwan* 인생관 view of life.

insam 인삼 ginseng.

insang 인상 impression. *insangjŏgin* 인상적인 impressive. *ch'ŏdinsang* 첫인상 first impression.

inse 인세 royalty; stamp duty.

inshim 인심 man's minds; people's hearts. *inshimi chot'a* 인심이 좋다 be good-hearted.

insol 인솔. *insorhada* 인솔하다 lead. *insolcha* 인솔 자 leader.

insu 인수. *insuhada* 인수하다 undertake; take charge of; accept.

inswae 인쇄 printing; print. *inswaehada* 인쇄하다 print. *inswaemul* 인쇄물 printed matter.

inwŏn 인원 number of persons[men]; staff; personnel.

inyang 인양 pulling up; salvage. *inyanghada* 인양하다 pull up; salvage.

inyŏm 이념 idea; ideology.

inyŏn 인연 affinity; connection; relation. *inyŏnŭl maetta* 인연을 맺다 form relations.

inyong 인용 quotation; citation. *inyonghada* 인용하다 quote; cite.

ioe 이외. *ioeŭi* 이외의 with the exception (of); except for. *ioee* 이외에 except; but; save.

iŏng 이엉 straw thatch.

ip 입 mouth. *ibŭl pŏllida[tamulda]* 입을 벌리다[다물다] open[shut] one's mouth.

ip 잎 leaf; foliage.

ipchang 입장 entrance; admission. *ipchanghada* 입장하다 enter; be admitted. *ipchangnyo* 입장료 admission fee. *ipchangkwon* 입장권 admission ticket.

ipch'e 입체 solid (body).

ipchu 입주. *ipchuhada* 입주하다 move in; live in.

ipchŭng 입증. *ipchŭnghada* 입증하다 prove; give proof; testify.

ipku 입구 entrance; way in. *ipkuesŏ* 입구에서 at the entrance[door].

ipkuk 입국 entrance into a country. *ipkuk'ada* 입국하다 enter a country. *ipkuk sachŭng* 입국 사증 entry visa. *ipkuk chŏlch'a* 입국 절차 formalities for entry.

ipkŭm 입금 receipts; receipt of money. *ipkŭmhada* 입금하다 receive (some money).

ipkwan 입관. *ipkwanhada* 입관하다 place in a

coffin.

ip'ak 입학 entrance. *ip'ak'ada* 입학하다 enter a school. *ip'ak shihŏm* 입학 시험 entrance examination.

ipch'al 입찰 tender (*Eng.*); bid(*Am.*). *ipch'arhada* 입찰하다 tender[bid] for.

ip'ida 입히다 ① dress; clothe; put on ② plate; coat; gild.

ip'oe 입회 admission; joining. *ip'oehada* 입회하다 join[enter]; become a member of.

ippŏrŭt 입버릇 way[habit] of saying; one's manner of speech.

ip'yŏn 이편 this side[way].

ipsa 입사. *ipsahada* 입사하다 enter[join] a company. *ipsa shihŏm* 입사 시험 employment examination.

ipsagwi 잎사귀 leaf; leaflet.

ipsang 입상 winning a prize. *ipsanghada* 입상하다 win[get] a prize.

ipshi 입시 entrance examination. →**ip'ak shihŏm** 입학 시험.

ipsŏn 입선. *ipsŏnhada* 입선하다 be accepted; be selected.

ipsongmal 입속말 murmur; mutter. *ipsongmarhada* 입속말하다 mutter; grumble; murmur.

ipsu 입수. *ipsuhada* 입수하다 receive; get; obtain.

ipsul 입술 lip. *win[araen] ipsul* 윗[아랫] 입술 upper[lower] lip.   [ed].

ipsŏn 입선. *ipsŏnhada* 입선하다 (be) accepted[select-

ipta 입다 ① put on; wear; be dressed in ② owe; be indebted to.

iptae 입대 enlistment. *iptaehada* 입대하다 join

[enter] the army.

iptam 입담 skill at talking; eloquence.

ip'ubo 입후보. *ip'ubohada* 입후보하다 stand for; run for. *ip'uboja* 입후보자 candidate.

irang 이랑 ridge and furrow.

ire 이레 the seventh day (of the month); seven days.

irhada 일하다 work; labor; do one's work.

irhaeng 일행 party; company; one's suite; troupe.

irhal 일할 ten percent; 10%.

irho 일호 number one; No. 1.

irhŭn 일흔 seventy; three score and ten.

irhwa 일화 anecdote; episode.

irhwa 일화 Japanese money.

iri 이리 wolf. *iritte* 이리떼 pack of wolves.

irijŏri 이리저리 this way and that; here and there; up and down.

irin 일인 one person. *irindang* 일인당 for each (person); per head.

irŏn 이런 such; like this; of this kind.

irŏk'e 이렇게 thus; like; this; in this way; so.

iron 이론 theory. *ironsang*[*jŏgŭro*] 이론상[적으로] theoretically; in theory.

irŏnada 일어나다 ① rise; get up; stand up; arise ② happen; occur; break out.

irŏnajŏrŏna 이러나저러나 at any rate; in any case; anyway; anyhow.

irŏsŏda 일어서다 stand up; rise(to one's feet); get up.

iru 이루 second base. *irusu* 이루수 second baseman.

iruda 이루다 accomplish; achieve; attain.

irŭda 이르다 ① (be) early; premature. *irŭn ach'im*

이른 아침 early morning ② arrive.

irŭk'ida 일으키다 ① raise[set] up ② wake up; awake ③ establish; found.

irŭm 이름 name; full name.

irŭnba 이른바 so-called; what is called.

irwi 일위 first[foremost] place; first rank; No. 1.

irwol 일월 January.

iryoil 일요일 Sunday. *taŭm[chinan] iryoire* 다음 [지난] 일요일에 next[last] Sunday.

iryŏk 이력 one's personal history; one's career[record]. *iryŏksŏ* 이력서 personal history.

iryong 일용 everyday[daily] use. *iryongp'um* 일용품 daily necessities.

iryu 이류. *iryŭi* 이류의 second-class[rate]; minor; inferior. *iryu hot'el* 이류 호텔 second-class hotel.

isa 이사 removal; moving. *isahada* 이사하다 move.

isa 이사 director; trustee. *isahoe* 이사회 board of directors.

isam 이삼 two or three; few. *isamil* 이삼일 two or three[few] days.

isan 이산. *isanhada* 이산하다 be scattered; be dispersed. *isan kajok* 이산 가족 dispersed[separated] families. *isan kajok ch'atki undong* 이산 가족 찾기 운동 Campaign for reunion of dispersed family members.

isang 이상 strangeness; abnormality. *isangsŭrŏun* 이상스러운 odd; strange; queer.

isang 이상 ideal. *isangjŏg(ŭro)* 이상적(으로) ideal(ly). *isangjuŭi* 이상주의 idealism.

isang 이상 more than; over; above; beyond. *shimnyŏn isang* 십년 이상 more than 10 years.

isŏ 이서 endorsement. *isŏhada* 이서하다 endorse.

isŏng 이성 reason. *isŏngjŏgin* 이성적인 rational.

isŏng 이성 the other[opposite] sex.

issushigae 이쑤시개 toothpick.

isŭl 이슬 dew; dewdrops.

isŭlbi 이슬비 drizzle; mizzle; misty rain.

itchok 이쪽 this side[way]; our side.

itta 있다 ① be; there is [are]; exist ② stay; remain ③ stand; be situated; be located ④ consist (in); lie (in).

itta 잇다 join; put together; connect; link.

itta 잊다 ① forget; slip one's mind ② leave behind. *ijŭl su ŏmnŭn* 잊을 수 없는 unforgettable.

ittae 이때 (at) this time[moment]; then. *ittaekkaji* 이때까지 until now; to this time.

ittagŭm 이따금 from time to time; now and then; at times.

it'ŭl 이틀 ① two days ② second day (of month).

it'ŭnnal 이튿날 next[following] day.

iut 이웃 neighbo(u)rhood. *iutchip* 이웃집 neighbo(u)ring house; next door.

iwol 이월 February.

iyagi 이야기 talk; conversation; chat. *iyagihada* 이야기하다 speak; talk; have a chat.

iyŏk 이역 foreign[alien] country[land].

iyong 이용 use; utilization. *iyonghada* 이용하다 make use of; utilize.

iyu 이유 reason; cause; motive; grounds; pretext; why. *iyu ŏpshi* 이유없이 without (good) reason. ···*ŭi iyuro* ···의 이유로 by reason of ···. *iyurŭl mutta* 이유를 묻다 inquire into the reason of.

iyul 이율 (the rate of) interest.

iyun 이윤 profit; gain. →**iik** 이익.

K

ka, kajangjari 가, 가장자리 edge; verge; brink; margin.

ka- 가- temporary; provisional. *kagyeyak* 가계약 provisional contract.

-k(g)a -가 street; district. *oga* 5가 the fifth street.

kabal 가발 wig; false hair.

kabang 가방 bag; satchel; trunk; suitcase. *sonkabang* 손가방 valise; handbag.

kabong 가봉 basting; fitting. *kabonghada* 가봉하다 baste; tack.

kabo 가보 family treasure; heirloom.

kabot 갑옷 suit[piece] of armor. *kabotkwa t'ugu* 갑옷과 투구 armor and helmet.

kabul 가불 advance; advance payment.

kabyŏpke 가볍게 lightly; slightly; rashly.

kabyŏpta 가볍다 (be) light; not heavy; not serious.

kach'i 가치 value; worth; merit. *kach'i innŭn* 가치 있는 valuable; worthy. *kach'i ŏmnŭn* 가치 없는 worthless; of no value.

kach'i 같이 ① like; as; likewise; similarly; in the same way; equally ② (along, together) with; in company with.

kach'ida 갇히다 be confined; be shut in (up); be kept indoors; be imprisoned.

kach'uk 가축 domestic cattle; livestock. *kach'uk pyŏngwon* 가축 병원 veterinary hospital; pet's hospital.

kach'ul 가출 disappearance from home. *kach'urhada* 가출하다 run away from home. *kach'ul sonyŏ*

가출 소녀 runaway girl.

kach'urok 가출옥 release on parole; provisional release.

kada 가다 go; proceed; visit.

kadong 가동 operation; work. *kadonghada* 가동하다 operate; run.

kadu 가두 street. *kadu yŏnsŏl* 가두 연설 wayside speech.

kaduda 가두다 shut in (up); lock in (up); confine; imprison.

kadŭk 가득 full *kadŭk ch'ada* 가득 차다 be full to the brim.

kae 개 dog; hound; puppy. *suk'ae* 수캐 male dog *amk'ae* 암캐 bitch.

kae 개 piece; unit. *pinu tasŏt kae* 비누 다섯. 개 five pieces[cakes] of soap.

kaebal 개발 exploitation; reclamation; development. *kaebarhada* 개발하다 develop; exploit; improve.

kaebang 개방. *kaebanghada* 개방하다 (leave) open; throw open (a place) to the public.

kaebi 개비 piece (of split wood); stick. *sŏngnyang-kaebi* 성냥개비 matchstick.

kaebok susul 개복 수술 abdominal operation; celiotomy.

kaebong 개봉 (cinema) release. *kaebonghada* 개봉하다 release (a film).

kaech'al 개찰 examination of tickets. *kaech'arhada* 개찰하다 examine[punch] tickets. *kaech'algu* 개찰구 wicket; ticket gate.

kaech'oe 개최. *kaech'oehada* 개최하다 hold; have; open. *kaech'oeil* 개최일 the day fixed for a meeting; fixture. *kaech'oeji*[*changso*] 개최지[장소] site (of an exposition).

kaech'ŏk 개척 cultivation; reclamation; clearing; exploitation. *kaech'ŏk'ada* 개척하다 open up; bring (land) under cultivation; exploit.

kaech'ŏnjŏl 개천절 the National Foundation Day (of Korea); the Foundation Day of Korea.

kaeda 개다 fold (up); wrap up. *ibujarirŭl kaeda* 이부자리를 개다 fold up[turn down] the beddings[bedclothes].

kaeda 개다 knead (flour); mix up; work. *milkarurŭl kaeda* 밀가루를 개다 knead dough.

kaeda 개다 clear up; become clear. *Piga kaetta* 비가 갰다 The rain is over.

kaegak 개각 cabinet reshuffle; cabinet shake-up.

kaegan 개간 reclamation; land cleaning. *kaeganhada* 개간하다 clear (the land); reclaim.

kaegang 개강. *kaeganghada* 개강하다 open a course; begin a series of one's lecture.

kaegi 개기 total eclipse. *kaegi il*[*wol*]*shik* 개기 일[월]식 total solar[lunar] eclipse.

kaegolch'ang 개골창 ditch; drain; gutter.

kaegujangi 개구장이 naughty boy; urchin.

kaeguri 개구리 frog. *shigyong kaeguri* 식용 개구리 edible frog; table frog.

kaegwan 개관 general survey[view]; outline. *kaegwanhada* 개관하다 survey; take a bird's-eye view of.

kaegyo 개교 opening of a school. *kaegyohada* 개교하다 open a school

kaehak 개학 beginning of school. *kaehak'ada* 개학하다 begin school; school begins.

kaehoe 개회. *kaehoehada* 개회하다 open a meeting; go into session. *kaehoesa* 개회사 opening address. *kaehoeshik* 개회식 opening ceremony.

kaehŏn 개헌 constitutional amendment[revision]. *kaehŏnhada* 개헌하다 revise a constitution.

kaehwa 개화 enlightenment; civilization. *kaehwahada* 개화하다 get civilized[enlightened]. *kaehwahan* 개화한 civilized; enlightened.

kaehyŏk 개혁 reform; innovation. *kaehyŏk'ada* 개혁하다 reform; innovate.

kaein 개인 individual; private person. *kaeinjŏk* 개인적 individual; private; personal.

kaeinjŏn 개인전 one-man show; private exhibition.

kaeinjuŭi 개인주의 individualism. *kaeinjuŭija* 개인주의자 individualist. *kaeinjuŭijŏgin* 개인주의적인 individualistic.

kaeip 개입 intervention; meddling. *kaeip'ada* 개입하다 intervene in; meddle in.

kaejashik 개자식 son-of-bitch.

kaejo 개조 remodeling; reconstruction; rebuilding. *kaejohada* 개조하다 remodel; reorganize; rebuild.

kaejŏm 개점 opening[establishment] of a shop [store]. *kaejŏmhada* 개점하다 open[start] a shop [store]; set up in business.

kaejŏng 개정 revision. *kaejŏnghada* 개정하다 revise. *kaejŏngp'an* 개정판 revised edition; revision.

kaejugŭm 개죽음 throwing away one's life. *kaejugŭmhada* 개죽음하다 die in vain; die to no purpose.

kaekch'a 객차 passenger car[train]; coach (*Am.*).

kaekchi 객지 strange[alien] land; one's staying place on a journey.

kaek'ida 개키다 fold (up). *ibujarirŭl kaek'ida* 이부자리를 개키다 fold up beddings.

kaekkwan 객관. *kaekkwanjŏk* 객관적 objective. *kaekkwanshik shihŏm* 객관식 시험 objective test.

kaekshil 객실 (*hotel*) guest room; (*boat, etc.*) passenger cabin.

kaeksŏk 객석 seat for a guest.

kaemak 개막 raising the curtain. *kaemak'ada* 개막하다 raise the curtain; commence[begin] the performance.

kaemi 개미 ant. *kaemitte* 개미떼 swarm of ants. *kaemit'ap* 개미탑 ant hill.

kaemŏri 개머리 gunstock; butt. *kaemŏrip'an* 개머리판 the butt of a rifle.

kaenari 개나리 golden forsythia.

kaeng 갱 pit; shaft. *kaengdo* 갱도 drift; gallery.

kaengji 갱지 pulp paper; rough paper.

kaengnyŏn-gi 갱년기 the turn[change] of (one's) life; climacteric.

kaengshin 갱신 renewal; renovation.

kaenyŏm 개념 concept; general idea; notion.

kaeŏp 개업 opening[commencement] of business [trade]. *kaeŏp'ada* 개업하다 open[start] business; begin business; (*lawyer, docter*) start[set up a] practice.

kaep'ittŏk 개피떡 rice-cake stuffed with bean jam.

kaep'yo 개표 ballot counting; official canvass of the votes (*Am.*). *kaep'yohada* 개표하다 count the ballots [votes]; make a canvass (*Am.*).

kaeron 개론 outline; introduction; survey; general remarks. *yŏngmunhak kaeron* 영문학 개론 an introduction to English literature.

kaeryak 개략 outline; summary; resume.

kaeryang 개량 improvement; reform. *kaeryanghada* 개량하다 improve; reform; (make) better.

kaesalgu 개살구 wild apricot.

kaeshi 개시 opening; beginning; start. *kaeshihada* 개시하다 begin; commence; open (game).

kaeshik 개식 the opening ceremony. *kaeshiksa* 개식사 opening address[speech].

kaesŏn 개선 improvement; betterment. *kaesŏnhada* 개선하다 improve; amend; reform.

kaesŏng 개성 individuality; personality; individual character.

kaesunmul 개숫물 dishwater; slops.

kaesut'ong 개수통 dishpan; slop-basin.

kaet'an 개탄 deploring; lamentation; regret. *kaet'anhada* 개탄하다 deplore; lament. *kaet'anhal manhan* 개탄할 만한 deplorable; lamentable.

kaetka 갯가 shore of an estuary.

kaet'ong 개통. *kaet'onghada* 개통하다 be opened to [for] traffic; be installed. *kaet'ongshik* 개통식 opening ceremony.

kaettongbŏlle 개똥벌레 firefly; glowworm.

kaeul 개울 brook; rivulet; creek; streamlet.

kaeunhada 개운하다 feel refreshed[relieved, well].

kaeyo 개요 outline; summary; epitome.

kage 가게 shop; store (*Am.*). *kumŏng kage* 구멍 가게 penny candy store.

kago 각오 preparedness; resolution. *kagohada* 각오하다 be ready[prepared] for.

kagok 가곡 song; lied. *kakokchip* 가곡집 collection of songs.

kagong 가공 processing. *kagonghada* 가공하다 process; work upon. *kagong shikp'um* 가공 식품 processed foodstuffs.

kagu 가구 furniture; upholstery. *kagujŏm[sang]* 가구점[상] furniture store.

kagŭk 가극 opera; lyric drama. *kagŭktan* 가극단 opera company.

kagye 가계 housekeeping. *kagyebu* 가계부 housekeeping book.

kagyŏk 가격 price; cost. *tomae[somae] kagyŏk* 도매[소매] 가격 wholesale[retail] price.

kahada 가하다 add (up); sum up. *amnyŏgŭl kahada* 압력을 가하다 give [apply] pressure (to).

kahok 가혹. *kahok'an* 가혹한 severe; cruel; harsh; merciless.

kahun 가훈 family precept; family code of conduct.

kaip 가입 joining; affiliation; subscription. *kaip'ada* 가입하다 join; become a member of; affiliate oneself with; subscribe for.

kajae 가재 household goods; furniture and effects.

kajak 가작 fine piece of work; work of merits.

kajang 가장 disguise; masquerade. *kajanghada* 가장하다 disguise oneself. *kajang haengnyŏl* 가장 행렬 fancy procession.

kajang 가장 most; extremely; exceedingly. *kajang arŭmdaun* 가장 아름다운 the most beautiful.

kajangjari 가장자리 edge; verge; margin; border.

kaji 가지 eggplant; egg apple.

kaji 가지 kind; sort; class. *se kaji* 세 가지 three kinds. *kajigajiŭi* 가지가지의 various; diverse; sundry.

kaji 가지 branch; bough; limb.

kajida 가지다 have; hold; carry; possess.

kajigaksaek 가지각색 (of) every kind and description. *kajigaksaegŭi* 가지각색의 various; of all kinds.

kajirŏnhada 가지런하다 (be) trim; even; equal; uniform. *kajirŏnhi* 가지런히 trimly; evenly.

kajok 가족 family; members of a family. *kajok kyehoek* 가족 계획 family planning.

kajŏn chep'um 가전 제품 electric home appliance.

kajŏng 가정 home; family. *kajŏng kyosa* 가정 교사 private teacher. *kajŏng kyoyuk* 가정 교육 home education; discipline.

kajŏng 가정 housekeeping; household management. *kajŏngkwa* 가정과 department of domestic science. *kajŏngbu* 가정부 housekeeper.

kajŏng 가정 assumption; supposition. *kajŏnghada* 가정하다 assume; suppose; presume.

kajuk 가죽 skin; hide; leather.

kajŭn 갖은 all; all sorts of; every. *kajŭn kosaeng* 갖은 고생 all sorts of hardship.

kajyŏgada 가져가다 take[carry] away; take along; carry.

kajyŏoda 가져오다 bring (over); bring (a thing with one); take (a thing) along; fetch.

kak 각 each; every. *kakkuk* 각국 every country; each nation.

kak 각 ① horn ② corner; turn ③ angle.

kak'a 각하 (2 *nd person*) Your Excellency; (3 *rd person*) His[Her] Excellency. *taet'ongnyŏng kak'a* 대통령 각하 Your[His] Excellency the President.

kakcha 각자 each; each[every] one; individually; respectively.

kakchi 각지 every[each] place; various places

[quarters].

kakch'ŏ 각처 every[each] place; various places. *kakch'ŏe* 각처에 everywhere; in all[various] places.

kakchong 각종 every kind; various kinds; all kinds[sorts]. *kakchongŭi* 각종의 all sorts of; various.

kakch'ŭng 각층 ① each[every] floor ② each stratum (of society).

kakkaein 각개인 each one[individual]; each; each person.

kakkai 가까이 near; close by[to]; nearly; almost. *kakkai oda* 가까이 오다 come up close. *paengmyŏng kakkai* 백명 가까이 nearly one hundred persons.

kakkak 각각 separately; respectively; apart. *kakkagŭi* 각각의 respective.

kakkapta 가깝다 (be) near; be close by; be at home.

kakki 각기 beriberi. *kakkie kŏllida* 각기에 걸리다 have an attack of beriberi.

kakkŭm 가끔 occasionally; from time to time; now and then.

kakkwang 각광 footlights; highlight. *kakkwangŭl patta* 각광을 받다 be in the limelight.

kakkye 각계 all walks of life; every field[sphere] of life.

kakp'a 각파 each party; all political parties [groups]; each faction; all sects; all schools.

kak pangmyŏn 각 방면 every direction [quarter]; all directions. *sahoe kak pangmyŏn* 사회 각 방면 all strata of society.

kakpon 각본 playbook; scenario; script.

kakpu 각부 each section; every department[ministry].

kak pubun 각 부분 each[every] part; various parts.

kaksat'ang 각사탕 cube[lump] sugar; sugar cubes.

kakshi 각시 maiden doll; doll bride.

kaksŏ 각서 memorandum; memo; note.

kaksŏnmi 각선미 beauty of leg line.

kakto 각도 angle; degrees of an angle.

kaltŭng 갈등 complications; discord; trouble(s).

kalbi 갈비 ribs. *kalbit'ang* 갈비탕 beef-rib soup.

kalch'ae 갈채 cheer; applause. *kalch'aehada* 갈채
하다 applause; cheer; give cheer.

kalchŭng 갈증 thirst. *kalchŭngi nada* 갈증이 나다
feel thirsty.

kalda 갈다 ① sharpen; grind ② polish; burnish
③ rub; chafe.

kalda 갈다 change; replace; substitute; alter.

kalda 갈다 till; cultivate; plow.

kalgamagwi 갈가마귀 jackdaw.

kalgamŏkta 갉아먹다 nibble (at); gnaw (upon);
bite (at).

kalgida 갈기다 ① strike; beat ② kick ③ cut;
slash ④ scrawl; scribble; dash off.

kalgorangi 갈고랑이 hook; crook; gaff.

kalgyŏssŭda 갈겨쓰다 scrawl; scribble; dash off.

kallae 갈래 fork; branch; division. *se kallae kil*
세 갈래 길 three forked[trifurcated] road; junction.

kallajida 갈라지다 ① split; cleave; crack ② part;
fork ③ be divided ④ be separated.

kallida 갈리다 (be) divided into; break into; fork.
kallimkil 갈림길 branch road; forked road.

kalmaegi 갈매기 (sea) gull.

kalmanghada 갈망하다 be anxious (for); long [yearn, thirst, crave] (for).

kalp'angjilp'ang 갈팡질팡 confusedly; in a flurry; pellmell; this way and that. *kalp'angjilp'anghada* 갈팡질팡하다 go this way and that; run pellmell; be at a loss.

kalsaek 갈색 brown. *kalsaek injong* 갈색 인종 brown races.

kalsurok 갈수록 as time goes by; more and more. *nari kalsurok* 날이 갈수록 as days go by.

kaltae 갈대 reed. *kaltaebal* 갈대발 reed blind.

kam 감 persimmon.

kam 감 material; stuff. *otkam* 옷감 (dress) material; cloth.

kama 가마 palanquin; sedan chair.

kama(sot) 가마(솥) iron pot; kettle; oven; kiln.

kamanhi 가만히 still; quietly; silently. *kamanhi itta* 가만히 있다 keep still; be[remain] motionless [quiet].

kamani 가마니 straw bag; bale; sack.

kama ollida 감아 올리다 roll up; wind up; hoist.

kambang 감방 cell; ward.

kamch'al 감찰 license plate; license. *yŏngŏp kamch'al* 영업 감찰 trade[business] license.

kamch'o 감초 licorice root. *yakpangŭi kamch'o* 약방의 감초 Jack-of-all-trades.

kamch'ok 감촉 touch; feeling. *kamch'ogi pudŭrŏpta* 감촉이 부드럽다 It feels soft(to the touch).

kamchŏm 감점 demerit mark. *kamchŏmhada* 감점하다 give (a person) a demerit mark.

kamch'uda 감추다 ① hide; conceal; put out of

sight; keep secret ② cover; veil; cloak; disguise.

kamch'ida 감치다 hem; sew up.

kamdok 감독 superintendence; supervision. *yŏnghwa kamdok* 영화 감독 director of a film.

kamdong 감동 deep emotion; impression. *kamdonghada* 감동하다 (be) impressed (with, by); (be) moved[touched, affected] (by).

kamgae 감개 deep emotion. *kamgae muryanghada* 감개 무량하다 My heart is filled with deep emotion.

kamgak 감각 sense; sensation; feeling; sensibility. *kamgagi yemin[tun]hada* 감각이 예민[둔]하다 have keen[dull] senses.

kamgi 감기 cold; influenza; flu. *kamgie kŏllida* 감기에 걸리다 catch[take] (a) cold.

kamgŭm 감금 confinement; detention. *kamgŭmhada* 감금하다 confine; detain; imprison.

kamgyŏk 감격 deep emotion; strong feeling. *kamgyŏk'ada* 감격하다 be deeply moved[touched].

kamhada 감하다 decrease; deduct; reduce; subtract; diminish; decline; fall off.

kamhaeng 감행 decisive[resolute] action. *kamhaenghada* 감행하다 venture; dare; carry out resolutely.

kamhi 감히 boldly; daringly. *kamhi ...hada* 감히 ...하다 dare[venture] to (do).

kamhwa 감화 influence; (moral) reform. *kamhwarŭl patta* 감화를 받다 be influenced[affected] (by). *kamhwahada* 감화하다 influence; exert influence upon (a person).

kamihada 가미하다 season; flavor.

kamja 감자 potato; white potato.

kamjilnada 감질나다 feel insatiable; never feel satisfied; feel tantalized.

kamjŏn 감전 (receiving) an electric shock. *kamjŏn-doeda* 감전되다 receive an electric shock.

kamjŏng 감정 judgment; appraisal. *kamjŏnghada* 감정하다 judge; appraise.

kamjŏng 감정 feeling; emotion; passion; sentiment. *kamjŏngjŏk* 감정적 emotional; sentimental.

kamjŏng 감정 ill feeling; grudge. *kamjŏngŭl sada* 감정을 사다 earn[incur] (a person's) grudge.

kamjŏngga 감정가 judge; connoisseur; appraiser.

kamjŏngin 감정인 →**kamjŏngga** 감정가.

kamnigyo 감리교 Methodist church. 「이 prison life.

kamok 감옥 prison; gaol (*Eng.*). *kamoksari* 감옥살

kamsa 감사 inspection; audit. *kamsahada* 감사하다 inspect; audit (accounts).

kamsa 감사 thanks; gratitude; appreciation. *kamsahada* 감사하다 thank; feel grateful[thankful].

kamsa 감사 inspector; auditor; supervisor.

kamsaek 감색 dark[deep, navy] blue; indigo.

kamsang 감상 appreciation. *kamsanghada* 감상하다 appreciate; enjoy.

kamsang 감상 sentimentality. *kamsangjŏgin* 감상적 인 sentimental. *kamsangjuŭija* 감상주의자 sentimentalist.

kamshi 감시 watch; lookout; vigil; observation *kamshihada* 감시하다 watch; keep watch (on, over); observe.

kamso 감소 diminution; decrease; decline; drop. *kamsohada* 감소하다 diminish; decrease; lessen.

kamsŏng 감성 sensitivity; sense; sensibility.

kamssada 감싸다 protect; shield; shelter; take (a person) under one's wing.

kamsu 감수. *kamsuhada* 감수하다 submit to; put up

with; be ready to suffer.

kamta 감다 wind; roll (up); coil; twine.

kamta 감다 shut[close] (one's eyes).

kamta 감다 wash; bathe; have a bath. *mŏrirŭl kamta* 머리를 감다 wash one's hair.

kamt'an 감탄 admiration; wonder. *kamt'anhada* 감탄하다 admire; marvel (at); wonder (at). *kamt'anhal manhan* 감탄할 만한 admirable; wonderful.

kamtchokkatta 감쪽같다 ① be perfect in (mending); be just as it was ② (be) complete; perfect.

kamt'oe 감퇴 decrease; decline; recession. *kamt'oehada* 감퇴하다 decrease; fall of. *chŏngnyŏgŭi kamt'oe* 정력의 감퇴 decline in energy.

kamt'u 감투 government post; high office. *kamt'urŭl ssŭda* 감투를 쓰다 assume office; hold a prominent post.

kamulda 가물다 (be) droughty; dry; have a spell of dry weather.

kamulgŏrida 가물거리다 ① (*light*) flicker; gleam ② (*spirit*) have a dim consciousness[memory].

kamun 가문 one's family; birth; lineage.

kamurŏjida, kkamurŏjida 가무러지다, 까무러지다 faint; swoon; lose one's senses.

kamwon 감원 personnel cut; reduction of staff. *kamwonhada* 감원하다 lay off; reduce the personnel.

kamyŏm 감염 infection; contagion. *kamyŏmhada [doeda]* 감염하다[되다] get infected(with); catch.

kamyŏn 가면 mask; disguise; cloak. *kamyŏnŭl ssŭda* 가면을 쓰다 wear a mask; make one's face.

kamyŏng 가명 assumed name; alias.

kan 간 ① liver ② courage; pluck. *kanam* 간암

cancer of the liver; liver cancer.

kan 간 seasoning; salty taste; saltiness. *kanŭl ch'ida* 간을 치다 apply salt (to); season.

kanan 가난 poverty; want. *kananhada* 가난하다 (be) poor; needy.

kananbaengi 가난뱅이 poor man; pauper.

kanbam 간밤 last night[evening].

kanbu 간부 members of the executive; the managing staff.

kanbu 간부 (*male*) adulterer; (*female*) adulteress.

kanch'ŏk 간척 land reclamation (by drainage).

kanch'ŏng 간청 entreaty; earnest request. *kanch'ŏnghada* 간청하다 entreat; implore; solicit.

kanch'ŏp 간첩 spy; secret[espionage] agent. *mujang kanch'ŏp* 무장 간첩 armed espionage agent.

kandan 간단 brevity; simplicity. *kandanhan* 간단한 brief; simple; light. *kandanhan shiksa* 간단한 식사 light meal; quick meal; snack (lunch).

kandejokchok 간데족족 everywhere; wherever one goes.

kandŭlgŏrida 간들거리다 ① (*wind*) blow gently; breeze ② (*behavior*) act coquettishly; put on coquettish air.

kandŭrŏjida 간드러지다 (be) charming; coquettish; fascinating. *kandŭrŏjige utta* 간드러지게 웃다 laugh coquettishly.

kang 강 river. *kang kŏnnŏ* 강 건너 across the river. *kangŭl ttara* 강을 따라 along a river.

kangaji 강아지 pup; puppy.

kan-gani 간간이 occasionally; now and then; from time to time; at times.

kangap 강압 oppression; repression; coercion;

pressure. *kangapchŏgin* 강압적인 oppressive; highhanded.

kangbyŏn 강변 riverside; riverbank. *kangbyŏn toro* 강변 도로 riverside road[drive].

kangch'ŏl 강철 steel. *kangch'ŏlp'an* 강철판 steel plate[plank].

kangch'uwi 강추위 spell of dry cold weather; intense[bitter] cold.

kangdaehada 강대하다 (be) big and strong; mighty; powerful. *kangdaeguk* 강대국 powerful country; big power.

kangdan 강단 (lecture) platform; rostrum.

kangdang 강당 (lecture) hall; auditorium (*Am.*); assembly hall (*Eng.*).

kangdo 강도 burglar; robber. *kwŏnch'ong kangdo* 권총 강도 holdup (man).

kangdo 강도 intensity; degree of strength. *kangdoŭi* 강도의 intense; strong; powerful.

kanggan 강간 rape; violation; outrage. *kangganhada* 강간하다 violate; rape.

kanggŏn 강건 robustness; sturdiness. *kanggŏnhada* 강건하다 (be) strong; robust; healthy.

kangguk 강국 great[strong] power.

kanghada 강하다 (be) strong; powerful; mighty. *kanghage* 강하게 hard; severely; strongly.

kanghwa 강화 peace; peace negotiations. *kanghwahada* 강화하다 make[conclude] peace (with).

kangja 강자 strong man; the powerful. *kangjawa yakcha* 강자와 약자 the strong and the weak.

kangjangje 강장제 tonic; invigorant; restorative.

kangje 강제 compulsion; coercion; constraint. *kangjehada* 강제하다 force; compel; coerce. *kangje·*

jŏgin 강제적인 compulsory; forced.

kangjo 강조 stress; emphasis. *kangjohada* 강조하다 stress; emphasize; accentuate.

kangjwa 강좌 lecture; course. *radio Yŏngŏ kangjwa* 라디오 영어 강좌 radio English course.

kangka 강가 riverside; riverbank. →**kangbyŏn** 강변.

kangmae 강매 high-pressure salesmanship (*Am.*). *kangmaehada* 강매하다 force a sale (on); force (a thing) upon (a person).

kangmul 강물 river; stream; river water.

kangnamk'ong 강남콩 kidney bean; French bean.

kangnyo 각료 Cabinet members[ministers]; ministers of state.

kangnyŏng 강령 general principles; platform. *chŏngdangŭi kangnyŏng* 정당의 강령 party platform.

kangp'an 강판 grater.

kangparam 강바람 river wind; dry wind.

kangp'ung 강풍 strong[high] wind; gale.

kangsa 강사 lecturer; instructor *shigan*[*chŏnim*] *kangsa* 시간[전임] 강사 part-time[full-time] lecturer.

kangshimje 강심제 heart stimulant; cardiac; cordial.

kangsŭp 강습 short training course. *kangsŭbŭl patta* 강습을 받다 take a course (in). *kangsŭpso* 강습소 institute; training school.

kangt'a 강타 heavy[hard] flow; fatal blow. *kangt'ahada* 강타하다 give[deal] (a person) a heavy blow.

kangt'al 강탈 seizure; extortion; robbery; plunder. *kangt'arhada* 강탈하다 plunder[loot; despoil; rob]

kangtcha 강짜. *kangtchaburida* 강짜부리다 show

unreasonable jealousy.

kangtuk 강둑 river imbankment; levee.

kangu 강우 rainfall. *kanguryang* 강우량 amount of rainfall.

kangŭi 강의 lecture; discourse. *kangŭihada* 강의하다 lecture (on); give a lecture.

kangŭm 강음 accent; stress. *kangŭm puho* 강음 부호 accent mark.

kangyo 강요 enforcement; extortion; exaction *kangyohada* 강요하다 exact; force; compel.

kan-gyŏk 간격 space; interval; gap. *imit'ŏ kan-gyŏgŭro* 2미터 간격으로 at intervals of two meters.

kan-gyŏl 간결 conciseness; brevity. *kan-gyŏrhada* 간결하다 (be) concise; terse; brief.

kangyŏn 강연 lecture; address; discourse. *kangyŏnhada* 강연하다 (give a) lecture; address (an audience). *kangyŏnhoe* 강연회 lecture meeting.

kanhaeng 간행 publication. *kanhaenghada* 간행하다 publish; issue; bring out.

kanho 간호 nursing; care (of the sick). *kanhohada* 간호하다 nurse; tend.

kanhok 간혹 sometimes; occasionally; now and then; once in a while.

kani 간이 simplicity. *kani shiktang* 간이 식당 quick-lunch room; snack bar; cafeteria.

kanjang 간장 liver. *kanjangpyŏng* 간장병 liver troubles[complaint]. *kanjangyŏm* 간장염 inflammation of the liver; hepatitis.

kanjang 간장 soy; soybean sauce.

kanjik'ada 간직하다 ① keep; store; save; treasure (up) ② hold in mind; cherish; entertain.

kanjirida 간질이다 tickle; titillate.

kanjirŏpta 간지럽다 (be) ticklish; feel ticklish.

kanjittae 간짓대 (long) bamboo pole.

kanjŏp 간접 indirectness. *kanjŏpchŏgin* 간접적인 indirect; roundabout. *kanjŏpchŏgŭro* 간접적으로 indirectly.

kanjugok 간주곡 interlude; intermezzo.

kanmagi 간막이 ① partition; division ② screen.

kanman 간만 ebb and flow.

kan match'uda 간 맞추다 salt properly; season well.

kanmul 간물 salty water; brine.

kanp'an 간판 signboard; billboard.

kanp'yŏn 간편 convenience; handiness. *kanp'yŏnhada* 간편하다 (be) convenient; simple; easy.

kansa 간사 executive secretary; manager. *kansajang* 간사장 chief secretary.

kansahada 간사하다 (be) cunning; sly; foxy.

kanse 간세 indirect tax.

kanshik 간식 eating between meals; snack. *kanshik'ada* 간식하다 have a snack.

kanshinhi 간신히 with difficulty; barely; narrowly.

kanso 간소 simplicity. *kansohada* 간소하다 (be) simple; plain.

kansŏn 간선 trunk[main] line. *kansŏn toro* 간선 도로 trunk road.

kansŏp 간섭 interference; intervention. *kansŏp'ada* 간섭하다 interfere; intervene. *muryŏk kansŏp* 무력 간섭 armed[military] intervention.

kansu 간수 (prison) guard; warder; jailer (*Am.*); gaoler (*Eng.*).

kant'ong 간통 adultery; illicit intercourse. *kant'onghada* 간통하다 commit adultery (with).

kanŭlda 가늘다 (be) thin; fine; slender. *kanŭn*

moksori 가는 목소리 thin voice. *kanŭn shil* 가는 실 fine thread. *kanŭn hŏri* 가는 허리 slender waist.

kanŭm 간음 adultery; illicit intercourse. *kanŭmhada* 간음하다 commit adultery.

kanŭng 가능. *kanŭnghan* 가능한 possible. *kanŭnghadamyŏn* 가능하다면 if (it is) possible.

kanyŏm 간염 hepatitis; inflammation of the liver.

kanyu 간유 (cod-)liver oil. *kanyugu* 간유구 sugar-coated cod-liver oil pills.

kaok 가옥 house; building. *kaokse* 가옥세 house tax.

kap 값 price; cost; charge. *kapshi ssada[pissada]* 값이 싸다[비싸다] be cheap[expensive].

kap 갑 casket; box; pack. *tambaetkap* 담뱃갑 cigarette case; tobacco box.

kapchŏl 갑절→**pae** 배.

kapkap'ada 갑갑하다 (be) tedious; stuffy; irksome; boring. *kasŭmi kapkap'ada* 가슴이 갑갑하다 feel heavy in the chest.

kapkapchŭng 갑갑증 ennui; boredom; tedium.

kapp'an 갑판 deck. *kapp'an sŭngganggu* 갑판 승강구 hatchway. *kapp'anjang* 갑판장 boatswain.

kappŭda 가쁘다 be out of breath; be short of wind; pant.

kappu 갑부 the richest man; millionaire; plutes (*Am.*).

kap'arŭda 가파르다 (be) steep; precipitous.

kapchagi 갑자기 suddenly; all of a sudden; all at once; abruptly.

kapsa 갑사 fine gauze.

kapsangsŏn 갑상선 thyroid gland. *kapsangsŏn horŭ-*

mon 갑상선 호르몬 thyroxine.

kapta 갚다 ① pay back; repay ② return; give (something) in return; reward ③ retaliate;. revenge.

kap'ulmak 가풀막 steep slope[ascent].

kap'ung 가풍 family tradition[custom].

karaanta 가라앉다 sink; go down; go to the bottom.

karae 가래 spade; plow; plough.

karae 가래 phlegm; sputum. *karaerŭl paetta* 가래 를 뱉다 spit (out).

karaech'im 가래침 spit; spittle.

karaipta 갈아입다 change (one's) clothes.

karakchi 가락지 ring; set of twin rings.

karangbi 가랑비 drizzle.

karangi 가랑이 fork; crotch.

karangnun 가랑눈 fine[powdery] snow.

karat'ada 갈아타다 change cars[trains]; transfer (to another train).

karida 가리다 hide; conceal; screen; cover.

karigae 가리개 twofold screen.

karik'ida 가리키다 point to; indicate; point out; show.

karo 가로 street; road. *karodŭng* 가로등 street lamp. *karosu* 가로수 street[roadside] trees.

karo 가로 width; breadth. *karo ip'it'ŭ* 가로 2피 트 two feet in width.

karomakta 가로막다 interrupt; hinder; block.

karu 가루 flour; meal; powder; dust. *karupinu* 가 루비누 powder soap.

karŭch'ida 가르치다 teach; instruct; educate.

karŭda 가르다 divide; part; sever; split; distribute.

karyŏpta 가렵다 (be) itchy; itching; feel itchy.

kasa 가사 household affairs; domestic duties; family concerns.

kasa 가사 words[text] of a song.

kasang 가상 imagination; supposition. *kasanghada* 가상하다 imagine; suppose. *kasang chŏk* 가상 적 imaginary enemy.

kashi 가시 thorn; prickle; bur. *kashidŏmbul* 가시 덤불 thorn thicket.

kashich'ŏl 가시철 barbed wire. *kashich'ŏlmang* 가 시철망 (barbed) wire entanglement.

kasok 가속 acceleration. *kasokto* 가속도 degree of acceleration.

kasŏkpang 가석방 release on parole.

kasŏl 가설 construction; installation. *kasŏrhada* 가 설하다 build; construct; install; lay on.

kasŏl 가설 hypothesis. *kasoljŏgin* 가설적인 hypothetical.

kasŏl 가설 temporary installation. *kasŏrhada* 가설 하다 install temporarily. *kasŏl kŭkchang* 가설 극장 temporary theater.

kasollin 가솔린 gasoline; gas.

kasu 가수 singer; (*female*) songstress; vocalist. *yuhaeng kasu* 유행 가수 popular song singer; crooner (*Am.*).

kasŭ 가스 gas; natural gas; coal gas. *kasŭ chungdok* 가스 중독 gas-poisoning.

kasŭm 가슴 breast; chest. *kasŭmi ap'ŭda* 가슴이 아 프다 have a pain in the chest.

kasŭmari 가슴앓이 heartburn; pyrosis.

kasŭmdulle 가슴둘레 girth of chest; bust.

kat 갓 Korean top hat (made of horsehair).

kat'aek susaek 가택 수색 house-searching.

katcha 가짜 imitation; sham; bogus; fake.

katch'uda 갖추다 ① get ready; prepare; furnish; equip; provide ② possess; have; be endowed (with). *chunbirŭl katch'uda* 준비를 갖추다 prepare for; make full preparation.

katkaji 갖가지 various kinds; all sorts; every kind.

kat'ollikkyo 가톨릭교 Catholicism. *kat'ollik kyodo* 가톨릭 교도 (Roman) Catholic.

katta 같다 ① be the same; (be) identical ② (be) equal (to); uniform; equivalent ③ similar; like; alike. *ttokkatta* 똑같다 be the very same; be just the same.

kat'ŭn kapshimyŏn 같은 값이면 if...at all; other things being equal; if it is all the same.

kaŭl 가을 autumn; fall (*Am.*). *kaŭl param* 가을 바람 autumn wind.

kaunde 가운데 ① middle; midway; center ② interior; inside ③ between; among.

kaundessonkarak 가운뎃손가락 middle finger.

kawi 가위 scissors; shears; clippers.

kawinnal 가윗날 →**ch'usŏk** 추석.

kayagŭm 가야금 Korean harp.

kayo 가요 song; ballad; lied. *kayoje* 가요제 popular song festival. ⌈miserable.

kayŏpta 가엾다 (be) poor; pitiable; pitiful; sad;

ke 게 crab. *kettakchi* 게딱지 crust of a crab.

kedaga 게다가 besides; moreover; what is more; in addition (to that).

kejae 게재. *kejaehada* 게재하다 publish[print] (in a newspaper); insert (an advertisement in a magazine).

kera 게라 printing galley; galley proof[sheet].

kerilla 게릴라 guerrilla. *kerillajŏn* 게릴라전 guerrilla warfare.

keshi 게시 notice; bulletin. *keshihada* 게시하다 post [put up] a notice. *keship'an* 게시판 bulletin [board].

keuda 게우다 vomit; throw up; fetch up.

keŭllihada 게을리하다 neglect (one's work); be negligent (of duty).

keŭrŭda 게으르다 (be) idle; lazy; indolent.

keŭrŭm 게으름 laziness; idleness; indolence. *keŭrŭmp'iuda* 게으름피우다 be lazy; be idle.

keŭrŭmbaengi 게으름뱅이 idler; lazybone; idle [lazy] fellow.

keyang 게양. *keyanghada* 게양하다 hoist; raise; fly; display (a flag).

ki 기 flag; banner; colo(u)rs. *kirŭl talda[naerida]* 기를 달다[내리다] hoist[lower] a flag.

kia 기아 abandoned child; foundling.

kiak 기악 instrumental music.

kiap 기압 atmospheric pressure. *ko[chŏ]giap* 고[저] 기압 high[low] atmospheric pressure.

kibon 기본 foundation; basis. *kibonjŏgin* 기본적인 fundamental; basic; standard.

kibu 기부 contribution; donation. *kibugŭm* 기부금 contribution; subscription.

kibun 기분 feeling; humor; mood.

kibyŏl 기별 notice; information. *kibyŏrhada* 기별 하다 inform[notify].

kibyŏng 기병 cavalryman; horseman; cavalry.

kich'a 기차 train; railway carriage; railroad car (*Am.*). *kich'aro* 기차로 by train.

kich'im 기침 cough; coughing. *kich'imhada* 기침하 다 have a cough.

kich'o 기초 foundation; basis; base.

kida 기다 crawl; creep; go on all fours.

kidae 기대 expectation; anticipation. *kidaehada* 기대하다 expect; look forward to.

kidaeda 기대다 lean(against); rest against; recline on; lean over. 「forward to.

kidarida 기다리다 wait for; await; expect; look

kido 기도 prayer; grace. *kidohada* 기도하다 pray; offer〔give〕 prayers; say grace.

kidokkyo 기독교 Christianity; Christian religion 〔faith〕. *kidokkyoŭi* 기독교의 Christian. *kidokkyodo* 기독교도 Christian.

kidongch'a 기동차 diesel train.

kidung 기둥 pillar; pole; post.

kigan 기간 period; term.

kigo 기고 contribution. *kigohada* 기고하다 contribute (to); write (for).

kigu 기구 utensil; implement; apparatus. *chŏn-gi kigu* 전기 기구 electrical appliance.

kigu 기구 structure; organization; machinery. *kukche kigu* 국제 기구 international organization.

kigŭm 기금 fund; foundation; endowment.

kigwan 기관 organ. *kamgak kigwan* 감각 기관 sense organs.

kigwan 기관 ① engine; machine ② organ; means; facilities. *kyoyuk kigwan* 교육 기관 educational facilities.

kigwanch'a 기관차 engine(*Eng.*); locomotive(*Am.*). *chŏn-gi kigwanch'a* 전기 기관차 electric locomotive.

kigwanch'ong 기관총 machine gun.

kigye 기계 machine; machinery. *kigyejŏgin* 기계적 인 mechanical. *kigyejŏguro* 기계적으로 mechanically; automatically.

kigye 기계 instrument; appliance; apparatus.

kigyo 기교 art; technique; trick; technical skill.

kiyŏ 기여 contribution; service. *kiyŏhada* 기여하다 contribute; render services.

kihan 기한 term; period; time limit.

kihang 기항. *kihanghada* 기항하다 put in; call. *kihangji* 기항지 port of call.

kiho 기호 mark; sign; symbol. *hwahak kiho* 화학 기호 chemical symbol.

kihoe 기회 opportunity; chance. *kihoerŭl chapta* 기회를 잡다 seize a chance. *kihoejuŭija* 기회주의 자 opportunist.

kihoek 기획 planning; plan. *kihoek'ada* 기획하다 (make a) plan; work out a program.

kihu 기후 weather; climate.

kiil 기일 fixed date; time limit; appointed day.

kiip 기입 entry. *kiip'ada* 기입하다 enter; fill up.

kija 기자 journalist; pressman (*Eng.*); newspaper- man (*Am.*).

kiji 기지 base. *haegun kiji* 해군 기지 naval base.

kijil 기질 disposition; temper; nature; spirit. *hak- saeng kijil* 학생 기질 spirit of the student.

kijŏgwi 기저귀 diaper; (baby's) napkin.

kijŏk 기적 (steam) whistle; siren (*Am.*).

kijŏk 기적 miracle; wonder. *kijŏkchŏk(-ŭro)* 기적 적 (으로) miraculous(ly).

kijŏl 기절 fainting; swoon. *kijŏrhada* 기절하다 faint (away); go faint; swoon.

kijun 기준 standard; basis. *kijunŭi* 기준의 stand- ard; basic; base.

kijŭng 기증 contribution; donation. *kijŭnghada* 기

증하다 present; contribute; donate.

kijunggi 기중기 crane; derrick; hoist.

kikkŏi 기꺼이 willingly; with pleasure; readily.

kikkŏt'aeya 기껏해야 at (the) most; at (the) best; at the outside.

kikwon 기권 abstention; renunciation. *kikwonhada* 기권하다 abstain; withdraw one's entry.

kil 길 road; way; street. *kanŭn kire* 가는 길에 on the way. *kirŭl mutta* 길을 묻다 ask the way.

kilda 길다 (be) long; lengthy. *kin tari* 긴 다리 long legs.

kildŭrida 길들이다 ① tame; domesticate; train; break in. ② accustom; acclimate[acclimatize].

kim 김 steam; vapor. *kimi nada* 김이 나다 steam; reek. *kimppajida* 김 빠지다 lose its flavo(u)r.

kim 김 laver; dried laver.

kima 기마 horse riding.

kimak'ida 기막히다 ① stifle; feel stifled[suffocated; choked] ② (be) amazed; stunned.

kimch'i 김치 pickles; pickled vegetables.

kimin 기민 smartness, sharpness. *kiminhan* 기민한 quick; prompt; sharp. ⌜curious.

kimyo 기묘. *kimyohan* 기묘한 strange; queer; odd;

kin-gŭp 긴급 emergency; urgency. *kin-gŭp'an* 긴급한 urgent; pressing; emergent.

kinjang 긴장 tension; strain. *kinjanghada* 긴장하다 become tense; be strained. *kinjangdoen* 긴장된 strained; tense.

kinmil 긴밀. *kinmirhan* 긴밀한 close[intimate].

kinŭng 기능 ability; capacity; skill. *kinŭng ollimp'ik* 기능 올림픽 Olympics in Technology.

kinyŏm 기념 commemoration; memory. *kinyŏmha-*

da 기념하다 commemorate; honor the memory of. *kinyŏmŭro* 기념으로 in memory[commemoration] of.

kiŏk 기억 memory; remembrance. *kiŏk'ada* 기억하다 remember; bear in mind.

kion 기온 temperature. *kion pyŏnhwa* 기온 변화 change of[in] temperature.

kiŏp 기업 enterprise; undertaking. *kiŏpka* 기업가 enterpriser.

kip'i 기피 evasion. *kip'ihada* 기피하다 evade; shirk; dodge.

kipŏp 기법 techniques.

kippŭda 기쁘다 (be) glad; delightful; happy; pleased.

kipta 깊다 (be) deep; profound; close. *kip'i* 깊이 deep(ly).

kipta 깁다 sew (together); stitch; patch up.

kiri 길이 length; extent.

kirin 기린 giraffe.

kiroe 기뢰 mine. *kiroerŭl pusŏrhada* 기뢰를 부설하다 lay[place] mines (in the sea).

kirok 기록 record; document; archives. *kirok'ada* 기록하다 record; write down; register.

kirŭda 기르다 ① bring up; rear; breed; raise ② keep; grow; cultivate.

kirŭm 기름 ① oil ② fat; lard ③ grease; pomade.

kiryŏk 기력 energy; spirit; vigo(u)r. *kiryŏgi wangsŏnghan* 기력이 왕성한 energetic; vigorous.

kiryu 기류 air current. *sangsŭng[hagang] kiryu* 상승[하강] 기류 ascending[descending] current.

kisa 기사 engineer; technician. *t'omok kisa* 토목 기사 civil engineer.

kisa 기사 article; account; news. *shinmun kisa* 신문 기사 newspaper account.

kiso 기소 prosecution; litigation. *kisohada* 기소하다 prosecute; indict.

kisuk 기숙. *kisuk'ada* 기숙하다 lodge[board] (at, with a person) *kisuksa* 기숙사 dormitory.

kisul 기술 art; technique; skill. *kisulcha* 기술자 technician; engineer.

kit 깃 feather; plume.

kitpal 깃발 flag; banner. →**ki** 기.

kittae 깃대 flagstaff; flagpole.

kiulda 기울다 incline (to); lean(to); slant; tilt.

kiun 기운 ① (physical) strength; energy; force ② vigor; spirit. *kiunch'an* 기운찬 vigorous; energetic.

kiuttunggŏrida 기우뚱거리다 sway from side to side; rock; totter.

kkaburŭda 까부르다 winnow; fan.

kkach i 까치 magpie.

kkada 까다 peel; husk; pare. *kyurŭl kkada* 귤을 까다 peel an orange.

kkadak 까닭 reason; why; cause. *musŭn kkadalgŭro* 무슨 까닭으로 why; for what reason.

kkadaropta 까다롭다 (be) particular; fastidious; overnice.

kkae 깨 sesame. *ch'amkkae* 참깨 sesame. *tŭlkkae* 들깨 wild sesame.

kkaech'ida 깨치다 learn; understand; comprehend; master. *han-gŭrŭl kkaech'ida* 한글을 깨치다 learn [master] Korean language.

kkaeda 깨다 break; crush; smash. *kŭrŭsŭl kkaeda* 그릇을 깨다 break a dish.

kkaeda 깨다 ① wake up; awake ② become sober; sober (up) ③ have one's eyes opened.

kkaeda 깨다 (be) hatched; hatch.

kkaedatta 깨닫다 see; perceive; realize; understand; sense; be aware of.

kkaejida 깨지다 ① break; be broken[smashed] ② fail; come to a rupture ③ be spoiled.

kkaekkŭshi 깨끗이 clean(ly); neatly; tidily. *kkaekkŭshi takta* 깨끗이 닦다 wipe (a thing) cleanly.

kkaekkŭt'ada 깨끗하다 ① (be) clean; cleanly; tidy; neat ② (be) pure; clean; innocent; chaste ③ (be) fair; clean.

kkaemulda 깨물다 bite (on); gnaw (at). *ipsurŭl kkaemulda* 입술을 깨물다 bite[gnaw] one's lips.

kkaenada 깨나다 return to consciousness; recover one's senses; come to oneself; awake from.

kkaesogŭm 깨소금 powdered sesame mixed with salt; sesame-salt.

kkaettŭrida 깨뜨리다 ① break; crush; destroy; crash; smash ② baffle; frustrate; disturb; spoil.

kkaeuch'ida 깨우치다 wake up; awake; (a)rouse; call (a person's) attention.

kkaeuda 깨우다 ① wake up; awaken; arouse ② bring (a person) to his sense; get[make] sober.

kkaji 까지 ① till; until; up to; by (*time*) ② to; up to; as far as (*place*) ③ even; so far as (*extent*).

kkakchŏngi 깍정이 miser; skinflint; crafty fellow.

kkakkŭragi 까끄라기 awn; beard.

kkakta 깎다 shave; sharpen; cut down.

kkaktugi 깍두기 white-radish pickles.

kkalboda 깔보다 make light of; look down upon.

kkalda 깔다 ① spread; stretch ② pave; cover ③ sit on (a cushion).

kkalgae 깔개 cushion.

kkalkkal 깔깔. *kkalkkal utta* 깔깔 웃다 laugh loudly [aloud].

kkalkkarhada 깔깔하다 (be) coarse; rough.

kkalkkŭmhada 깔끔하다 ① (be) smart; neat and tidy ② sharp; harsh.

kkalttaegi 깔때기 funnel.

kkamagwi 까마귀 crow; raven.

kkambakkŏrida 깜박거리다 twinkle; blink; flicker; glitter.

kkamkkamhada 깜깜하다 ① (be) pitch-dark ② (be) ignorant.

kkamtchakkamtchak 깜짝깜짝 with repeated starts. *kkamtchakkamtchak nollada* 깜짝깜짝 놀라다 be startled again and again.

kkamtchakkŏrida 깜짝거리다 blink repeatedly; wink.

kkamtchik'ada 깜찍하다 (be) clever for one's age; (be) precocious.

kkamtchiksŭrŏpta 깜찍스럽다 →**kkamtchik'ada** 깜찍하다.

kkangsul 깡술 drink without any food. *kkangsurŭl mashida* 깡술을 마시다 drink liquor without food.

kkangt'ong 깡통 can (*Am.*); tin (can) (*Eng.*). *kkangt'ong ttagae* 깡통 따개 can[tin] opener. *pin kkangt'ong* 빈 깡통 empty can[tin].

kkattagŏpta 까딱없다 (be) safe and sound.

kkat'uri 까투리 hen pheasant.

kkida 끼다 ① hold (a thing) (under) ② put on; pull on; wear.

kkiŏnta 끼었다 pour; shower; splash.

kkiuda 끼우다 put[hold] between; insert; fit into.

kkoch'aengi 꼬챙이 spit; skewer; p.·od.

kkoda 꼬다 ① twist; twine ② writhe; wriggle. *saekkirŭl kkoda* 새끼를 꼬다 make[twist] a rope.

kkouŭgida 꼬드기다 incite; urge; egg [set] (a person on to do).

kkoe 꾀 ① wit; resources ② trick; trap; artifice.

kkoebyŏng 꾀병 feigned[pretended] illness; fake sickness (*Am.*).

kkoeda 꾀다 tempt; entice; lure; seduce.

kkoekkori 꾀꼬리 (Korean) nightingale; oriole.

kkŏjida 꺼지다 ① go[die] out; be put out; be extinguished ② cave[fall] in; sink; subside.

kkojipta 꼬집다 pinch; nip.

kkok 꼭 ① tightly; firmly; fast ② exactly; just ③ surely; without fail.

kkokchi 꼭지 ① (stop) cock; tap; spigot; faucet ② knob; nipple ③ stalk; stem.

kkokkaot 꼬까옷 children's gala dress.

kkokkurajida 꼬꾸라지다 ① fall; drop ② die.

kkŏkta 꺾다 ① break (off); snap ② make a turn; turn. *orŭnp'yŏnŭro kkŏkta* 오른편으로 꺾다 turn to the right; turn right.

kkoktaegi 꼭대기 top; summit; peak; crown.

kkoktukkakshi 꼭둑각시 puppet; dummy.

kkol 꼴 ① shape; form; appearance ② state; condition; situation ③ sight; spectacle. *chamdamhan kkol* 참담한 꼴 horrible sight[spectacle]. *kkolsanaun* 꼴사나운 unsightly; shabby.

kkŏlkkŏl 껄껄 ha-ha; haw-haw. *kkŏlkkŏl utta* 껄껄 웃다 laugh aloud; roar with laughter.

kkŏlkkŭrŏpta 껄끄럽다 (be) rough; coarse.

kkŏllŏngp'ae 껄렁패 good-for-nothing crew; shiftless lot.

kkolsanapta 꼴사납다 (be) ugly; unbecoming; unsightly.

kkoltchi 꼴찌 the last; the bottom; the tail end.

kkoma 꼬마 boy; (little) kid; baby miniature. *kkoma chadongch'a* 꼬마 자동차 baby car. *kkoma chŏn-gu* 꼬마 전구 miniature bulb.

kkomkkomhada 꼼꼼하다 very careful; methodical.

kkŏmkkŏmhada 껌껌하다 (be) pitch-dark; be as dark as pitch.

kkomtchak mot'ada 꼼짝 못하다 be unable to move an inch.

kkŏnaeda 꺼내다 pull[draw] out; take[bring] out; produce; whip out; pick out.

kkŏngch'ung 껑충 with a jump[leap].

kkongmuni 꽁무니 rear (end); tail (end); last.

kkŏpchil 껍질 ① bark ② rind; peel ③ husk; shell. *sagwa kkopchil* 사과 껍질 (the) rind of (an) apple.

kkŏptegi 껍데기 husk; hull; shell. →**kkŏpchil** 껍질.

kkoraksŏni 꼬락서니 (*slang*) state; condition; appearance; spectacle.

kkori 꼬리 tail; tag; brush (of fox); scut (of rabbit). *kkorirŭl chapta* 꼬리를 잡다 find (a person's) weak point; catch (a person) tripping.

kkŏrida 꺼리다 ① dislike; abhor ② avoid; shun ③ hesitate.

kkŏrimch'ik'ada 꺼림칙하다 feel uncomfortable [uneasy] (about).

kkorip'yo 꼬리표 address tag; label. *kkorip'yorŭl talda* 꼬리표를 달다 put on a tag.

kkot 꽃 flower; blossom; bloom. *kkoch'ŭi* 꽃의 floral. *kkottaun* 꽃다운 flowery; flowerlike. *kkotkage* 꽃가게 flowershop. *kkottabal* 꽃다발 bouquet; bunch of flowers.

-kkŏt -껏 as far as possible; to the best (of); to the utmost (of). *sŏngŭikkŏt* 성의껏 heartily; from one's heart *himkkŏt* 힘껏 as far as possible; to the best of one's ability.

kkotta 꽂다 ① stick; put[fix] in (to); prick; pin ② insert ③ drive into.

kkuda 꾸다 borrow; have[get] the loan (of).

kkŭda 끄다 put out; extinguish; flow out.

kkujitta 꾸짖다 scold; rebuke; chide.

kkujunhada 꾸준하다 (be) steady; untiring; constant. *kkujunhi* 꾸준히 untiringly; steadily.

kkul 꿀 honey; nectar. *kkulbŏl* 꿀벌 honeybee. *kkulmul* 꿀물 honeyed water.

kkŭl 끌 chisel.

kkŭlda 끌다 ① draw; pull; tug; drag ② attract; catch ③ delay; protract.

kkult'a 꿇다 kneel (down); fall[drop] on one's knees.

kkŭlt'a 끓다 boil; simmer; seethe.

kkum 꿈 ① dream ② vision; illusion. *kkum kat'ŭn* 꿈 같은 dreamlike. *kkumŭl kkuda* 꿈을 꾸다 dream; have a dream.

kkumida 꾸미다 ① decorate; ornament; adorn ② feign; pretend ③ invent; fabricate.

kkŭmtchik'ada 끔찍하다 ① (be) awful; terrible; cruel ② (be) very hearty; warm. *kkŭmtchigi* 끔찍이 ① awfully; terribly ② warmly; wholeheartedly.

kkumulgŏrida 꾸물거리다 ① wriggle; squirm; wiggle ② move slowly; dawdle.

kkŭnabul 끄나불 piece of string.

kkŭnimŏpta 끊임없다 (be) continuous; ceaseless; incessant. *kkŭnimŏpshi* 끊임없이 constantly; continually.

kkŭnnada 끝나다 (come to an) end; close; be over (up); be finished; expire.

kkŭnnaeda 끝내다 end; go[get] through (with); finish; complete.

kkŭnt'a 끊다 ① cut; cut off; sever ② give up; leave off.

kkŭnjŏkkŏrida 끈적거리다 be sticky; be greasy.

kkurida 꾸리다 pack[wrap] up; bundle. *chimŭl kkurida* 짐을 꾸리다 make a bundle[package].

kkŭrida 끓이다 ① boil (water); heat ② cook.

kkŭrŏanta 끌어안다 hug; embrace; draw (a person) close to one's breast.

kkŭrŏdŭrida 끌어들이다 ① draw in; pull in ② win (a person) over to one's side.

kkurŏmi 꾸러미 bundle; package; parcel. *ot kkurŏmi* 옷 꾸러미 bundle of clothes.

kkŭrŭda 끄르다 undo; untie; loosen; unfasten.

kkŭt 끝 ① end; close; final; last ② point; tip ③ result; consequence.

kkutkkut'ada 꿋꿋하다 (be) upright; firm; solid; steady.

kkwae 꽤 fairly; pretty; considerably.

kkwak 꽉 ① tightly; fast; closely ② to the full. *munŭl kkwak chamgŭda* 문을 꽉 잠그다 shut a door fast; lock a door tight.

kkweda 꿰다 run[pass] (a thing) through. *panŭre shirŭl kkweda* 바늘에 실을 꿰다 run[pass] a thread through a needle.

kkwemaeda 꿰매다 sew; stitch; darn; patch up.

kkwettult'a 꿰뚫다 pierce; pass[run] through; penetrate; shoot through.

kkyŏanta 껴안다 embrace; hug; hold (a person) in one's arms.

kkyŏipta 껴입다 wear (a coat) over another.

-ko -고 ① height ② amount; sum. *p'yogo[haebal]* 표고[해발] above the sea-level. *sanch'ulgo* 산출고 product; output. *maesanggo* 매상고 the amount sold. ⌈Dr. Kim.

ko 고 the late. *ko Kim paksa* 고 김 박사 the late

koa 고아 orphan. *koawon* 고아원 orphanage; orphan asylum.

kŏaek 거액 big[colossal] sum; large amount.

koap 고압 ① high pressure ② high tension; high voltage. *koapchŏgin* 고압적인 high-handed. *koapsŏn* 고압선 high-tension[-voltage] wire.

kobaek 고백 confession. *kobaek'ada* 고백하다 confess.

kobal 고발 prosecution; indictment; complaint. *kobarhada* 고발하다 prosecute; indict.

kobi 고비 climax; crest; height; crucial moment. *kobirŭl nŏmgida* 고비를 넘기다 pass the crisis.

kobon 고본 second-hand book. *kobon kage* 고본 가게 second-hand bookshop.

kŏbu 거부 millionaire; billionaire.

kŏbu 거부 refusal; denial; rejection. *kŏbuhada* 거부하다 deny; refuse; reject; veto (a bill). *kŏbukwon* 거부권 veto; veto power.

kŏbuk 거북 tortoise; terrapin; turtle.

kŏbuk'ada 거북하다 feel awkward; feel ill at ease; feel uncomfortable.

kŏbuksŏn 거북선 "Turtle Boat."

kobun 고분 old[ancient] tomb.

koch'ida 고치다 ① cure; heal; remedy ② mend; repair; fix (up) ③ correct; reform; rectify.

kŏch'ida 거치다 pass by[through]; go by way of.

kŏch'ida 걷히다 clear up[away, off]; lift. *Kurŭmi kŏch'yŏtta* 구름이 걷혔다. The clouds have cleared away.

kŏch'ilda 거칠다 (be) coarse; rough; harsh; violent.

kŏch'imŏpta 거침없다 without a hitch; without hesitation.

koch'u 고추 red pepper; cayenne pepper. *koch'ujang* 고추장 hot pepper paste.

kŏch'ujangsŭrŏpta 거추장스럽다 (be) burdensome; cumbersome; troublesome.

koch'ŭng 고층 higher stories; upper floors. *koch'ŭng kŏnmul* 고층 건물 high[lofty] building.

koch'wihada 고취하다 inspire(a person with); instil.

kodae 고대 ancient[old] times; antiquity. *kodaeŭi* 고대의 ancient; antique.

kŏdae 거대. *kŏdaehan* 거대한 huge; gigantic; enormous; colossal.

kodaehada 고대하다 wait impatiently (for); long for; eagerly look forward to.

kodalp'ŭda 고달프다 (be) exhausted; tired out; done up.

kodam 고담 old tale[story]; folklore.

kodanhada 고단하다 (be) tired; fatigued.

kodo 고도 ① altitude; height ② high power[degree]. *kodoŭi* 고도의 high; high power.

kodo 고도 desert[isolated] island.

kodo 고도 ancient city; former capital.

kŏdŏch'ada 걷어차다 kick hard; give (a person) a hard kick.

kŏdŏch'iuda 걷어치우다 ① put[take] away; clear off; remove ② stop; quit; shut[close] up. *hadŏn irŭl kŏdŏch'iuda* 하던 일을 걷어치우다 stop doing a job.

kodoeda 고되다 (be) hard; painful. *kodoen il* 고된 일 hard work; toil.

kodok 고독 solitude; loneliness. *kodok'ada* 고독하다 (be) solitary; lonely; lone; isolated.

kodong 고동 beat; pulsation; palpitation. *kodongch'ida* 고동치다 beat; palpitate; throb; pulsate.

kodong 고동 steam whistle; syren; siren (*Am.*).

kodongsaek 고동색 brown; reddish brown.

kŏdot 겉옷 outer garment.

kŏdu 거두 leader; magnate. *chŏnggyeŭi kŏdu* 정계의 거두 political leader

kŏduda 거두다 ① gather; collect; harvest ② gain; obtain ③ die; expire.

kŏdŭlda 거들다 help; give help (to); assist.

kŏdŭlmŏkkŏrida 거들먹거리다 mount the high horse; give oneself airs; swagger.

kodung 고둥 roll shell; spiral shellfish.

kodŭng 고등 high grade; high class. *kodŭngŭi* 고등의 high; higher; advanced. *kodŭng hakkyo* 고등학교 high school.

kodŭngŏ 고등어 mackerel.

kŏdŭp 거듭 (over) again; repeatedly. *kŏdŭp'ada* 거듭하다 repeat; do again

kodŭrŭm 고드름 icicle.

kŏdŭrŭm 거드름 haughty air. *kŏdŭrŭm p'iuda* 거드

름 피우다 act proudly; hold one's head high.

koehan 괴한 ruffian; suspicious[strange] guy.

koemul 괴물 monster; goblin.

koengjanghada 굉장하다 grand; magnificent; splendid. *koengjanghi* 굉장히 magnificently; awfully; terribly.

koeropta 괴롭다 ① (be) troublesome; hard ② (be) onerous; distressing ③ (be) awkward; embarrassing.

koesang 괴상. *koesanghan* 괴상한 strange; queer; odd.

koetcha 괴짜 odd person; crank.

kogae 고개 ① nape; scruff ② (mountain) pass ③ crest; summit; peak; climax.

kogaek 고객 customer; client; patron. *oraen kogaek* 오랜 고객 old[regular] customer.

kŏgankkun 거간꾼 broker; middleman; agent.

kogi 고기 ① meat ② fish. *takkogi* 닭고기 chicken. *twaejigogi* 돼지고기 pork. *soegogi* 쇠고기 beef.

kŏgi 거기 that place; there. *kŏgie[esŏ]* 거기에[에서] in that place; there. *kŏgiro* 거기로 to that place; there. *kŏgisŏbut'ŏ[robutŏ]* 거기서부터[로부터] from there.

kogiap 고기압 high atmospheric pressure.

kogijabi 고기잡이 ① fishing; fishery ② fisherman; fisher.

kogitpae 고깃배 fishing boat; fisherboat.

kogohak 고고학 arch(a)eology *kogohakcha* 고고학자 archeologist.

kogong 고공 high sky; high altitude. *kogong pihaeng* 고공 비행 high altitude flight[flying].

kŏgu 거구 gigantic[massive] figure; big body.

koguk 고국 one's native land[country]; one's home land.

kogung 고궁 ancient[old] palace.

koguma 고구마 sweet potato *kun koguma* 군 고구마 roast[baked] sweet potato.

kogŭp 고급 high-class[-grade]; higher; senior. *kogŭp kwalli* 고급 관리 higher[high-ranking] officials. *kogŭp ch'a* 고급 차 deluxe car.

kogwan 고관 high officer[official]; dignitary. *kogwandŭl* 고관들 high functionaries; high-ups.

kogwi 고귀. *kogwihada* 고귀하다 (be) noble; high-born. *kogwihan saram* 고귀한 사람 high personage.

kogye 곡예 (acrobatic) feats; stunts; tricks. *kogyesa* 곡예사 acrobat; tumble.

kogyŏl 고결. *kogyŏrhada* 고결하다 (be) noble; lofty; noble-minded. *kogyŏrhan inkyŏk* 고결한 인격 lofty [noble, high] character.

kohyang 고향 one's home; one's native place; one's birthplace.

kohyŏrap 고혈압 high blood pressure; hypertension.

koin 고인 the deceased[departed]; the dead.

kŏin 거인 giant; Titan; great man.

kojang 고장 ① hitch; hindrance ② accident; break-down. *kojangnada* 고장나다 get out of order; break down; go wrong.

kojang 고장 ① locality; district ② place of production ③ native place.

kŏji 거지 beggar; mendicant.

kŏjinmal 거짓말 lie; falsehood; fabrication; fake. *kŏjinmarhada* 거짓말하다 tell a lie; lie.

kojip 고집 stubbornness; abstinacy. *kojip'ada* 고집하다 hold fast (to); adhere. *kojip sen* 고집 센

stubborn; abstinate.

kojobu 고조부 one's great-great-grandfather.

kojŏk 고적 historic remains; place of historical interest.

kŏjŏk 거적 (straw) mat. *kŏjŏgŭl kkalda* 거적을 깔다 spread a mat.

kŏjŏl 거절 refusal; rejection. *kŏjŏrhada* 거절하다 refuse; reject.

kojŏn 고전 classics. *kojŏnjŏk* 고전적 classic(al).

kŏju 거주 residence; dwelling. *kŏjuhada* 거주하다 dwell; reside; inhabit; live.

kŏjuk 거죽 ① surface; face ② right side ③ exterior.

kok 곡 tune; air; music; strains.

kŏkchŏng 걱정 ① anxiety; apprehensions ② uneasiness; fear ③ care; worry; trouble. *kŏkchŏnghada* 걱정하다 be anxious (about); be worried (by); trouble oneself about.

kŏkkuro 거꾸로 reversely; (in) the wrong way; inside out; upside down; topsyturvy.

kŏkkurŏjida 거꾸러지다 fall; fall down[over]; fall headfirst; tumble down.

kŏkkurŏttŭrida 거꾸러뜨리다 make fall flat[headfirst]; throw down; knock[strike] down.

kokkwaengi 곡괭이 pick; picker; pickax(e).

koksŏn 곡선 curve; curved line. *koksŏnmi* 곡선미 beauty of a curve line.

kol 골 anger; temper. *kori nada* 골이 나다 be angry. *kollaeda* 골내다 get[become] angry.

kŏlchak 걸작 masterpiece; fine piece of work.

kŏlch'ida 걸치다 extend (over); spread (over); range; cover.

kolda 골다 snore. *k'orŭl kolmyŏ chada* 코를 골며 자다 sleep with (loud) snores.

kŏlda 걸다 ① hang; suspend ② speak to ③ pick; provoke ④ call to; ring up; telephone.

kŏlda 걸다 ① (be) rich; fertile ② abundant; plentiful; sumptuous.

kŏlgŏrhada 걸걸하다 (be) openhearted; free and easy. *sŏngmiga kŏlgŏrhada* 성미가 걸걸하다 be a freehearted fellow. 「고루.

kolgoru 골고루 evenly among all; equally. →**koru**

kolgyŏk 골격 frame; build; bone structure.

kollan 곤란 difficulty; trouble; embarrassment. *kollanhan* 곤란한 difficult; hard; troublesome.

kŏlle 걸레 floor cloth; dustcloth; mop. *kŏllejirhada* 걸레질하다 wipe with a damp cloth; mop (the floor).

kŏllida 걸리다 ① hang ② fall ill ③ be caught ④ take ⑤ make (a person) walk.

kŏllŏ 걸러 at intervals of; skipping. *haru kŏllŏ* 하루 걸러 every other[second] day.

kolmaru 골마루 narrow corridor[hallway].

kŏlmŏjida 걸머지다 ① shoulder; bear ② contract a debt.

kolmok 골목 side street; alley; byway. *twitkolmok* 뒷골목 back street.

kŏlp'it'amyŏn 걸핏하면 too often; readily; quickly; without any reason.

kŏlsang 걸상 bench; stool; couch.

kŏlsoe 걸쇠 latch; hasp.

koltchagi 골짜기 valley; vale; ravine; dale.

kŏltchuk'ada 걸쭉하다 (be) thick; heavy. *kŏltchuk'an kuk* 걸쭉한 국 thick soup.

kŏlt'ŏanta 걸터앉다 sit (on, in); sit astride.

koltong, koltongp'um 골동, 골동품 curio; antique. *koltongp'um kage* 골동품 가게 curio store[shop].

kom 곰 bear.

kŏm 검 sword. *ch'onggŏm* 총검 bayonet. *tan-gŏm* 단검 dagger.

kŏmabi 거마비 traffic expenses; carriage.

kŏman 거만 arrogance; haughtiness; self-importance *kŏmanhada* 거만하다 be arrogant; haughty.

komapta 고맙다 ① (be) thankful; grateful ② (be) kind; nice; appreciated.

kombo 곰보 pockmarked person.

kŏmbŏsŏt 검버섯 dark spots on an old man's skin.

kŏmbukta 검붉다 (be) dark red; blackish red.

kŏmch'al 검찰. *kŏmch'algwan* 검찰관 public prose-cutor[procurator]. *kŏmch'alch'ŏng* 검찰청 the (Public) Prosecutor's Office.

kŏmdaeng 검댕 soot. *kŏmdaengi mutta* 검댕이 묻다 be smeared with soot.

kŏmdo 검도 art of fencing.

kŏmdungi 검둥이 dark skinned person; Negro; nigger.

kŏmi 거미 spider. *kŏmijul* 거미줄 cobweb.

komin 고민 agony; anguish. *kominhada* 고민하다 (be) in agony; agonize.

kŏminjŏng, kŏmjŏng 검인정, 검정 official approv-al; authorization. *kŏminjŏng kyogwasŏ* 검인정 교과서 authorized textbook.

kŏmjin 검진 medical examination. *kŏmjinhada* 검진하다 give a medical examination; examine.

komkuk 곰국 thick beef soup.

kŏmmun 검문 examination; inspection; checkup (*Am.*). *kŏmmunhada* 검문하다 check up (passers-by). *kŏmmunso* 검문소 check point.

komo 고모 paternal aunt; one's father's sister.

komobu 고모부 husband of one's (paternal) aunt.

kŏmŏjwida 거머쥐다 grasp; grip; grab (up); seize.

komok 고목 old[aged] tree.

kŏmŏri 거머리 leech.

kŏmŏt'a, kkŏmŏt'a 거멓다, 꺼멓다 (be) deep black; jet-black.

komp'angi 곰팡이 mold; mildew; must.

kŏmp'urŭda 검푸르다 (be) dark blue; blue-black.

kŏmp'yo 검표 examination of tickets. *kŏmp'yohada* 검표하다 clip[examine] tickets.

kŏmsa 검사 public prosecutor; the prosecution. *pujang kŏmsa* 부장 검사 chief public prosecutor.

kŏmsa 검사 inspection; examination; test. *kŏmsahada* 검사하다 inspect; examine; audit; condition (merchandise).

kŏmsaek 검색 reference; search. *kŏmsaek'ada* 검색하다 refer to (a dictionary); search (a house).

kŏmsan 검산. *kŏmsanhada* 검산하다 verify[check] accounts; check one's figures.

kŏmso 검소. *kŏmsohada* 검소하다 (be) simple; frugal; plain. *kŏmsohan saenghwal* 검소한 생활 plain living.

kŏmsul 검술 fencing; swordmanship.

kŏmta 검다 (be) black; dark; sooty.

kŏmt'o 검토 examination; scrutiny. *kŏmt'ohada* 검토하다 examine; scrutinize.

komu 고무 rubber. *komugong* 고무공 rubber ball.

komushin 고무신 rubber shoes.

komul 고물 second-hand articles; used articles. *komulsang* 고물상 second-hand shop[store].

kŏmul 거물 leading[prominent] figure; bigwig.

komun 고문 adviser; counsel(l)or; consultant. *kisul komun* 기술 고문 technical adviser.

komurae 고무래 rake.

kŏmusŭrŭmhada 거무스름하다 (be) darkish; blackish.

kŏmyak 검약 thrift; (practice) economy; frugality. *kŏmyak'ada* 검약하다 economize (in); be thrifty.

kŏmyŏk 검역 quarantine; medical inspection.

kŏmyŏl 검열 censorship; inspection; review. *kŏmyŏrhada* 검열하다 censor; inspect; examine.

komyŏngttal 고명딸 the only daughter among one's many sons.

-kŏna -거나 whether...or; whatever; however; whenever. *nŏya choahagŏna malgŏna* 너야 좋아하거나 말거나 whether you like it or not.

kŏnahada 거나하다 (be) mellow; tipsy; slightly drunk[intoxicated].

konan 고난 hardship; suffering; affliction. *konanŭl kyŏkta* 고난을 겪다 undergo hardships.

kŏnban 건반 keyboard. *kŏnban akki* 건반 악기 keyboard instruments.

kŏnbangjida 건방지다 (be) impertinent; insolent; haughty. *kŏnbangjin t'aedo* 건방진 태도 haughty bearing.

konbong 곤봉 club; cudgel; stick; truncheon.

kŏnch'o 건초 hay; dry grass.

kŏnch'uk 건축 building; construction. *kŏnch'uk'ada* 건축하다 build; contruct; erect. *kŏnch'ukka* 건축

가 architect. *kŏnch'uk hoesa* 건축 회사 building company. *kŏnch'ukpŏp* 건축법 building regulation.

konch'ung 곤충 insect; bug. *konch'ung ch'aejip* 곤충 채집 insect collecting.

kŏndal 건달 libertine; scamp. *kŏndalp'ae* 건달패 a group of scamps[sluggards].

kŏndŏgi 건더기 ingredients; a piece of meat[vegetables] in soup; a piece of solid in liquid.

kŏndŭrida 건드리다 ① touch; jog ② provoke; tease; irritate.

kong 공 ball; handball. *kongŭl ch'ada* 공을 차다 kick a ball.

kŏn-gang 건강 health. *kŏn-ganghada* 건강하다 (be) well; healthy; sound. *kŏn-gang chindan* 건강 진단 medical examination.

kongbak 공박 refutation; wordy attack; charge. *kongbak'ada* 공박하다 refute; confute; argue against.

kongbi 공비 red[communist] guerillas. *mujang kongbi* 무장 공비 armed red guerillas.

kongbok 공복 empty stomach; hunger.

kongbŏm 공범 complicity; conspiracy. *kongbŏmja* 공범자 accomplice; confederate.

kongbu 공부 study; learning. *kongbuhada* 공부하다 study; work at[on]. *shihŏm kongbu* 시험 공부 study for an examination

kongbyŏng 공병 engineer; sapper. *kongbyŏngdae* 공병대 engineer corps.

kongch'ae 공채 public loan[debt]. *kongch'ae shijang* 공채 시장 bond market.

kongch'aek 공책 notebook.

kongch'ang 공창 licence prostitution.

kongch'ŏn 공천 public nomination[recommendation]. *kongch'ŏnhada* 공천하다 nominate publicly.

kongch'ŏnghoe 공청회 public[opening] hearing.

kongdong 공동 association; cooperation; union. *kongdongŭi* 공동의 common; joint; public. *kongdong pyŏnso* 공동 변소 public lavatory. *kongdong myoji* 공동 묘지 public cemetery.

konggal 공갈 threat; intimidation; blackmail. *konggarhada* 공갈하다 threaten; blackmail.

konggan 공간 space; room. *shigan-gwa konggan* 시간과 공간 time and space.

konggi 공기 air; atmosphere. *konggi oyŏm* 공기 오염 air pollution.

konggu 공구 tool; implement. *konggujŏm* 공구점 machine parts supplier.

konggŭm 공금 public money[funds].

konggun 공군 air force. *konggun kiji* 공군 기지 air base.

konggŭp 공급 supply; provision. *konggŭp'ada* 공급하다 supply[furnish, provide] (a person) with.

konggwan 공관 official residence. *chaeoe konggwan* 재외 공관 diplomatic establishment abroad.

konghae 공해 public nuisance[hazard, harm]; pollution. *maeyŏn konghae* 매연 공해 pollution caused by exhaust smoke.

konghak 공학 coeducation (*Am.*); mixed education (*Eng.*). *konghakche* 공학제 coeducationalism.

konghak 공학 engineering; technology. *t'omok[kigye, chŏn-gi] konghak* 토목[기계, 전기] 공학 civil [mechanical, electrical] engineering.

konghang 공항 airport. *kukche konghang* 국제 공항 international airport. *Kimp'o konghang* 김포공항

Kimpo Airport.

konghŏn 공헌 contribution; service. *konghŏnhada* 공헌하다 contribute (to); make a contribution (to); render services (to, for).

konghwang 공황 panic; crisis; consternation. *kŭmnyung konghwang* 금융 공황 financial crisis *segye konghwang* 세계 공황 world crisis.

konghyuil 공휴일 legal holiday; red-letter day.

kongil 공일 ① Sunday ② holiday.

kongim 공임 wage, wages; pay.

kongja 공자 Confucius.

kongjak 공작 peacock; peahen.

kongjak 공작 prince; duke (*Eng.*). *kongjak puin* 공작 부인 princess; duchess.

kongjang 공장 factory; plant; mill; workshop. *kunsu kongjang* 군수 공장 munitions factory. *kongjang p'yesu* 공장 폐수 industrial sewage.

kongji 공지 vacant lot; vacant land.

kongjŏngdae 공정대 air-borne troops; paratroops.

kongju 공주 (royal) princess.

kongjung 공중 public. *kongjungŭi* 공중의 public; common. *kongjung chŏnhwa* 공중 전화 public telephone.

kongkwa 공과. *kongkwa taehak* 공과 대학 engineering college.

kongma 곡마 circus; equestrian feats. *kongmadan* 곡마단 circus (troupe).

kongmok 곡목 program; selection; repertoire; number.

kongmo 공모 conspiracy; collusion. *kongmohada* 공모하다 conspire with; plot together.

kongmu 공무 official business[duties]. *kongmuwŏn*

공무원 public official[servant].

kongmun 공문 official document. *kongmunsŏ* 공문서 official document.

kongnip 공립 public; communal. *kongnip hakkyo* 공립 학교 public school.

kongno 공로 meritorious service; merits. *kongnoja* 공로자 person of merit. *kongnosang* 공로상 distinguished service medal.

kongno 공로 airway; air route. *kongnoro* 공로로 by plane[air].

kongŏp 공업 industry. *kongŏbŭi* 공업의 industrial; technical. *kongŏp tanji* 공업 단지 industrial complex. *kongŏp hakkyo* 공업 학교 technical school. *chung[kyŏng]gongŏp* 중[경]공업 heavy[light] industry.

kongp'o 공포 fear; terror; dread; horror. *kongp'o-echillin* 공포에 질린 terror-[horror-, panic-] stricken. *kongp'ochŭng* 공포증 phobia; morbid fear.

kongp'o 공포 blank shot[cartridge]. *kongp'orŭl ssoda* 공포를 쏘다 fire a blank shot.

kongp'yŏng 공평. *kongp'yŏnghada* 공평하다 (be) fair; impartial; even-handed. *kongp'yŏnghage* 공평하게 fairly; impartially; justly.

kongsa 공사 (diplomatic) minister. *kongsagwan* 공사관 legation.

kongsa 공사 construction work. *kongsabi* 공사비 cost of construction. *kongsajang* 공사장 site of construction.

kongsandang 공산당 Communist Party. *kongsandangwŏn* 공산당원 communist. *kongsanjuŭi* 공산주의 communism.

kongsang 공상 idle fancy; daydream. *kongsang-*

hada 공상하다 fancy; daydream.

kongsanp'um 공산품 industrial products[goods].

kongshik 공식 formula. *kongshigŭi* 공식의 formal; official.

kongsŏl 공설. *kongsŏrŭi* 공설의 public; municipal. *kongsŏl kigwan* 공설 기관 public institution.

kongson 공손. *kongsonhan* 공손한 polite; courteous; civil. *kongsonhi* 공손히 politely; humbly; courteously.

kongsŭp 공습 air raid[attack]. *kongsŭp'ada* 공습 하다 make an air attack (on); air-raid.

kongsup'yo 공수표 ① wind bill; fictitious bill; bad [dishonored] check. ② empty talks.

kongtcha 공짜 thing got for nothing; free charge; gratuitousness.

kongt'ong 공통. *kongt'onghada* 공통하다 be common (to). *kongt'ongŭi* 공통의 common; mutual; general.

kongŭi 공의 community doctor[physician].

kŏn-guk 건국 foundation of a country. *kŏn-guk kinyŏmil* 건국 기념일 National Foundation Day.

kongwon 공원 park; public garden. *kungnip kongwon* 국립 공원 national park.

kongyak 공약 public pledge[promise]. *kongyak'ada* 공약하다 pledge[commit] oneself (publicly).

kongye 공예 industrial arts; technology. *kongyega* 공예가 technologist. *kongyep'um* 공예품 industrial art products.

kon-gyŏng 곤경 awkward position; predicament; fix; adversity; difficult situation.

koni 고니 swan. *hŭkkoni* 흑고니 black swan.

kŏnilda 거닐다 walk[stroll] aimless; saunter; wander about.

kŏnjang 건장. *kŏnjanghan* 건장한 strong; stout; robust; sturdy. *kŏnjanghan ch'egyŏk* 건장한 체격 tough[robust] constitution.

kŏnjida 건지다 ① take[bring] out of water; pick up ② save[rescue] a person from.

kŏnjo 건조. *kŏnjohan* 건조한 dry; dried; arid. *kŏnjogi* 건조기 drier; desiccator.

kŏnjŏn 건전. *kŏnjŏnhada* 건전하다 (be) healthy; sound; wholesome. *kŏnjŏnhan sasang* 건전한 사상 wholesome ideas.

kŏnjŏnji 건전지 dry cell; battery.

kŏnmangchŭng 건망증 amnesia.

kŏnmoyang 겉모양 outward appearance; outlook; show; outside view.

kŏnmul 건물 building; structure. *sŏkcho[mokcho] kŏnmul* 석조[목조] 건물 stone[wooden] building.

kŏnnejuda 건네주다 ① pass[set] (a person) over [across]; take[ferry] over ② hand (over); deliver.

kŏnnŏgada 건너가다 go[pass] over; go across; cross (over)

kŏnnŏp'yŏn 건너편 the opposite side; the other side. *kŏnnŏp'yŏne* 건너편에 on the opposite[other] side.

kŏnnŭkta 겉늙다 look older than one's age; look old for one's age.

konoe 고뇌 suffering; distress; affliction; agony.

kŏnp'odo 건포도 raisins; dried grapes.

kŏnp'yŏng 건평 floor space; building area.

kŏnshil 건실. *kŏnshirhada* 건실하다 (be) steady; sound; reliable. *kŏnshirhan saram* 건실한 사람 steady[reliable] person.

kŏnsŏl 건설 construction; building. *kŏnsŏrhada* 건설하다 construct; build; establish. *kŏnsŏljŏgin* 건설적인 constructive.

kŏn 건 affair; subject; item. *tonan kŏnsu* 도난 건수 number of cases of theft.

kŏnŭi 건의 proposal; suggestion. *kŏnŭihada* 건의하다 propose; recommend.

kŏnŭrida 거느리다 have (with one); lead; head; command.

kop 곱 double; times. *kop'ada* 곱하다 multiply; double. *tu kop* 두 곱 double; twice; twofold.

kŏp 겁 ① cowardice; timidity ② fear; awe; fright. *kŏbi nada* 겁이 나다 be seized with fear.

kopch'ang 곱창 chitterlings; small intestines (of cattle).

kŏpchangi 겁장이 coward; pudding heart.

koppaegi 곱배기 double measure (of wine); double-the-ordinary dish.

koppi 고삐 reins; bridle; halter.

kopsadŭngi 곱사등이 hunchback; humpback.

kopta 곱다 ① (be) beautiful; lovely; fair; fine; nice ② (be) tender; kindly. *koun maŭmssi* 고운 마음씨 tender heart.

kŏpt'al 겁탈 plunder; rape. *kŏpt'arhada* 겁탈하다 plunder; rape.

kŏp'u 거푸 again and again; over again; repeatedly.

kop'ŭda 고프다 (be) hungry. *paega kop'ŭda* 배가 고프다 feel hungry.

kŏp'um 거품 bubble; foam; froth. *mulgŏp'um* 물거품 water bubble.

korae 고래 whale. *koraejabi* 고래잡이 whale fishing.

kŏrae 거래 transactions; dealings; business; trade.

kŏraehada 거래하다 do[transact] business (with); have an account with.

korak 고락 pleasure and pain; joys and sorrows.

korang 고랑 furrow; trough.

korang 고랑 handcuffs; shackles.

kori 고리 ring; link; loop. *kwigori* 귀고리 earring.

kori 고리 high interest; usury. *kori taegŭmŏpcha* 고리 대금업자 usurer; loanshark (*Am.*).

kŏri 거리 street; road; town; quarter *shijang kŏri* 시장 거리 market street.

kŏri 거리 distance; range; interval.

kŏrikkida 거리끼다 be afraid (of doing); hesitate (to do); refrain from (doing).

korinnae 고린내 bad[foul] smell; stinking smell.

korip 고립 isolation. *korip'ada* 고립하다 stand along; be isolated; be friendless. *koriptoen* 고립된 isolated; solitary; helpless.

koritchak 고리짝 wicker trunk.

koru 고루 equally; evenly. *koru nanuda* 고루 나누다 divide equally.

kŏrŭda 거르다 filter; leach; percolate; strain (through cloth).

kŏrŭda 거르다 skip (over); omit; go without. *haru kŏllŏsŏ* 하루 걸러서 every other day.

koruk'ada 거룩하다 (be) divine; sacred; holy.

korŭm 고름 pus; (purulent) matter.

kŏrŭm 걸음 walking; stepping; step; pace. *pparŭn kŏrŭmŭro* 빠른 걸음으로 at a rapid pace.

kŏrŭm 거름 manure; muck; fertilizer.

kŏrŭmma 걸음마. *kŏrŭmmarŭl hada* 걸음마를 하다 toddle; find its feet.

kŏrutpae 거룻배 barge; lighter; sampan.

koryo 고료 fee[payment] for a manuscript.

koryŏ 고려 consideration; deliberation *koryŏhada* 고려하다 consider; deliberate; bear in mind.

Koryŏ chagi 고려 자기 Koryo ceramics; ancient Korean pottery.

koryŏng 고령 advanced age; ripe old age. *koryŏngja* 고령자 person of advanced age.

kŏryu 거류. *kŏryumin* 거류민 (foreign) residents. *kŏryu oegugin* 거류 외국인 resident foreigners.

kosa 고사 examination; test. *yebi kosa* 예비 고사 preliminary examination.

kosaeng 고생 ① hard[tough] life; hardships; sufferings ② toil; labor; pain. *kosaenghada* 고생하다 go through hardship.

kosan 고산 high[lofty] mountain; alp. *kosan shingmul* 고산 식물 alpine plant.

kosang 고상. *kosanghan* 고상한 noble; lofty; high; elegant; refined.

kosap'o 고사포 anti-aircraft gun; A.A. gun

kosari 고사리 fernbrake; bracken.

kŏse 거세 castration; emasculation. *kŏsehada* 거세하다 castrate.

kŏseda 거세다 (be) rough; wild; violent. *kŏsen yŏja* 거센 여자 unruly woman

koshi 고시 examination; test. *kodŭng koshi* 고등 고시 higher civil service examination.

kŏshil 거실 sitting room; living room (*Am.*).

koso 고소 accusation; complaint; charge. *kosohada* 고소하다 accuse; bring a charge (against).

kosŏ 고서 old[ancient] books; classics.

kosok 고속 high-speed; rapid transit. *kosok toro* 고속 도로 express highway; superhighway. *kosok* *pŏsŭ* 고속 버스 express bus.

kosŏngnŭng 고성능 high efficiency[performance]. *kosŏngnŭng sushin-gi* 고성능 수신기 high-fidelity receiver.

kŏsŭllida 거슬리다 (be) against one's taste; be unpleasant.

kŏsŭllŏ ollagada 거슬러 올라가다 ① go up stream ② go back (to the past).

kŏsŭrŏmi 거스러미 (*of finger*) agnail; hangnail; (*of lumber*) splinter.

kŏsŭrŭda 거스르다 ① oppose; go against; run counter to ② give (back) the change.

kŏsŭrŭmton 거스름돈 change.

kot 곧 ① at once; immediately; instantly ② easily; readily.

kot 곳 place; scene; locality. *kose ttara* 곳에 따라 in some places. *kotkose* 곳곳에 here and there.

kŏt 겉 face; surface; right side; exterior; outward appearance.

kŏtchang 겉장 front page; cover of a book.

kŏtch'ijang 겉치장. *kŏtch'ijanghada* 겉치장하다 dress up outside; make outward show.

kŏtch'ire 겉치레 outward show; ostentation; ostensible decoration. *kŏtch'iryehada* 겉치레하다 dress up; show off.

kotkam 곶감 dried persimmons.

kot'ong 고통 pain; suffering; agony; anguish. *kot'ongsŭrŏun* 고통스러운 painful; afflicting.

kŏtpong 겉봉 envelope. *kŏtpongŭl ttŭtta* 겉봉을 뜯다 open[break open] an envelope.

kotta 곧다 ① (be) straight; upright; erect ② (be) honest; upright.

kŏtta 걷다 walk; go on foot; stroll; trudge. *kŏrirŭl kŏtta* 거리를 걷다 walk the street.

kŏtta 걷다 ① tuck[roll] up (one's sleeves); gather up (curtains); fold up ② take away; remove. *ppallaerŭl kŏtta* 빨래를 걷다 gather up the laundry.

koŭi 고의. *koŭiŭi* 고의의 intentional; deliberate. *koŭiro* 고의로 intentionally; on purpose.

kŏŭi 거의 ① almost; nearly; practically ② hardly; scarcely; little. *kŏŭi chŏnbu* 거의 전부 almost all.

kŏul 거울 mirror; looking glass; speculum. *sonkŏul* 손거울 hand mirror. *kŏurŭl poda* 거울을 보다 look in a glass.

kowi 고위 high rank. *kowi kwalli* 고위 관리 ranking government official.

kŏwi 거위 goose (*pl.* geese).

koyak 고약 plaster; ointment.

koyangi 고양이 cat; puss(y). *koyangi saekki* 고양이 새끼 kitten; kitty.

koyo 고요. *koyohada* 고요하다 (be) quiet; still; tranquil; calm.

kŏyŏk 거역. *kŏyŏk'ada* 거역하다 disobey; oppose; offend; go against.

koyong 고용. *koyonghada* 고용하다 hire; employ; engage. *koyongin* 고용인 employee. *koyongju* 고용주 employer.

ku 구, 9 nine. *chegu* 제구 the ninth. →**ahop** 아홉.

ku 구 former; ex-; old. *kusedae* 구세대 the old generation.

kŭ 그 that; it. *kŭ saram* 그 사람 that man[woman]; he; she. *kŭŭi* 그의 his; her.

kŭ 그 that; those; the; its. *kunal* 그날 that[the] day. *kŭttae* 그때 that time; then. *kŭgach'i* 그같

이 thus; so; like that.

kuae 구애 courtship; love-making. *kuaehada* 구애하다 court; woo; make love to.

kubi 구비. *kubihada* 구비하다 possess; have; be fully equipped. *kubi sŏryu* 구비 서류 required documents.

kubun 구분 division; demarcation; classification. *kubunhada* 구분하다 divide; classify; partition.

kuburŏjida 구부러지다 bend; curve; stoop.

kubyŏl 구별 distinction; difference; discrimination; division. *kubyŏrhada* 구별하다 distinguish; discriminate.

kŭbyu 급유 oil supply; refueling. *kŭbyuhada* 급유하다 supply oil; refuel. *kŭbyuso* 급유소 oil station; gas station.

kŭch'ida 그치다 stop; cease; halt; be over; end.

kuch'uk'am 구축함 (torpedo) destroyer.

kŭdaero 그대로 as it is[stands]; intact; just like that.

kudŏgi 구더기 maggot; grub; worm.

kudok 구독 subscription. *kudok'ada* 구독하다 subscribe.

kudŏngi 구덩이 hollow; depression; pit.

kudu 구두 shoes; boots. *kudurŭl shinta[pŏtta]* 구두를 신다[벗다] put on[take off, remove] shoes. *kududakki* 구두닦기 shoeshine boy.

kudusoe 구두쇠 miser; stingy[grasping] fellow; close-fisted man.

kugak 국악 Korean classic music.

kugimsal 구김살 creases; rumples; folds.

kugŏ 국어 language; one's mother tongue; Korean language.

kugŭp 구급 relief; first-aid. *kugŭpch'a* 구급차 ambulance. *kugŭp hwanja* 구급 환자 emergency cases.

kugwang 국왕 king; monarch; sovereign.

kŭgyak 극약 powerful drug; deadly poison.

kugyo 구교 Roman Catholicism; Catholic Church. *kugyodo* 구교도 (Roman) Catholic.

kugyŏng 국영 state operation[management]. *kugyŏngŭi* 국영의 state-operated[-run].

kugyŏnghada 구경하다 see (a play); watch (a game); do the sights (of). *shinaerŭl kukyŏnghada* 시내를 구경하다 do the sights of a city.

kugyŏngkkun 구경꾼 sightseer; onlooker; spectator.

kuhada 구하다 ① pursue; ask for ② save; rescue.

kuho 구호 slogan; motto; catch phrase.

kuhon 구혼 proposal[offer] of marriage; courtship. *kuhonhada* 구혼하다 propose (to); court.

kŭ hu 그 후 after that; thereafter; (ever) since; since then.

kui 구이 meat [fish] roasted[broiled] with seasonings. *saengsŏn kui* 생선 구이 baked fish. *kalbi kui* 갈비 구이 roasted ribs.

kŭi 그이 that person; he.

kuil 구일 the ninth day. →**ahŭre** 아흐레.

kuip 구입 purchase; buying. *kuip'ada* 구입하다 purchase; buy. *kuipcha* 구입자 purchaser.

kuje 구제 relief; succor; help; aid. *kujehada* 구제하다 relieve; succor; deliver (a person) from.

kujik 구직 seeking work; job-hunting.

kujo 구조 rescue; aid; relief; succor. *kujohada* 구조하다 save; rescue; relieve.

kŭjŏkke 그저께 the day before yesterday.

kujŏn 구전 commission; brokerage (fee).

kŭjŏn 그전 former days[times]; the past.

kujŏng 구정 lunar New Year's Day.

kŭjŭŭm 그즈음 about that time; around then.

kujwa 구좌 account. →kyejwa 계좌.

kuk 국 soup; broth. *kugŭl mashida* 국을 마시다 sip soup.

kŭk 극 drama; play. *kŭkchŏgin* 극적인 dramatical. *kŭkchŏgŭro* 극적으로 dramatically.

kŭk 극 ① pole(s) ② height; extreme; climax. ···*ŭi kŭge tarhada* ···의 극에 달하다 reach the climax.

kukch'ae 국채 national debt; national loan; government bond

kukchang 국장 director of a bureau.

kŭkchang 극장 theater; playhouse.

kukche 국제. *kukchejŏk* 국제적 international; world. *kukchejŏgŭro* 국제적으로 internationally; universally.

kukche yŏnhap 국제 연합 United Nations (U.N.).

kŭkchin 극진. *kŭkchinhada* 극진하다 (be) very cordial; devoted. *kŭkchinhi* 극진히 kindly; cordially.

kukchŏk 국적 nationality; citizenship. *kukchŏk pulmyŏngŭi* 국적 불명의 of unknown nationality.

kukchŏn 국전 the National Art Exhibition.

kŭk'i 극히 extremely; highly; most; quite.

kŭkchak 극작 play writing. *kŭkchakka* 극작가 dramatist; playwright.

kukka 국가 state; nation; country. *kukkajŏk* 국가적 national; state.

kukka 국가 national anthem.

kukki 국기 national flag[colors].

kukkun 국군 national army. *kukkunŭi nal* 국군의 날 (ROK) Armed Forces Day.

kŭ kot 그 곳 that place; there. *kŭ kose* 그 곳에 in that place; there.

kukkyŏng 국경 border; national boundary

kukkyŏngil 국경일 national holiday.

kuk'oe 국회 National Assembly. *kuk'oe ŭiwŏn* 국회 의원 member of National Assembly [Congressman].

kukpang 국방 national defense. *kukpangbu* 국방부 Ministry of National Defense.

kukpap 국밥 rice-and-meat soup.

kukpi 국비 national expenditure [expenses] *kukpi yuhaksaeng* 국비 유학생 government student abroad.

kŭkpin 극빈 extreme poverty. *kŭkpinja* 극빈자 needy [destitute] person; pauper.

kukpo 국보 national treasure [heirloom].

kŭkpok 극복 conquest. *kŭkpok'ada* 극복하다 overcome; conquer

kuksa 국사 national history; history of Korea.

kuksan 국산 home [domestic] production. *kuksanŭi* 국산의 homemade. *kuksanp'um* 국산품 home products; homemade articles.

kukta 굵다 (be) big; thick. *kulgŭn p'al* 굵은 팔 big arm.

kŭkta 긁다 ① scratch; scrape (off, out) ② rake up; gather up.

kŭktan 극단 dramatical [theatrical] company; theatrical troupe.

kŭktan 극단 extreme; extremity. *kŭktanŭi* 극단의 extreme. *kŭktanŭro* 극단으로 extremely.

kukt'o 국토 country; territory; domain. *kukt'o pangwi* 국토 방위 national defense.

kŭkto 극도 extreme. *kŭktoŭi* 극도의 extreme; utmost. *kŭktoro* 극도로 extremely; to the utmost.

Kŭktong 극동 the Far East.

kuk'wa 국화 chrysanthemum.

kuk'wa 국화 national flower.

kul 굴 oyster. *kult'wigim* 굴튀김 fried oysters.

kul 굴 ① cave; cavern ② den; lair ③ tunnel.

kŭl 글 writings; composition; prose; sentence; letter.

kulbok 굴복 submission; surrender. *kulbok'ada* 굴복하다 submit[surrender, yield, give in].

kŭlcha 글자 letter; character; ideography.

kŭlkwi 글귀 passage; line; words; terms.

kulle 굴레 bridle. *kullerŭl ssŭiuda* 굴레를 씌우다 bridle. *kullerŭl pŏtta* 굴레를 벗다 take off a bridle.

kŭlp'i 글피 two days after tomorrow.

kŭlssi 글씨 letter; character; writing; penmanship.

kulttuk 굴뚝 chimney.

kŭm 금 gold. *kŭmŭi* 금의 gold; golden; auric. *kŭmshigye* 금시계 gold watch.

kŭm 금 ① line ② fold; crease ③ crevice; crack.

kŭmanduda 그만두다 stop; cease; quit; discontinue.

kŭmaek 금액 amount of money; sum (of money).

kŭmbal 금발 golden hair; blonde (of female); blond (of male).

kŭmbang 금방 →panggŭm 방금.

kŭmgangsŏk 금강석 diamond.

kŭmgo 금고 safe; strongbox; cash box; vault.

kŭmgoe 금괴 gold bullion; gold ingot; gold bar.

kŭmhada 금하다 ① → kŭmjihada 금지하다 ② suppress; restrain; check.

Kumi 구미 Europe and America; the West.

kŭmil 금일 today; this day. →onŭl 오늘.

kŭmji 금지 prohibition; ban; embargo. *kŭmjihada* 금지하다 prohibit; forbid; ban.

kŭmjŏn 금전 money; cash; gold coin. *kŭmjŏnsang-ŭi* 금전상의 monetary; financial; pecuniary.

kŭmju 금주 abstinence (from drink); total abstinence.

kŭmju 금주 this week. *kŭmju chunge* 금주 중에 some time this week.

kumjurida 굶주리다 be[go] hungry; starve; thirst (for, after).

kŭmmyŏnggan 금명간 in a day or two.

kŭmnyo 급료 pay; salary; wages. →**ponggŭp** 봉급, **imgŭm** 임금.

kŭmnyŏn 금년 this year; the current year. →**orhae** 올해.

kŭmnyu 급류 swift stream; torrents; rapids.

kŭmnyung 금융 money market; finance; monetary circulation. *kŭmnyunggye* 금융계 financial circles.

kumŏng 구멍 hole; opening; chink. *panŭl kumŏng* 바늘 구멍 eye of a needle. *kumŏngŭl ttult'a* 구멍을 뚫다 make[bore, drill] a hole.

kumŏng kage 구멍 가게 small shop[store].

kŭmp'um 금품 money and goods. *kŭmp'umŭl chuda* 금품을 주다 bribe (a person) with money and other valuables.

kŭmni 금리 interest; money rates.

kŭmsok 금속 metal. *kyŏnggŭmsok* 경금속 light metals. *kwigŭmsok* 귀금속 precious metals.

kŭmsu 금수 embargo on the exportation[importation]. *kŭmsup'ŭm* 금수품 contraband (goods).

kumta 굶다 starve; go hungry. *kulmŏ chukta* 굶어 죽다 starve to death; die of hunger.

kumt'ŭlgŏrida 굼틀거리다 wriggle; squirm; writhe.

kŭmul 그물 net; dragnet; netting.

kŭmŭmnal 그믐날 the last day (of the month).

kŭmyoil 금요일 Friday.

kun 군 ① army; force; troops ② team. *che p'algun* 제8군 the Eighth Army. *paekkun* 백군 white team.

kunae 구내 premises; precincts; compound. *kunae shiktang* 구내 식당 refectory.

kunak 군악 military music. *kunaktae* 군악대 military[naval] band.

kunbi 군비 armaments. *kunbi kyŏngjaeng* 군비 경쟁 armament race. *kunbi ch'ukso[hwakchang]* 군비 축소[확장] reduction[expansion] of armaments.

kunbok 군복 service[military, naval] uniform.

kŭnbon 근본 foundation; basis; origin. *kŭnbonjŏk (ŭro)* 근본적 (으로) fundamental(ly); basical(ly).

kŭnch'ŏ 근처 neighborhood; vicinity. *kŭnch'ŏŭi* 근처의 neighboring; nearby; close by. *kŭnch'ŏe* 근처에 in the neighborhood[vicinity].

kunch'uk 군축 reduction of armaments; disarmament. *kunch'uk'ada* 군축하다 reduce armament.

kŭndae 근대 modern ages; recent times. *kŭndaejŏgin* 근대적인 modernistic. *kŭndaehwahada* 근대화 하다 modernize.

kundan 군단 corps; army corps.

kundo 군도 saber; service-sword.

kŭne 그네 swing; trapeze. *kŭnerŭl t'ada* 그네를 타 다 get on a swing.

kungdungi 궁둥이 buttocks; hips; rump; ass.

kun-gi 군기 colors; standard.

kungji 궁지 difficult situation; predicament; fix.

kungjie ppajida 궁지에 빠지다 be in a fix[sad plight].

kŭngji 궁지 pride; dignity.

kungjŏn 궁전 (royal) palace.

kungmin 국민 nation; people. *kungminŭi* 국민의 national. *kungmin sodŭk* 국민 소득 national income.

kungmun 국문 national[Korean] language. *kungmunpŏp* 국문법 Korean grammar.

kŭngnak 극락 paradise. *kŭngnak segye* 극락 세계 abode of perfect bliss.

kungnip 국립. *kungnibŭi* 국립의 national; state. *kungnip kŭkchang[kongwŏn]* 국립 극장[공원] national theater[park].

kungnyŏk 국력 national power. *kungnyŏgŭl kirŭda* 국력을 기르다 build up national power.

kŭn-gŏ 근거 basis; base; foundation; ground. *kŭngŏga ŏmnŭn* 근거가 없는 groundless; baseless.

kungsul 궁술 archery; bowmanship.

kŭn-gyo 근교 suburbs; outskirts.

kŭnhae 근해 neighboring[home] waters; near [adjacent] seas.

kunham 군함 warship; battleship.

kunhwa 군화 military shoes; combat boats.

kunin 군인 serviceman; soldier; sailor; airman. *chigŏp kunin* 직업 군인 professional soldier.

kŭnjirŏpta 근지럽다 →**karyŏpta** 가렵다.

kunjung 군중 crowd; masses; multitude. *kunjung taehoe* 군중 대회 (mass) rally.

kunmaejŏm 군매점 canteen; post exchange (P. X.).

kŭnmu 근무 service; duty; work. *kŭnmuhada* 근무하다 serve; work.

kunpap 군납 supply of goods and services to the

military. *kunnap ŏpcha* 군납 업자 military goods supplier.

kunpŏp 군법 military law. *kunpŏp hoeŭi* 군법 회의 court-martial.

kunsa 군사 military affairs. *kunsa komundan* 군사 고문단 the Military Advisory Group.

kŭnsa 근사. *kŭnsahan* 근사한 ① approximate; closely resembled ② fine; nice; splendid. *kŭnsahan saenggak* 근사한 생각 splendid idea.

kunsaryŏnggwan 군사령관 army commander.

kŭnshi 근시. *kŭnshiŭi* 근시의 shortsighted; nearsighted. *kŭnshi an-gyŏng* 근시 안경 glasses for short sight.

kunsu 군수. *kunsu kongjang* 군수 공장 munition factory. *kunsu sanŏp* 군수 산업 war industry.

kunŭi 군의 army[naval] doctor[surgeon]. *kunŭigwan* 군의관 medical officer.

kŭnŭl 그늘 shade. *namu kŭnŭl* 나무 그늘 shade of a tree.

kŭnwon 근원 origin; source; root; cause.

kŭnyang 그냥 as it is; as you find it; in that condition.

kŭnyŏ 그녀 she. *kŭnyŏŭi*[*rŭl*, *ege*] 그녀의[를, 에게] her.

kunyong 군용 military use. *kunyongŭi* 군용의 military. *kunyonggi* 군용기 military plane.

kŭnyuk 근육 muscle; sinews.

kup 굽 hoof; heel. *kubi nop'ŭn*[*najŭn*] *kudu* 굽이 높은[낮은] 구두 high-[low-]heeled shoes.

kŭp 급 class; grade.

kŭp'aeng 급행. *kŭp'aeng yŏlch'a* 급행 열차 express train.

kŭp'ada 급하다 (be) urgent; pressing; hasty. *kŭp'i* 급히 quickly; rapidly; hastily.

kup'ida 굽히다 bend; bow; stoop.

kŭppi 급비 supply of expenses. *kŭppisaeng* 급비생 scholar (*Eng.*); scholarship holder (*Am.*).

kŭpsu 급수 water supply[service]. *kŭpsuhada* 급수하다 supply (a town) with water.

kupta 굽다 roast; broil; bake. *chal kuwŏjin* 잘 구워진 well-done; well baked. *tŏl kuwŏjin* 덜 구워진 medium. *sŏl kuwojin* 설 구워진 rare.

kurenarut 구레나룻 whiskers.

kuri 구리 copper. *kuritpit* 구릿빛 copper-colored. *kuri ch'ŏlsa* 구리 철사 copper wire.

kŭrida 그리다 yearn after[for]; long[pine] for [after]; thirst for[after].

kŭrida 그리다 picture; draw; paint; sketch.

kŭrim 그림 picture; painting; drawing. *kŭrim yŏpsŏ* 그림 엽서 picture[post] card. *kŭrim kat'ŭn* 그림 같은 picturesque.

kŭrimja 그림자 shadow; silhouette.

kŭrŏch'i anŭmyŏn 그렇지 않으면 otherwise; unless; if...not so; (or) else.

kŭrŏk'omalgo 그렇고말고 indeed; of course; certainly.

kŭrŏlssahada 그럴싸하다 (be) plausible; likely.

kŭrŏl tŭt'ada 그럴 듯하다 →**kŭrŏlssahada** 그럴싸하다.

kŭrŏmŭro 그러므로 so; hence; therefore.

kŭrŏmyŏn 그러면 if so; in that case; then.

kŭrŏna 그러나 but; still; however; and yet.

kurŏngi 구렁이 big snake; huge serpent.

kŭru 그루 stump; stock. *namu han kŭru* 나무 한

그루 a stump of tree.

kŭrŭch'ida 그르치다 spoil; ruin; destroy; err.

kurŭm 구름 cloud. *kurŭm kkin* 구름 낀 cloudy. *kurŭm ŏmnŭn* 구름 없는 cloudless.

kurŭmdari 구름다리 overpass; land bridge.

kŭrŭrŏnggŏrida 그르렁거리다 wheeze; purr.

kŭrŭt 그릇 vessel; container. *notkŭrŭt* 놋그릇 brazen vessel.

kuse 구세 salvation (of the world). *kusegun* 구세군 the Salvation Army. *kuseju* 구세주 Savior; Messiah.

kushil 구실 excuse; pretext; pretense. *...ŭl kushillo sama* …을 구실로 삼아 on the pretext of.

kusok 구속 ① restriction; restraint ② detention; binding. *kusok'ada* 구속하다 restrict; restrain; detain (a person) in custody.

kusŏk 구석 corner; nook. *kusŏge* 구석에 in a corner.

kusŏng 구성 constitution; composition; organization. *kusŏnghada* 구성하다 constitute; organize.

kusŭl 구슬 bead; gem.

kŭsŭllida 그슬리다 burn; scorch; singe.

kusŭlp'ŭda 구슬프다 (be) sad; sorrowful; doleful.

kut'o 구토 vomiting; nausea. *kut'ohada* 구토하다 vomit; throw up.

kŭ tongan 그 동안 the while; during that time; these[those] days.

kutta 궂다 ① (be) cross; bad ② (be) foul; nasty; rainy. *kujŭn nalssi* 궂은 날씨 nasty weather.

kŭŭlda 그을다 be sunburned; be scorched[tanned]; be sooted (up).

kuyak sŏngsŏ 구약 성서 Old Testament.

kŭyamallo 그야말로 indeed; really; quite.

kuyŏkchil 구역질 nausea. *kuyŏkchillada* 구역질나다 feel nausea; feel sick.

kwa 과 course; department; faculty. *Yŏngŏkwa* 영어과 English course[department].

kwa 과 ① lesson; subject ② section; department; division. *che igwa* 제 2 과 Lesson two. *ch'ongmukwa(jang)* 총무과 (장) (chief[head] of a) general affairs section.

kwabu 과부 widow.

kwadae 과대 exaggeration. *kwadaehada* 과대하다 exaggerate; overstate. →**kwajang** 과장.

kwadogi 과도기 transition(al) period[stage]; age of transition.

kwaench'ant'a 괜찮다 ① (be) passable; not so bad; will do ② do not care; be all right.

kwaengi 괭이 hoe; pick. *kwaengiro p'ada* 괭이로 파다 hoe up the soil.

kwagŏ 과거 the past (days); bygone days. *kwagŏŭi* 과거의 past; bygone.

kwahada 과하다 levy (a tax); impose; assign; set; inflict. *segŭmŭl kwahada* 세금을 과하다 levy [impose] a tax on.

kwahak 과학 science. *kwahakchŏk(ŭro)* 과학적 (으로) scientific(ally). *kwahak kisul* 과학 기술 science and technology. *kwahakcha* 과학자 scientist.

kwail 과일 (edible) fruit. *kwail kage* 과일 가게 fruit shop[stand]. →**kwashil** 과실.

kwaja 과자 confectionery; cake; sweets; candy. *kwajajŏm* 과자점 sweetshop; candy store(*Am.*).

kwajang 과장 exaggeration. *kwajanghada* 과장하다 exaggerate; overstate; magnify.

kwallam 관람 inspection; viewing. *kwallamhada*

관람하다 see; view; inspect. *kwallamkwŏn* 관람권 admission ticket. *kwallamnyo* 관람료 admission fee. *kwallamgaek〔kwan-gaek〕* 관람객〔관객〕 spectator; visitor.

kwalli 관리 government official; public servant.

kwalli 관리 management; administration. *kwallihada* 관리하다 administer; manage. *kwalliin〔ja〕* 관리인〔자〕 manager; superintendent.

kwallye 관례 custom; usage; precedent.

kwamok 과목 subject; lesson; course. *p'ilsu〔sŏnt'aek〕 kwamok* 필수〔선택〕과목 required〔optional, elective〕 subject.

kwan 관 coffin; casket. *kwane nŏt'a* 관에 넣다 lay (a corpse) in a coffin.

kwanak 관악 pipe-music. *kwanakki* 관악기 wind instrument.

kwanbo 관보 official gazette.

kwanch'ŭk 관측 observation; survey. *kwanch'ŭk'ada* 관측하다 observe; make〔take〕 an observations. *kwanch'ŭkso* 관측소 observatory.

kwandae 관대. *kwandaehada* 관대하다 (be) generous; broad-minded. *kwandaehan* 관대한 broad-minded; generous; liberal. *kwandaehi* 관대히 generously; tolerantly.

kwang 광 storeroom; storehouse; cellar.

kwan-gaek 관객 spectator; audience.

kwangbu 광부 miner; mine worker; pitman.

kwangdae 광대 clown; feat actor; acrobatic performer.

kwanggo 광고 advertisement. *kwanggohada* 광고하다 advertise; announce.

kwanggyŏng 광경 spectacle; sight; scene; view.

kwanghak 광학 optics; optical science.

kwangjang 광장 open space; (public) square; plaza.

kwangmaek 광맥 vein of ore; deposit.

kwangmul 광물 mineral. *kwangmul chawŏn* 광물 자원 mineral resources.

kwan-gongsŏ 관공서 government and public offices.

kwangŏp 광업 mining (industry).

kwangsan 광산 mine. *kwangsan kisa* 광산 기사 mining engineer. *kwangsan nodongja* 광산 노동자 mine worker; miner.

kwangshin 광신 religious fanaticism. *kwangshinja* 광신자 fanatic.

kwangsŏn 광선 light; ray; beam. *t'aeyang kwangsŏn* 태양 광선 sunlight. *eksŭ kwangsŏn* 엑스 광선 X rays.

kwangt'aek 광택 luster; gloss; shine. *kwangt'aegŭl naeda* 광택을 내다 polish; shine.

kwan-gwang 관광 sightseeing. *kwan-gwanghada* 관광하다 go sightseeing; do the sights (of). *kwan-gwanggaek* 관광객 sightseer; tourist. *kwan-gwang pŏsŭ* 관광 버스 sightseeing bus. *kwan-gwang yŏhaeng* 관광 여행 sightseeing tour. *kwan-gwangji* 〔hot'el〕 관광지〔호텔〕 tourist resort〔hotel〕.

kwan-gye 관계 relation; concern(ment); connection. *kwan-gyehada* 관계하다 relate to; concern; participate in; be concerned in.

kwanhyŏn 관현 wind and string instrument. *kwanhyŏnak* 관현악 orchestra music. *kwanhyŏnaktan* 관현악단 orchestra (band).

kwannyŏm 관념 ① idea; notion ② sense.

kwansa 관사 official residence.

kwanse 관세 customs; customs duties. *suip*〔*such'ul*〕

kwanse 수입〔수출〕관세 import〔export〕duties.
kwansech'ŏng 관세청 the Office of Customs Administration.

kwanshim 관심 concern; interest. ···*e kwanshimŭl kajida* ···에 관심을 가지다 be concerned (about).

kwanyŏk 과녁 target; mark.

kwanyong 관용. *kwanyongŭi* 관용의 common; customary. *kwanyongŏ* 관용어 idiom; idiomatic expression.

kwao 과오 fault; mistake; error. *kwaorŭl pŏmhada* 과오를 범하다 make a mistake; blunder.

kwarho 괄호 parenthesis; bracket; brace.

kwashik 과식 overeating. *kwashik'ada* 과식하다 eat too much; overeat.

kwashil 과실 fruit. *kwashilju* 과실주 fruit wine.

kwashil 과실 fault; mistake; blunder. *kwashil ch'isa* 과실 치사 accidental homicide.

kwasuwon 과수원 orchard; fruit garden.

kwetchak 궤짝 box; chest. *sagwa han kwetchak* 사과 한 궤짝 a box of apples.

kweyang 궤양 ulcer. *wigweyang* 위궤양 ulcer of the stomach.

kwi 귀 ear. *kwiga mŏlda* 귀가 멀다 be hard of hearing.

kwibin 귀빈 guest of honor; important guest. *kwibinsŏk〔shil〕* 귀빈석〔실〕 room for VIPs.

kwibuin 귀부인 (titled) lady; noble woman.

kwich'ant'a 귀찮다 (be) annoying; irksome. *kwich'ank'e* 귀찮게 annoyingly.

kwiguk 귀국. *kwiguk'ada* 귀국하다 return to one's country; go home.

kwigŭmsok 귀금속 precious metals.

kwihada 귀하다 ① (be) noble; honorable ② (be) deer; lovable ③ (be) rare; uncommon.

kwihwa 귀화 naturalization. *kwihwahada* 귀화하다 be naturalized.

kwijok 귀족 noble(man); peer. *kwijogŭi* 귀족의 noble; titled; aristocratic. *kwijok sahoe* 귀족 사회 aristocracy; nobility.

kwijunghada 귀중하다 (be) precious; valuable. *kwijungp'um* 귀중품 valuables.

kwimŏgŏri 귀머거리 deaf person.

kwisun 귀순 submission; allegiance. *kwisunhada* 귀순하다 defect; submit (to).

kwitkumŏng 귓구멍 ear-hole; opening of the ear; ear.

kwitpyŏng 귓병 ear disease.

kwitturami 귀뚜라미 cricket; grig.

kwiyŏpta 귀엽다 (be) lovely; charming; attractive; cute.

kwiyŏwŏhada 귀여워하다 love; pet; caress; hold (a person) dear.

kwolli 권리 right; claim; title; privilege.

kwollyŏk 권력 power; authority. *kwollyŏk innŭn* 권력 있는 influential; powerful. *kwollyŏkka* 권력 가 man of power.

kwollyŏn 궐련 cigarette.

kwonch'ong 권총 pistol; revolver; gun(*Am.*). *kwonch'ong kangdo* 권총 강도 armed robber; gunman.

kwonhada 권하다 ① recommend ② advise; ask ③ invite; urge.

kwonse 권세 power; influence; authority. *kwonserŭl purida* 권세를 부리다 wield power.

kwont'ae 권태 weariness; fatigue; languor.

kwont'u 권투 boxing. *kwont'u shihap* 권투 시합 boxing match[bout]; prize-fight.

kwonwi 권위 authority; power; dignity. *kwonwi innŭn* 권위 있는 authoritative.

kwonyu 권유 inducement; solicitation; canvassing. *kwonyuhada* 권유하다 induce; canvass; solicit.

kyaltchuk'ada 걀쭉하다 somewhat long and slender; oval.

kyarŭmhada 갸름하다 somewhat long; (be) pleasantly oval. *kyarŭmhan ŏlgul* 갸름한 얼굴 oval face.

kye 계 ① section (in an office) ② charge; duty. *ch'ullapkye* 출납계 cashier's section.

kye 계 ① system ② family line; lineage ③ faction; clique. *t'aeyanggye* 태양계 solar system.

kye 계 mutual-aid society; loan club; guild. *kyeju* 계주 principal of a loan club.

-kye -계 notice; report. *kyŏlsŏkkye* 결석계 absence report. *samanggye* 사망계 notice of death.

-kye -계 circles; community; world; kingdom. *shirŏpkye* 실업계 business circle.

kyebu 계부 stepfather.

kyech'aek 계책 stratagem; plot; trick; scheme. *kyech'aegŭl ssŭda* 계책을 쓰다 adopt[use] a stratagem.

kyech'ŭng 계층 class; social stratum; walk of life.

kyedan 계단 stairs; staircase; doorstep.

kyegan 계간 quarterly publication. *kyeganji* 계간 지 quarterly.

kyegi 계기 meter; gauge; scale; instrument.

kyegok 계곡 valley; glen; dale; canyon.

kyegŭp 계급 class; caste. *sangnyu[chungnyu, ha-*

ryu〕 *kyegŭp* 상류〔중류, 하류〕 계급 upper〔middle, lower〕 class(es).

kyehoek 계획 plan; project; scheme; program(me). *kyehoek'ada* 계획하다 plan; project; scheme; intend. *kyehoekchŏgin* 계획적인 intentional; planned. *kyehoekchŏguro* 계획적으로 intentionally; deliberately.

kyejang 계장 chief clerk; chief.

kyejip 계집 (*slang*) woman; female; one's wife. *kyejibai* 계집아이 girl; lass.

kyejŏl 계절 season. *kyejŏrŭi* 계절의 seasonal.

kyeju kyŏnggi 계주 경기 relay (race). *ch'ŏnmit'ŏ kyeju kyŏnggi* 1,000 미터 계주 경기 1,000 meter relay race.

kyejwa 계좌 account. *kyejwarŭl yŏlda* 계좌를 열다 open an account(with a bank).

kyemo 계모 stepmother.

kyemong 계몽 enlightenment; education. *kyemonghada* 계몽하다 enlighten; educate.

kyeŏmnyŏng 계엄령 martial law.

kyeran 계란 egg. →**talgyal** 달걀.

kyerisa 계리사 chartered accountant; certified public accountant.

kyeryanggi 계량기 meter; gauge; scale.

kyesan 계산 calculation; reckoning; counting; computation. *kyesanhada* 계산하다 count; sum up; calculate; reckon. *kyesan-gi* 계산기 adding machine; calculating machine. *kyesansŏ* 계산서 bill; account.

kyeshi 계시 revelation; apocalypse. *kyeshihada* 계시하다 reveal.

kyeshida 계시다 (*honorific*) be; stay.

kyesok 계속 continuance; continuation. *kyesok'ada*
계속하다 continue; last; go on with. *kyesokchŏgin*
계속적인 continuous; continual.

kyesu 계수 younger brother's wife; sister-in-law.

kyesŭng 계승 succession; inheritance. *kyesŭnghada*
succeed to; inherit.

kyet'ong 계통 ① system ② lineage ③ party.
kyet'ongjŏk 계통적 systematic. *kyet'ongjŏguro*
계통적으로 systematically.

kyewon 계원 clerk in charge; section man. *chŏpsu
kyewon* 접수 계원 information clerk.

kyeyak 계약 contract; compact; covenant. *kyeyak'a-
da* 계약하다 contract; make a contract. *kyeyak-
kŭm* 계약금 contract deposit. *kyeyaksŏ* 계약서
(written) contract.

kyŏ 겨 chaff, hulls〔husks〕 of grain; bran.

kyoch'a 교차 intersection; crossing. *kyoch'ahada*
교차하다 cross〔intersect〕 (each other). *kyoch'aro*
교차로 crossroads; intersection.

kyodae 교대 alternation; change. *kyodaehada* 교
대하다 take turns; alternate. *kyodaero* 교대로
by turns; alternately.

kyodan 교단 platform. *kyodane sŏda* 교단에 서다
teach a class; be a teacher.

kyodoso 교도소 prison; jail.

kyŏdŭrangi 겨드랑이 armpit; axilla.

kyoga 교가 school〔college〕 song; Alma Mater song.

kyŏgil 격일. *kyŏgillo* 격일로 every other day; on
alternate days.

kyŏgŏn 격언 maxim; proverb; saying.

kyogwasŏ 교과서 textbook. *kŏmjŏng kyogwasŏ* 검
정 교과서 authorized textbook.

kyŏgwol 겨월 every other month. *kyŏgwol kan-haengmul* 격월 간행물 bimonthly (publication).

kyohoe 교회 church; chapel; cathedral. *kyohoe-dang* 교회당 church; chapel.

kyohun 교훈 instruction; precept; lesson.

kyohwal 교활. *kyohwarhan* 교활한 cunning; crafty; sly. *kyohwarhan nom* 교활한 놈 old fox; sly dog.

kyohwan 교환 exchange; interchange; barter. *kyohwanhada* 교환하다 exchange; barter; interchange.

kyohyangak 교향악 symphony. *kyohyangaktan* 교향악단 symphony orchestra.

kyoin 교인 believer; adherent; follower. *Kŭrisŭdo* [*kidok*] *kyoin* 그리스도[기독] 교인 believer in christianity; christian.

kyŏja 겨자 mustard.

kyojang 교장 schoolmaster; headmaster (of primary school); principal (of junior high school); director (of high school).

kyoje 교제 association; intercourse. *kyojehada* 교제하다 associate with; hold intercourse with; keep company with.

kyojŏng 교정 school grounds; campus (*Am.*); school playground.

kyojŏng 교정 proofreading. *kyojŏnghada* 교정하다 read proofs; correct (the press).

kyŏkcha 격자 lattice. *kyŏkcha munŭi* 격자 무늬 cross stripes; check.

kyŏkch'an 격찬 high praise. *kyŏkch'anhada* 격찬하다 praise highly; extol; speak highly of.

kyŏkch'im 격침 sinking, destruction. *kyŏkch'imha-da* 격침하다 (attack and) sink (a ship); send (a ship) to the bottom.

kyŏkchŏn 격전 hot fight; fierce battle; hot contest.

kyŏkchu 격주. *kyŏkchuŭi* 격주의 fortnightly; bi-weekly.

kyŏkch'u 격추. *kyŏkch'uhada* 격추하다 shoot (airplanes) down; bring down.

kyŏkpun 격분 wild rage; vehement indignation. *kyŏkpunhada* 격분하다 be enraged.

kyŏkpyŏn 격변 sudden change; revulsion. *kyŏkpyŏnhada* 격변하다 change violently.

kyŏkta 겪다 ① undergo; suffer; experience ② receive; entertain.

kyŏkt'oe 격퇴 repulse. *kyŏkt'oehada* 격퇴하다 repulse; drive[beat] back.

kyŏktol 격돌 crash; violent collision. *kyŏktorhada* 격돌하다 crash into[against].

kyŏkt'u 격투 grapple; (hand-to-hand) fight; scuffle. *kyŏkt'uhada* 격투하다 grapple with.

kyŏk'wa 격화. *kyŏk'wahada* 격화하다 grow more intense[violent]; intensify.

kyŏl 결 grain; texture. *pidankyŏl* 비단결 silky texture. *salkyŏl* 살결 texture of the skin.

kyŏlbaek 결백 purity; innocence; integrity. *kyŏlbaek'ada* 결백하다 (be) pure; upright; innocent.

kyŏlbu 결부. *kyŏlbushik'ida* 결부시키다 connect (A) with (B); link together.

kyŏlchae 결재 sanction; approval *kyŏlchaehada* 결재하다 decide (upon); approve; sanction.

kyŏlchŏm 결점 fault; defect; flaw.

kyŏlchŏng 결정 decision; determination; conclusion; settlement. *kyŏlchŏnghada* 결정하다 decide (upon); conclude; settle.

kyŏlguk 결국 after all; in the end; finally; in the long run; eventually.

kyŏlgŭn 결근 absence (from). *kyŏlgŭnhada* 결근하다 be absent[absent oneself] (from).

kyŏlgwa 결과 result; consequence; effect; fruit. …*ŭi kyŏlgwa* …의 결과 as a[the] result of.

kyŏlk'o 결코 never; by no means; not in the least.

kyŏllida 결리다 feel a stitch; get stiff.

kyŏllon 결론 conclusion. *kyŏllonŭl naerida* 결론을 내리다 draw[form] a conclusion.

kyŏllyŏl 결렬 rupture; breakdown. *kyŏllyŏrhada* 결렬하다 break down; be broken off.

kyŏlmal 결말 end; conclusion; result; settlement. *kyŏlmallada* 결말나다 be settled; come to a conclusion.

kyŏlsa 결사 *kyŏlsajŏk[ŭi]* 결사적[의] desperate; death-defying. *kyŏlsadae* 결사대 forlorn hope.

kyŏlsan 결산 settlement of accounts. *kyŏlsanhada* 결산하다 settle[balance] an account.

kyŏlshim 결심 determination; resolution. *kyŏlshimhada* 결심하다 determine; be resolved; make up one's mind.

kyŏlsŏk 결석 absence. *kyŏlsŏk'ada* 결석하다 be absent[absent oneself] (from). → kyŏlgŭn 결근.

kyŏlson 결손 loss; deficit. *kyŏlsonŭl naeda* 결손을 내다 run a deficit; suffer[incur] a loss.

kyŏlsŭng 결승 decision (of a contest). *kyŏlsŭngjŏn* 결승전 final game[match].

kyŏltan 결단 decision; determination; resolution. *kyŏltanŭl naerida* 결단을 내리다 reach[come to] a definite decision. ⌈duel.

kyŏlt'u 결투 duel. *kyŏlt'uhada* 결투하다 fight a

kyŏm 겸 and; in addition; concurrently. *ach'im kyŏm chŏmshim* 아침 겸 점심 brunch. *ch'imshil kyŏm kŏshil* 침실 겸 거실 bed-sitting room. *susang kyŏm oesang* 수상 겸 외상 Prime Minister and (concurrently) Foreign Minister.

kyoman 교만 pride; elation; haughtiness. *kyomanhada* 교만하다 (be) proud; haughty; arrogant.

kyŏmbi 겸비. *kyŏmbihada* 겸비하다 combine (one thing) with (another); have both.

kyomi 교미 copulation; coition. *kyomihada* 교미하 다 copulate.

kyŏmim 겸임. *kyŏmimhada* 겸임하다 hold an additional post[office].

kyŏmson 겸손 modesty; humility. *kyŏmsonhada* 겸 손하다 (be) modest; humble.

kyomun 교문 school gate. ⌈deft.

kyomyo 교묘 *kyomyohan* 교묘한 clever; skil(l)ful;

kyŏn 견 silk. *kyŏnsa* 견사 silk-thread.

kyonae 교내 campus. *kyonaeŭi* 교내의 interclass. *kyonaeesŏ* 교내에서 on[within] the campus.

kyŏnbon 견본 sample; specimen.

kyŏndida 견디다 ① bear; endure; stand ② wear; last; be good for; be equal to.

kyŏng 경 about; toward(s); around. *seshigyŏng* 세시경 about three o'clock.

kyŏng 경 Lord; Sir; you.

kyŏng 경 ① Chinese classics of Confucianism ② sutra; Buddhist scripture.

kyŏngbi 경비 expenses; cost; expenditure. *kyŏngbi chŏryak[chŏlgam]* 경비 절약[절감] curtailment of expenditure.

kyŏngbi 경비 defense; guard. *kyŏngbihada* 경비

하다 defend; keep watch.

kyŏngbo 경보 alarm; warning. *kyŏnggye kyŏngbo* 경계 경보 air defense alarm. *kongsŭp kyŏngbo* 공습 경보 air raid alarm.

kyŏngbŏmchoe 경범죄 minor[light] offense[crime]; misdemeanor.

kyŏngch'al 경찰 the police. *kyŏngch'alsŏ* 경찰서 police station. *kyŏngch'algwan* 경찰관 policeman; police officer. *kyŏngch'algwan p'ach'ulso* 경찰관 파출소 police box[station branch].

kyŏngch'i 경치 scenery; landscape; view.

kyŏngch'ing 경칭 honorific; term of respect.

kyŏngch'uk 경축 congratulation; celebration. *kyŏngch'uk'ada* 경축하다 congratulate; celebrate. *kyŏngch'ugil* 경축일 national holiday; fête day.

kyŏngdae 경대 dressing stand[table]; vanity (*Am.*); toilet table (*Eng.*).

kyŏngdan 경단 rice cake dumpling.

kyŏnggi 경기 game; match; contest; event. *kyŏnggihada* 경기하다 have[play] a game. *kyŏnggijang* 경기장 ground; field; stadium.

kyŏnggi 경기 ① business(condition); market ② the times; things. *pulgyŏnggi* 불경기 depression; recession. *hogyŏnggi* 호경기 boom; prosperity.

kyŏnggigwanch'ong 경기관총 light machine gun.

kyŏnggo 경고 warning; caution. *kyŏnggohada* 경고하다 warn(a person) against (of); give warning (to).

kyŏnggŏn 경건 piety; devotion. *kyŏnggŏnhada* 경건하다 (be) devout; pious.

kyŏnggongŏp 경공업 light industry.

kyŏnggu 경구 epigram; aphorism; witticism.

kyŏnggŭmsok 경금속 light metals.

kyŏnggwa 경과 ① progress (of a case); development (of an event) ② lapse (of time). *kyŏnggwahada* 경과하다 elapse; pass; go by; expire.

kyŏnggwan 경관 policeman; constable (*Eng.*); cop.

kyŏnggye 경계 guard; lookout; watch; precaution. *kyŏnggyehada* 경계하다 guard against; look out [watch] (for).

kyŏnggye 경계 boundary; border; frontier. *kyŏnggyesŏn* 경계선 boundary line; border line.

kyŏnghap 경합 concurrence; conflict; competition. *kyŏnghap'ada* 경합하다 concur; compete (with).

kyŏngho 경호 guard; escort. *kyŏnghohada* 경호하다 guard; convoy; escort. *kyŏnghowon* 경호원 bodyguard.

kyŏnghŏm 경험 experience. *kyŏnghŏmhada* 경험하다 experience; go through; undergo. *kyŏnghŏmi itta* 경험이 있다 have experience (in).

kyŏnghwahak kongŏp 경화학 공업 light chemical industry.

kyŏnghyang 경향 tendency; trend. *…ŭi kyŏnghyangi itta* …의 경향이 있다 tend towards; tend to (do); have a tendency to.

kyŏngi 경이 wonder; miracle. *kyŏngijŏk (in)* 경이적 (인) wonderful; marvelous; sensational.

kyŏngjaeng 경쟁 competition; rivalry; contest. *kyŏngjaenghada* 경쟁하다 compete with; contest; vie; cope.

kyŏngjak 경작 cultivation; tillage; farming. *kyŏngjak'ada* 경작하다 cultivate; till; plow; farm.

kyŏngje 경제 economy; finance. *kyŏngjeŭi* 경제의 economic; financial. *kyŏngjejŏk (ŭro)* 경제적 (으로)

economical(ly). *kyŏngjehak* 경제학 economics; political economy.

kyŏngji 경지 cultivated field[area]; arable land.

kyŏngjil 경질 change; replacement; reshuffle. *kyŏngjirhada* 경질하다 change; reshuffle.

kyŏngjŏk 경적 alarm whistle; police whistle; horn. *kyŏngjŏgŭl ullida* 경적을 울리다 whistle a warning.

kyŏngjŏn 경전 sacred books; scriptures.

kyŏngjong 경종 alarm bell; warning. *kyŏngjongŭl ullida* 경종을 울리다 ring[sound] an alarm bell.

kyŏngju 경주 race; run. *kyŏngjuhada* 경주하다 have[run] a race (with).

kyŏngk'wae 경쾌. *kyŏngk'waehada* 경쾌하다 (be) light; nimble; lighthearted.

kyŏngma 경마 horse race[racing]. *kyŏngmajang* 경마장 horse race track; turf.

kyŏngmae 경매 auction; public sale. *kyŏngmaehada* 경매하다 sell by[at] auction.

kyŏngmang 경망 *kyŏngmanghada[surŏpta]* 경망하다 [스럽다] (be) thoughtless; rash; imprudent; fickle; frivolous; flippant.

kyŏngmun 격문 manifesto; written appeal.

kyŏngmyŏl 경멸 contempt; scorn. *kyŏngmyŏrhada* 경멸하다 despise; disdain; scorn; look down upon; hold (a person) in contempt.

kyŏngnae 경내 compound; precincts; premises.

kyŏngnapko 격납고 hangar; air plane[aviation] shed.

kyŏngni 경리 accounting; management.

kyŏngni 격리 isolation; segregation(*Am.*); quarantine. *kyŏngnihada* 격리하다 isolate; segregate;

quarantine.

kyŏngno 경로 respect for the aged. *kyŏngnohoe* 경로회 respect-for-age meeting.

kyŏngnon 격론 heated argument; high words.

kyŏngnyang 경량 light weight. *kyŏngnyangkŭp* 경량급 lightweight division.

kyŏngnye 경례 salutation; salute; bow. *kyŏngnyehada* 경례하다 salute; bow; make a salute.

kyŏngnyŏ 격려 encouragement; urging. *kyŏngnyŏhada* 격려하다 encourage; spur (a person) on; cheer up.

kyŏngnyŏk 경력 career; record; personal history.

kyŏngnyŏn 경련 convulsions; spasm; fit. *kyŏngnyŏni irŏnada* 경련이 일어나다 fall into convulsions; have a spasm.

kyŏngŏ 경어 honorific (expression, word).

kyŏngp'um 경품 premium; free gift. *kyŏngp'umkwon* 경품권 premium ticket; gift coupon.

kyŏngsa 경사 inclination; slant. *kyŏngsajida* 경사지다 incline; slant; slope.

kyŏngsa 경사 police sergeant.

kyŏngsang 경상 slight wound. *kyŏngsangŭl ipta* 경상을 입다 be slightly injured[wounded].

kyŏngshi 경시. *kyŏngshihada* 경시하다 make light [little] of; despise; neglect.

kyŏngshin 경신 renewal. *kyŏngshinhada* 경신하다 renew; renovate. *kyeyagŭl kyŏngshinhada* 계약을 경신하다 renew a contract.

kyŏngsol 경솔. *kyŏngsorhada* 경솔하다 (be) rash; hasty; careless. *kyŏngsorhage[hi]* 경솔하게[히] rashly; hastily; thoughtlessly.

kyŏngt'an 경탄 wonder; admiration. *kyŏngt'an-*

hada 경탄하다 wonder[marvel] (at); admire.
kyŏngt'anhal manhan 경탄할 만한 wonderful; admirable; marvelous.

kyŏngu 경우 occasion; time; circumstances; case. *kŭrŏn kyŏngu* 그런 경우 in such a case. *ŏttŏn kyŏnguedo* 어떤 경우에도 under any circumstances. *kyŏngue ttarasŏnŭn* 경우에 따라서는 according to [under some] circumstances.

kyŏngŭi 경의 respect; regard; homage. *kyŏngŭirŭl p'yohada* 경의를 표하다 pay one's respects.

kyŏngŭi 경의. *kyŏngŭishil* 경의실 dressing[locker] room.

kyŏngŭmak 경음악 light music.

kyŏngun-gi 경운기 cultivator.

kyŏngwi 경위 police lieutenant.

kyŏngyŏn 경연 contest. *kyŏngyŏnhada* 경연하다 compete (on the stage). *minyo kyŏngyŏn taehoe* 민요 경연 대회 folk song concours.

kyŏngyŏng 경영 management; administration. *kyŏngyŏnghada* 경영하다 manage; run; keep.

kyŏngyu 경유. *kyŏngyuhada* 경유하다 go by way of; pass[go] through. ···*ŭl kyŏngyuhayŏ* ···을 경유하여 via; by way of; through.

kyŏnhae 견해 opinion; one's view.

kyŏnhak 견학 inspection; study; observation. *kyŏnhak'ada* 견학하다 inspect; visit (a place) for study.

kyŏnjang 견장 shoulder strap; epaulet (te).

kyŏnje 견제 restraint; check. *kyŏnjehada* 견제하다 check; restrain; divert; curb.

kyŏnji 견지 point-of-view; standpoint; viewpoint; angle. →**ipchang** 입장.

kyŏnjingmul 견직물 silk fabrics; silk goods.

kyŏnjŏk 견적 estimate; estimation; assessment. *kyŏnjŏk'ada* 견적하다 estimate (at).

kyŏnjuda 견주다 compare (A) with (B); measure (one thing) against (another).

kyŏnmun 견문 information; knowledge. *kyŏnmuni nŏlta[chopta]* 견문이 넓다[좁다] be well informed [poorly informed].

kyŏnnun 곁눈 side glance. *kyŏnnunjirhada* 곁눈질하다 look askance[sideways] (at).

kyŏnsŭp 견습 apprenticeship; probation; apprentice. *kyŏnsŭpsaeng* 견습생 apprentice; trainee.

kyŏnuda 겨누다 ① (take) aim at; level (a gun) at ② compare (A with B); measure.

kyooe 교외 suburbs; outskirts. *kyooe saenghwal* 교외 생활 suburban life. *kyooesŏn* 교외선 suburban railway.

kyŏp 겹 fold *tu kyŏp* 두 겹 two fold. *yŏrŏ kyŏp* 여러 겹 many folds.

kyŏpch'ida 겹치다 pile[heap] up; put one upon another; overlap.

kyŏpkyŏbi 겹겹이 in many folds; fold and fold.

kyoran 교란 disturbance; derangement. *kyoranhada* 교란하다 disturb; derange; stir up.

kyŏre 겨레 brethren; one's countrymen; compatriots.

kyŏrhaek 결핵 tuberculosis; consumption. *kyŏrhaek hwanja* 결핵 환자 tuberculosis[T.B.] patient.

kyŏrham 결함 defect; fault; shortcoming; deficiency. *yukch'ejŏk[chŏngshinjŏk] kyŏrham* 육체적[정신적] 결함 physical[mental] defect[deficiency].

kyŏrhap 결합 combination; union. *kyŏrhap'ada* 결합하다 unite[combine] (with); joint together.

kyŏrhon 결혼 marriage; matrimony; wedding. *kyŏrhonhada* 결혼하다 marry; be[get] married (to). *kyŏrhonshik* 결혼식 wedding[marriage] ceremony. *kyŏrhon p'iroyŏn* 결혼 피로연 wedding reception.

kyŏruda 겨루다 compete with; contend; pit (one's skill against).

kyŏrŭi 결의 resolution; decision; vote.

kyŏrŭl 겨를 leisure; leisure time; free time; time to spare. *kyŏrŭri ŏpta* 겨를이 없다 have no leisure[time to spare].

kyŏrwon 결원 vacancy; vacant post[position].

kyŏryŏn 결연 forming a relationship. *kyŏryŏnhada* 결연하다 form a connection(with). *chamae kyŏryŏn* 자매 결연 establishment of sisterhood ties.

kyoryu 교류 interchange. *kyoryuhada* 교류하다 interchange. *Hanmi munhwa kyoryu* 한미 문화 교류 cultural exchange between Korea and America.

kyosa 교사 teacher; instructor.

kyosa 교사 school house; school building.

kyoshil 교실 classroom. *hwahak kyoshil* 화학 교실 chemistry room.

kyosŏp 교섭 negotiation(s). *kyosŏp'ada* 교섭하다 negotiate; approach (a person on a matter).

kyŏssang 곁상 side table.

kyosu 교수 ① teaching; instruction; tuition ② professor. *pugyosu* 부교수 associate professor. *chogyosu* 조교수 assistant professor.

kyŏt 곁 side. *kyŏt'e* 곁에 by (the side of). *paro kyŏt'e* 바로 곁에 hard[near, close] by.

kyot'ae 교태 coquetry; coquettish behavior[attitude]. *kyot'aerŭl purida* 교태를 부리다 play the coquette.

kyot'ong 교통 traffic; communication.

kyŏtpang 곁방 ① side chamber ② rented room. *kyŏtpangsari* 곁방살이 living in a rented room.

kyŏu 겨우 barely; narrowly; with difficulty; only.

kyŏul 겨울 winter. *kyŏurŭi*〔*kat'ŭn*〕 겨울의〔같은〕 wintry. *kyŏul panghak* 겨울 방학 winter vacation.

kyŏunae 겨우내 throughout the winter; all winter through. 〔instructor.

kyowon 교원 teacher; schoolteacher; schoolmaster;

kyoyang 교양 culture; education; refinement. *kyoyangi innŭn* 교양이 있는 educated; cultured; refined. *kyoyangi omnŭn* 교양이 없는 uneducated; uncultured.

kyoyuk 교육 education; schooling; instruction; training. *kyoyuk'ada* 교육하다 educate; instruct; train. *kajŏng kyoyuk* 가정 교육 home training 〔breeding〕.

kyuch'ik 규칙 rule; regulations. *kyuch'ikchŏk*〔*ŭro*〕 규칙적〔으로〕 regular〔ly〕; systematical〔ly〕.

kyul 귤 orange. *kyulkkŏpchil* 귤껍질 orange peel.

kyumo 규모 scale; scope; structure. *taegyumoro* 대규모로 on a large scale.

kyun 균 bacillus; germ; bacterium.

kyut'an 규탄 censure; denunciation. *kyut'anhada* 규탄하다 censure; denounce.

⟡ **K'** ⟡

k'aeda 캐다 dig up〔out〕; unearth.

k'al 칼 knife; sword; saber.

k'alguksu 칼국수 knife-cut noodles.

k'allal 칼날 blade of a knife[sword].

k'amk'amhada 캄캄하다 (be) dark; pitch-black.

k'i 키 stature; height. *k'iga k'ŭda*[*chakta*] 키가 크다[작다] be tall[short].

k'i 키 winnow; winnowing fan. *k'ijirhada* 키질 하다 winnow.

k'ingk'inggŏrida 킹킹거리다 whine; whimper.

k'iuda 키우다 bring up; rear; raise; breed.

k'o 코 nose. *tŭlch'angk'o* 들창코 turned-up nose. *maeburik'o* 매부리코 Roman[aquiline] nose.

k'ogolda 코골다 snore.

k'ŏjida 커지다 grow big[large]; grow up; expand.

k'okkiri 코끼리 elephant.

k'ŏlk'ŏrhada 컬컬하다 (be) thirsty; dry.

k'ollokkŏrida 콜록거리다 keep coughing[hacking].

k'ong 콩 beans; peas; soybean. *k'ongkkaenmuk* 콩 깻묵 bean cake.

k'ongnamul 콩나물 bean sprouts.

k'onnorae 콧노래 humming; hum. *k'onnoraehada* 콧노래하다 hum.

k'op'i 코피 nosebleed. *k'op'iga hŭrŭda* 코피가 흐르 다 bleed at the nose.

k'otkumŏng 콧구멍 nostrils.

k'ossuyŏm 콧수염 moustache.

k'ousŭm 코웃음 sneer. *k'ousŭmch'ida* 코웃음치다 sneer.

k'ŭda 크다 (be) big; large; great. *nŏmu k'ŭda* 너무 크다 be too large.

k'ŭgi 크기 size; dimensions. *kat'ŭn k'ŭgiŭi* 같은 크기의 of the same size.

k'ŭn-gil 큰길 main street[road]; highway; thoroughfare; avenue (*Am.*).

k'ŭnil 큰일 important affair; serious matter. *k'ŭnil-nada* 큰일 나다 serious thing happens.

k'ŭnsori 큰소리 ① loud voice; yell ② big talk; bragging.

k'waehwal 쾌활. *k'waehwarhan* 쾌활한 cheerful; gay; lively. *k'waehwarhage* 쾌활하게 cheerfully; gaily.

k'waerak 쾌락 pleasure; enjoyment. *insaengŭi k'waerak* 인생의 쾌락 pleasures[joys] of life.

k'wik'wihada 퀴퀴하다 (be) fetid; stinking; foul-smelling.

k'yŏda 켜다 light; kindle; turn[switch] on.

k'yŏlle 켤레 pair. *kudu han k'yŏlle* 구두 한 켤레 a pair of shoes.

⊷ M ⊷

mabi 마비 paralysis; palsy; numbness. *mabidoeda* 마비되다 be paralyzed. *shimjang mabi* 심장 마비 heart failure.

mabu 마부 groom; stableman; coachman.

mach'a 마차 carriage; coach; cab. *chimmach'a* 짐마차 horse and van.

mach'al 마찰 friction; rubbing; trouble. *mach'arhada* 마찰하다 rub(against); chafe (the skin).

mach'i 마치 as if[though]; just like.

mach'ida 마치다 finish; complete. *hagŏbŭl mach'ida* 학업을 마치다 finish a school course.

mach'im 마침 luckily; fortunately; just in time.

mach'imnae 마침내 finally; at last; eventually.

mach'imp'yo 마침표 period; full stop.

madang 마당 garden; yard; court. *ammadang* 앞 마당 front yard. *anmadang* 안마당 courtyard.

madi 마디 joint; knot; knob.

mae 매 whip; rod; cane.

maebu 매부 husband of one's sister; one's brother-in-law.

maech'un 매춘 prostitution; harlotry. *maech'unbu* 매춘부 prostitute; street girl; courtesan.

maeda 매다 tie (up); bind; fasten.

maedŭp 매듭 knot; tie; joint; macrame.

maegi p'ullida 맥이 풀리다 fall into low spirits; be dispirited.

maegŏpshi 맥없이 weakly; tiredly; helplessly.

maehok 매혹 fascination. *maehokchŏgin* 매혹적인 charming; fascinating. *maehoktoeda* 매혹되다 be charmed〔fascinated〕.

maeil 매일 everyday; each day; daily. *maeirŭi* 매일의 everyday; daily. *maeil maeil* 매일 매일 day after day; day by day.

maejang 매장. *maejanghada* 매장하다 bury in the ground.

maejŏm 매점 stand; stall; booth.

maeju 매주 every week; each week; weekly.

maek 맥 pulse; pulsation. *maegi ttwida* 맥이 뛰다 pulsate; pulse beats.

maek'aehada 매캐하다 ① (be) smoky ② (be) musty; mouldy.

maekchu 맥주 beer; ale. *pyŏngmaekchu* 병맥주 bottled beer. *saengmaekchu* 생맥주 draft beer.

maekko moja 맥고 모자 straw hat.

maekkŭrŏpta 매끄럽다 (be) smooth; slimly; slippery.

maekpak 맥박 pulse; pulsation.

maemae 매매 trade; dealing; bargain. *maemae-hada* 매매하다 deal[trade] (in).

maemanjida 매만지다 smooth down; trim; dress.

maenbal 맨발 bare feet; barefoot. *maenballo* 맨발로 with bare[naked] feet.

maengmok 맹목 blindness. *maengmokchŏk(ŭro)* 맹목적(으로) blind(ly); reckless(ly).

maengse 맹세 oath; pledge; vow. *maengsehada* 맹세하다 swear; vow; take an oath.

maengsu 맹수 fierce animal; beast of prey.

maenyŏn 매년 every[each] year; annually; yearly.

maepshi 맵시 figure; shapeliness; smartness. *maepshi innŭn* 맵시 있는 smart; shapely; well-formed. *onmaepshi* 옷맵시 style of dressing.

maep'yoso 매표소 ① ticket[booking] office ② box office.

maeryŏk 매력 charm; fascination. *maeryŏk innŭn* 매력 있는 charming; attractive.

maesanggo, maech'uraek 매상고, 매출액 amount sold; sales; proceeds (of sale).

maesŏpta 매섭다 (be) fierce; severe; strict; stern.

maesuhada 매수하다 bribe[buy over] (a person).

maetta 맺다 ① tie (up); (make a) knot ② bear fruit ③ contract; enter relations (with).

maeu 매우 very (much); greatly; awfully.

maeŭm 매음 prostitution. →**maech'un** 매춘.

maeunt'ang 매운탕 pepper-pot soup; hot chowder.

maewol 매월 every month; each month; monthly.

magae 마개 stopper; cork; plug; stopcock. *magae-rŭl ppopta* 마개를 뽑다 uncork.

magu 마구 recklessly; at random.

magu 마구 harness; horse-equipment[furniture].

magyŏnhada 막연하다 (be) vague; obscure; ambiguous.

mahŭn 마흔 forty. →**saship** 사십.

majak 마작 mahjong(g). *majak'ada* 마작하다 play mahjong(g).

majimak 마지막 the last; the end.

maju 마주 face to face; visavis. *maju poda* 마주 보다 look at each other.

majuch'ida 마주치다 collide with; clash with; run against.

majung 마중 meeting; reception. *majung nagada* 마중 나가다 go to meet (a person).

majŭnp'yŏn 맞은편 opposite side.

mak 막 ① curtain; hanging screen ② shed; hut; shack.

mak 막 just; just now; (be) about to.

mak 막 the last. *mangnae* 막내 the lastborn. *makch'a* 막차 the last train.

mak'ida 막히다 be stopped by; be clogged [chocked].

makkŏlli 막걸리 unrefined [raw] rice liquor [wine].

makp'an 막판 the last round; the final scene; the last moment.

makpŏrikkun 막벌이꾼 day laborer; odd-jobber.

maksa 막사 camp; barracks.

makta 막다 ① stop (up); plug ② intercept; block ③ defend; keep off [away].

makta 맑다 (be) clear; clean; pure (*water*); (be) resonant (*sound*); (be) fine; clear (*weather*).

maktaegi 막대기 stick; rod; bar; club.

mal 말 horse. *marŭl t'ada* 말을 타다 ride [get on] a horse. *chongma* 종마 stallion.

mal 말 word; speech; language; term.

malch'amgyŏn 말참견 interfering; meddling. *malch'amgyŏnhada* 말참견하다 interfere; meddle in.

maldaekku 말대꾸 retort; severe reply. *maldaekkuhada* 말대꾸하다 retort.

maldat'um 말다툼 dispute; quarrel; argument. *maldat'umhada* 말다툼하다 dispute; quarrel; have an argument with.

maldŏdŭmta 말더듬다 →**tŏdŭmgŏrida** 더듬거리다.

malgup 말굽 horse's hoof; horseshoe.

malgwallyangi 말괄량이 romp; tomboy; flapper.

malkkŭmhada 말끔하다 (be) clean; neat; tidy.

mallida 말리다 dissuade (a person from doing); stop. *ssaumŭl mallida* 싸움을 말리다 stop a quarrel.

mallida 말리다 make dry; dry. *pure mallida* 불에 말리다 dry (a thing) over the fire.

mallu 만루 full base.

mallyŏn 말년 ① one's last days; the last period. ② one's declining years.

malpŏrŭt 말버릇 manner of speaking; way of talking.

malssŏng 말썽 trouble; complaint; dispute. *malssŏngŭl purida* 말썽을 부리다 complain; cause trouble.

malssuk'ada 말쑥하다 (be) clean; neat; smart.

malttuk 말뚝 pile; stake; post.

mamuri 마무리 finish; finishing (touches). *mamurihada* 마무리하다 finish (up); complete.

man 만 ten thousand; myriad. *suman* 수만 tens of thousands. *sushimman* 수십만 hundreds of thousands.

mananim 마나님 ① madam ② your lady.

manch'an 만찬 supper; dinner. *manch'anhoe* 만찬
회 dinner party.

manchŏm 만점 full marks.

mandam 만담 comic chat[dialogue]. *mandamga*
만담가 comedian.

mandŭlda 만들다 make; manufacture; create;
form.

mang 망 ① net; casting net ② network. *t'ongshin-*
[*pangsong*]*mang* 통신[방송]망 communication
[radio] network.

mangboda 망보다 keep watch; look out for; stand
guard.

mangch'i 망치 hammer.

mangch'ida 망치다 spoil; ruin; destroy; make a
mess (of).

manggŭrŏjida 망그러지다 break; be broken; be
destroyed; ruined.

manghada 망하다 go to ruin; be ruined; perish.

man-gi 만기 expiration (of a term); maturity (of a
bill).

mangmyŏng 망명 flight. *mangmyŏnghada* 망명하
다 seek[take] refuge; exile oneself.

mangnyŏnhoe 망년회 year-end party.

mangshin 망신 shame; disgrace. *mangshinhada*
망신하다 disgrace oneself; be put to shame.

mangsŏrida 망설이다 hesitate; scruple; be at a
loss.

mangwon-gyŏng 망원경 telescope.

manhoe 만회 recovery; retrieval. *manhoehada* 만
회하다 recover; restore; revive.

manhwa 만화 caricature; cartoon.

mani 많이 much; lots; plenty; in abundance.

manil 만일 if; in case; supposing (that).

manjok 만족 satisfaction; contentment. *manjok'ada* 만족하다 be satisfied with.

mannada 만나다 see; meet; interview.

mannal 만날 always; all the time; everyday.

mannyŏnp'il 만년필 fountain pen.

manse 만세 ① cheers; hurrah ② long live.

mant'a 많다 (be) many; much; lots of; plenty of.

manŭl 마늘 garlic.

manwon 만원 full[packed] house; capacity audience. *manwon pŏsŭ* 만원 버스 jam-packed bus.

marhada 말하다 talk (about); speak; converse; state; tell; say; mention.

mari 마리 number of animals; head.

maril 말일 the last day; the end. *shiwol marire* 10월 말일에 at the end of October.

marŭda 마르다 (be) dry (up); get dry; run dry.

maryŏnhada 마련하다 prepare; arrange; raise; make shift.

maryŏpta 마렵다 feel an urge to urinate.

massŏda 맞서다 ① stand opposite each other ② stand against.

massŏn poda 맞선 보다 meet[see] each other with a view to marriage.

masul 마술 magic; black art. *masulsa* 마술사 magician; sorcerer.

mat 맛 taste; flavor; savor. *matchoŭn* 맛좋은 tasty; savory; delicious.

match'uda 맞추다 fix[fit] into; assemble; put together.

matkida 맡기다 place in custody; deposit with; put in charge of.

matpuditch'ida 맞부딪치다 hit against; run into [against].

matta 맞다 ① be right[correct] ② become; match ③ fit; suit ④ agree (with).

matta 맡다 ① be entrusted with ② take[be in] charge of.

mattanghi 마땅히 naturally; properly; justly.

matton 맞돈 cash (payment); hard cash; ready money.

maŭl 마을 village; hamlet. *maŭl saram* 마을 사람 villagers.

maŭm 마음 mind; spirit; heart; will. *maŭmsogŭro* 마음속으로 inwardly; in one's heart.

maŭmdaero 마음대로 as one pleases[likes, wishes].

maŭmssi 마음써 turn of mind; temper; disposition. *maŭmssiga choťa[nappŭda]* 마음써가 좋다[나쁘다] be good-natured[ill-natured].

mayak 마약 narcotic; dope. *mayak chungdokcha* 마약 중독자 drug addict.

meari 메아리 echo. *mearich'ida* 메아리치다 echo; be echoed; resound.

mech'uragi, mech'uri 메추라기, 메추리 quail.

meda 메다 shoulder; carry on one's shoulder [back].

melppang 멜빵 shoulder strap[belt]; braces; suspenders.

mesŭkkŏpta 메스껍다 feel nausea; feel sick.

mettugi 메뚜기 grasshopper; locust.

meuda 메우다 fill up[in]; stop (up); reclaim.

mi 미 beauty; grace. *yukch'emi* 육체미 physical beauty. *chayŏnmi* 자연미 natural beauty.

mia 미아 lost[stray, missing] child.

mianhada 미안하다 (be) sorry; regrettable; repentant.

mich'ida 미치다 go mad[crazy]; become insane; lose one's senses.

mich'igwangi 미치광이 madman; lunatic; crazy [insane] man.

midaji 미닫이 sliding door.

midŏpta 미덥다 (be) trustworthy; reliable; dependable; promising; hopeful.

migae 미개 *migaehan* 미개한 uncivilized; savage; barbarous. *migaein* 미개인 barbarian.

migok 미곡 rice. *migoksang* 미곡상 rice dealer.

Miguk 미국 (the United States of) America; U.S. A. *Migugŭi* 미국의 American; U.S.

Migun 미군 U.S. Armed Forces; American Forces. *chuhan Migun* 주한 미군 American Forces stationed in Korea.

migyŏl 미결. *migyŏrŭi* 미결의 unsettled; undecided; pending.

mihon 미혼. *mihonŭi* 미혼의 unmarried; single. *mihonmo* 미혼모 unwed[unmarried] mother.

mihwa 미화 American money[currency]; American dollar.

miin 미인 beautiful woman[girl]; beauty.

mijangwon 미장원 beauty salon[parlor, shop].

Mije 미제. *Mijeŭi* 미제의. American[U.S.] made; made in U.S.A.

mijigŭnhada 미지근하다 (be) tepid; lukewarm.

mikki 미끼 ① bait ② decoy; lure; allurement.

mikkŭrŏjida 미끄러지다 slide; glide; slip; fail (in) an examination.

mikkŭrŏpta 미끄럽다 (be) smooth; slippery.

mil 밀 wheat. *milkaru* 밀가루 wheat flour.

milchip 밀짚 (wheat) straw. *milchip moja* 밀짚 모자 straw hat. →**maekko moja** 맥고 모자.

milchŏp 밀접. *milchŏp'an* 밀접한 close; intimate.

milda 밀다 push; shove; thrust; jostle.

milgam 밀감 mandarin orange.

millim 밀림 dense forest; jungle.

milsu 밀수 smuggling. *milsuhada* 밀수하다 smuggle. *milsup'um* 밀수품 smuggled goods.

mimangin 미망인 widow. *chŏnjaeng mimangin* 전 쟁 미망인 war widow.

mimo 미모 beautiful[handsome] face; good looks. *mimoŭi* 미모의 beautiful; good-looking; handsome.

mimyohada 미묘하다 (be) delicate; subtle; nice.

minamja 미남자 handsome man; good-looking fellow.

minbangwi 민방위 civil defense. *minbangwidae* 민 방위대 Civil Defense Corps unit.

minch'ŏp 민첩 agility, quickness. *minch'ŏp'ada* 민 첩하다 (be) quick; agile; nimble; prompt.

min-gan 민간. *min-ganŭi* 민간의 civil; civilian; nongovernment.

minjok 민족 race; nation; people. *minjok undong* 민족 운동 national movement.

minju 민주 democracy. *minjujŏgin* 민주적인 democratic. *minjujuŭi* 민주주의 democracy.

minjung 민중 people; masses.

minkwŏn 민권 people's rights; civil rights.

minsok 민속 folklore; folkways. *minsok pangmulgwan* 민속 박물관 folklore museum.

minwŏn 민원 civil appeal. *minwŏn sangdamso* 민

원 상담소 civil affairs office.

minyo 민요 folk song; ballad.

minyŏ 미녀 beautiful woman; beauty; belle.

mion 미온. *mionjŏgin* 미온적인 lukewarm; tepid; half-hearted.

mipta 밉다 (be) hateful; abominable; detestable.

mirae 미래 future; time to come. *miraeŭi* 미래의 future; coming; to come. *miraee* 미래에 in the future. *miraep'a* 미래파 futurism.

miri 미리 beforehand; in advance; previously; in anticipation; prior to; earlier than.

miruda 미루다 ① put off; postpone; delay; defer ② shift; shuffle off.

misaengmul 미생물 microorganism; microbe; germ. *misaengmurhak* 미생물학 microbiology.

misail 미사일 missile. *misail kiji* 미사일 기지 missile base[station].

mishin 미신 superstition; superstitious belief.

miso 미소 smile. *misohada* 미소하다 smile; beam.

Miso 미소. *Misoŭi* 미소의 American-Soviet; Russo-American. *Miso kwan-gye* 미소 관계 American-Soviet relations.

misŏngnyŏn 미성년 minority; under age. *misŏngnyŏnja* 미성년자 minor.

misul 미술 art; fine arts. *misurŭi* 미술의 artistic. *misulga* 미술가 artist.

mit 밑 lower part; bottom; base; foot. *mit'ŭi* 밑의 lower; subordinate; inferior. *mit'ŭro* 밑으로 down(ward). *mit'ŭrobut'ŏ* 밑으로부터 from under[below].

mit 및 and; also; as well as; in addition.

mitch'ŏn 밑천 capital; funds; principal; costprice.

mitta 믿다 believe; be convinced; trust; credit.
midŭl su innŭn 믿을 수 있는 believable.

miwansŏng 미완성. *miwansŏngŭi* 미완성의 incomplete; unfinished.

miwohada 미워하다 hate; detest; loathe.

miyŏk 미역 (outdoor) bathing; swimming; swim.
miyŏk kamta 미역 감다 bathe; have a swim; swim.

miyok 미역 brown-seaweed.

miyong 미용. *miyongsa* 미용사 beautician(*Am.*).
miyong ch'ejo 미용 체조 beauty exercise.

mo 모 certain person; Mr. So-and-so; certain; some.
Kim mossi 김 모씨 certain Kim.

mobang 모방 imitation; mimicry. *mobanghada* 모방하다 imitate; copy (from, after).

mobŏm 모범 model; example; pattern. *mobŏmjŏk* 모범적 exemplary; model; typical.

moch'in 모친 →*ŏmŏni* 어머니.

modok 모독 profanation. *modok'ada* 모독하다 profane; defile.

mŏdŏpta 멋없다 (be) not smart[stylish]; insipid.

modu 모두 ① all; everything; everybody; everyone ② in all; all told ③ altogether.

modŭn 모든 all; every; each and every.

mogi 모기 mosquito. *mogijang* 모기장 mosquito net. *mogihyang* 모기향 mosquito stick[coil].

mŏgi 먹이 feed; food; fodder.

mŏgida 먹이다 let someone eat; feed (cattle on grass).

moguk 모국 one's mother country; one's native country. *mogugŏ* 모국어 one's mother tongue.

mogŭm 모금 fund raising; collection of subscriptions. *mogŭmhada* 모금하다 raise a fund.

mogyo 모교 one's alma mater; one's old school.

mogyok 목욕 bathing; bath. *mogyok'ada* 목욕하다 bathe (oneself) in; take[have] a bath.

mohŏm 모험 adventure; risk. *mohŏmhada* 모험하다 adventure; take a risk[chance]. *mohŏmjŏgin* 모험적인 adventurous; risky.

mohyŏng 모형 model; pattern; mold. *mohyŏng chut'aek* 모형 주택 model house.

moida 모이다 gather; come[get] together; flock; crowd.

moja 모자 hat, cap. *mojarŭl ssŭda[pŏtta]* 모자를 쓰다[벗다] put on[take off] a[one's] hat.

mojarada 모자라다 be not enough; be insufficient; be short of.

mojip 모집 collection; raising. *mojip'ada* 모집하다 collect; raise.

mojori 모조리 all; wholly; entirely; altogether; without (an) exception.

mok 목 neck.

mok 몫 share; portion; lot; allotment. *nae mok* 내 몫 my share.

mŏk 먹 inkstick; Chinese ink; Indian ink.

mokch'a 목차 (table of) contents.

mokchae 목재 wood; timber; lumber(*Am.*).

mokchang 목장 pasture; stockfarm; meadow; ranch(*Am.*).

mokcho 목조 *mokchoŭi* 목조의 wooden; made of wood. *mokcho kaok* 목조 가옥 wooden house.

mokch'o 목초 grass; pasturage. *mokch'oji* 목초지 meadow; grass land.

mokchŏk 목적 purpose; aim; object; end. *mokchŏgŭl talssŏnghada* 목적을 달성하다 attain one's object; fulfil one's purpose.

mokch'uk 목축 stock farming; cattle raising. *mokch'ugŏp* 목축업 stock raising.

mokkong 목공 woodworker; carpenter. *mokkongso* 목공소 woodworking shop[plant]; sawmill.

mokkŏri 목걸이 necklace; neckwear; neckpiece. *chinju mokkŏri* 진주 목걸이 pearl necklace.

mokkumŏng 목구멍 throat; gullet; windpipe.

mŏkkurŭm 먹구름 black cloud; dark clouds.

mokkyŏk 목격 observation; witnessing. *mokkyŏk'ada* 목격하다 witness; observe.

mokp'yo 목표 mark; target; object; aim. *mokp'yohada* 목표하다 aim at; set the goal at.

moksa 목사 pastor; minister; parson; clergyman; vicar; rector; chaplain.

moksori 목소리 voice; tone (of voice).

moksu 목수 carpenter. →mokkong 목공.

moksum 목숨 life. *moksumŭl kŏlgo* 목숨을 걸고 at the risk of one's life.

mŏkta 먹다 eat; take; have. *pabŭl mŏkta* 밥을 먹다 eat rice; take a meal.

moktŏlmi 목덜미 nape of the neck.

moktong 목동 shepherd boy; cowboy; cowherd; herdboy; cowpuncher (*Am.*).

moktori 목도리 muffler; neckerchief; comforter; shawl; scarf; boa.

molda 몰다 drive; urge; chase; run after. *ch'arŭl molda* 차를 몰다 drive a car.

mollae 몰래 secretly; stealthily; in secret.

mollak 몰락 ruin; fall. *mollak'ada* 몰락하다 fall; go to ruin; be ruined.

mollyŏdanida 몰려다니다 go[move] about in crowds

[groups].

mŏlmi 멀미 nausea; sickness. *paenmŏlmi* 뱃멀미 seasickness.

molsangshik 몰상식. *molsangshik'an* 몰상식한 wanting in common sense; senseless. *molsangshik'ada* 몰상식하다 be lacking in common sense; have no common sense.

molsu 몰수 confiscation; seizure. *molsuhada* 몰수하다 confiscate; seize.

mom 몸 body; physique; build; frame. *momi k'ŭn* 몸이 큰 big-bodied.

momburim 몸부림. *momburimch'ida* 몸부림치다 struggle; writhe; wriggle; flounder.

momchip 몸집 body; size; frame; build.

momchit 몸짓 gesture; motion. *momchit'ada* 몸짓 하다 make gestures.

mŏmch'uda 멈추다 stop; cease; put a stop; halt.

momdanjanghada 몸단장하다 dress oneself.

momttungi 몸뚱이 body; frame. *momttungiga chakta* 몸뚱이가 작다 be small of frame.

mŏmurŭda 머무르다 stay; stop; put up (at an inn). *hot'ere mŏmurŭda* 호텔에 머무르다 stop[put up] at a hotel.

momyŏn 모면 evasion; escape. *momyŏnhada* 모면 하다 evade; shirk; escape.

mŏndong 먼동 dawning sky. *mŏndongi t'ŭda* 먼 동이 트다 Day breaks.

mongdungi 몽둥이 stick; club; cudgel.

mongnok 목록 catalog(ue); list.

mongttang 몽땅 all; completely; entirely; wholly; in full; perfectly.

mŏnjŏ 먼저 first; first of all; above all.

monnani 못난이 stupid person; no-good; simpleton.

mop'i 모피 fur; skin.

mopshi 몹시 very (much); hard; greatly; awfully; extremely.

morae 모래 sand; grit. *moraettang* 모래땅 sandy soil. *moraet'op* 모래톱 sand-bank.

moranaeda 몰아내다 expel; drive out; eject; oust.

moranŏt'a 몰아넣다 ① drive in[into]; push into; chase into. ② corner up; drive into a corner.

more 모레 the day after tomorrow.

mŏri 머리 ① head ② brain ③ hair.

mŏrik'arak 머리카락 hair. *hŭin mŏrik'arak* 흰 머리카락 white hair.

mŏritkirŭm 머릿기름 hair oil; pomade.

morŭda 모르다 do not know; be ignorant.

moryak 모략 plot; trick; stratagem. *moryak sŏnjŏn* 모략 선전 strategical propaganda.

mosaek'ada 모색하다 grope (for); feel one's way.

mossalge kulda 못살게 굴다 tease; treat badly.

mosŭm 머슴 farm hand; farmer's man.

mosun 모순 contradiction; conflict; inconsistency. *mosundoeda* 모순되다 be inconsistent (with).

mosŭp 모습 appearance; one's features; one's image; face; look. *yenmosŭp* 옛모습 one's former self.

mot 못 nail; peg. *mosŭl ch'ida[ppaeda]* 못을 치다[빼다] drive in[pull out] a nail.

mŏt 멋 dandyism; foppery. *mŏdinnŭn* 멋있는 smart-looking; stylish; chic.

mot'ada 못하다 (be) inferior; be worse than; fall behind.

mŏtchangi 멋장이 dandy; fop; cockscomb; dude.

motpon ch'ehada 못본 체하다 pretend not to see.

mŏttaero 멋대로 in one's own way; wilfully; self-ishly.

mot'ungi 모퉁이 corner; turn; turning. *kil mot'ungi* 길모퉁이 street corner.

mŏttŭrŏjida 멋들어지다 (be) nice; smart; stylish. *mŏttŭrŏjige* 멋들어지게 smartly; nicely.

moŭda 모으다 ① gather; get (things, people) together; collect ② concentrate; focus.

moyang 모양 shape; form; appearance; figure. *k'omoyang* 코모양 shape of one's nose.

moyok 모욕 insult; contempt. *moyok'ada* 모욕하다 insult.

muanhada 무안하다 be ashamed; feel shame; lose face.

mubŏp 무법. *mubŏbŭi* 무법의 unlawful; unjust; unreasonable. *mubŏpcha* 무법자 ruffian; outlaw.

much'abyŏl 무차별 indiscrimination. *much'abyŏrŭi* 무차별의 indiscriminate.

mudae 무대 stage; sphere; field. *mudae changch'i* 무대 장치 stage setting; set(s).

mudang 무당 witch; sorceress; exorcist.

mudida 무디다 ① (be) blunt; dull ② curt ③ slow; thick-headed.

mudo 무도 dance; dancing. *mudogok* 무도곡 dance music. *mudohoe* 무도회 dancing party.

mudŏgi 무더기 heap; pile; mound.

mudŏm 무덤 grave; tomb.

mudŏnhada 무던하다 (be) generous; broad-minded.

mudŏpta 무덥다 (be) sultry; sweltering; muggy.

muge 무게 weight; heaviness; burden. *mugerŭl talda* 무게를 달다 weigh (a thing).

mugi 무기 arms; weapon; ordnance.

mugimyŏng 무기명. *mugimyŏngŭi* 무기명의 unregistered; unsigned; uninscribed. *mugimyŏng t'up'yo* 무기명 투표 secret ballot[vote].

mugŏpta 무겁다 (be) heavy; weighty. *mugŏun chim* 무거운 짐 heavy[weighty] burden.

mugunghwa 무궁화 rose of Sharon (*national flower of Korea*).

mugwan 무관 military[naval, air force] officer.

mugwan 무관. *mugwanhan* 무관한 unrelated; irrelevant (to).

mugwanshim 무관심 indifference; unconcern. *mugwanshimhada* 무관심하다 (be) indifferent (to); unconcerned (with, at, about). 「fig tree.

muhwagwa 무화과 fig. *muhwagwanamu* 무화과나무

muhan 무한 infinity. *muhanhan* 무한한 limitless; endless; infinite.

muhŭi 무희 dancing girl; dancer.

muhyo 무효 invalidity; ineffectiveness. *muhyoŭi* 무효의 invalid; unavailable.

muindo 무인도 desert island; uninhabited island.

mujagyŏk 무자격 disqualification; incapacity. *mujagyŏgŭi* 무자격의 disqualified.

mujang 무장 arms; armament. *mujanghada* 무장하다 arm; be under arms; equip (an army). *mujanghan* 무장한 armed.

muji 무지 ignorance; illiteracy. *mujihada* 무지하다 (be) ignorant; illiterate.

mujilsŏ 무질서 disorder. *mujilsŏhada* 무질서하다 (be) disordered; chaotic; lawless.

mujoe 무죄 innocence; being not guilty. *mujoeŭi* 무죄의 innocent; guiltless.

mujokŏn 무조건. *mujokŏnŭi* 무조건의 unconditional; unqualified. *mujokŏnŭro* 무조건으로 unconditionally; without reservation.

mujŏn 무전 *mujŏn yŏhaeng* 무전 여행 penniless journey; travel without money.

mujŏnghada 무정하다 (be) hard; heartless; pitiless; coldhearted.

mukta 묶다 bind; tie; fasten (together).

muksarhada 묵살하다 take no notice (of); ignore.

mul 물 water. *ch'anmul* 찬물 cold water. *tŏunmul* 더운물 hot water.

mulcha 물자 goods; commodities; (raw) materials.

mulch'e 물체 body; object.

mulchil 물질 matter; substance. *mulchiljŏgin* 물질 적인 material; physical.

mulchip 물집 (water) blister. *mulchibi saenggida* 물집이 생기다 get a blister.

mulda 물다 ① bite; snap; sting ② hold[put] in the mouth.

muldŭrida 물들이다 dye; color; tint; paint.

mulgunamusŏda 물구나무서다 stand on one's (head and) hands; stand on end.

mulka 물가 prices (of commodities). *mulkago* 물 가고 high prices of commodities.

mulki 물기 moisture. *mulkiga itta* 물기가 있다 be moist; damp; wet; succulent.

mulkogi 물고기 fish. →*saengsŏn* 생선.

mulkyŏl 물결 wave; billow; surf; ripple.

mullan 문란 disorder; confusion; corruption. *mullanhada* 문란하다 be in disorder.

mullebanga 물레방아 water mill.

mulli 문리 liberal arts and science(s). *mullikwa*

taehak 문리과 대학 College of Liberal Arts and Science (s).

mullich'ida 물리치다 ① decline; refuse; reject ② drive back[away]; beat off[back] ③ keep away.

mullida 물리다 get bitten. *mogie mullida* 모기에 물리다 be bitten by a mosquito.

mullihak 물리학 physics; physical science.

mullŏgada 물러가다 move backward; step back; retreat; withdraw.

mullon 물론 of course; to say nothing of; not to speak of; no doubt; needless to say; naturally.

mullyak 물약 liquid medicine.

mullyŏbatta 물려받다 inherit; take over.

mullyŏjuda 물려주다 hand[make] over; transfer; bequeath.

mulpangul 물방울 drop of water; water drop.

mulp'um 물품 articles; things; goods; commodities.

mulsaek'ada 물색하다 look for; search for; hunt for[up].

mulso 물소 buffalo.

mult'ong 물통 water pail[bucket].

mumo 무모. *mumohada* 무모하다 (be) rash; thoughtless; reckless. *mumohage* 무모하게 recklessly; rashly; imprudently.

mumyŏng 무명 cotton. *mumyŏngshil* 무명실 cotton thread. *mumyŏngot* 무명옷 cotton clothes.

mun 문 gate; door; gateway. *chadongmun* 자동문 automatic door. *am[twin]mun* 앞[뒷]문 front [back] door.

munbanggu 문방구 stationery; writing materials. *munbanggujŏm* 문방구점 stationery shop; stationer's.

muncha 문자 letters; character; alphabet.

mungch'i 뭉치 bundle; roll; lump.

mungch'ida 뭉치다 ① lump; mass ② unite; combine.

munggaeda 뭉개다 crumple; mash; squash.

mungnyŏm 묵념 silent[tacit] prayer. *mungnyŏmhada* 묵념하다 pray silently.

mun-gongbu, munhwa kongbobu 문공부, 문화 공보부 Ministry of Culture and Information.

mungttuk'ada 뭉뚝하다 stubby; (be) stumpy; blunt.

mun-gwan 문관 civilian; civil officer.

mun-gyobu 문교부 Ministry of Education.

munhak 문학 literature; letters. *munhagŭi* 문학의 literary. *munhakcha* 문학자 literary man.

munhwa 문화 culture; civilization. *munhwa saenghwal* 문화 생활 cultural life. *munhwa chut'aek* 문화 주택 modern[up-to-date] house.

munjang 문장 sentence; composition; writing.

munje 문제 question; problem; issue. *sahoe munje* 사회 문제 social problem.

munjigi 문지기 gatekeeper; janitor; gateman; doorman; porter; guard.

munjip 문집 collection of works; anthology.

munmyŏng 문명 civilization; culture. *munmyŏnghan* 문명한 civilized; enlightened.

munŏjida 무너지다 crumble; collapse; go[fall] to pieces; give way.

munp'ae 문패 doorplate; name plate.

munpŏp 문법 grammar.

munshin 문신 tattoo. *munshinhada* 문신하다 tattoo.

munsŏ 문서 document; paper. *munsŏro* 문서로 in writing.

munŭi 무늬 pattern; design; figure.

munŭng 무능. *munŭnghan* 무능한 incapable; incompetent; good-for-nothing.

munye 문예 literary arts; art and literature. *munyeran* 문예란 literary column.

muŏn-gŭk 무언극 pantomime; dumb show.

muot 무엇 what; something; anything. *muŏshidŭn* 무엇이든 anything; whatever. *muŏtpodado* 무엇보다도 above all (things); first of all.

muri 무리. *murihan* 무리한 unreasonable; unjust; immoderate.

muroehan 무뢰한 rogue; ruffian; scoundrel; rowdy; hooligan; rascal.

murŏjuda 물어주다 pay (for); compensate.

murori 물오리 wild duck; drake.

murye 무례. *muryehan* 무례한 rude; discourteous; impolite; insolent.

muryo 무료. *muryoŭi* 무료의 free (of charge); gratuitous; cost-free.

muryŏk 무력 military power; force (of arms). *muryŏgŭro* 무력으로 by force (of arms).

muryŏk 무력. *muryŏk'an* 무력한 powerless; helpless; incompetent; impotent.

muryŏp 무렵 time; about; around; towards. *haejil muryŏbe* 해질 무렵에 toward evening.

musa 무사 warrior; soldier; knight.

musa 무사 safety; peace. *musahada* 무사하다 (be) safe; peaceful; quiet. *musahi* 무사히 safely.

musang 무상 *musangŭi* 무상의 gratis; for nothing.

mushimushihada 무시무시하다 (be) dreadful; awful; frightful; horrible.

musŏn 무선 wireless; radio. *musŏn kisa* 무선 기사 wireless[radio] operator.

musŏnghada 무성하다 (be) thick; dense; luxuriant.

musŏpta 무섭다 (be) fearful; terrible; dreadful; horrible.

musosok 무소속. *musosogŭi* 무소속의 independent; neutral. *musosok ŭiwŏn* 무소속 의원 independent member; nonaffiliated members.

musŏwŏhada 무서워하다 (be) afraid (of); fear; be fearful (of); be frightened (at).

musul 무술 military arts.

musŭn 무슨 what; what sort[kind] of. *musŭn illo* 무슨 일로 on what business.

musŭngbu 무승부 draw; drawn game; tie. *musŭngburo kkŭnnada* 무승부로 끝나다 end in a tie [draw].

mut 뭍 land; the shore.

mut 뭇 many; numerous. *mussaram* 뭇사람 people of all sorts.

mutta 묻다 ask; question; inquire.

mutta 묻다 bury; inter.

mut'ŏktaego 무덕대고 blindly; recklessly.

muŭishik 무의식 unconsciousness. *muŭishikchŏk (ŭro)* 무의식적 (으로) unconscious (ly).

muyŏk 무역 trade; commerce. *muyŏk'ada* 무역하다 trade(with); engage in foreign trade.

muyong 무용 dancing; dance. *muyonghada* 무용하다 dance; perform a dance.

myo 묘 grave; tomb. *myochari* 묘자리 grave site.

myobi 묘비 tombstone; gravestone. *myobimyŏng* 묘비명 epitaph; inscription (on tomb).

myŏch'il 며칠 what day of the month; how many days; how long; a few days. *myŏch'il chŏn* 며칠 전 a few days ago.

myogi 묘기 exquisite skill; wonderful performance.

myoji 묘지 graveyard; cemetery. *kongdong myoji* 공동 묘지 public cemetery.

myŏksal 멱살 throat; collar. *myŏksarŭl chapta* 멱살을 잡다 seize (a person) by the collar.

myŏlmang 멸망 fall; ruin; destruction. *myŏlmanghada* 멸망하다 fall; be ruined; be destroyed.

myŏlshi 멸시 contempt; disdain. *myŏlshihada* 멸시하다 despise; disdain.

myomok 묘목 young plant; sapling; seedling.

myŏn 면 cotton.

myŏndam 면담 interview; talk. *myŏndamhada* 면담하다 have an interview (with).

myŏndo 면도 shaving. *myŏndohada* 면도하다 shave oneself; get a shave. *myŏndok'al* 면도칼 razor.

myŏngbok 명복 heavenly bliss.

myŏngch'al 명찰 identification tag; name plate.

myŏngch'ang 명창 great[noted] singer.

myŏngdan 명단 list of names; roll; roster.

myŏnggok 명곡 famous music; musical classics.

myŏngham 명함 (name) card; visiting card; calling card(*Am.*); business card.

myŏngjak 명작 masterpiece; excellent work.

myŏngjŏl 명절 festival[festive] days; gala days.

myŏngju 명주 silk. *myŏngjushil* 명주실 silk thread.

myŏngjung 명중 hit. *myŏngjunghada* 명중하다 hit (the mark); strike.

myŏngmok 명목 name; title; pretext. *myŏngmoksangŭi* 명목상의 nominal; in name only.

myŏngmul 명물 special product; speciality.

myŏngnang 명랑. *myŏngnanghan* 명랑한 gay; merry; bright; light-hearted.

myŏngnyŏng 명령 order; command. *myŏngnyŏnghada* 명령하다 order; command.

myŏngsa 명사 man of note; distinguished〔noted, celebrated〕 person; celebrity.

myŏngsesŏ 명세서 detailed statement〔account〕; specifications.

myŏngso 명소 noted place; beauty〔scenic〕 spot; sights.

myŏngsŏng 명성 fame; reputation; renown. *myŏngsŏngŭl ŏtta* 명성을 얻다 gain〔win〕 fame〔a reputation〕.

myŏngsŭng 명승 *myŏngsŭng kojŏk* 명승 고적 places of scenic beauty and historic interest. *myŏngsŭngji* 명승지 beautiful place.

myŏngye 명예 honor; credit; glory. *myŏngyeroun* 명예로운 honorable.

myŏnhada 면하다 escape; avoid; get rid of.

myŏnhŏ 면허 license; permission. *myŏnhŏchŭng* 면허증 license card.

myŏnhoe 면회 interview. *myŏnhoehada* 면회하다 meet; see; have an interview.

myŏnjŏk 면적 area. *kyŏngjak myŏnjŏk* 경작 면적 area under cultivation.

myŏnmok 면목 ① countenance; looks; features ② face; honor; prestige; credit. *myŏnmok ŏpta* 면목 없다 be ashamed of oneself.

myŏnmyŏt 몇몇 some; several.

myŏnse 면세 tax exemption. *myŏnsehada* 면세하다 exempt(a person) from taxes. *myŏnsep'um* 면세품 tax-exempt〔free〕 articles.

myŏnŭri 며느리 daughter-in-law; one's son's wife.

myŏnyŏk 면역 immunity. *myŏnyŏgi toeda* 면역이
되다 become[be] immune (from).

myosa 묘사 description; depiction. *myosahada* 묘
사하다 draw; sketch; paint; describe.

myŏt 몇 ① some; a few; several ② how many;
how much.

※※※ **N** ※※※

na 나 I; myself. *naŭi* 나의 my. *na-ege[rŭl]* 나에
게[를] me.

naagada 나아가다 advance; proceed; march; go
forward; move on.

naajida 나아지다 become[get] better; improve;
make a good progress.

nabal 나발 trumpet. →**nap'al** 나팔.

nabi 나비 butterfly.

nabukkida 나부끼다 flutter; flap; wave.

nach'e 나체 naked body; nudity.

nach'imban 나침반 compass.

nada 나다 ① be born ② be out; come into(*bud,
leaf*) ③ produce; yield ④ smell; taste.

nadal 낟알 grain.

nadŭri 나들이 going out; outing. *nadŭrihada* 나들
이하다 go on a visit.

nae 내 stream; brook; creek(*Am.*).

naebin 내빈 guest. *naebinsŏk* 내빈석 guests' seat.
naebinshil 내빈실 reception room.

naebonaeda 내보내다 ① let out; let go out ②
dismiss; fire (*Am.*).

naebu 내부 inside; interior. *naebuŭi* 내부의 inside;
internal; inner. *naebue* 내부에 inside; within.

naehunyŏn 내후년 the year after next.

naeil 내일 tomorrow. *naeil chŏnyŏk* 내일 저녁 to-morrow evening.

naejang 내장 internal organs; intestines.

naeju 내주 next week. *naeju woryoil* 내주 월요일 Monday next week; next Monday.

naejuda 내주다 ① take[bring] (a thing) out and give it; give away ② resign[surrender] (one's seat to a person).

naemak 내막 inside facts; private circumstances; the inside.

naemsae 냄새 smell; odo(u)r; scent; fragrance; perfume; stink; reek. *naemsaenada* 냄새나다 smell (of tobacco). *choŭn[nappŭn] naemsae* 좋은 [나쁜] 냄새 sweet[bad] smell.

naemu 내무 home[domestic] affairs. *naemubu* 내무부 Ministry of Home Affairs; Home Office (*Eng.*); Department of Interior (*Am.*).

naengbang 냉방 unheated room. *naengbang changch'i* 냉방 장치 air-conditioning; air conditioner; air cooler.

naengch'a 냉차 iced tea; ice[cold] tea.

naengdae 냉대 →**p'udaejŏp** 푸대접.

naengdong 냉동 refrigeration, freezing. *naengdonghada* 냉동하다 cool down; refrigerate. *naengdong shikp'um* 냉동 식품 frozen foodstuffs.

naenggak 냉각 cooling; refrigeration. *naenggakki* 냉각기 freezer.

naengjang 냉장 cold storage; refrigeration. *naengjanggo* 냉장고 refrigerator; freezer; icebox.

naengjŏn 냉전 cold war.

naengjŏng 냉정 calmness; composure; coolness.

naengjŏnghan 냉정한 calm; cool. *naengjŏnghi* 냉정히 calmly; cooly.

naengsu 냉수 cold water. *naengsu mach'al* 냉수 마찰 cold-water rubbing.

naeppaeda 내빼다 free; run away.

naeppumta 내뿜다 gush out; spout; shoot up (smoke).

naerida 내리다 ① descend; come down; get off; dismount ② drop; fall.

naeshil 내실 inner room; women's quarters.

naesŭp 내습 attack; raid. *naesŭp'ada* 내습하다 attack; raid.

naetchotta 내쫓다 ① expel; turn[send, drive] out ② dismiss; fire.

naetka 냇가 riverside; bank[edge] of a river.

naeŭi 내의 undergarment; undershirt; underwear.

naewang 내왕 comings and goings; traffic; intercourse. *naewanghada* 내왕하다 come and go; pass.

naeyong 내용 contents; substance.

nagada 나가다 go[come, get] out; be present; leave.

nagŭne 나그네 travel(l)er; vagabond; tourist.

nagwi 나귀 donkey; ass.

nagwon 낙원 paradise; Eden.

nagyŏp 낙엽 fallen[dead] leaves.

nahŭl 나흘 four days; the fourth day of the month.

nai 나이 age; years.

najŏn 나전 mother of pearl (*Am.*); nacre. *najŏn ch'ilgi* 나전 칠기 lacquerwork inlaid with mother of pearl.

najung 나중. *najunge* 나중에 later (on); afterwards;

after some time. *najung kŏt* 나중 것 the latter.

nak'asan 낙하산 parachute; chute. *nak'asan pudae* 낙하산 부대 paratroops; parachute troop.

nakch'al 낙찰 successful bid. *nakch'arhada* 낙찰하다 make a successful bid.

nakche 낙제 failure in an examination. *nakchehada* 낙제하다 fail in an exam.

nakchin 낙진 fallout. *pangsasŏng nakchin* 방사성 낙진 (radioactive) fallout.

nakkwan 낙관 optimism. *nakkwanhada* 낙관하다 be optimistic.

nakshijil 낚시질 angling; fishing. *nakshijirhada* 낚시질하다 fish; angle.

naksŏ 낙서 scribble; scrawl.

naksŏn 낙선 *naksŏnhada* 낙선하다 be defeated in an election. *naksŏnja* 낙선자 unsuccessful candidate.

nakta 낡다 ① (be) old; used; worn ② (be) old-fashioned; be out of date.

nakt'a 낙타 camel.

nakt'ae 낙태 abortion; miscarriage. *nakt'ae* 낙태하다 have an abortion.

nakto 낙도 remote island.

nak'wasaeng 낙화생 peanut; ground nut; monkey-nut(*Eng.*). →**ttangk'ong** 땅콩.

nal 날 ① day; date; time ② time when; in time of. *nallo* 날로 day by day.

nal 날 edge; blade. *k'allal* 칼날 blade of a knife.

nalch'igi 날치기 snatching; snatcher (person). *nalch'igirŭl tanghada* 날치기를 당하다 have (a purse) snatched.

nalchimsŭng 날짐승 fowls; birds; the feathered

tribe.

nalda 날다 fly; soar; flutter[flit] about.

nalgae 날개 wing. *nalgae tallin* 날개 달린 winged.

nalk'aropta 날카롭다 (be) sharp; keen; acute; pointed. *nalk'aropke* 날카롭게 sharply; stingingly.

nallim 날림 slipshod work; careless manufacture. *nallim kongsa* 날림 공사 jerry-building.

nanip 난입 intrusion; trespass(ing). *nanip'ada* 난입하다 break into; intrude; trespass.

nallo 난로 stove; fireplace; heater.

nalmada 날마다 every day; day after day; day by day.

nalp'um 날품 day labo(u)r; daywork. *nalp'um-p'arikkun* 날품팔이꾼 day laborer.

nalssaeda 날쌔다 (be) quick; swift; nimble. *nalssaege* 날쌔게 quickly; speedily; swiftly.

nalssi 날씨 weather; weather condition.

nalssinhada 날씬하다 (be) slender; slim.

naltcha 날짜 date. *kyeyak naltcha* 계약 날짜 date of a contract.

nam 남 another person; others; unrelated person; stranger; outsider.

nam 남 south. *namŭro* 남으로 to the south. *namtchoge* 남쪽에 in the south.

nammae 남매 brother and sister.

nambi 남비 pot; cook-pot; pan; saucepan.

nambu 남부 southern part[district, section].

nambuk 남북 north and south. *nambuk taehwa* 남북 대화 the South-North dialogue. *nambuk t'ongil* 남북 통일 reunification of Korea.

nambukkŭrŏpta 남부끄럽다 (be) ashamed; feel

shameful.

namdaemun 남대문 the South Gate (of Seoul).

namdan 남단 the southern extremity.

namgida 남기다 ① leave (behind); bequeath ② make[get, obtain, realize] a profit (of).

Namhan 남한 South Korea.

namja 남자 man; male. *namjaŭi* 남자의 male; masculine. *namjadaun* 남자다운 manly.

namnyŏ 남녀 man and woman; male and female.

namŏji 나머지 ① the rest; the remainder; the balance ② excess.

namp'yŏn 남편 husband; one's man; one's worse half.

namsŏng 남성 male (sex); the masculine gender. *namsŏngjŏk(in)* 남성적(인) manly; virile.

namta 남다 be left over; remain.

namu 나무 ① tree; plant ② wood; timber; lumber. *namunnip* 나뭇잎 leaf; foliage.

namurada 나무라다 scold; reproach; reprimand.

namyong 남용 misuse; abuse. *namyonghada* 남용하다 misuse; abuse.

nan 난 column. *kwanggonan* 광고난 advertisement column. *tokchanan* 독자난 reader's column.

nanbang 난방 heating; heated room. *nanbang changch'i* 난방 장치 heating apparatus.

nanbong 난봉 dissipation; debauchery. *nanbongburida* 난봉부리다 live a fast life. *nanbongkkun* 난봉꾼 libertine; prodigal son.

nanch'o 난초 orchid; orchis.

nanch'ŏ 난처. *nanch'ŏhada* 난처하다 (be) awkward; be at a loss.

nandong 난동 disturbance; commotion; riot. *nan-*

dongŭl purida 난동을 부리다 raise a disturbance; stir up a riot.

nan-gan 난간 railing; rail; parapet; balustrade.

nangbi 낭비 waste; extravagance. *nangbihada* 낭비하다 waste; squander.

nangnong 낙농 dairy; dairy farming.

nangttŏrŏji 낭떠러지 precipice; cliff.

nanmal 낱말 word; vocabulary.

nanp'a 난파 shipwreck. *nanp'ahada* 난파하다 be wrecked; wreck. *nanp'asŏn* 난파선 wrecked ship.

nanp'ok 난폭 violence; outrage. *nanp'ok'ada* 난폭하다 (be) violent; outrageous.

nant'u 난투 confused fight; scuffle.

nanuda 나누다 ① divide ② share ③ classify.

naoda 나오다 go[come, get] out; be present; leave.

nap 납 wax; beeswax.

nap'al 나팔 bugle; trumpet. *nap'alsu* 나팔수 bugler; trumpeter.

napchak'ada 납작하다 (be) flat.

napchakk'o 납작코 flat nose; snub nose.

napch'i 납치 hijacking; kidnapping. *napch'ihada* 납치하다 kidnap; hijack.

nappajida 나빠지다 grow worse; go bad.

nappu 납부 delivery; payment. *nappuhada* 납부하다 pay; deliver; supply (goods).

nappŭda 나쁘다 bad; evil; wrong; wicked; inferior (*quality*); unwell (*health*); poor, weak (*memory*); nasty, foul (*weather*).

napse 납세 tax payment. *napse kojisŏ* 납세 고지서 tax notice[papers]. *napseja* 납세자 taxpayer.

naptŭk 납득 understanding. *naptŭk'ada* 납득하다 understand; persuade oneself.

nara 나라 ① country; state; land; nation ② world; realm. *uri nara* 우리 나라 our country. *tallara* 달나라 lunar world.

naranhi 나란히 in a row[line]; side by side.

narin 날인. *narinhada* 날인하다 seal; affix one's seal. *sŏmyŏng narinhada* 서명 날인하다 sign and seal.

narŭda 나르다 carry; convey; transport.

narŭnhada 나른하다 (be) languid; weary; dull.

narutpae 나룻배 ferryboat.

nasa 나사 screw. *nasamot* 나사못 screw nail.

nassŏlda 낯설다 (be) strange; unfamiliar.

nat 낯 face; features; looks. →**ŏlgul** 얼굴.

nat 낮 daytime. *naje* 낮에 in the daytime.

nat 낫 sickle; scythe.

nat'a 낳다 ① bear; give birth to; be delivered of (a child) ② produce.

nat'anada 나타나다 come out; turn up; appear.

natcham 낮잠 nap; siesta. *natcham chada* 낮잠 자다 take a nap[siesta].

natta 낫다 (be) better (than); preferable.

natta 낫다 recover; get well; be cure (of); heal up.

natta 낮다 ① (be) low ② humble.

natton 낱돈 small[loose] money.

ne 네 four. *ne saram* 네 사람 four people.

ne 네 ① you ② your. *ne adŭl* 네 아들 your son.

ne 네 (*answer*) yes; certainly. →**ye** 예.

negŏri 네거리 crossroads; street crossing.

nemo 네모 square. *nemonan* 네모난 four-cornered; square.

netchae 네째 the fourth; No. 4; the fourth place.

no 노 oar; paddle; scull.

nŏbi 너비 width; breadth.

noch'onggak 노총각 old bachelor.

noch'ŏnyŏ 노처녀 old maid; spinster.

nodaji 노다지 ① rich mine; bonanza (*Am.*) ② run of luck; great[big, smash] success[hit].

nodong 노동 labor; work. *nodonghada* 노동하다 labor; work; toil.

nodong chohap 노동 조합 labor union(*Am.*); trade union(*Eng.*).

nodongja 노동자 laborer; worker; workingman; labor.

noe 뇌 brain; brains. *noeŭi* 뇌의 cerebral.

noeirhyŏl 뇌일혈 (cerebral) apoplexy.

noemul 뇌물 bribe; corruption.

noesŏng 뇌성 thunder; peal[rumbling] of thunder.

nogolchŏk 노골적 plain; frank; outspoken. *nogolchŏguro* 노골적으로 openly; broadly.

nogŭm 녹음 sound recording. *nogŭmhada* 녹음하다 record; phonograph. *nogŭmgi* 녹음기 (tape) recorder. *nogŭm t'eip'ŭ* 녹음 테이프 recording tape.

nŏguri 너구리 racoon dog.

nŏgŭrŏpta 너그럽다 (be) lenient; generous. *nŏgŭrŏi* 너그러이 generously; leniently.

nŏhŭi 너희 you all; you people[folk].

noim 노임 wages; pay. *noim insang* 노임 인상 rise [raise] in wages; wage increase (*Am.*)

noin 노인 old[aged] man. *noinpyŏng* 노인병 disease of old age.

nojŏm 노점 street-stall; booth.

nŏk 넋 soul; spirit; ghost. *nŏksŭl ilt'a* 넋을 잃다

be absent-minded.

nokchi 녹지 green track of land. *nokchidae* 녹지
대 green belt[zone].

nokkŭn 노끈 string; small cord.

noksaek 녹색 green; green color.

nokta 녹다 melt; dissolve; thaw.

noktu 녹두 small green peas.

nŏkturi 넋두리 *nŏkturihada* 넋두리하다 make com
plaints; grumble (at, over).

nok'wa 녹화 afforestation. *nok'wahada* 녹화하다
plant trees (in).

nok'wa 녹화 video (tape) recording; videotape.

nol 놀 glow. *chŏnyŏngnŏl* 저녁놀 evening glow.

nolda 놀다 play; amuse oneself.

nŏlda 널다 spread out; stretch.

nollada 놀라다 be surprised[astonished]; be star
tled; be stunned. *nollal manhan* 놀랄 만한 sur
prising; amazing.

nolli 논리 logic. *nollijŏk(ŭro)* 논리적(으로) logica
(ly). *nollihak* 논리학 logic.

nŏlli 널리 widely; far and wide; generally.

nollida 놀리다 tease; kid; laugh at; make fur
of; banter; chaff; rally; ridicule.

nŏlp'ida 넓히다 widen; enlarge; broaden; extend.

nŏlppanji 널빤지 board; plank.

nŏlta 넓다 (be) broad; wide; roomy; extensive.

nŏlttwigi 널뛰기 seesaw(ing); teeter. *nŏlttwida* 널
뛰다 play at seesaw.

nom 놈 fellow; chap; guy; creature.

nŏmch'ida 넘치다 ① overflow; flow[run] over; be
full of ② exceed; be above[beyond].

nŏmgida 넘기다 ① hand (over); turn over; transfer; pass ② throw down; overthrow ③ pass; exceed ④ turn a page.

nŏmŏ 너머 opposite[other] side; across; beyond.

nŏmŏgada 넘어가다 ① cross; go across[over] ② sink; set; go down ③ be transferred ④ fall; be thrown down ⑤ be swallowed.

nŏmŏjida 넘어지다 fall (down); come down; tumble down.

nŏmŏttŭrida 넘어뜨리다 throw[tumble] down; overthrow; pull down; push down.

nŏmshilgŏrida 넘실거리다 surge; roll; swell.

nŏmta 넘다 ① cross; go over; go[get] beyond ② exceed; pass.

nŏmu 너무 too (much); over; excessively.

nonga 농아 deaf and dumb; deaf-mute.

nongak 농악 instrumental music of peasants. *nongaktae* 농악대 farm band.

nongbu 농부 farmer; peasant; farm hand.

nongch'on 농촌 farm village; rural community.

nongdam 농담 joke; jest; fun; prank. *nongdamhada* 농담하다 joke; jest; crack a joke.

nongdo 농도 thickness; density.

nongga 농가 farmhouse; farm household.

nonggu 농구 basketball. *nonggu sŏnsu* 농구 선수 basketball player.

nongjang 농장 farm; plantation.

nongjangmul 농작물 crops; harvest; farm produce.

nŏngk'ul 넝쿨 vine. →*tŏngul* 덩굴.

nŏngma 넝마 rags; tatters.

nongmin 농민 farmer; peasant.

nŏngnŏk'ada 넉넉하다 (be) enough; sufficient. *nŏngnŏk'i* 넉넉히 enough; sufficiently; fully.

nongŏp 농업 agriculture; farming. *nongŏbŭi* 농업의 agricultural.

nongsanmul 농산물 agricultural products; farm produce.

nongttaengi 농땡이 lazybones; do-little. *nongttaengi purida* 농땡이 부리다 shirk one's duty.

nongyak 농약 agricultural medicines[chemicals].

nonjaeng 논쟁 dispute; controversy. *nonjaenghada* 논쟁하다 dispute; argue; contend.

nonkil 논길 paddy path.

nonmun 논문 treatise; essay; dissertation; thesis.

nonsŏl 논설 discourse; leading article; editorial (*Am.*) *nonsŏl wiwon* 논설 위원 editorial writer.

nonyŏn 노년 old age; declining years.

nop'a 노파 old woman *nop'ashim* 노파심 grandmotherly solicitude.

nop'i 높이 ① (*noun*) height; altitude ② (*adverb*) high; highly.

nop'ittwigi 높이뛰기 (running) high jump.

nopta 높다 (be) high; tall; lofty; elevated.

norae 노래 song; ballad; singing. *noraehada* 노래하다 sing (a song).

norat'a 노랗다 (be) yellow.

nori 놀이 play; game; sport. *kkonnori* 꽃놀이 flower viewing. *norit'ŏ* 놀이터 playground; pleasure resort.

norida 노리다 stare at; watch (for); fix the eye on; aim at.

norigae 노리개 ① pendent trinket ② plaything; toy.

nŏrŭda 너르다 (be) wide; vast; extensive; spacious; roomy.

norŭm 노름 gambling; gaming; betting. *norŭm-hada* 노름하다 gamble; play for money. *norŭm-kkun* 노름꾼 gambler; gamester.

norŭnja(wi) 노른자(위) yolk of an egg.

noryŏk 노력 endeavo(u)r; effort. *noryŏk'ada* 노력하다 endeavor; strive; make efforts.

noryŏnhan 노련한 experienced; veteran; expert; skilled.

nosŏn 노선 route; line. *pŏsŭ nosŏn* 버스 노선 bus service route.

not'a 놓다 ① put; place; lay; set ② let go; set free; release.

nŏt'a 넣다 ① put in[into]; set[let] in; stuff ② send[put] (to); admit.

notkŭrŭt 놋그릇 brassware.

nŏulgŏrida 너울거리다 ① wave; roll ② flutter; undulate; waver.

noye 노예 slave; slavery. *noye kŭnsŏng* 노예 근성 servile spirit.

noyŏum 노여움 anger; offence; displeasure. *noyŏumŭl sada* 노여움을 사다 incur (a person's) displeasure.

nuda 누다 ① make[pass] water; urinate ② evacuate; relieve nature.

nŭdadŏpshi 느닷없이 abruptly; all of a sudden; unexpectedly.

nudŏgi 누더기 rags; tatters.

nue 누에 silkworm.

nugu 누구 who. *nuguŭi* 누구의 whose. *nugurŭl* 누구를 whom.

nugŭrŏjida 누그러지다 get milder; calm down; abate; subside.

nui 누이 sister; elder sister; younger sister.

nuidongsaeng 누이동생 younger[little] sister.

nujŏn 누전 electric leakage. *nujŏnhada* 누전하다 short-circuit; electricity leaks.

nŭkchangburida 늑장부리다 dawdle (over); linger; be tardy; be slow.

nŭkkida 느끼다 ① feel; be aware[conscious](of) ② be impressed (by, with).

nŭkkol 늑골 rib; costa.   ⌈placid.

nukta 눅다 ① (be) soft; limp; flabby ② (be) genial;

nŭkta 늙다 grow old; age; advance in age.

nŭktae 늑대 wolf. *nŭktae[iri]ŭi* 늑대〔이리〕의 lupine.

nŭl 늘 →*ŏnjena* 언제나.

nŭllida 늘리다 ① increase; add to; multiply ② extend; enlarge.

nŭlssinhada 늘씬하다 (be) slender; slim; slender and elegant.

nun 눈 snow; snowfall. *nunŭi* 눈의 snowy.

nun 눈 eye. *nunŭl ttŭda[kamta]* 눈을 뜨다〔감다〕 open[close] one's eyes.

nŭng 능 royal mausoleum[tomb].

nŭnghada 능하다 (be) skillful; good at; proficient.

nŭnghi 능히 well; easily; ably.

nŭngmak 늑막 pleura. *nŭngmangnyŏm* 늑막염 (dry, moist) pleurisy.

nungnuk'ada 눅눅하다 (be) damp; humid.

nŭngnyŏk 능력 ability; capacity; faculty. *nŭngnyŏge ttara* 능력에 따라 according to ability. *nŭngnyŏgi itta* 능력이 있다 be able to do.

nŭngnyul 능률 efficiency. *nŭngnyulchŏgin* 능률 적인 efficient.

nŭrinnŭrit 느릿느릿 slowly; sluggishly; idly.

nŭrŏnot'a 늘어놓다 ① scatter about; leave (things) lying about ② arrange; place (things) in a row.

nŭrŏsŏda 늘어서다 stand in a row; form in a line; stand abreast.

nŭrŏttŭrida 늘어뜨리다 hang down; suspend; droop.

nurŭda 누르다 ① press (down); weigh‐on; hold (a person) down ② stamp; seal.

nusŏrhada 누설하다 reveal; divulge; disclose; let out. *pimirŭl nusŏrhada* 비밀을 누설하다 let out [leak] a secret.

nŭsŭnhada 느슨하다 be loose; slack; relaxed.

nŭtcham 늦잠 late rising; morning sleep. *nŭtcham-jada* 늦잠자다 rise [get up] late.

nŭtch'uda 늦추다 ① loosen; unfasten; slacken ② put off; postpone; delay; defer.

nŭtta 늦다 (be) late; behind time; be slow. *nŭtke* 늦게 late. *nŭjŏdo* 늦어도 at (the) latest.

nyŏsŏk 녀석 fellow; guy; chap; boy. *I pabo nyŏsŏk* 이 바보 녀석 You fool!

❖❖◗ O ◖❖❖

o 오, 5 five; *cheo* 제 5 the fifth.

ŏani bŏngbŏnghada 어안이 벙벙하다 be dumfounded; be struck dumb; be confused.

ŏbŏi 어버이 parents; father and mother. *ŏbŏiŭi* 어버이의 parental.

ŏbu 어부 fisherman; fisher.

ocha 오자 wrong word; erratum; misprint.

och'an 오찬 luncheon; lunch. *och'anhoe* 오찬회 luncheon party.

ŏch'ŏguniŏpta 어처구니없다 (be) amazing; dumfounded; absurd. →ŏiŏpta 어이없다.

ŏch'on 어촌 fishing village.

oda 오다 come; come up[down]; come over[along].

ŏdi 어디 where; what place. 어디에나 *ŏdiena* 어디
에나 anywhere; everywhere.

odumak 오두막 hut; shed; hovel; shanty.

ŏdupta 어둡다 (be) dark; dim; gloomy.

oebak 외박. *oebak'ada* 외박하다 stay[stop, sleep]
out; lodging out.

oebu 외부 outside; exterior. *oebuŭi* 외부의 outside;
outward; external.

oech'ida 외치다 shout out; cry(out); exclaim.

oech'ul 외출 going out. *oech'urhada* 외출하다 go
out. *oech'ulbok* 외출복 street wear[clothes].

oeda 외다 recite from memory; learn by heart;
memorize(*Am.*); commit to memory.

oedŭng 외등 outdoor lamp.

oega 외가 one's mother's family[home].

oegojip, onggojip 외고집, 옹고집. *oegojibŭi* 외고집
의 obstinate; stubborn; obdurate.

oeguk 외국 foreign country[land]. *oegugŭi* 외국
의 foreign; alien. *oegugin* 외국인 foreigner.
oegugŏ 외국어 foreign language.

oegwan 외관 (external) appearance; outside view.
oegwansang 외관상 externally; seemingly.

oegyo 외교 diplomacy. *oegyo munje* 외교 문제 diplomatic problem. *oegyo chŏngch'aek* 외교 정책 diplomatic policy. *oegyogwan* 외교관 diplomat.

oegyŏn 외견 →**oegwan** 외관.

oehwa 외화 foreign currency[money].

oein 외인 foreigner. →**oegugin** 외국인. *oein sangsa*
외인 상사 foreign(business) firm. *oein pudae* 외인

부대 foreign legion.

oeji 외지 foreign land; oversea(s) land.

oekwa 외과 surgery; surgical department. *oekwa ŭisa* 외과 의사 surgeon.

oemo 외모 (outward) appearance; external feature.

oemu 외무 foreign affairs. *oemubu* 외무부 Ministry of Foreign Affairs.

oenson 왼손 left hand. *oensonjabi* 왼손잡이 left-handed person; southpaw (*baseball*).

oentchok 왼쪽 left (side). *oentchogŭi* 왼쪽의 left (-hand). *oentchoge* 왼쪽에 on the left side.

oerae 외래. *oeraeŭi* 외래의 foreign; imported. *oeraep'um* 외래품 imported goods.

oeropta 외롭다 (be) lonely; lonesome; solitary.

oesang 외상 credit; trust. *oesang kŏrae* 외상 거래 credit transaction.

oeshik 외식. *oeshik'ada* 외식하다 dine[eat] out; board out(*Am.*).

oeshin 외신 foreign news; foreign message[telegram].

oettal 외딸 only daughter.

oettanjip 외딴집 isolated house; solitary house.

oet'u 외투 overcoat; greatcoat; topcoat.

ogak'yŏng 오각형 pentagon.

ŏgap 억압 oppression; suppression. *ŏgap'ada* 억압하다 hold[keep] down; oppress.

ŏgida 어기다 go against; disobey; break.

ogoe 옥외. *ogoeŭi* 옥외의 outdoor; out-of-door; openair, *ogoeesŏ* 옥외에서 in the open air.

ogok 오곡 ① five grains[rice·barley·millet·bean etc.] ② grain(*Am.*); corn(*Eng.*); cereal.

ŏgu 어구 phrase; words and phrases.

ŏgul 억울. *ŏgurhada* 억울하다 suffer unfairness; feel victimized.

ŏgŭnnada 어긋나다 ① cross each other ② pass each other ③ go amiss; go wrong with.

ogŭrida 오그리다 curl up; crouch; huddle.

ŏgŭrŏjida 어그러지다 be[act] contrary to; be a-gainst; guess wrong.

ŏgwi 어귀 entrance; entry(*Am.*) *maŭl ŏgwi* 마을 어귀 entrance to a village.

ohae 오해 misunderstanding; misconception. *ohae-hada* 오해하다 misunderstand.

ŏhak 어학 language study; philology; linguistics.

ohan 오한 chill; cold fit.

ohiryŏ 오히려 rather; preferably; on the contrary; instead.

ohu 오후 afternoon; p. m.; P. M.

ŏhwi 어휘 vocabulary; glossary.

oi 오이 cucumber. *oiji* 오이지 cucumbers pickled in salt.

oil 오일 five days; the fifth day (of the month).

oin 오인. *oinhada* 오인하다 misconceive; mistake [take] (A) for (B).

ŏiŏpta 어이없다 be struck dumb; be amazed (at).

ŏje 어제 yesterday. *ŏje ach'im* 어제 아침 yester-day morning.

ŏjirŏpta 어지럽다 (be) dizzy; feel giddy.

ŏjirŭda 어지르다 scatter (about); put in disorder.

ojŏn 오전 forenoon; morning; a. m.; A. M.

ŏjŏnggŏrida 어정거리다 walk leisurely along; stroll [ramble] about.

ŏjŏngtchŏnghada 어정쩡하다 (be) suspicious; doubt-ful; dubious; vague.

ojum 오줌 urine; piss. *ojum nuda* 오줌 누다 urinate.

ok 옥 jade. *okkarakchi* 옥가락지 jade ring.

ŏk 억 one hundred million. *shibŏk* 십억 milliard; billion(*Am.*).

ŏkche 억제 control; constraint. *ŏkchehada* 억제하다 check; control; restrain.

ŏkchiro 억지로 by force; forcibly.

ŏkkae 어깨 shoulder. *ŏkkaerŭl ŭssŭk'ada* 어깨를 으쓱하다 perk up[raise] one's shoulders.

okp'yŏn 옥편 Chinese-Korean dictionary.

oksang 옥상 roof; rooftop. *oksangesŏ* 옥상에서 on the roof.

ŏkseda 억세다 (be) strong; tough; sturdy.

ŏkta 얽다 get[be] pockmarked. *ŏlgŭn chaguk* 얽은 자국 pockmarks.

ol 올 ply; texture; strand.

ŏl 얼 spirit; mind; soul.

ŏlbŏmurida 얼버무리다 speak ambiguously;quibble.

olch'aengi 올챙이 tadpole.

olch'i 옳지 Good!; Right!; Yes!.

ŏlda 얼다 freeze; be frozen (over); be benumbed with cold.

olgamaeda 옭아매다 tie up.

olgami 올가미 trap. *olgamirŭl ssŭiuda* 올가미를 씌우다 put the rope on; trap.

olganaeda 옭아내다 cheat out of; squeeze from.

ŏlgani 얼간이 fool; half-wit; ass; dunce.

ŏlgul 얼굴 face; features; looks. *olgurŭl tollida* 얼굴을 돌리다 look away; look aside. *ŏlgurŭl pulk'ida* 얼굴을 붉히다 blush.

ŏlgulpit 얼굴빛 complexion; countenance.

ŏlgŭmbaengi 얼금뱅이 pockmarked person.

ŏlgŭnhada 얼근하다 ① (be) tipsy; slightly intoxicated ② be rather hot[peppery].

olk'e 올케 girl's sister-in-law; wife of a girl's brother.

ŏlk'ida 얽히다 be[get] entangled; get intertwined.

ŏlk'ŭnhada 얼큰하다 (be) intoxicated; be a bit spicy.

ollagada 올라가다 go up; mount; climb; rise; ascend.

ŏlle 얼레 reel; spool.

ollida 올리다 raise; lift up; put[hold] up; elevate; hoist.

ŏllon 언론 speech. *ŏllonŭi chayu* 언론의 자유 freedom of speech.

ŏlluk 얼룩 stain; spot; blot. *ŏllukchin* 얼룩진 spotted; stained; smeared.

ŏllŭn 얼른 fast; quickly; rapidly; promptly; at once.

ŏlma 얼마 ① how much; what price ② how many; what number[amount].

olmagada 옮아가다 move away; change quarters.

ŏlmana 얼마나 ① how much; what; how many ② how (far, large, old, etc.).

olppaemi 올빼미 owl.

ŏlppajida 얼빠지다 (be) stunned; get absent-minded. *ŏlppajin* 얼빠진 silly; half-witted.

ŏlssaanta 얼싸안다 hug fondly; embrace.

ŏlssinmot'ada 얼씬못하다 dare not come around.

olt'a 옳다 ① (be) right; rightful ② (be) righteous; just ③ (be) correct; accurate ④ (be) proper.

ŏlttŏlttŏrhada 얼떨떨하다 (be) confused; bewildered; puzzle.

om 옴 itch; scabies.

omaksari 오막살이 living in a grass hut; hovel life.

oman 오만. *omanhan* 오만한 haughty; arrogant; overbearing.

ŏmbŏl 엄벌 severe[heavy] punishment. *ŏmbŏrhada* 엄벌하다 punish severely.

ŏmch'ŏngnada 엄청나다 (be) surprising; extraordinary; awful. *ŏmch'ŏngnage* 엄청나게 awfully; terribly.

omgida 옮기다 remove; move; transfer.

ŏmji 엄지 *ŏmjisonkarak* 엄지손가락 thumb.

ŏmkyŏk 엄격 *ŏmkyŏk'ada* 엄격하다 (be) strict; stern.

ŏmma 엄마 ma; mama; mammy; mummy.

ŏmmu 업무 business. *ŏmmuyong* 업무용 for business use.

omok'ada 오목하다 (be) hollow; dented; sunken.

ŏmŏna 어머나 Oh! Oh my! Dear me!

ŏmŏni 어머니 mother. *ŏmŏniŭi* 어머니의 mother's; motherly; maternal.

omp'ok'ada 옴폭하다 (be) hollow; sunken; dented.

ŏmsuk 엄숙 solemnity; gravity. *ŏmsuk'ada* 엄숙하다 (be) grave; solemn *ŏmsuk'age* 엄숙하게 solemnly.

omul 오물 filth; dust; dirt; garbage. *omulch'a* 오물차 garbage car.

ŏmul 어물 fishes; dried fish; stockfish. *ŏmulchŏn* 어물전 fish shop; dried-fish shop.

omulgòrida 오물거리다 mumble; chew on.

omŭrida 오므리다 pucker; purse.

omyŏng 오명 disgrace; dishonor; infamy. *omyŏngŭl ssitta* 오명을 씻다 wipe off a dishonor.

on 온 all; whole. *on sesang* 온 세상 all the world. *on chiban* 온집안 whole family.

onch'ŏn 온천 hot spring; spa. *onch'ŏnjang* 온천장 hot bath〔spring〕 resort; spa.

ondae 온대 Temperate Zone; warm latitudes.

ondo 온도 temperature. *ondogye* 온도계 thermometer; mercury.

ŏndo 언도 →**sŏn-go** 선고.

ondol 온돌 hypocaust; hot floor. *ondolpang* 온돌방 hotfloored room; ondol room.

on-gat 온갖 all; every; all sorts of; various.

ŏngdŏngi 엉덩이 buttocks; hips.

onggi 옹기 pottery; earthenware.

ŏnggida 엉기다 congeal; curdle; clot.

ongi 옹이 knot; gnarl.

ŏngk'ŭmhada 엉큼하다 (be) wily〔insidious〕; crafty.

ŏngmaeda 얽매다 bind〔tie〕 up; fetter; restrict.

ŏngmang 엉망 *ŏngmangi toeda* 엉망이 되다 be spoiled; get confused; get out of shape.

ongnae 옥내. *ongnaeŭi* 옥내의 indoor. *ongnae-esŏ* 옥내에서 indoors; within doors.

ŏngnurŭda 억누르다 suppress; control; hold down.

ŏngnyu 억류 detention; detainment. *ŏngnyuhada* 억류하다 detain〔keep〕 by force.

ŏngsŏnghada 엉성하다 (be) thin; sparse; loose.

ŏngt'ŏri 엉터리 ① fake; sham ② ground; foundation. *ŏngt'ŏri ŭisa* 엉터리 의사 quack (doctor). *ŏngt'ŏriŏmnŭn* 엉터리없는 groundless; absurd.

ŏn-gŭp 언급. *ŏn-gŭp'ada* 언급하다 refer (to); allude (to); mention.

onhwa 온화. *onhwahan* 온화한 gentle; mild; quiet; genial.

ŏnje 언제 when. *ŏnjerado* 언제라도 at any time.

ŏnjebut'ŏ 언제부터 from what time; since when.

ŏnjedŭnji 언제든지 (at) any time; whenever; always.

ŏnjekkaji 언제까지 how long; till when; by what time.

ŏnjena 언제나 always; all the time; usually.

ŏnjen-ga 언젠가 some time; some day.

onjiban 온집안 whole family; all the family.

onjongil 온종일 all day (long); whole day.

ŏnjŏri 언저리 edge; brim; bounds. *ibŏnjŏrie* 입언저리에 about one's mouth.

ŏnni 언니 elder sister.

ŏnŏ 언어 language; speech; words. *ŏnŏ changae* 언어 장애 speech defect.

onshil 온실 greenhouse; hothouse; glasshouse.

onsunhan 온순한 gentle; meek; obedient; docile.

ŏntchant'a 언짢다 (be) displeased; bad-tempered.

ont'ong 온통 all; wholly; entirely; completely.

ŏnta 얹다 put on; place[lay, set] on; load.

ŏnŭ 어느 ① a; one; certain; some ② which; what *ŏnŭ nal* 어느 날 one day. *ŏnŭ ch'aek* 어느 책 which book.

ŏnŭ chŏngdo 어느 정도 to some degree; somewhat.

onŭl 오늘 today; this day.

onŭn 오는 next; coming; to come. *onŭn t'oyoil* 오는 토요일 next Saturday.

ŏnŭsae 어느새 ① already; now; by this time ② before one knows; unnoticed.

onyuwol 오뉴월 May and June.

ŏŏp 어업 fishery; fishing (industry).

ŏpcha 업자 businessmen concerned; traders.

ŏpchŏk 업적 achievements; results.

ŏpchirŭda 엎지르다 spill; slop.

ŏp'ŏjida 엎어지다 be upset; be turned over.

ŏpshi 없이 without. *hyuildo ŏpshi* 휴일도 없이 without holidays.

ŏpta 없다 ① There is no …; cannot be found ② have no …; lack.

ŏpta 업다 carry on one's back.

ŏpta 엎다 overturn; turn over; turn upside down.

ŏptŭrida 엎드리다 prostrate oneself; lie flat.

orae 오래 long; for a long while[time].

oraettongan 오랫동안 for a long time[while].

orak 오락 amusement(s); recreation; pastime. *orakshil* 오락실 amusement hall.

orhae 올해 this year; the current year.

orida 오리다 cut off[away]; cut out.

ŏrida 어리다 (be) young; juvenile; infant; childish.

ŏridungjŏrhada 어리둥절하다 ① (be) dazed[stunned]; bewildered ② (be) puzzled.

ŏrini 어린이 child; little one; youngster; infant.

ŏrisŏkta 어리석다 (be) foolish; silly; stupid.

ŏroe 어뢰 torpedo. *ŏroejŏng* 어뢰정 torpedo boat.

oroji 오로지 alone; only; solely; exclusively.

orŭda 오르다 go up; climb; ascend; rise; mount.

ŏrŭda 어르다 humo(u)r; fondle; amuse.

ŏrŭm 얼음 ice. *sarŏrŭm* 살얼음 thin ice. *ŏrŭm chumŏni* 얼음 주머니 ice pack[bag].

ŏrumanjida 어루만지다 stroke; caress; rub.

ŏrŭmjich'ida 얼음지치다 skate; do skating.

orŭn 오른. *orŭntchok* 오른쪽 right side. *orŭntchoge*

오른쪽에 on the right (side of). *orŭntchogŭro* 오른쪽으로 to the right (of). *orŭnson* 오른손 right hand.

ŏrŭn 어른 man; adult; grown-up (person). *ŏrŭnŭi* 어른의 adult; grown-up.

orŭnaerida 오르내리다 go up and down.

ŏrŭn-gŏrida 어른거리다 flicker; glimmer.

ŏryŏmp'ushi 어렴풋이 dimly; faintly; vaguely.

ŏryŏpta 어렵다 (be) hard; difficult.

ŏsaek 어색. *ŏsaek'ada* 어색하다 feel awkward[embarrassed]; clumsy.

oshik 오식 misprint; printer's error.

oship 오십, 50 fifty. *oshimnyŏn* 50년 fifty years.

ŏsŏ 어서 ① quickly; without delay ② (if you) please; right. *Ŏsŏ tŭrŏoshipshio* 어서 들어오십시오 Come right in, please.

osŏnji 오선지 music paper.

ossak 오싹. *ossak'ada* 오싹하다 feel[have] a chill; shiver; thrill.

ŏsŭllŏnggŏrida 어슬렁거리다 hang about[around]; wander about; loiter.

ŏsuruk'ada 어수룩하다 (be) naive; simple; unsophisticated.

ŏsusŏnhada 어수선하다 be in disorder[confusion].

ot 옷 clothes; dress; garment.

ot 옻 lacquer.

ŏtchaesŏ 어째서 why; for what reason; how.

ŏtchaettŭn 어쨌든 anyhow; anyway; at any rate.

otchang 옷장 wardrobe; clothes chest.

otcharak 옷자락 skirt; train.

otch'arim 옷차림 one's attire; personal appearance.

ŏtchi 어찌 how; in what way; by what means.

ŏtchihaesŏdŭnji 어찌해서든지 by all means; in any way.

ŏtchŏnji 어쩐지 somehow; without knowing why.

ŏtkallida 엇갈리다 pass[cross] each other.

otkam 옷감 cloth; stuff; dry goods.

otkŏri 옷걸이 coat hanger; clothes rack.

ŏtkŭje 엊그제 the day before yesterday; a few days ago.

ŏtta 얻다 get; gain; obtain; earn; achieve; win.

ŏttŏk'e 어떻게 how; in what manner[way]. *ŏttŏk'e haesŏrado* 어떻게 해서라도 at any cost; by any means.

ŏttŏn 어떤 what; what like; what sort[kind] of; any. *ŏttŏn iyuro* 어떤 이유로 why; for what reason.

ŏullida 어울리다 become; match; be becoming[suitable, fitting].

ŏŭm 어음 draft; bill; note. *yaksok ŏŭm* 약속 어음 promissory note. *pudo ŏŭm* 부도 어음 dishonored bill.

oyŏk 오역 mistranslation. *oyŏk'ada* 오역하다 mistranslate.

oyŏm 오염 pollution. *oyŏmhada* 오염하다 pollute.

◄◄ **P** ►►

pabo 바보 fool; ass; idiot; dunce. *pabo kat'ŭn* 바보 같은 silly; foolish.

pach'ida 바치다 give; offer; present; dedicate.

pada 바다 sea; ocean. *pada kŏnnŏ* 바다 건너 beyond[across] the sea.

padak 바닥 flat surface; bottom; bed.

pae 배 vessel; ship; boat; steamer. *paero* 배로 by ship.

pae 배 belly; abdomen; bowels; stomach.

pae 배 pear. *paenamu* 배나무 pear tree.

paeban 배반 betrayal. *paebanhada* 배반하다 betray.

paech'i 배치 arrangement; disposition. *paech'ihada* 배치하다 arrange; distribute; post.

paech'u 배추 Chinese cabbage. *paech'u kimch'i* 배추 김치 pickled cabbage.

paeda 배다 soak into[through]; spread; permeate.

paeda 배다 conceive; become pregnant. *airŭl paeda* 아이를 배다 conceive a child; be pregnant.

paedal 배달. *paedarhada* 배달하다 deliver; distribute. *paedalbu* 배달부 deliveryman; carrier; mailman.

paedang 배당 allotment; dividend. *paedanghada* 배당하다 allot; pay a dividend.

paegin 백인 white (man); Caucasian. *paeginjong* white race; the whites.

paegop'ŭda 배고프다 (be) hungry; feel hungry.

paegu 배구 volleyball.

paegŭm 배금 money worship. *paegŭmjuŭi* 배금주의 mammonism. *paegŭmjuŭija* 배금주의자 mammonist.

paegŭp 배급 distribution; rationing. *paegŭp'ada* 배급하다 distribute; ration.

paegyŏng 배경 ① background; setting ② backing; pull.

paehap 배합 combination; mixture; harmony. *paehap'ada* 배합하다 combine; match; harmonize.

paehu 배후 rear; back. *paehue* 배후에 at the back

〔rear〕; behind. *paehu inmul* 배후인물 wirepuller.

paeje 배제 exclusion; elimination. *paejehada* 배제하다 exclude; eliminate; remove.

paekchak 백작 count; earl (*Eng.*). *paekchak puin* 백작 부인 countess.

paekchi 백지 white paper; blank sheet of paper.

paekch'i 백치 idiocy; idiot; imbecile.

paekkop 배꼽 navel; belly button.

paekku 백구 white (sea) gull.

paekkwa sajŏn 백과 사전 encyclopedia.

paekpal 백발 white〔grey〕 hair.

paeksŏ 백서 white paper; white book. *kyŏngje paeksŏ* 경제 백서 economic white book.

paektong 백동 nickel.

paekkŭm 백금 platinum; white gold.

paek'wajŏm 백화점 department store.

paem 뱀 snake; serpent.

paemjangŏ 뱀장어 eel.

paenang 배낭 knapsack; rucksack.

paengman 백만 million.

paengnyŏn 백년 one hundred years; a century.

paenmŏlmi 뱃멀미 seasickness. *paenmŏlmihada* 뱃멀미하다 get seasick.

paennori 뱃놀이 boating; boat ride.

paesang 배상 compensation; recompense; reparation. *paesanghada* 배상하다 recompense; compensate.

paesŏl 배설 excretion. *paesŏrhada* 배설하다 excrete; discharge.

paessagong 뱃사공 boatman.

paetchang 배짱 boldness; nerve; courage.

paetta 뱉다 spit out. *ch'imŭl paetta* 침을 뱉다

spit (out).

paeu 배우 actor; actress; player, *yŏnghwa〔yŏn-gŭk〕 paeu* 영화〔연극〕 배우 film〔stage〕 actor.

paeuda 배우다 learn; take lessons (in, on); be taught; study.

paeuja 배우자 spouse; match; life partner.

paeung 배웅. *paeunghada* 배웅하다 see off; show out; give a send-off.

paguni 바구니 basket. *changpaguni* 장바구니 market〔shopping〕 basket.

paji 바지 trousers; pants(*Am.*).

pak 박 gourd; calabash.

pak 밖 ① →**pakkat** 바깥 ② outside of; exception of; except; but.

pak'a 박하 peppermint; mint.

pak'ae 박해 persecution. *pak'aehada* 박해하다 persecute; oppress.

pakcha 박자 time; rhythm; beat.

pakch'a 박차 spur. *pakch'arŭl kahada* 박차를 가하다 spur (one's horse, a person).

pakkat 바깥 outside; exterior; out-of-doors. *pakkat'ŭi* 바깥의 outside; outdoor; outer; external. *pakkat'esŏ* 바깥에서 in the open (air).

pakkuda 바꾸다 ① change; exchange; barter ② replace; alter; shift.

pakpong 박봉 small〔scanty〕 salary; poor pay.

paksa 박사 doctor〔Dr.〕; doctorate. *paksa hagwi* 박사 학위 doctor's degree.

pakshik 박식 wide knowledge; erudition. *pakshik'an* 박식한 erudite; learned; well-informed.

paksu 박수 hand clapping. *paksuch'ida* 박수치다 clap one's hands.

pakta 박다 drive in; hammer (in); set; inlay.

pakta 밝다 (be) light; bright.

pak'wi 바퀴 wheel; round[turn]. *ap[twit]pak'wi* 앞[뒷]바퀴 front[back] wheel.

pal 발 ① foot; paw; leg ② blind.

palchaguk 발자국 footprint; footmark; track (*Am.*).

palchŏn 발전 development; growth. *palchŏnhada* 발전하다 develop; grow.

palgul 발굴 excavation. *palgurhada* 발굴하다 dip up[out]; excavate; unearth.

palgyŏn 발견 discovery. *palgyŏnhada* 발견하다 find(out); discover.

paljach'wi 발자취 →**palchaguk** 발자국.

palkŏrŭm 발걸음 gait; step.

palkkŭt 발끝 tip of the toes; tiptoe.

pallan 반란 revolt; rebellion.

pallon 반론 counterargument; refutation. *pallonhada* 반론하다 argue against; refute.

palmyŏng 발명 invention. *palmyŏnghada* 발명하다 invent; devise.

palp'yo 발표 announcement; publication. *palp'yohada* 발표하다 announce; make public.

palsa 발사 firing; discharge. *palsahada* 발사하다 discharge; fire; blast-off.

palsaeng 발생 occurrence; outbreak; origination; generation. *palsaenghada* 발생하다 occur; break out; originate.

palt'op 발톱 toenail; claw.

paltal 발달 development; growth; progress; advance. *paltarhada* 발달하다 develop; grow; advance; make progress.

paltwikkumch'i, paltwich'uk 발뒤꿈치, 발뒤축

heel.

pam 밤 night; evening. *pame* 밤에 at night.

pamnat 밤낮 night and day. *pamnajŭro* 밤낮으로 round-the-clock.

pamsaedorok 밤새도록 all night(long); overnight; all through the night.

pamsaeuda 밤새우다 sit[stay] up all night.

pan 반 half; halfway; partial. *pan shigan* 반 시 간 half an hour; half hour.

panaek 반액 half the amount[sum, price, fare]; half-price[fare].

panbak 반박 refutation; retort; confutation. *panbak'ada* 반박하다 refute; confute.

panbal 반발 repulsion. *panbarhada* 반발하다 repel; repulse; resist.

panbanhada 반반하다 (be) smooth; even; flat.

panbok 반복 repetition; reiteration. *panbok'ada* 반복하다 repeat; reiterate.

panch'an 반찬 sidedish. *kogi panch'an* 고기 반찬 meat dish. *panch'an kage* 반찬가게 grocery store.

panch'anggo 반창고 plaster. *panch'anggorŭl puch'ida* 반창고를 붙이다 apply a plaster.

pandae 반대 contrary; opposition; reverse; objection. *pandaehada* 반대하다 oppose; object to. *pandaeŭi* 반대의 opposite; contrary. *pandaero* 반대로 on the contrary.

panditpul 반딧불 glow of firefly.

pando 반도 peninsula. *Hanbando* 한반도 Peninsula of Korea.

pandong 반동 reaction; rebound. *pandongjŏk* 반동적 reactionary. *pandong punja* 반동 분자 reactionary elements.

pandŭshi 반드시 certainly; surely; without fail; necessarily; by all means. *pandŭshi …hajinŭn ant'a* 반드시 …하지는 않다 not always; not necessarily.

pang 방 room; chamber; apartment *setpang* 셋방 room to let.

panga 방아 mill. *mulbanga* 물방아 water mill.

pan-gam 반감 antipathy; ill feeling.

pan-gapta 반갑다 (be) happy; glad; be pleased [delighted].

pangbŏp 방법 way; method; means.

pangch'im 방침 course; line; policy; principle. *yŏngŏp pangch'im* 영업 방침 business policy.

pangch'ŏng 방청 hearing; attendance. *pangch'ŏng-hada* 방청하다 hear; attend; listen to.

panggong 방공 air defense. *panggongho* 방공호 dugout; air-raid shelter. *panggong yŏnsŭp* 방공 연습 anti-air raid[air defense] drill.

panggŭm 방금 just now; a moment ago.

panggwi 방귀 wind; fart. *panggwi kkwida* 방귀 꾸다 break wind; fart.

panghae 방해 obstruction; disturbance. *panghae-hada* 방해하다 obstruct; disturb; interrupt.

panghwa 방화 fire prevention. *panghwa chugan* 방화 주간 Fire Prevention Week.

panghyang 방향 direction; course.

pan-gida 반기다 rejoice (at, over); be glad (of); be delighted[pleased] (at).

pangji 방지 prevention; check. *pangjihada* 방지하다 prevent; check; stop.

pangjŏk 방적 spinning. *pangjŏk kongjang* 방적 공장 cotton(spinning) mill.

pangmangi 방망이 club; cudgel; mallet.

pangmulgwan 박물관 museum. *kungnip pangmulgwan* 국립박물관 National Museum.

pangmun 방문 call; visit. *pangmunhada* 방문하다 (pay a) visit; make a call on; call at.

pangmyŏn 방면 direction; quarter; district. *Cheju pangmyŏn* 제주 방면 the Cheju districts.

pangmyŏng 방명 your (honored) name. *pangmyongnok* 방명록 list of names; visitors' register[list].

pan-gong(juŭi) 반공(주의) anti-Communism.

pangnamhoe 박람회 exhibition; exposition(EXPO); fair (*Am.*) *pangnamhoejang* 박람회장 fair ground.

pangsa 방사 radiation; emission. *pangsahada* 방사하다 radiate; emit.

pangsong 방송 broadcasting; broadcast. *pangsonghada* 방송하다 broadcast; go on the air.

pangul 방울 ① bell ② drop. *mulpangul* 물방울 water drops.

pangwi 방위 defense; protection. *pangwihada* 방위하다 defend; protect.

pan-gyŏk 반격 counterattack. *pan-gyŏk'ada* 반격하다 make a counterattack; strike back.

panhada 반하다 fall[be] in love (with); take a fancy (to); fall for (*Am.*).

panhang 반항 resistance; opposition; defiance. *panhanghada* 반항하다 resist; oppose; rebel (against).

panjep'um 반제품 half-finished goods; partly manufactured articles.

panji 반지 ring. *panjirŭl kkida* 반지를 끼다 put a ring on one's finger. *kyŏrhon[yak'on] panji* 결혼[약혼] 반지 wedding[engagement] ring.

panjitkori 반짇고리 work-box; housewife.

panju 반주 accompaniment. *panjuhada* 반주하다 accompany.

panmyŏn 반면 the other side; the reverse. *panmyŏne* 반면에 on the other hand.

pansa 반사 reflection. *pansahada* 반사하다 reflect; reverberate.

pansomae 반소매 half-sleeve; half-length sleeve. *pansomae syŏssŭ* 반소매 셔쓰 shirt with short (-length) sleeves.

pansŏng 반성 reflection; self-examination. *pansŏnghada* 반성하다 reflect on (oneself); reconsider.

panŭjil 바느질 needlework; sewing. *panŭjirhada* 바느질하다 sew; do needlework.

panŭl 바늘 needle; pin; hook. *ttŭgae panŭl* 뜨개 바늘 knitting needle. *nakshi panŭl* 낚시 바늘 fishhook. *panŭl pangsŏk* 바늘 방석 uncomfortable situation.

panyŏk 반역 treason; rebellion. *panyŏk'ada* 반역 하다 rebel (against); rise in revolt. *panyŏkcha* 반역자 traitor.

panyŏng 반영 reflection. *panyŏnghada* 반영하다 reflect; be reflected (in). 「다 cook[boil] rice.

pap 밥 boiled[cooked] rice. *pabŭl chitta* 밥을 짓

papkŭrŭt 밥그릇 rice bowl.

pappŏri 밥벌이 breadwinning. *pappŏrihada* 밥벌 이하다 make a living; earn one's daily bread.

pappŭda 바쁘다 (be) busy; (be) pressing; urgent. *pappŭge* 바쁘게 busily; hurriedly.

papsot 밥솥 rice pot[kettle].

papta 밟다 ① step[tread] on ② set foot on.

paraboda 바라보다 see; look (at); look out over; watch; gaze (at).

parada 바라다 ① expect; hope for; look forward to ② want; wish; desire ③ beg; request.

paraeda 바래다 fade; discolor; bleach.

param 바람 wind; breeze; gale; storm. *parami pulda* 바람이 불다 wind blows.

parammatta 바람맞다 be fooled[cheated]; be taken in; be rejected.

parhaeng 발행 publication; issue. *parhaenghada* 발행하다 publish; issue; bring out.

paro 바로 ① rightly; correctly; straight ② just; exactly ③ at once; immediately; right away.

parŏn 발언 utterance; speaking. *parŏnhada* 발언 하다 utter; speak.

parŭda 바르다 ① (be) straight; upright ② (be) right; righteous; just; correct.

parŭm 발음 pronunciation; articulation. *parŭm- hada* 발음하다 pronounce; articulate.

parŭnmal 바른말 truth; reasonable word; candid remark; plain word.

pasuda 바수다 break; smash; crush; grind.

pat'ang 바탕 ① nature; character; natural dispo- sition ② texture; ground.

pat 밭 field; farm. *oksusubat* 옥수수밭 corn field.

patta 받다 receive; accept; be given[granted].

pawi 바위 rock; crag.

payahŭro 바야흐로 *payahŭro ...haryŏ hada* 바야흐 로 …하려 하다 be going[about] to (do); be on the point of (doing).

peda 베다 cut; chop; saw; carve.

pegae 베개 pillow.

pe 베 hemp. *pet'ŭl* 베틀 loom.

pi 비 rain *piga oda[mŏtta]* 비가 오다[멎다] (It) rains

[stops raining]. *pie chŏtta* 비에 젖다 get wet with rain.

pi 비 broom; besom. *pitcharu* 빗자루 broom stick.

pi 비 monument. *pirŭl seuda* 비를 세우다 errect a monument.

piae 비애 sorrow; sadness; grief. *piaerŭl nŭkkida* 비애를 느끼다 feel sad.

pibida 비비다 ① rub; chafe ② make round; roll ③ mix. *sonŭl pibida* 손을 비비다 chafe[rub] one's hands.

pich'am 비참. *pich'amhan* 비참한 miserable; wretched; tragic; distressful.

pich'ida 비치다 ① shine ② be reflected[mirrored] (in) ③ show through.

pich'uda 비추다 ① shed[throw] light (on); light (up); illuminate ② reflect; mirror ③ hint; suggest.

pidan 비단 silk fabrics; silks.

pidulgi 비둘기 dove; pigeon. *pidulgip'a* 비둘기파 the doves; soft-liner.

pidŭm 비듬 dandruff; scurf.

pigida 비기다 end in a tie[draw].

pigongshik 비공식 informality. *pigongshikchŏgin* 비공식적인 unofficial; informal.

pigŏp 비겁. *pigŏp'an* 비겁한 cowardly; mean.

pigŭk 비극 tragedy. *pigŭkchŏk* 비극적 tragic.

pigul 비굴. *pigurhan* 비굴한 mean; servile.

pigwan(non) 비관(론) pessimism. *pigwanhada* 비관하다 be pessimistic.

pigyo 비교 comparison. *pigyohada* 비교하다 compare (A with B). *pigyojŏk(ŭro)* 비교적 (으로) comparative(ly).

pigyŏl 비결 secret (of); key (to); tip (for).

pihaeng 비행 flying; flight; aviation. *pihaenghada* 비행하다 fly; make a flight; take the air.

pihaenggi 비행기 aeroplane(*Eng.*); airplane(*Am.*); aircraft.

pihaengjang 비행장 airfield; airport; airdrome (*Am.*); aerodrome(*Eng.*).

pihaengsŏn 비행선 airship.

pihappŏpchŏk 비합법적 (being) illegal; unlawful; illicit.

pijopta 비좁다 (be) narrow and close[confined]; cramped.

pik'ida 비키다 avoid; shun; dodge; get out of the way; evade; shirk; step aside (from).

pikkoda 비꼬다 ① twist; twine ② make cynical remarks; speak ironically.

pilda 빌다 ① pray; wish ② beg; solicit ③ ask; request; entreat.

pilda, pillida 빌다, 빌리다 borrow; have[get] the loan (of); hire; rent; lease; charter.

pimaep'um 비매품 article not for sale; not for sale.

pimangnok 비망록 memorandum; memo.

pimil 비밀 secrecy; secret. *pimirŭi* 비밀의 secret; confidential.

pimujang 비무장. *pimujangŭi* 비무장의 demilitarized. *pimujang chidae* 비무장지대 demilitarized zone(DMZ).

pimun 비문 epitaph; inscription.

pimyŏng 비명 scream; shriek. *pimyŏngŭl chirŭda* 비명을 지르다 scream; shriek.

pinan 비난 blame; censure. *pinanhada* 비난하다

blame; censure; accuse.

pinbang 빈방 empty room; vacant room.

pinbŏn 빈번. *pinbŏnhan* 빈번한 frequent; incessant. *pinbŏnhi* 빈번히 frequently.

pinbu 빈부 wealth and poverty. *pinbuŭi ch'a* 빈부의 차 the gap between the rich and the poor.

pindae 빈대 housebug; bedbug(*Am.*).

pindaek'o 빈대코 flat nose.

pindaettŏk 빈대떡 mung bean[green-bean] pancake.

pinggwa 빙과 ices; ice creams; ice cakes.

pin-gon 빈곤 poverty; want; need. *pin-gonhan* 빈곤한 poor; needy; destitute.

pinjari 빈자리 vacant seat; vacant position. → **kongsŏk** 공석.

pinnada 빛나다 ① shine; be bright; gleam ② be brilliant.

pinnaeda 빛내다 light up; make (a thing) shine; brighten.

pinnagada 빗나가다 turn away[aside]; wander[deviate] (from); miss.

pinnong 빈농 poor farmer[peasant].

pint'ŏlt'ŏri 빈털터리 penniless person.

pint'ŭm 빈틈 opening; gap; chink; crack.

pinu 비누 soap. *karu pinu* 가루 비누 soap powder.

pinŭl 비늘 scale. *pinŭri innŭn* 비늘이 있는 scaly.

pinyak'an 빈약한 poor; scant; meager. *pinyak'an chishik* 빈약한 지식 poor[scanty] knowledge.

piok 비옥. *piok'ada* 비옥하다 (be) fertile; rich; productive.

pip'an 비판 criticism. *pip'anhada* 비판하다 criticize; comment (on); pass[give] judgment (on).

pip'yŏng 비평 review; comment; critique. *pip'yŏng-*

hada 비평하다 criticize; review.
pirida 비리다 (be) fishy; (be) bloody.
pirinnae 비린내 fishy smell; bloody smell.
pirok 비록 though; if; even if.
piroso 비로소 for the first time; not … until[till].
pirye 비례 proportion; ratio. *piryehada* 비례하다 be in proportion (to).
piryo 비료 fertilizer; manure.
pisang 비상. *pisanghada* 비상하다 (be) unusual; uncommon; extraordinary.
pisŏ 비서 (private) secretary. *pisŏshil* 비서실 secretariat (office).
pisŏk 비석 tombstone; stone monument.
pissada 비싸다 (be) expensive; costly; dear; high.
pisu 비수 dagger; dirk.
pisŭt'ada 비슷하다 (be) like; similar; look like.
pit 빛 ① light; rays; beam ② color; hue.
pit 빚 debt; loan. *pijŭl chida* 빚을 지다 run[get] into debt; borrow money.
pit 빗 comb. *pitchil* 빗질 combing. *pitchirhada* 빗질하다 comb (one's hair).
pit'al 비탈 slope; incline. *pit'alkil* 비탈길 slope.
pitchang 빗장 bolt; crossbar; bar.
pitkkal 빛깔 color; shade; hue; tint.
pitmatta 빗맞다 miss the mark; guess wrong.
pitpangul 빗방울 raindrops.
pitta 빚다 ① brew (*wine*) ② shape dough for (*rice cakes*) ③ cause; give rise to; bring about.
pitturŏjida 비뚤어지다 get crooked; slant; incline; be tilted; bent; be jealous of.
pit'ŭlda 비틀다 twist; wrench; screw.
pit'ŭlgŏrida 비틀거리다 stagger; totter; reel.

piutta 비웃다 laugh at; deride; jeer (at).

piyak 비약 leap; jump. *piyak'ada* 비약하다 leap; make rapid progress.

piyŏl 비열 meanness; baseness. *piyŏrhada* 비열하다 (be) mean; base; cowardly.

piyong 비용 cost; expense(s).

piyul 비율 ratio; percentage; rate. ⋯*ŭi piyullo* ⋯의 비율로 at the rate[ratio] of.

pobae 보배 treasure; precious things.

pŏbin 법인 juridical[legal] person; corporation. *pŏbinse* 법인세 corporation tax.

pobok 보복 retaliation; revenge. *pobok'ada* 보복하다 retaliate; revenge oneself on.

pŏbwon 법원 court; tribunal. *pŏbwonjang* 법원장 president of a court.

pobyŏng 보병 infantry; infantryman; foot soldier.

poch'ung 보충 supplement; replacement. *poch'unghada* 보충하다 supplement; fill up.

poda 보다 see; look at; witness; stare[gaze] at; watch; read; look over; view.

podap 보답 recompense; reward; compensation. *podap'ada* 보답하다 return; repay; reward; recompense; return; compensate.

podo 보도 report; news; information.

podo 보도 sidewalk(*Am.*); pavement(*Eng.*); footpath. *hoengdan podo* 횡단 보도 marked crossing (*Am.*).

podŭmda 보듬다 embrace; hug; clasp (a person) to one's bosom.

pogi 보기 example; instance.

pogo 보고 report; information. *pogohada* 보고하다 report; inform. *pogosŏ* 보고서 report.

pogŏn 보건 (preservation of) health; sanitation;

hygienics. *segye pogŏn kigu* 세계 보전 기구 World Health Organization(WHO).

pogŭm 복음 gospel. *pogŭm kyohoe* 복음 교회 Evangelical church.

pogŭp 보급 diffusion; popularization. *pogŭp'ada* 보급하다 diffuse; pervade; popularize.

pogwan 보관 custody; (safe) keeping. *pogwanhada* 보관하다 take custody[charge] of; take [have] (a thing) in charge.

pogyŏl 보결 supplement; substitute. *pogyŏrŭi* 보결의 supplementary.

pogyong 복용. *pogyonghada* 복용하다 take (medicine); use internally.

poho 보호 protection; safeguard. *pohohada* 보호하다 protect; shelter; safeguard.

pohŏm 보험 insurance. *pohŏmnyo* 보험료 premium. *pohŏm hoesa* 보험 회사 insurance company.

poida 보이다 ① see; catch sight of; be seen[visible]; appear ② show; let (a person) see.

pojang 보장 guarantee; security. *pojanghada* 보장하다 guarantee; secure. *sahoe pojang* 사회 보장 social security.

pojogŭm 보조금 subsidy; bounty; grant-in-aid.

pojon 보존 preservation; conservation. *pojonhada* preserve; conserve.

pŏjŏt'ada 버젓하다 (be) fair and square; be open. *pŏjŏshi* 버젓이 fairly; overtly.

pojŭng 보증 guarantee; assurance; security. *pojŭnghada* guarantee; assure; warrant. *pojŭng sup'yo* 보증 수표 certified check. *pojŭngin* 보증인 guarantor; surety.

pok 복 felicity; bliss; blessing; good luck. *poktoen*

복된 happy; blessed.

pokchang 복장 dress; attire; clothes.

pokchap 복잡 complexity; complication. *pokchap'an* 복잡한 (be) complicated; complex; tangled.

pokchi 복지 (public) welfare; well-being. *pokchi shisŏl* 복지 시설 welfare facilities.

pokchik 복직 resumption of office; reappointment. *pokchik'ada* 복직하다 resume office; be reinstalled.

pokchong 복종 obedience; submission. *pokchonghada* 복종하다 obey; submit.

pokkwon 복권 lottery ticket.

pokp'an 복판 middle; center; midst; heart. *pokp'ane* 복판에 in the middle of.

poksa 복사 reproduction; reprint. *poksahada* 복사하다 reproduce; copy.

poksu 복수 revenge; avenge; vengeance. *poksuhada* 복수하다 revenge oneself (on).

poksunga 복숭아 peach. *poksungakkot* 복숭아꽃 peach blossoms.

pokta 볶다 parch; roast; fry.

pokto 복도 corridor; passage; lobby; hallway (*Am.*).

poktŏkpang 복덕방 real estate agency.

pol 볼 cheek. *polmen sori* 볼멘 소리 angry voice.

pŏl 벌 bee. *pŏltte* 벌떼 swarm of bees. *pŏlchip* 벌집 beehive; honeycomb.

pŏl 벌 punishment; penalty. *pŏrhada[chuda]* 벌하다〔주다〕 punish; penalize.

pŏl 벌 set; suit. *ot han pol* 옷 한 벌 a suit of clothes.

pŏlda 벌다 earn; make (money); gain.

polgi 볼기 buttock; hip; rump.

pŏlgŭm 벌금 fine; penalty; forfeit.

pollae 본래 originally; primarily; naturally; by nature. *pollaeŭi* 본래의 original; natural.

pŏlle 벌레 insect; bug; worm; moth. *pŏlle mŏgŭn* 벌레 먹은 worm[moth]-eaten; vermicular.

pŏllida 벌리다 open; widen; leave space.

polmanhada 볼만하다 be worth seeing; be worthy of notice.

pom 봄 spring(time). *pomŭi* 봄의 spring; vernal.

pŏm 범 tiger; tigress. →**horangi** 호랑이.

pŏmhaeng 범행 crime; offense.

pŏmin 범인 criminal; offender; culprit.

pŏmjoe 범죄 crime; criminal act. *pŏmjoeŭi* 범죄의 criminal.

pŏmnyul 법률 law; statute. *pŏmnyurŭi* 법률의 legal. *pŏmnyulga* 법률가 jurist; lawyer.

pomo 보모 nurse; nursery attendant; kindergarten teacher; kindergartner.

pŏmpŏp 범법 violation of the law. *pŏmpŏp'ada* 범법하다 violate[break] the law.

pomul 보물 treasure; jewel; valuables.

pŏmwi 범위 extent; scope; sphere; range; limit; bounds. *pŏmwi nae[oe]e* 범위 내[외]에 within [beyond] the limits[scope].

ponaeda 보내다 send; forward; transmit.

ponbogi 본보기 example; model; pattern.

pŏnbŏni 번번이 every[each] time; whenever; as often as; always.

ponbu 본부 headquarters; main[head] office.

pŏnch'ang 번창 prosperity. *pŏnch'anghada* prosper; thrive; flourish.

pŏn-gae 번개 (flash of) lightning.

ponggŏn 봉건 feudalism; feudal system. *ponggŏn-*

jŏk 봉건적 feudal. *ponggŏnjuŭi* 봉건주의 feudalism. *ponggŏn chedo* 봉건 제도 feudal system.

ponggŭp 봉급 salary; pay; wages.

ponghwa 봉화 signal[beacon] fire; rocket.

pongji 봉지 paper bag.

pongmyŏn 복면 mask; disguise; veil. *pongmyŏnŭi* 복면의 masked; in disguise. *pongmyŏn kangdo* 복면 강도 masked robber.

pongori 봉오리 bud. *pongorirŭl maetta* 봉오리를 맺다 have[bear] buds. →**kkotpongori** 꽃봉오리.

pŏngŏri 벙어리 dumb person; mute.

pongsa 봉사 service; attendance. *pongsahada* 봉사하다 serve; render service; attend on.

pongsŏnhwa 봉선화 (garden) balsam; touch-me-not.

pongt'u 봉투 envelope.

ponguri 봉우리 peak; summit; top. *sanponguri* 산봉우리 mountain top[peak].

pŏnho 번호 number; mark. *pŏnhop'yo* 번호표 number ticket[plate].

ponjil 본질 essence; true[intrinsic] nature.

ponjŏk 본적 one's domicile; one's place of register.

ponjŏm 본점 ① head[main] office ② this office.

ponjŏn 본전 principal (sum); capital; prime cost.

ponin 본인 the person in question; the person himself[herself]; principal.

pŏnjida 번지다 spread; run; blot.

ponmun 본문 body (of a letter); text (of a treaty).

ponnŭng 본능 instinct. *ponnŭngjŏk[ŭro]* 본능적 [으로] instinctive[ly].

ponsa 본사 head office; main office.

ponshim 본심 one's real intention; one's heart.

pont'o 본토 mainland; the country proper.

pŏnyŏk 번역 translation. *pŏnyŏk'ada* 번역하다 translate〔render〕into; put (into).

pŏp 법 law; rule; custom; practice.

pŏpch'ik 법칙 law; rule.

poram 보람 worth; effect; result. *poram innŭn* 보람 있는 fruitful; effective.

poratpit 보랏빛 purple; violet. *yŏnboratpit* 연보랏빛 lilac.

pori 보리 barley. *porich'a* 보리차 barley tea.

pŏrida 버리다 ① throw〔cast, fling〕away ② abandon; forsake; give up.

pŏrŏjida 벌어지다 ① split; crack ② open; smile ③ occur; come about ④ become wide.

porŭm 보름 half a month.

pŏrŭt 버릇 habit; acquired tendency; propensity. *…hanŭn pŏrŭshi itta* …하는 버릇이 있다 have a habit of doing.

poryu 보류 reservation. *poryuhada* 보류하다 reserve; shelve.

posalp'ida 보살피다 take care of; look after; tend.

posang 보상 compensation; indemnity. *posanghada* 보상하다 compensate for; make up for.

posŏk 보석 jewel; gem; precious stone. *posŏksang* 보석상 jewel's (shop).

posŏk 보석 bail; bailment. *posŏk'ada* 보석하다 release (a person) on bail; bail.

pŏsŏn 버선 Korean socks.

pŏsŏt 버섯 mushroom; toadstool; fungus.

posu 보수 remuneration; reward; fee; pay.

posu 보수. *posujuŭi* 보수주의 conservatism. *posudangwŏn* 보수당원 Conservative; Tory (*Eng.*).

pŏt 벗 friend; companion; mate; company.

pot'aeda 보태다 ① supplement; make up (for); help out ② add (up); sum up.

pŏt'ida 버티다 endure; stand; bear.

pŏtkida 벗기다 ① peel; rind; pare ② take[strip] off; strip of; help off.

pot'ong 보통 ordinarily; commonly; normally. *pot'ongŭi* 보통의 usual; ordinary; common.

pŏtta 벗다 take[put] off; slip[fling] off.

poyak 보약 restorative; tonic; bracer.

poyŏjuda 보여주다 show; let (a person) see; display.

ppaeatta 빼앗다 take away from; snatch from; plunder; deprive of.

ppaeda 빼다 ① pull[take] out; draw; extract ② subtract[deduct] (from) ③ remove; wash off ④ omit; exclude.

ppaekppaek'ada 빽빽하다 (be) close[dense, thick].

ppaengsoni 뺑소니 flight; escape. *ppaengsonich'ida* 뺑소니치다 run away; take (to) flight.

ppajida 빠지다 fall[get] into; sink; go down.

ppalda 빨다 ① sip; suck; lick ② wash.

ppallae 빨래 wash; washing. *ppallaehada* 빨래하다 wash. *ppallaetchul* 빨랫줄 clothesline.

ppalli 빨리 quickly; fast; rapidly; in haste; soon; immediately.

ppaltae 빨대 straw; sipper.

ppang 빵 bread. *ppangŭl kupta* 빵을 굽다 bake [toast] bread.

ppappat'ada 빳빳하다 ① (be) stiff; straight ② (be) headstrong; unyielding.

pparŭda 빠르다 ① (be) quick; fast; swift; speedy ② (be) early; premature.

ppattŭrida 빠뜨리다 throw into (a river); trap;

tempt; lure.

ppŏkkugi, ppŏkkuksae 뻐꾸기, 뻐꾹새 cuckoo.

ppong 뽕 mulberry. *ppongnip* 뽕잎 mulberry leaves. *ppongnamu pat* 뽕나무 밭 mulberry field.

ppopta 뽑다 ① pull[take] out; draw; extract ② select; pick[single] out; elect ③ enlist; enroll.

ppŏtta 뻗다 ① lengthen; stretch; extend ② collapse; knock out ③ develop.

ppumta 뿜다 belch; emit; spout; spurt; gush out.

ppun 뿐 only; alone; merely. *ppunman anira* 뿐 만 아니라 besides; moreover; in addition.

ppuri 뿌리 root. *ppuri kip'ŭn* 뿌리 깊은 deep-rooted.

ppurida 뿌리다 sprinkle; strew; scatter; diffuse.

ppyam 뺨 cheek. *ppyamŭl ch'ida* 뺨을 치다 slap (a person) on the cheek.

ppyŏ 뼈 bone. *ppyŏdae* 뼈대 frame.

pubu 부부 man[husband] and wife; married couple.

pubun 부분 part; portion; section. *pubunjŏguro* 부분적으로 partially.

puch'ae 부채 fan; folding fan.

puch'ida 붙이다 ① put[fix, stick] ② attach[fasten]; paste ③ apply.

puch'ida 부치다 send; mail; remit; forward. *tonŭl puch'ida* 돈을 부치다 remit money.

Puch'ŏ 부처 Buddha.

puch'ongni 부총리 Deputy Prime Minister.

puch'ugida 부추기다 incite; instigate; agitate.

pudae 부대 unit; corps; detachment. *pudaejang* 부대장 commander.

pudakch'ida 부닥치다 come upon[across]; hit upon; encounter; meet with.

pudam 부담 burden; charge; responsibility. *pudam-*

hada 부담하다 bear; shoulder; stand; share.

pudang 부당. *pudanghada* 부당하다 (be) unjust; unfair; unreasonable.

pudi 부디 without fail; by all means; in any cost.

pudich'ida 부딪히다 collide with; bump against [into].

pudo 부도 dishonor. *pudonada* 부도나다 be dishonored. *pudo sup'yo* 부도 수표 dishonored check.

pudongsan 부동산 immovable property; real estate; realty. *pudongsanŏpcha* 부동산업자 realtor (*Am.*)

pudu 부두 quay; pier; wharf; water front.

pudŭrŏpta 부드럽다 (be) soft; tender; mild; gentle. *pudŭrŏpke* 부드럽게 softly; mildly; tenderly.

pugi 부기 book-keeping.

pugo 부고 obituary; announcement of death.

pugun 부군 one's husband.

pugŭn 부근 neighborhood; vicinity. *pugŭnŭi* 부근 의 neighboring; nearby; adjacent.

pugyŏl 부결 rejection. *pugyŏrhada* 부결하다 reject; turn down; decide against; vote down.

puha 부하 subordinate; follower.

puho 부호 rich man; man of wealth.

puho 부호 sign; mark; cipher; symbol.

puhŭng 부흥 revival; reconstruction; restoration; rehabilitation; renaissance. *puhŭnghada* 부흥하다 be reconstructed; be revived.

puim 부임. *puimhada* 부임하다 leave[start] for one's (new) post.

puin 부인 woman; lady. *puinpyŏng* 부인병 women's disease[ailments].

puin 부인 Mrs.; Madam; wife; lady. *Kimssi puin* 김씨 부인 Mrs. Kim.

puin 부인 denial; disapproval. *puinhada* 부인하다 deny; disapprove; say no.

puja 부자 rich man; man of wealth.

pujang 부장 head[chief, director] of a department.

puji 부지 (building) site; plot; lot. *kŏnch'uk puji* 건축 부지 building site.

pujirŏnhada 부지런하다 (be) industrious; diligent. *pujirŏnhi* 부지런히 diligently; industriously; hard.

pujo 부조 ① help; aid; support ② congratulatory gift; condolence money.

pujok 부족 shortage; deficiency; deficit; lack. *pujok'ada* 부족하다 be short (of); lack.

pujŏktang 부적당 unfitness; unsuitableness. *pujŏktanghada* 부적당하다 (be) unfit (for).

pujŏng 부정 injustice; dishonest; unlawfulness. *pujŏnghan* 부정한 unjust; foul; unlawful.

pujŏnggi 부정기. *pujŏnggiŭi* 부정기의 irregular; nonscheduled.

pukkŭk 북극 the North Pole. *pukkŭgŭi* 북극의 arctic; polar. *pukkŭksŏng* 북극성 polestar.

pukkŭrŏpta 부끄럽다 (be) shameful; disgraceful.

pukta 붉다 (be) red; crimson; scarlet.

pul 불 fire; flame; blaze. *purŭl puch'ida* 불을 붙이다 light a fire.

pulch'injŏl 불친절 unkindness. *pulch'injŏrhan* 불친절한 unkind; unfriendly.

pulch'ungbun 불충분 insufficiency; inadequacy *pulch'ungbunhan* 불충분한 insufficient; not enough.

pulda 불다 blow; breathe. *nap'arŭl pulda* 나팔을 불다 blow a trumpet.

pulganŭng 불가능 impossibility. *pulganŭnghada* 불가능하다 (be) impossible[unattainable].

pulgil 불길. *pulgirhan* 불길한 unlucky; ominous.

pulgong 불공 Buddhist mass.

pulgongp'yŏng 불공평. *pulgongp'yŏnghada* 불공평
하다 (be) partial; unfair; unjust.

pulgu 불구 deformity. *pulguŭi* 불구의 deformed;
cripple; disabled. *pulguja* 불구자 disabled[deformed] person; cripple.

pulgusok 불구속. *pulgusogŭro* 불구속으로 without
physical restraint.

pulgyo 불교 Buddhism. *pulgyodo* 불교도 Buddhist.

pulgyŏl 불결. *pulgyŏrhada* 불결하다 (be) dirty;
unclean; filthy; unsanitary.

pulgyŏnggi 불경기 hard[bad] time; slump; dullness; depression.

pulgyuch'ik 불규칙 irregularity. *pulgyuch'ik'ada*
불규칙하다 (be) irregular; unsystematic.

puljadongch'a 불자동차 →**sobangch'a** 소방차.

pulk'wae 불쾌 unpleasantness; displeasure. *pulk'waehada* 불쾌하다 feel unpleasant[displeased].

pulli 분리 separation; segregation. *pullihada* 분
리하다 separate (from); isolate; segregate.

pullyang 분량 quantity; measure; dose.

pulman 불만 dissatisfaction; discontent. *pulmanŭi*
불만의 dissatisfied.

pulmo 불모. *pulmoŭi* 불모의 barren; sterile. *pulmoji* 불모지 barren[waste] land.

pulmyŏnchŭng 불면증 insomnia. *pulmyŏnchŭng
hwanja* 불면증 환자 insomniac.

pulmyŏngye 불명예 dishonor; disgrace; shame.
pulmyŏngyehan 불명예한 dishonorable; shameful;
disgraceful.

pulp'iryo 불필요 *pulp'iryohan* 불필요한 unnecessary; needless. *pulp'iryohage* 불필요하게 unnecessarily; needlessly.

pulpŏp 불법 unlawfulness; illegality. *pulpŏbŭi* 불법의 unlawful; illegal; unjust. *pulpŏp ipkuk* 불법 입국 illegal entry[immigration].

pulp'yŏn 불편 inconvenience. *pulp'yŏnhada* 불편하다 (be) inconvenient.

pulp'yŏng 불평 discontent; complaint; grievance. *pulp'yŏnghada* 불평하다 grumble; complain.

pulp'yŏngdŭng 불평등 inequality. *pulp'yŏngdŭnghada* 불평등하다 (be) unequal; unfair.

pulsang 불상 image of Buddha; Buddhist image.

pulson 불손 insolence. *pulsonhan* 불손한 insolent; haughty; arrogant.

pulssanghada 불쌍하다 (be) poor; pitiful; pitiable; miserable.

pulssuk 불쑥 suddenly; unexpectedly; abruptly.

pult'ada 불타다 burn; blaze; be on fire[in flames].

pultan 불단 Buddhist altar.

pumbida 붐비다 (be) crowded; congested; jammed; packed; thronged.

pumo 부모 father and mother; parents. *pumoŭi* 부모의 parental.

pumun 부문 section; department; class; group; category.

pun 분 minute (of an hour). *shibobun* 15분 quarter; fifteen minutes.

punbae 분배 distribution; sharing. *punbaehada* 분배하다 distribute; divide; allot.

punch'im 분침 minute hand.

pun-gae 분개 indignation; resentment. *pun-gaehada* 분개하다 (be) indignant; resent.

pungdae 붕대 bandage; dressing. *pungdaerŭl kamta* 붕대를 감다 apply a bandage (to); dress (a wound).

punhae 분해 analysis. *punhaehada* 분해하다 analyze; dissolve.

punhyang 분향. *punhyanghada* 분향하다 burn [offer] incense (for the dead).

punjae 분재 potted plant; pot-planting.

punjang 분장 make up; disguise. *punjanghada* 분장하다 make[dress] up as; disguise oneself as.

punji 분지 basin; hollow; valley.

punjŏm 분점 branch shop; branch office.

punju 분주. *punjuhada* 분주하다 (be) busy; busily engaged.

punmal 분말 powder; flour; dust

punmyŏng 분명 clearness. *punmyŏnghada* 분명하다 (be) clear; distinct; obvious. *punmyŏnghi* 분명히 clearly; apparently.

punno 분노 fury; rage; indignation. *punnohada* 분노하다 get[be] angry; be enraged.

punp'il 분필 chalk.

punshik 분식 powdered food; flour.

punshil 분실 loss. *punshirhada* 분실하다 lose; be lost; be missing.

punsŏk 분석 analysis. *punsŏk'ada* 분석하다 assay; analyze; make an analysis (of).

punsu 분수 fountain; jet (of water).

punswae 분쇄 *punswaehada* 분쇄하다 shatter (a thing) to pieces; crush; smash.

punwigi 분위기 atmosphere; surroundings.

punya 분야 sphere; field; province. *yŏn-gu punya* 연구 분야 field[area] of study.

punyŏ 부녀 father and daughter.

punyŏja 부녀자 woman; womenfolk; fair sex.

puŏk 부엌 kitchen.

puŏp 부업 sideline; subsidiary business.

pup'ae 부패 putrefaction; rotting. *pup'aehada* 부
패하다 rot; addle.

pup'i 부피 bulk; volume; size.

purak 부락 village; village community. *purangmin*
부락민 village folk.

puran 불안 uneasiness; anxiety; unrest. *puranhan*
불안한 uneasy; anxious.

purhaeng 불행 unhappiness; misfortune; ill-luck.
purhaeng 불행한 unhappy; unfortunate. *pur-
haenghi(do)* 불행히 (도) unfortunately.

purhamni 불합리 *purhamnihan* 불합리한 irrational;
illogical; unreasonable.

purhapkyŏk 불합격 failure; rejection. *purhapkyŏ-
k'ada* 불합격하다 (be) disqualified; fail to pass.

purhwa 불화 trouble; discord. *purhwahada* 불화
하다 be on bad terms (with); be in discord
(with); be at strife[odds] (with).

purhwang 불황 depression; slump; recession. *pur-
hwangŭi* 불황의 inactive; dull; stagnant.

puri 부리 bill; beak.

purida 부리다 ① keep (person, horse, etc.) at
work; set[put] to work; hire; employ ② manage;
handle; run ③ exercise; yield.

purip 불입 payment. *purip'ada* 불입하다 pay in;
pay up. *puripkŭm* 불입금 money due.

purŏ 부러 on purpose; intentionally; deliberately.
purŏ kŏjinmarhada 부러 거짓말하다 lie deliberately. → **ilburŏ** 일부러.

purok 부록 supplement; appendix (to a book).

purŏnada 불어나다 increase; gain; grow.

purŏpta 부럽다 (be) enviable. *purŏun dŭshi* 부러운 듯이 enviously; with envy.

purŭda 부르다 ① call; hail ② name; designate ③ bid; offer ④ sing ⑤ shout ⑥ send for; invite ⑦ full; inflated.

purŭjitta 부르짖다 shout; cry; exclaim.

purun 불운 misfortune; ill-luck. *purunhan* 불운한 unfortunate; unlucky.

purut'unghada 부루퉁하다 ① (be) swollen; bloated ② (be) sulky. *purut'unghan ŏlgul* 부루퉁한 얼굴 swollen face; sulky look.

purwanjŏn 불완전 imperfection; incompleteness. *purwanjŏnhan* 불완전한 imperfect; incomplete.

puryaburya 부랴부랴 hurriedly; in a great hurry.

pusang 부상 wound; injury; cut; bruise. *pusanghada* 부상하다 be wounded; get hurt.

pusanmul 부산물 by-product; residual product.

pushida 부시다 dazzling; glaring.

pusŏjida 부서지다 break; be smashed [broken, wrecked]; go [fall] to pieces.

pusok 부속. *pusok'ada* 부속하다 belong (to); be attached to. *pusogŭi* 부속의 attached; belonging to; dependent.

pusu 부수 number of copies; circulation.

pusuip 부수입 additional [side] income.

pusŭrŏgi 부스러기 bit; fragment; scraps; adds and ends; crumbs; chips.

pusŭrŏm 부스럼 boil; ulcer; abscess; tumor.

put 붓 writing brush; brush; pen.

putta 붙다 stick (to); adhere [cling] (to); attach

oneself to; glue; paste.

putta 붓다 pour (into, out); fill with; put (water in a bowl); feed (a lamp with oil).

putta 붓다 swell; become swollen; bloat.

put'ak 부탁 request; favor; solicitation. *put'ak'ada* 부탁하다 ask; request; beg.

putchapta 붙잡다 seize; grasp; catch; take hold of.

puttŭlda 붙들다 ① catch; seize; take hold of; grasp[grab] ② arrest; capture.

puŭi 부의 obituary gift. *puŭigŭm* 부의금 condolence money. ⌈staff man.

puwŏn 부원 member of the staff; staff (member);

puyang 부양 support; maintenance. *puyanghada* 부양하다 support; maintain. *puyang kajok* 부양 가족 dependent family.

puyu 부유. *puyuhada* 부유하다 be rich; wealthy.

pyŏ 벼 rice plant; paddy.

pyŏk 벽 wall; partition. *pyŏkpo* 벽보 bill; poster.

pyŏl 별 star. *pyŏlpit* 별빛 starlight.

pyŏlchang 별장 villa; country house; cottage(*Am.*).

pyŏlgwan 별관 annex; extension; outhouse.

pyŏllo 별로 especially; particularly; in particular.

pyŏndong 변동 change; fluctuation. *pyŏndonghada* 변동하다 change; alter.

pyŏnduri 변두리 outskirts; border. *Sŏurŭi pyŏnduri* 서울의 변두리 outskirts of Seoul.

pyŏng 병 bottle; jar.

pyŏng 병 disease; sickness (*Am.*); illness (*Eng.*). *pyŏngdŭn* 병든 sick (*Am.*); ill (*Eng.*); unwell.

pyŏngguwan 병구완 nursing; tending (a sick person).

pyŏn-gi 변기 chamber pot; night stool.

pyŏngja 병자 sick person; patient.

pyŏngp'ung 병풍 folding screen.

pyŏngsa 병사 soldier; private.

pyŏngshil 병실 sickroom; (sick) ward; sick bay.

pyŏngshin 병신 deformed person; cripple; disabled person.

pyŏngwŏn 병원 hospital; nursing home. *pyŏngwŏne ibwŏnhada* 병원에 입원하다 go into hospital.

pyŏngyŏk 병역 military service.

pyŏn-gyŏng 변경 change; alteration. *pyŏn-gyŏnghada* 변경하다 change; alter.

pyŏnhada 변하다 change; undergo a change; vary. *pyŏnhagi shwiun* 변하기 쉬운 changeable.

pyŏnho 변호 defense; justification. *pyŏnhohada* 변호하다 plead; defend; speak for.

pyŏnhosa 변호사 lawyer; attorney(*Am.*); barrist❍ the bar;

pyŏnhwa 변화 change; variation; alteration. *pyŏnhwahada* 변화하다 change; turn.

pyŏnjang 변장 disguise. *pyŏnjanghada* 변장하다 disguise oneself (as); be disguised (as).

pyŏnjŏl 변절 betrayal; treachery. *pyŏnjŏrhada* 변절하다 apostatize; change[turn] one's coat.

pyŏnjŏnso 변전소 (transformer) substation.

pyŏnsang 변상 payment; compensation. *pyŏnsanghada* 변상하다 pay for; reimburse.

pyŏnso 변소 lavatory; water closet; toilet room; rest room.

pyŏrak 벼락 thunder; thunderbolt. *pyŏrak kat'ŭn* 벼락 같은 thunderous.

pyŏrak puja 벼락 부자 mushroom[overnight] millionaire; upstart.

pyŏrang 벼랑 cliff; precipice; bluff.
pyŏru 벼루 inkstone; ink slab. *pyŏrutchip* 벼룻집 inkstone case.
pyŏsŭl 벼슬 government post[service].
pyŏt 볕 sunshine; sunlight.

ⵗ P ⵗ

p'a 파 ① branch of a family[clan] ② party; faction; sect. *churyup'a* 주류파 main stream faction.
p'a 파 Welsh onion.
p'abŏl 파벌 clique; faction.
p'abyŏng 파병 dispatch of forces[troops]. *p'abyŏnghada* 파병하다 dispatch troops[forces].
p'ach'ul 파출 *p'ach'urhada* 파출하다 dispatch; send out. *p'ach'ulbu* 파출부 visiting housekeeper. *p'ach'ulso* 파출소 police box.
p'ada 파다 dig; excavate; drill.
p'adakkŏrida 파닥거리다 flap; flutter; flop.
p'ado 파도 waves; billows; surge.
p'ae 패 ① tag; tablet ② group; gang; company.
p'aebae 패배 defeat; reverse.
p'aeda 패다 ① strike; batter ② chop firewood ③ come to ears ④ be dug[hollowed].
p'aejŏn 패전 defeat. *p'aejŏn-guk* 패전국 defeated nation. *p'aejŏn t'usu* 패전 투수 losing pitcher.
p'aemul 패물 personal ornament; trinkets.
p'aenggaech'ida 팽개치다 throw away[aside]; fling away; cast away.
p'agoe 파괴 destruction. *p'agoehada* 파괴하다 destroy; break. *p'agoejŏgin* 파괴적인 destructive. *p'agoeja* 파괴자 destroyer.

p'ahon 파혼. *p'ahonhada* 파혼하다 break (off) engagement.

p'al 팔 arm. *p'arŭl kkigo* 팔을 끼고 with folded arms; (walk) arm in arm (with).

p'alda 팔다 sell; deal in.

p'alkkumch'i 팔꿈치 elbow. ⌜eightieth.

p'alship 팔십, 80 eighty. *chep'alship* 제80 the

p'altchi 팔찌 bracelet; armlet(*Eng.*).

p'alttukshigye 팔뚝시계 wrist watch.

p'amutta 파묻다 bury; inter.

p'amyŏl 파멸 ruin; destruction. *p'amyŏrhada* 파멸하다 be ruined[wrecked]; go to ruin.

p'andan 판단 judgment; decision. *p'andanhada* 판단하다 judge.

p'an-gŏmsa 판검사 judges and public prosecutors.

p'an-gyŏl 판결 judgment; decision. *p'an-gyŏrhada* 판결하다 decide (on a case).

p'anja 판자 board; plank. *p'anjachip* 판자집 barrack; shack.

p'anmae 판매 sale; selling. *p'anmaehada* 판매하다 sell; deal in.

p'ansa 판사 judge; justice.

p'ansori 판소리 Korean (classical) solo opera drama.

p'aŏp 파업 strike; walkout(*Am.*). *p'aŏp'ada* 파업하다 go on strike; walk out.

p'ap'yŏn 파편 (broken) piece; fragment; splinter.

p'arae 파래 green laver; sea lettuce.

p'arang 파랑 blue(color); green. *p'arangsae* 파랑새 bluebird.

p'arat'a 파랗다 ① (be) blue; green ② (be) pale; pallid.

p'ari 파리 fly. *p'ariyak* 파리약 flypoison. *p'ari-*

ch'ae 파리채 fly flap.

p'arwol 팔월 August.

p'aryŏmch'i 파렴치. *p'aryŏmch'ihan* 파렴치한 ① shameless; infamous ② shameless fellow.

p'asan 파산 bankruptcy; insolvency. *p'asanhada* 파산하다 become bankrupt.

p'ason 파손 damage; injury; breakdown. *p'asondoeda* 파손되다 be damaged; break down.

p'ayŏl 파열 explosion; bursting. *p'ayŏrhada* 파열 하다 explode; burst (up); rupture.

p'i 피 blood. *p'iga nada* 피가 나다 bleed; blood runs[flows] out.

p'ibu 피부 skin. *p'ibusaek* 피부색 skin color.

p'igon 피곤 fatigue; tiredness. *p'igonhada* 피곤하 다 (be) tired; fatigued.

p'ihada 피하다 avoid; dodge; evade; keep away from; shirk; shun.

p'ihae 피해 damage; injury; harm. *p'ihaerŭl ipta* 피해를 입다 be damaged[injured] (by).

p'iim 피임 contraception. *p'iimnyak* 피임약 contraceptive. *p'iimhada* 피임하다 prevent conception.

p'ilsup'um 필수품 necessaries; requisites. *saenghwal p'ilsup'um* 생활 필수품 daily necessaries.

p'ilt'ong 필통 pencil[brush] case; brush[pen] stand.

p'inan 피난 refuge. *p'inanhada* 피난하다 take refuge. *p'inanmin* 피난민 refugee.

p'inggye 핑계 excuse; pretext. *p'inggyerŭl taeda* 핑계를 대다 make[find] an excuse.

p'injan 핀잔 *p'injanŭl chuda* 핀잔을 주다 rebuke; snub; scold.

p'iri 피리 pipe; flute. *p'iri sori* 피리 소리 sound

of a flute.

p'iro 피로 fatigue; weariness; exhaustion. *p'iro-han* 피로한 (be) tired; weary.

p'iryo 필요 necessity; need. *p'iryohan* 필요한 necessary; essential.

p'isŏ 피서 summering. *p'isŏ kada* 피서 가다 go to a summer resort.

p'iuda 피우다 ① make[build] a fire ② smoke; burn (incense) ③ bloom.

p'ŏbutta 퍼붓다 ① pour[shower, rain] upon ② rain in torrents.

p'odo 포도 grape. *p'odobat* 포도밭 vineyard. p'odo-ju 포도주 (grape)wine; port(wine).

p'ogi 포기 abandonment. *p'ogihada* 포기하다 give up; abandon.

p'ogŭnhada 포근하다 ① (be) mild; warm ② (be) soft and comfortable.

p'ogyo 포교 missionary work. *p'ogyohada* 포교하다 preach.

p'oham 포함. *p'ohamhada* 포함하다 contain; include. ···*ŭl p'ohamhayŏ* ···을 포함하여 including.

p'ojang 포장 packing. *p'ojanghada* 포장하다 pack; wrap (up). *p'ojangji* 포장지 packing[wrapping] paper.

p'ojang 포장 pavement; paving. *p'ojanghada* 포장하다 pave. *p'ojang toro* 포장 도로 pavement.

p'ŏjida 퍼지다 spread out; get broader; be propagated; get abroad.

p'ok 폭 width; breadth. *p'ogi nŏlbŭn* 폭이 넓은 wide; broad. *p'ogi chobŭn* 폭이 좁은 narrow.

p'ŏk 퍽 very (much); quite; awfully; highly.

p'ok'aeng 폭행 (act of) violence. *p'ok'aenghada*

폭행하다 do violence; commit an outrage.

p'okkun 폭군 tyrant; despot.

p'okkyŏk 폭격 bombing. *p'okkyŏk'ada* 폭격하다 bomb; make a bombing raid.

p'okpal 폭발 explosion. *p'okparhada* 폭발하다 explode; burst; blow up; erupt.

p'okp'o 폭포 waterfall; falls.

p'okp'ung 폭풍 storm; tempest; typhoon; hurricane. *p'okp'ung chuŭibo* 폭풍 주의보 storm alert.

p'okshinhada 폭신하다 (be) soft; spongy; cushiony.

p'okt'an 폭탄 bomb. *wonja[suso] p'okt'an* 원자[수소] 폭탄 atomic[hydrogen] bomb.

p'oktong 폭동 riot; uprising; disturbance.

p'ŏllŏkkŏrida, p'ŏllŏgida 펄럭거리다, 펄럭이다 flutter; flap; flicker; waver.

p'omok 포목 dry goods(*Am.*); drapery(*Eng.*). *p'omokchŏm* 포목점 dry goods store(*Am.*); draper's shop (*Eng.*).

p'ŏnaeda 퍼내다 bail[dip, scoop] out; pump out.

p'ongno 폭로 exposure; disclosure. *p'ongnohada* 폭로하다 expose; disclose; lay bare.

p'ongnyŏk 폭력 force; violence. *p'ongnyŏgŭro* 폭력으로 by force. *p'ongnyŏkpae* 폭력배 hooligans.

p'oro 포로 prisoner of war(POW). *p'oro suyongso* 포로 수용소 prisoner's[concentration] camp.

p'osu 포수 ① catch(er) ② gunner; shooter.

p'ot'al 포탈 evasion of tax. →**t'alse** 탈세.

p'ot'an 포탄 shell; cannonball.

p'ŏttŭrida 퍼뜨리다 spread; diffuse; circulate.

p'udaejŏp 푸대접 inhospitality; cold treatment. *p'udaejŏp'ada* 푸대접하다 treat coldly.

p'ul 풀 grass; weed. *p'ulppuri* 풀뿌리 grass root.

p'ullip 풀잎 grass leaf.

p'ul 풀 paste; starch. *p'ullo puch'ida* 풀로 붙이다 stick with paste; paste (up).

p'ulbat 풀밭 grass field; meadow; lawn.

p'ulda 풀다 ① untie; unpack; undo ② solve.

p'umta 품다 hold in one's bosom; embrace; hug.

p'umjil 품질 quality. *p'umjil kwalli* 품질 관리 quality control.

p'ungbu 풍부 abundance; plenty. *p'ungbuhan* 풍부한 abundant; rich; wealthy.

p'ungch'a 풍차 windmill; penwheel.

p'unggŭm 풍금 organ. *p'unggŭmŭl ch'ida* 풍금을 치다 play (on) the organ.

p'unggyŏng 풍경 landscape; scenery; view.

p'ungjak 풍작 good[rich] harvest.

p'ungmun 풍문 rumor; hearsay; (town) talk.

p'ungno 풍로 (portable) cooking stove; small kitchen range.

p'ungsok 풍속 manners; customs; public morals.

p'ungsŏn 풍선 balloon. *komu p'ungsŏn* 고무 풍선 rubber[toy] balloon.

p'ungsŭp 풍습 →**p'ungsok** 풍속.

p'ungt'o 풍토 natural features; climate.

p'unnagi 풋나기 greenhorn; novice; green hand.

p'unton 푼돈 loose cash; odd money; broken money; pennies.

p'unyŏm 푸념 idle complaint. *p'unyŏmhada* 푸념하다 complain; grumble; grievance.

p'urŏjuda 풀어주다 set (a person) free; liberate.

p'urŭda 푸르다 (be) blue; azure; pale.

p'ye 폐 lungs. *p'yeam* 폐암 cancer of lung. *p'yepyŏng*[*kyŏrhaek*] 폐병[결핵] tuberculosis.

p'yech'a 폐차 disused[useless] car; scrapped car [vehicle]; out-of-service car.

p'yegyŏrhaek 폐결핵 tuberculosis (T. B.).

p'yehoe 폐회 closing of meeting. *p'yehoesa* 폐회사 closing address.

p'yeji 폐지 abolition. *p'yejihada* 폐지하다 abolish; do away with; discontinue.

p'yemak 폐막. *p'yemak'ada* 폐막하다 end; close; come to a close; The curtain falls.

p'yemul 폐물 waste material; refuse; junk.

p'yeryŏm 폐렴 pneumonia. *kŭpsŏng p'yeryŏm* 급성 폐렴 acute pneumonia.

p'yo 표 table; list. *shiganp'yo* 시간표 time table. *chŏngkap'yo* 정가표 price list.

p'yobŏm 표범 leopard; panther.

p'yobon 표본 specimen; sample.

p'yŏda 펴다 spread (out); open; unfold.

p'yohyŏn 표현 expression. *p'yohyŏnhada* 표현하다 express; be representative[expressive] of.

p'yoje 표제 title; heading; caption (*Am.*).

p'yoji 표지 cover; binding. *kajuk p'yoji* 가죽 표지 leather cover.

p'yojŏng 표정 expression; look. *sŭlp'ŭn p'yojŏng* 슬픈 표정 sad expression.

p'yojun 표준 standard; level. *p'yojunŏ* 표준어 standard language.

p'yŏlli 편리 convenience; facilities. *p'yŏllihan* 편리한 convenient; expedient.

p'yŏnan 편안. *p'yŏnanhan* 편안한 peaceful; tranquil. *p'yŏnanhi* 편안히 peacefully; quietly.

p'yŏnch'ant'a 편찮다 (be) ill; unwell; indisposed.

p'yŏndo 편도 one way. *p'yŏndo sŭngch'akwon* 편

도 승차권 one-way ticket(*Am.*); single ticket
(*Eng.*).

p'yŏndŭlda 편들다 side; take sides with; stand
by; support; back; favor; assist.

p'yŏngbŏm 평범. *p'yŏngbŏmhan* 평범한 common;
ordinary; mediocre; flat; featureless.

p'yŏngdŭng 평등 equality; parity. *p'yŏngdŭnghan*
[*hage*] 평등한[하게] equal[ly]; even[ly].

p'yŏnghwa 평화 peace. *p'yŏnghwasŭrŏn* 평화스런
peaceful; tranquil. *p'yŏnghwajŏgŭro* 평화적으
로 peacefully; at[in] peace.

p'yŏngil 평일 weekday. *p'yŏngire(nŭn)* 평일에(는)
on weekdays; on business[ordinary] days.

p'yŏnggyun 평균 average. *p'yŏnggyunhayŏ* 평균
하여 on an[the] average.

p'yŏngka 평가 valuation; appraisal. *p'yŏngkahada*
평가하다 value; estimate; appraise.

p'yŏngmyŏn 평면 plane; level. *p'yŏngmyŏndo* 평
면도 plane figure.

p'yŏngnon 평론 review; criticism. *p'yŏngnonhada*
평론하다 review; criticize; comment (on).

p'yŏngp'an 평판 reputation; fame; popularity.

p'yŏngya 평야 plain; open field.

p'yŏn-gyŏn 편견 prejudice. *p'yŏn-gyŏn innŭn* 편견
있는 partial; prejudiced; biased.

p'yŏnhada 편하다 (be) comfortable; easy. *p'yŏn-
hage* 편하게 comfortably; at ease.

p'yŏnji 편지 letter. *p'yŏnjirŭl puch'ida* 편지를 부
치다 mail[post] a letter.

p'yŏnjip 편집 editing; compilation. *p'yŏnjip'ada*
편집하다 edit; compile.

p'yŏnmul 편물 knitting; knitwork; crochet. →ttŭgaejil 뜨개질.

p'yŏnŭi 편의 convenience; facilities. *p'yŏnŭisang* 편의상 for convenience' sake.

p'yoŏ 표어 motto; slogan; catchphrase; catchword.

radio 라디오 radio[*Am.*]; wireless(*Eng.*).

raemp'ŭ 램프 lamp. *sŏgyu raemp'ŭ* 석유 램프 oil lamp.

raengk'ing 랭킹 ranking. *raengk'ing irwi* 랭킹 1 위 the first ranking.

rait'ŏ 라이터 (cigarette) lighter. *rait'ŏ tol* 라이터 돌 lighter flint.

rait'ŭ 라이트 light. *rait'ŭrŭl k'yŏda* 라이트를 켜 다 switch on the light.

reink'ot'ŭ 레인코트 raincoat.

rek'odŭ 레코드 record.

renjŭ 렌즈 lens; lenses.

resŭt'orang 레스토랑 restaurant.

ribŏrŏllijŭm 리버럴리즘 liberalism.

ribon 리본 ribbon.

ridŭm 리듬 rhythm.

rillei 릴레이 relay (*race*).

rinch'i 린치 lynch; lynching.

ring 링 ring(*boxing*). *ringsaidŭ* 링사이드 ringside.

risepsyŏn 리셉션 reception. *risepsyŏnŭl yŏlda* 리셉 션을 열다 hold[give] a reception.

robot 로봇 robot.

rŏbŭ ret'ŏ 러브 레터 love letter.

Roma 로마 Rome. *Romacha* 로마자 Roman letters. *Roma sucha* 로마 수자 Roman numerals.

romaensŭ 로맨스 romance; love[romantic] affair.
rŏnch'i 런치 lunch; luncheon.
rŏning 러닝 running (*race*). *rŏning syassŭ* 러닝샤쓰 gym[athletic] shirt.
rŏshi 러시 rush. *rŏshi awo* 러시 아워 rush hours.
ruksaek 룩색 rucksack.
Rŭnesangsŭ 르네상스 Renaissance.
rut'ŭ 루트 route; channel. *chŏngshik rut'ŭ* 정식 루트 legal channels.

━━◆§◆━━

sa 사, 4 four. *chesa* 제4 the fourth.
sabang 사방 four sides; all directions[quarters].
sabip 삽입 insertion. *sabip'ada* 삽입하다 insert.
sabŏm 사범 teacher; master; coach. *kwont'u sabŏm* 권투 사범 boxing instructor.
sabŏp 사법 administration of justice. *sabŏbŭi* 사법의 judicial.
sabyŏn 사변 accident; incident. *yugio sabyŏn* 6·25 사변 the June 25th Incident of Korea; Korean
sabyŏng 사병 soldier; private. ⌞War.
sach'ae 사채 personal debt[loan]; private liabilities.
sach'ang 사창 unlicensed prostitution; streetwalker. *sach'anggul* 사창굴 brothel.
sach'i 사치 luxury; extravagance. *sach'isŭrŏpta* 사치스럽다 (be) luxurious; extravagant.
sach'inhoe 사친회 Parent-Teacher Association (P. T. A.)
sach'on 사촌 cousin. *oesach'on* 외사촌 cousin on the mother's side.
sachŭng 사증 visa; visé. *ipkuk[ch'ulguk] sa-*

chŭng 입국[출국] 사증 entry[exit] visa.

sach'un-gi 사춘기 adolescence; (age of) puberty.

sada 사다 buy; purchase.

sadaktari 사닥다리 ladder.

sadan 사단 (army) division. *sadanjang* 사단장 division(al) commander.

sadon 사돈 relatives by marriage.

sae 새 bird; fowl; poultry.

sae 새 new; fresh; novel; recent.

saeagi 새아기 one's new daughter-in-law; bride.

saeam 새암 jealousy; envy. *saeamhada* 새암하다 be jealous (of); be envious (of).

saebom 새봄 early spring; early springtime.

saebyŏk 새벽 dawn; daybreak. *saebyŏge* 새벽에 at dawn[daybreak].

saech'igi 새치기 cutting in. *saech'igihada* 새치기 하다 cut in (a line); break into the queue.

saech'imtegi 새침데기 indifferent person; ostensibly modest person.

saeda 새다 ① dawn; break ② leak(out); run.

saedal 새달 next month; the coming month.

saegida 새기다 ① sculpture; carve; engrave ② bear in mind.

saegin 색인 index.

saegŭn-gŏrida 새근거리다 ① gasp; pant ② feel a slight pain.

saehae 새해 new year; New Year.

saejang 새장 (bird) cage; birdcage.　「[house].

saejip 새집 ① nest; birdhouse ② new building

saek, saekch'ae 색, 색채 colo(u)r; hue; tint; tinge.

saekki 새끼 straw rope. *saekkirŭl kkoda* 새끼를 꼬 다 make[twist] a (straw) rope.

saekki 새끼 ① young; litter; cub ② guy; fellow. *kaesaekki* 개새끼 You beast!

saekshi 색시 ① bride ② wife ③ maiden; girl ④ barmaid; hostess.

saemaŭl undong 새마을 운동 the new community [village] movement; Saemaul Movement.

saemmul 샘물 spring water; fountain water.

saengae 생애 life; career; lifetime.

saengch'ae 생채 vegetable salad.

saenggak 생각 ① thinking; thought; ideas ② opinion ③ mind; intention.

saenggangnada 생각나다 come to mind; occur to one; be reminded of.

saenggida 생기다 ① get; obtain; come by ② arise; occur; happen ③ come into being.

saenggye 생계 livelihood; living. *saenggyebi* 생계비 cost of living; living expenses.

saenghwal 생활 life; living; livelihood. *saenghwarhada* 생활하다 live; make a living.

saengil 생일 birthday. *saengil chanch'i* 생일 잔치 birthday party.

saengjil 생질 one's sister's son; nephew.

saengjon 생존 existence; life. *saengjonhada* 생존하다 exist; live; survive.

saengmaekchu 생맥주 draught[draft] beer.

saengmul 생물 living thing; creature; life. *saengmurhak* 생물학 biology.

saengmyŏng 생명 life; soul; vitality.

saengni 생리 physiology. *saengnijŏk yokku* 생리적 욕구 physiological desire. *saengnihak* 생리학 physiology.

saengsa 생사 life and death.

saengsaek 생색. *saengsaengnaeda* 생색내다 ① make

a merit of ② patronizing; condescending.

saengsan 생산 production; manufacture.

saengshik 생식 reproduction; generation.

saengsŏn 생선 fish; fresh[raw] fish. *saengsŏnhoe* 생선회 sliced[slices of] raw fish.

saengnyak 생략 omission; abbreviation. *saengnyak'ada* 생략하다 omit; abbreviate.

saengnyŏnp'il 색연필 colored pencil.

saero 새로 newly; new; afresh; anew.

saeropta 새롭다 (be) new; fresh; vivid. *saeropke* 새롭게 newly; afresh.

saetkil 샛길 byway; side road; lane.

saeu 새우 lobster; prawn; shrimp. *saeujŏt* 새우젓 pickled shrimp.

saeuda 새우다 sit[stay] up all night; keep vigil.

saga 사가 historian; chronicler.

sagak 사각 square; rectangular. *sagak'yŏng* 사각형 square.

sagam 사감 dormitory dean[inspector]; housemother.

sagi 사기 swindle; fraud; deception. *sagihada* 사기하다 swindle; impose.

sagi 사기 china; chinaware; porcelain.

sago 사고 incident; accident; trouble.

sagong 사공 boatman; oarman; ferryman.

sagŭrajida 사그라지다 ① subside; go down ② melt away; decompose.

sagwa 사과 apple. *sagwaju* 사과주 cider.

sagwa 사과 apology. *sagwahada* 사과하다 apologize; beg (a person) pardon.

sagwan 사관 (military, naval) officer. *sagwan hakkyo* 사관 학교 military[naval] academy.

sagwida 사귀다 associate with; keep company with.

sagwolse 삭월세 monthly rent[rental]. *sagwolse-pang* 삭월세방 rented room.

sagyo 사교 social intercourse[life]. *sagyojŏgin* 사교적인 social.

sagyo 사교 bishop; pontiff.

sagyŏk 사격 firing; shooting. *sagyŏk'ada* 사격하다 shoot; fire at.

sahoe 사회 society; world; public. *sahoejŏk* 사회적 social.

sahŭl 사흘 ① three days ② →**sahŭnnal** 사흘날.

sahŭnnal 사흘날 the third day of the month.

sahyŏng 사형 death penalty[sentence]; capital punishment.

sai 사이 ① interval; distance; space ② time; during ③ between; among.

saim 사임 resignation. →**sajik** 사직.

sajae 사재 private funds[property].

sajang 사장 president (of company). *pusajang* 부사장 vice-president.

saje 사제 priest; pastor.

saji 사지 limbs; legs and arms; members.

sajik 사직 resignation. *sajik'ada* 사직하다 resign (from).

sajin 사진 photograph; picture; photo; snapshot. *sajinŭl tchikta* 사진을 찍다 take a photograph of. *sajin-ga* 사진가 photo artist; cameraman.

sajŏl 사절 emissary; delegate; envoy. *ch'insŏn sajŏl* 친선 사절 good-will envoy[mission].

sajŏl 사절 denial; refusal. *sajŏrhada* 사절하다 refuse; decline; turndown.

sajŏn 사전 dictionary; lexicon; wordbook. *sajŏnŭl*

ch'atta 사전을 찾다 consult[refer to] a dictionary.

sajŏng 사정 circumstances; conditions; reasons.

sajŏngŏpta 사정없다 (be) merciless; ruthless.

sak 삯 wages; pay; charge; fare. *sakchŏn* 삯전 wages; pay.

sakche 삭제 elimination; deletion. *sakchehada* 삭제하다 eliminate; strike[cross] out.

sakkam 삭감 reduction; curtailment.

sakŏn 사건 event; matter; occurrence; affair; case. *sarin sakŏn* 살인 사건 murder case.

sakpanŭjil 삯바느질 needle work for pay.

sal 살 flesh; muscles. *sari tchin* 살이 찐 fleshy; fat.

salda 살다 ① live; be alive ② make a living; get along ③ dwell; inhabit; reside.

salgu 살구 apricot.

salgŭmŏni 살그머니 furtively; stealthily; in secret.

sallida 살리다 save; spare (a person's) life.

sallim 살림 living; housekeeping. *sallimhada* 살림하다 run the house; manage a household.

sallim 산림 forest. *sallim poho* 산림 보호 forest conservation.

salp'ida 살피다 take a good look at; look about; inspect closely.

salp'o 살포 scattering; sprinkling. *salp'ohada* 살포하다 scatter; sprinkle.

sam 삼 hemp.

samagwi 사마귀 mole; wart.

samak 사막 desert.

samang 사망 death; decease. *samanghada* 사망하다 die; decease; pass away.

sambae 삼배 three times; thrice.

samch'on 삼촌 uncle (on the father's side). *oe-*

samch'on 외삼촌 uncle (on the mother's side). →
sukpu 숙부.

samch'ŭng 삼층 three stories[floors]; the third floor
(*Am.*); the second floor (*Eng.*).

samdae 삼대 three generations.

samdŭng 삼등 third class[rate]. *samdŭng yŏlch'a*
삼등 열차 third class compartment.

samgada 삼가다 ① be discreet[cautious] ② restrain
oneself.

samgak 삼각 triangle. *samgagŭi* 삼각의 triangular
samgak'yŏng 삼각형 triangle.

samgŏri 삼거리 three-way junction[intersection].

samta 삶다 boil; cook. *talgyarŭl samta* 달걀을 삶
다 boil an egg.

samilchŏl 삼일절 Anniversary of the Samil Independence Movement.

samil undong 삼일 운동 the 1919 Independence
Movement.

samin 삼인 three persons. *saminjo* 삼인조 trio.

samjung 삼중. *samjungŭi* 삼중의 threefold; triple.

samk'ida 삼키다 swallow; gulp down; gulp.

samnyŏn 삼년 three years. *samnyŏnmada* 삼년마
다 every three years.

samnyunch'a 삼륜차 tricycle.

samo 사모. *samohada* 사모하다 long for; yearn
after; burn with love.

samp'alsŏn 삼팔선 the 38th parallel.

samship 삼십, 30 thirty. *chesamship*(*ŭi*) 제30(의)
the thirtieth.

samship'altosŏn 38도선 38 degrees north latitude
→**samp'alsŏn** 삼팔선.

samu 사무 business; affairs; office work. *samu-*

shil 사무실 office (room). *samuwon* 사무원 clerk; deskworker.

samwol 삼월 March.

samyŏng 사명 mission; commission; errand. *samyŏnggam* 사명감 sense of duty.

san 산 mountain; hill.

san 산 acid.

sana 산아 newborn baby. *sana chehan* 산아 제한 birth control.

sanaeai 사내아이 boy; lad; kid.

sanai 사나이 man; male. *sanaidaun* 사나이다운 manly; manlike; manful.

sanapta 사납다 (be) fierce; wild; violent.

sanponguri 산봉우리 mountain peak.

sanbuinkwa 산부인과 obsterics and gynecology. *sanbuinkwa ŭisa* 산부인과 의사 ladies' doctor.

sang 상 prize; reward. *sangŭl t'ada* 상을 타다 win[get] a prize.

sang 상 figure; statue; image; portrait.

sang 상 (dining, eating) table; small table.

sanga 상아 ivory. *sangat'ap* 상아탑 ivory tower.

sangbanshin 상반신 upper half of the body; bust.

sangbok 상복 mourning clothes[dress]; sables.

sangch'i 상치 lettuce. *sangch'issam* 상치쌈 lettuce wrapped rice.

sangch'ŏ 상처 wound; injury; cut; scar.

sangdae 상대 ① companion; mate ② the other party; opponent.

sangdam 상담 consultation; counsel; conference. *sangdamhada* 상담하다 consult(with); confer.

sangdang 상당. *sangdanghan* 상당한 respectable; decent. *sangdanghi* 상당히 pretty; fairly; considerably.

sangdŭng 상등 first class; best grade. *sangdŭngp'um* 상등품 top grade article.

sangga 상가 downtown; business section[quarters, center].

sanggi 상기. *sanggihada* 상기하다 remember; recollect; call to mind.

sanggong 상공 commerce and industry. *sanggongbu* 상공부 Ministry of Commerce and Industry.

sanggong 상공 upper air; sky.

sanggŏrae 상거래 commercial transaction; business deal.

sanggŭm 상금 reward; prize money.

sanggwan 상관 senior[superior] officer; higher officer[official].

sanghae 상해 injury; harm. *sanghae ch'isa* 상해 치사 bodily injury resulting in death.

sangho 상호 firm[trade] name.

sangho 상호 mutually; each other; one another. *sanghoŭi* 상호의 mutual.

sanghoe 상회 company; firm. *Chongno sanghoe* 종로 상회 the Chongno company.

sanghwang 상황 state of things[affairs]; conditions; situation; circumstances.

sangi 상이. *sangi kunin* 상이 군인 wounded soldier; disabled veteran.

sangin 상인 merchant; trader; dealer; tradesman; shopkeeper.

sangja 상자 box; case.

sangjing 상징 symbol; emblem. *sangjinghada* 상징하다 symbolize.

sangjŏm 상점 shop; store (*Am.*). *sangjom chuin*

상점 주인 shopkeeper (*Eng.*); storekeeper (*Am*).

sangju 상주 chief mourner.

sangk'wae 상쾌. *sangk'waehan* 상쾌한 refreshing; exhilarating; invigorating; bracing.

sangmal 상말 vulgar words; vulgarism.

sangnyanghada 상냥하다 (be) gentle; tender; amiable; sweet.

sangnyu 상류 ① upper stream ② upper[higher] classes. *sangnyu sahoe* 상류사회 high society.

sangnyuk 상륙 landing. *sangnyuk'ada* 상륙하다 land (at); go on shore.

sango 상오 forenoon; morning; a. m.; A. M.

sangŏ 상어 shark. *sangŏ kajuk* 상어 가죽 sharkskin.

sangŏp 상업 commerce; trade; business. *sangŏbŭi* 상업의 commercial; business.

sangp'ae 상패 medal; medallion.

sangp'um 상품 goods; merchandise; commodity.

sangp'yo 상표 trademark; brand.

sangsa 상사 firm; trading company. *oeguk sangsa* 외국 상사 foreign firm.

sangsa 상사 sergeant.

sangsa 상사 superior authorities; one's superior.

sangsang 상상 imagination; fancy. *sangsanghada* 상상하다 imagine; fancy.

sangse 상세 details; particulars. *sangsehada* 상세하다 (be) detailed; particular. *sangsehi* 상세히 in detail; minutely.

sangshik 상식 common sense; good sense.

sangso 상소 appeal. *sangsohada* 상소하다 appeal to (a higher court).

sangsok 상속 succession; inheritance. *sangsok'ada* 상속하다 succeed (to); inherit.

sangsŭrŏpta 상스럽다 (be) vulgar; base; indecent.

sangt'ae 상태 condition; state; situation. *kŏn-gang sangt'ae* 건강 상태 state of health.

sangchang 상장 certificate of merit; honorary certificate.

sangt'u 상투 topknot. *sangt'ujangi* 상투장이 man with a topknot.

sangyŏgŭm 상여금 bonus; reward. *yŏnmal sangyŏgŭm* 연말 상여금 year-end bonus.

sangyong 상용. *sangyongŭro* 상용으로 on business. *sangyongmun* 상용문 commercial[business] correspondence[term].

sanho 산호 coral. *sanhoch'o* 산호초 coral reef.

sanji 산지 place of production. *ssarŭi sanji* 쌀의 산지 rice-producing district.

sankkoktaegi 산꼭대기 mountain top; top[summit] of a mountain.

sankoltchagi 산골짜기 mountain valley; ravine.

sanmaek 산맥 mountain range.

sanmaru 산마루 top of a mountain.

sanmul 산물 product; production; produce.

sanŏp 산업 industry. *sanŏbŭi* 산업의 industrial.

sansam 산삼 wild ginseng.

sanso 산소 oxygen.

sanso 산소 ancestral graveyard.

sansul 산술 arithmetic. *sansurŭi* 산술의 arithmetical.

santtŭt'ada 산뜻하다 (be) clean; fresh; bright. *santtŭt'an ot* 산뜻한 옷 neat dress.

sanyang 사냥 hunting; shooting. *sanyanghada* 사냥하다 hunt; shoot.

saŏp 사업 enterprise; undertaking; business. *saŏpka* 사업가 man of enterprise.

sap'wa 삽화 illustration; cut.

sarhae 살해 murder; killing. *sarhaehada* 살해하다 murder; kill; slay.

sarajida 사라지다 disappear; vanish; be gone.

saram 사람 man; person; human being.

sarang 사랑 love; affection. *saranghada* 사랑하다 love; be fond of; be attached to.

sarin 살인 murder; homicide. *sarinhada* 살인하다 commit murder.

sarip 사립 private establishment. *saribŭi* 사립의 private. *sarip hakkyo* 사립 학교 private school.

sarojapta 사로잡다 ① catch (an animal) alive; capture ② captivate.

saryŏng 사령 command. *saryŏnggwan* 사령관 commander. *saryŏngbu* 사령부 headquarters.

sasaek 사색 contemplation; meditation. *sasaek'ada* 사색하다 contemplate; speculate.

sasaenga 사생아 illegitimate child; bastard.

sasaenghwal 사생활 private[personal] life.

sasal 사살 shooting to death. *sasarhada* 사살하다 shoot (a person) dead[to death].

sasang 사상 thought; idea. *sasangga* 사상가 thinker. *sasangbŏm* 사상범 political offense[offender].

sasang 사상 death and injury; casualties. *sasangja(su)* 사상자(수) (number of) casualties.

sashil 사실 fact; actual fact; truth. *sashilsang* 사실상 in fact; actually.

sashin 사신 envoy. *oeguk sashin* 외국 사신 foreign envoys.

saship 사십, 40 forty. *chesaship* 제40 the fortieth.

sasŏl 사설 leading article; editorial; leader(*Eng.*).

sasŭl 사슬 chain.

sasŭm 사슴 deer; stag; buck. *sasŭm ppul* 사슴 뿔 antler. *sasŭm kajuk* 사슴 가죽 deer skin.

sat 샅 crotch; groin. *satpa* 샅바 Korean wrestler's thigh band.

sat'ae 사태 situation; state[position] of affairs.

sat'ang 사탕 sugar. →**sŏlt'ang** 설탕.

sat'oe 사퇴 ① declination; refusal ② resignation. *sat'oehada* 사퇴하다 ① decline; refuse to accept ② resign.

sat'uri 사투리 dialect; brogue; provincial accent.

sawi 사위 son-in-law.

sawol 사월 April.

sawon 사원 member; employee; clerk. *shinip sawon* 신입 사원 incoming partner[employee].

sayang 사양. *sayanghada* 사양하다 decline (with regrets); refuse courteously.

sayong 사용 use; employment. *sayonghada* 사용 하다 use; employ; apply.

sayu 사유 private ownership. *sayuhada* 사유하다 possess oneself of. *sayu chaesan* 사유 재산 private property.

se 세 tax; duty (on goods). *sodŭkse* 소득세 individual income tax.

se 세 rent; hire. *chip[pang]se* 집[방]세 house [room] rent.

se 세 three. *se saram* 세 사람 *three men*.

sebae 세배 New Year('s) greetings.

sech'a 세차 car washing. *sech'ahada* 세차하다 wash down a car.

seda 세다 count; calculate; enumerate.

seda 세다 (be) strong; powerful; mighty. *sege* 세게 hard; strongly.

sedae 세대 generation. *chŏlmŭn sedae* 젊은 세대 rising[younger] generation.

segi 세기 century. *ishipsegi* 20세기 the twenties century. *segimal* 세기말 the end of the century [fin-de-siècle.

segŭm 세금 tax. →se 세.

segwan 세관 customhouse; customs. *segwan chŏlch'a* 세관 절차 customs formalities.

segye 세계 world. *segyejŏk* 세계적 world-wide; international; universal.

segyun 세균 bacillus; germ; bacterium.

seje 세제 cleaning material; detergent.

semil 세밀. *semirhan* 세밀한 minute; detailed; elaborate. *semirhi* 세밀히 minutely; in detail.

sep'o 세포 cell. *sep'oŭi* 세포의 cellular.

serye 세례 baptism; christening. *seryemyŏng* 세례명 baptismal name.

seryŏk 세력 influence; power. *seryŏk innŭn* 세력 있는 powerful; influential.

sesang 세상 world; life; society. *sesange* 세상에 in the world; on earth.

sesu 세수. *sesuhada* 세수하다 wash oneself; have a wash.

set 셋 three. *setchae(ro)* 세째(로) third(ly).

set'ak 세탁 wash(ing); laundry. *set'ak'ada* 세탁하다 wash; do washing. *set'akki* 세탁기 washing machine.

setchip 셋집 house for rent (*Am.*); house to let (*Eng.*).

setpang 셋방 room to let; room for rent.

seuda 세우다 ① raise; set[put] up; erect ② stop; hold up ③ build; construct.

sewol 세월 time; time and tide; years.

shi 시 poetry; poem; verse.

shi 시 o'clock; hour; time. *tushi* 두시 two o'clock.

shi 시 city; town. *shiŭi* 시의 municipal; city. *shi-ch'ŏng* 시청 city hall.

shibi 십이, 12 twelve. *cheshibi* 제12 the twelfth.

shibiwol 십이월 December.

shibil 십일, 11 eleven. *cheshibil* 제11 the eleventh.

shibirwol 십일월 November.

shibo 십오, 15 fifteen. *cheshibo* 제15 the fifteenth.

shibumo 시부모 parents of one's husband.

shich'al 시찰 inspection. *shich'arhada* 시찰하다 inspect; observe.

shich'e 시체 corpse; dead body.

shida 시다 (be) sour; acid; tart.

shidae 시대. age; era; period; times; days. *uju shidae* 우주 시대 space age.

shido 시도 attempt. *shidohada* 시도하다 attempt; try out.

shidŭlda 시들다 wither; wilt; fade (away).

shiga 시가 streets of a city; city; town. *shigaji* 시가지 urban district.

shigan 시간 time; hour. *yŏngŏp shigan* 영업 시간 business hour. *shiganp'yo* 시간표 time table.

shikkŭrŏpta 시끄럽다 (be) noisy; boisterous. *shikkŭrŏpke* 시끄럽게 clamorously.

shigi 시기 season; time; period; occasion.

shigol 시골 country(side); rural district. *shigol saram* 시골 사람 country-man; rustic.

shigolttŭgi 시골뜨기 country bumpkin; hick; yokel.

shigŭmch'i 시금치 spinach; spinage.

shigungch'ang 시궁창 ditch; sink; cesspool.

shigye 시계 clock; watch. *sonmok shigye* 손목 시

계 wristwatch. *t'aksang shigye* 탁상 시계 table clock.

shigyok 식욕 appetite; desire to eat.

shigyong 식용. *shigyongŭi* 식용의 edible; eatable.

shihap 시합 →**kyŏnggi** 경기.

shihŏm 시험 examination; exam; test. *shihŏmhada* 시험하다 examine; test.

shihŏmgwan 시험관 test tube.

shiil 시일 ① time; days; hours ② date; the time. *shiilgwa changso* 시일과 장소 time and place.

shiin 시인 poet. *yŏryu shiin* 여류 시인 poetess.

shiin 시인 approval. *shiinhada* 시인하다 approve of; admit.

shijak 시작 beginning; commencement. *shijak'ada* 시작하다 begin; commence; start.

shijang 시장 market (place); fair.

shijang 시장 mayor. *Sŏul shijang* 서울 시장 Mayor of Seoul.

shijang 시장. *shijanghada* 시장하다 be hungry; feel empty.

shijip 시집 collection of poems; anthology.

shijo 시조 founder; originator; progenitor.

shijung 시중 attendance; service. *shijungdŭlda* 시중들다 attend; wait on; serve.

shikchang 식장 hall of ceremony; ceremonial hall.

shik'ida 시키다 make[let] a person do; have[get] a person do.

shik'ida 식히다 cool; let (a thing) cool.

shikki 식기 tableware; dinner set.

shikkwon 식권 meal[food]-ticket.

shikpi 식비 food expenses[cost].

shiksa 식사 meal; diet. *shiksahada* 식사하다 have

[take] a meal; dine.

shiksaenghwal 식생활 dietary[food] life.

shikta 식다 (become) cool; get cold; cool off.

shikt'ak 식탁 (dinner) table. *shikt'akpo* 식탁보 table cloth.

shiktan 식단 menu; bill of fare.

shiktang 식당 dining room[hall]; mess hall; restaurant; eating house; lunch counter.

shil 실 thread; yarn; string.

shilbi 실비 actual expense; (real) cost.

shilche 실제 truth; fact; reality. *shilcheŭi* 실제의 real; true; actual; practical. *shilchero* 실제로 really; actually.

shilchik 실직 →**shirŏp** 실업.

shilchŏk 실적 actual results[accomplishments]. *shilchŏgŭl ollida* 실적을 올리다 bring about good results.

shilch'ŏn 실천 practice. *shilch'ŏnhada* 실천하다 practice; put into practice.

shilchong 실종 disappearance; missing. *shilchonghada* 실종하다 disappear; be missing.

shilchŭng 싫증 dislike; detestation; tiredness. *shilchŭngnada* 싫증나다 get tired of; be weary[sick] of; get disgusted (with).

shilk'ŏt 실컷 to one's heart's content; as much as one wishes[likes].

shillae 실내 interior of a room. *shillaeŭi* 실내의 indoor.

shillang 신랑 bridegroom. *shillang shinbu* 신랑 신부 bride and bridegroom; new couple.

shilloe 신뢰 confidence; trust; reliance. *shilloehada* 신뢰하다 trust; believe in.

shillye 실례 example; instance; concrete case.

shillye 실례 rudeness; discourtesy.

shillyŏk 실력 real ability. *shillyŏgi innŭn* 실력이 있는 able; capable; talented.

shilmang 실망 disappointment. *shilmanghada* 실망하다 be disappointed in[at].

shilmari 실마리 clue. *shilmarirŭl ch'atta* 실마리를 찾다 find a clue to.

shilmul 실물 real thing; actual object.

shilp'ae 실패 failure; mistake; error; blunder. *shilp'aehada* 실패하다 fail; go wrong.

shilsaenghwal 실생활 real[actual] life; realities of life.

shilshi 실시 execution; enforcement. *shilshihada* 실시하다 enforce; put in operation[force].

shilsu 실수 mistake; blunder; fault. *shilsuhada* 실수하다 make a mistake; commit a blunder.

shilsŭp 실습 practice; exercise; drill. *shilsŭp'ada* 실습하다 practice; have(practical) training.

shilt'a 싫다 (be) disagreeable; disgusting; reluctant.

shimburŭm 심부름 errand; message. *shimburŭmhada* 심부름하다 go on an errand.

shimhada 심하다 (be) violent; intense; excessive; severe.

shimin 시민 citizen; townsmen; townfolks.

shimjang 심장 heart. *shimjang mabi* 심장마비 heart attack.

shimni 심리 mental state; psychology. *shimnijŏk (ŭro)* 심리적 (으로) mental(ly); psychological-(ly).

shimnihak 심리학 psychology.

shimnyuk 십육, 16 sixteen.

shimsa 심사 inspection; examination. *shimsahada* 심사하다 examine; judge; investigate.

shimshimhada 심심하다 be bored; feel ennui.

shimshimp'uri 심심풀이 killing time; passtime.

shimuruk'ada 시무룩하다 (be) sulky; sullen; ill-humo(u)red.

shin 신 shoes; boots. →**kudu** 구두.

shin 신 god. *yŏshin* 여신 goddess. *shinŭi* 신의 divine; godly.

shinae 시내 brook; creek; stream.

shinae 시내 (in, within) the city. *shinae pŏsŭ* 시내 버스 urban bus. *shinae chŏnhwa* 시내 전화 local phones.

shinang 신앙 faith; belief. *shinang saenghwal* 신앙 생활 life of faith; religious life.

shinbi 신비 mystery. *shinbihan* 신비한 mystic; mysterious.

shinbu 신부 (holy) father.

shinbu 신부 bride; newly-wed wife.

shinbun 신분 social position[standing, status].

shinch'e 신체 body. *shinch'eŭi* 신체의 bodily; physical. *shinch'e kŏmsa* 신체 검사 physical check-up (*Am.*).

shinch'ŏng 신청 application. *shinch'ŏnghada* 신청하다 apply (for). *shinch'ŏngsŏ* 신청서 (written) application. *shinch'ŏngin* 신청인 applicant.

shinch'ŏnji 신천지 new world.

shinch'ullagi 신출나기 newcomer; green hand; novice; beginner.

shindo 신도 →**shinja** 신자.

shindong 신동 (infant) prodigy; wonder child.

shin-gan 신간 new publication. *shin-ganŭi* 신간의 new; newly-published.

shin-girok 신기록 new record. *segye shin-girok* 세계 신기록 new world record.

shinggŏpta 싱겁다 (be) insipid; taste flat.

shingmin 식민 colonization; settlement. *shingminji* 식민지 colony.

shingmo 식모 kitchenmaid; domestic servant.

shingmok 식목 forestation; tree planting. *shingmogil* 식목일 Arbor Day.

shingmul 식물 plant; vegetation. *shingmurŭi* 식물의 vegetational.

shingnyang 식량 food; provisions; foodstuffs.

shin-go 신고 report; statement. *shin-gohada* 신고하다 state; report; make[file] a return.

shingshinghada 싱싱하다 (be) fresh; lively; full of life.

shin-gyŏng 신경 nerves. *shin-gyŏngsŏng(ŭi)* 신경성(의) nervous. *shin-gyŏngjil* 신경질 nervous temperament.

shinhak 신학 theology.

shinhakki 신학기 new (school) term; new semester.

shinho 신호 signal; signal(l)ing. *shinhohada* 신호하다 (make a) signal.

shinhon 신혼 new marriage. *shinhonŭi* 신혼의 newly married[wedded]. *shinhon yŏhaeng* 신혼 여행 honeymoon.

shinhwa 신화 myth; mythology.

shinja 신자 believer; devotee.

shinjang 신장 kidneys. *shinjangpyŏng* 신장병 kidney trouble.

shinjang 신장 stature; height.

shinjo 신조 creed; credo; principle. *saenghwal*

shinjo 생활 신조 one's principles of life.

shinjung 신중 prudence; discretion. *shinjunghan* 신중한 prudent; careful; cautious.

shinmun 신문 newspaper; paper; press.

shinmun 신문 examination. *shinmunhada* 신문하다 question; examine.

shinnada 신나다 get in high spirits; get elated.

shinnyŏm 신념 belief; faith; conviction.

shinnyŏn 신년 new year. →**saehae** 새해.

shinsa 신사 gentleman. *shinsajŏk* 신사적 gentlemanly; gentlemanlike.

shinsaenghwal 신생활 new life. *shinsaenghwal undong* 신생활 운동 new-life movement.

shinse 신세 debt of gratitude; favor. *shinserŭl chida* 신세를 지다 be indebted to; be obliged (to).

shinsegye 신세계 new world; the New World.

shinshik 신식 new style[type, method]. *shinshigŭi* 신식의 new (style, type); modern.

shinsok 신속. *shinsok'an* 신속한 rapid; swift. *shinsok'i* 신속히 rapidly; promptly; quickly.

shinsŏng 신성 sacredness; sanctity. *shinsŏnghan* 신성한 sacred; holy; divine.

shinta 신다 wear; put[have] on. *kudurŭl[yangmarŭl] shinta* 구두를[양말을] 신다 put on one's shoes[socks].

shint'ong 신통. *shint'onghada* 신통하다 (be) wonderful; marvelous.

shinwon 신원 one's identity. *shinwon chohoe* 신원 조회 personal inquiries.

shinyong 신용 confidence; trust. *shinyonghada* 신용하다 trust (in); give credit to; rely on.

shinyung 시늉 mimicry; imitation. *shinyunghada*

시늉하다 mimic; ape; feign.

shioe 시외 outskirts of a city; suburbs. *shioeŭi* 시외의 suburban.

ship 십, 10 ten. *cheship* 제10 the tenth.

shipchaga 십자가 cross; Holy Cross.

shipchang 십장 foreman; chief workman.

shipku 십구, 19 nineteen. *shipkusegi* 19세기 the nineteenth century. ⌜teenth.

shipsa 십사, 14 fourteen. *cheshipsa* 제14 the four-

shipsam 십삼, 13 thirteen. *cheshipsam* 제13 the thirteenth.

shipta 싶다 want, wish; hope; desire; would [should] like to (do).

shiptae 십대 teens. *shiptaeŭi ai* 십대의 아이 teen-ager; teen-age boy[girl].

shirhaeng 실행 practice; execution; fulfil(l)ment. *shirhaenghada* 실행하다 practice; carry out.

shirhŏm 실험 experiment; laboratory work. *shirhŏmhada* 실험하다 experiment (on).

shirhyŏn 실현 realization. *shirhyŏnhada* 실현하다 realize; materialize; come true.

shirip 시립. *shiribŭi* 시립의 city; municipal. *shirip pyŏngwon* 시립 병원 municipal hospital.

shirŏhada 싫어하다 dislike; hate; loathe; be un-

shirŏng 시렁 wall shelf; rack. ⌞willing.

shirŏp 실업 unemployment. *shirŏpcha* 실업자 man out of work; the unemployed; the jobless.

shiryŏk 시력 (eye) sight; vision. *shiryŏk kŏmsa* 시력 검사 eyesight test.

shiryŏn 시련 trial; test; ordeal.

shiryŏn 실연 disappointed love; broken heart. *shiryŏnhada* 실연하다 be disappointed in love.

shiryong 실용 practical use. *shiryongjŏgin* 실용
적인 practical; useful.

shishihada 시시하다 ① (be) dull; flat; uninterest-
ing ② (be) trifling; trivial ③ (be) worthless;
poor.

shisok 시속 speed per hour; velocityper hour.

shisŏl 시설 establishment; facilities; equipment.
shisŏrhada 시설하다 establish; equip.

shitta 싣다 load; take on; take on board; ship.

shiwi 시위 demonstration. *shiwihada* 시위하다
demonstrate; show off.

shiwonhada 시원하다 (be) feel cool[refreshing].

shiya 시야 visual field; one's view.

shwida 쉬다 rest; take a rest; lay off (*Am.*).

shwida 쉬다 get[grow] hoarse; become husky.

shwipsari 쉽사리 easily; readily; without difficulty.

shwipta 쉽다 ① (be) easy; simple; without difficulty
[effort] ② be apt to; be liable to.

so 소 cow; bull; ox; cattle.

soa 소아 infant; little child. *soa mabi* 소아 마비
infantile paralysis; poliomyelitis.

soakwa 소아과 pediatrics. *soakwa ŭisa* 소아과 의사
child specialist; pediatrician.

sobang 소방 fire fighting. *sobanggwan* 소방관
fireman; fire fighter. *sobangch'a* 소방차 fire
engine. *sobang yŏnsŭp* 소방 연습 fire drill.

sobi 소비 consumption. *sobihada* 소비하다 consume;
spend; expend.

sobyŏn 소변 urine; piss. *sobyŏnŭl poda* 소변을 보
다 urinate; pass urine[water].

soch'ong 소총 rifle; musket; small arms.

sŏda 서다 ① stand (up); rise (to one's feet) ②

stop; halt; run down ③ be built[erected].

sŏdo 서도 calligraphy.

sodok 소독 disinfection. *sodok'ada* 소독하다 disinfect; sterilize.

Sŏdok 서독 West Germany.

sodong 소동 disturbance; riot. *sodongŭl irŭk'ida* 소동을 일으키다 raise a disturbance.

sodŭk 소득 income; earnings. *kungmin sodŭk* 국민 소득 national income.

sŏdurŭda 서두르다 hurry (up); hasten; make haste. *sŏdullŏ* 서둘러 hurriedly; in haste.

soebuch'i 쇠붙이 metal things; ironware.

soegogi 쇠고기 beef. *soegogijŭp* 쇠고기즙 beef tea

soegorang 쇠고랑 handcuffs; manacles. ⌐[bouillon].

soegori 쇠고리 iron ring; clasp; metal hoop.

soemangch'i 쇠망치 iron hammer.

soeyak 쇠약 weakening; emaciation. *soeyak'an* 쇠약한 weak; weakened.

sŏga 서가 book shelf; bookstand.

sogae 소개 introduction. *sogaehada* 소개하다 introduce. *sogaechang* 소개장 letter of introduction.

sŏgi 서기 clerk; secretary. *sŏgijang* 서기장 head clerk; chief secretary.

sŏgi 서기 christian era; Anno Domini (A. D.).

sogida 속이다 deceive; cheat; swindle.

sogimsu 속임수 trickery; deception. *sogimsurŭl ssŭda* 속임수를 쓰다 cheat; play a trick on.

sogŏ 속어 slang; colloquial expression.

sŏgok 서곡 prelude; overture.

sogon-gŏrida 소곤거리다 whisper; talk in whispers.

sogot 속옷 underwear; underclothes; undergarment; undershirt (*Am.*).

Sŏgu 서구 Western Europe; the West; the Occident.

soguk 소국 small country; minor[lesser] power.

sogŭk 소극. sogŭkchŏk(ŭro) 소극적 (으로) negative (ly); passive(ly). 「hotbed of crime.

sogul 소굴 den; nest; lair. pŏmjoe sogul 범죄 소굴

sogŭm 소금 salt. sogŭme chŏrin 소금에 절인 salted; pickled with salt.

sogyŏng 소경 blind man. →changnim 장님.

sŏgyu 석유 oil; petroleum; kerosene. sŏgyu nallo 석유 난로 kerosene stove; oil stove.

sohaeng 소행 conduct; behavior. 「careless; rash.

sohol 소홀. sohorhada 소홀하다 (be) negligent;

sohwa 소화 digestion. sohwahada 소화하다 digest.

sŏhwa 서화 paintings and calligraphic works.

sohwan 소환 summons; call. sohwanhada 소환하다 summon; call.

sohyŏng 소형 small size. sohyŏngŭi 소형의 small (-sized); tiny; pocket(-size).

soit'an 소이탄 incendiary; incendiary bomb.

sŏjae 서재 study; library.

sojak 소작 tenancy. sojak'ada 소작하다 tenant.

sojang 소장 major general (army); rear admiral (navy); air commodore (air-force).

sŏjang 서장 head; chief; marshal. kyŏngch'alsŏjang 경찰서장 chief of police station.

soji 소지 possession. sojihada 소지하다 have; possess. sojip'um 소지품 one's belongings.

sojil 소질 making(s); character; tendency; aptitude.

sojip 소집 call; summons; convocation; levy. sojip'ada 소집하다 call; convene; summon.

sŏjŏk 서적 books; publications. sŏjŏksang 서적상 bookshop; bookstore.

sŏjŏm 서점 bookshop; bookstore; bookseller's.

soju 소주 (distilled) spirits; 'soju'.

sok 속 interior; inner part; inside. *soge* 속에 in; within; amid(st).

sok'ada 속하다 belong (to); appertain (to).

sokch'ima 속치마 underskirt; chemise.

sokkae 속개 resumption. *sokkaehada* 속개하다 resume; continue.

sŏkkan 석간 evening paper; evening edition (of).

sokki 속기 shorthand; stenography.

sŏkko 석고 plaster; gypsum. *sŏkkosang* 석고상 plaster bust[statue].

sŏk'oe 석회 lime. *sŏk'oesŏk* 석회석 limestone.

sokkuk 속국 dependency; subject[tributary] state.

sokkye 속계 earthly world; mundane world.

sokpak 속박 restriction. *sokpak'ada* 속박하다 restrict; restrain.

sŏkp'an 석판 lithography; lithograph.

sŏkpang 석방 release; acquittal. *sŏkpanghada* 석방하다 set (a person) free; release.

sokpo 속보 prompt[quick] report; (news) flash.

sokp'yŏn 속편 sequel; follow-up; serial film.

sŏksa 석사 Master. *munhak sŏksa* 문학 석사 Master of Arts(M. A.).

soksagida 속삭이다 ① whisper; speak in a whisper. ② murmur; ripple.

sokta 속다 be cheated[deceived, fooled].

sokta 솎다 thin (out); weed out.

sŏkta 섞다 mix; blend; mingle.

soktal 속달 express[special] delivery.

soktam 속담 proverb; (common) saying; maxim.

sŏkt'an 석탄 coal. *sŏkt'anchae* 석탄재 coal cinders.

sokto 속도 speed; velocity; tempo.

sol 솔 pine (tree). *sollip* 솔잎 pine needle.

sol 솔 brush. *soljil* 솔질 brushing. *sollo t'ŏlda* 솔로 털다 brush off.

sŏl 설 New Year's Day; New Year.

sŏlbi 설비 equipment(s); arrangements; facilities. *sŏlbihada* 설비하다 equip; provide; install.

sŏlch'i 설치 establishment; institution. *sŏlch'ihada* 설치하다 establish; set up; found.

sŏlgye 설계 plan; design. *sŏlgyehada* 설계하다 plan; design; layout.

sŏlgyo 설교 sermon; preaching. *sŏlgyohada* 설교하다 preach. *sŏlgyosa* 설교사 preacher.

sŏllip 설립 foundation; establishment. *sŏllip'ada* 설립하다 found; establish.

sŏllo 선로 railroad[railway] line; railroad track.

sŏlmyŏng 설명 explanation. *sŏlmyŏnghada* 설명하다 explain; account for.

sŏlsa 설사 diarrhea; loose bowels. *sŏlsahada* 설사하다 have loose bowels.

sŏlt'ang 설탕 sugar. *kaksŏlt'ang* 각설탕 lump [cube] sugar. *hŭksŏlt'ang* 흑설탕 muscovado.

solchik 솔직 *solchik'an* 솔직한 plain; frank; candid; straight and honest.

som 솜 cotton; cotton wool.

sŏm 섬 island; isle.

somae 소매 retail (sale). *somaehada* 소매하다 retail; sell at[by] retail.

somae 소매 sleeve. *somaega kin[tchalbŭn]* 소매가 긴[짧은] long[short]-sleeved.

somaech'igi 소매치기 pickpocket. *somaech'igidanghada* 소매치기당하다 have one's pocket picked.

somo 소모 consumption. *somohada* 소모하다 consume; use up.

sonmok 손목 wrist. *sonmogŭl chapta* 손목을 잡다 take (a person) by the wrist.

sŏmŏk'ada 서먹하다 feel awkward[embarrassed]; (be) unfamiliar; be ill at ease.

somssi 솜씨 skill; make; workmanship. *somssi innŭn* 솜씨 있는 skillful; dexterous; tactful.

sŏmu 서무 general affairs. *somukwa* 서무과 general affairs section.

somun 소문 rumo(u)r; report; hearsay. *somunnan* 소문난 (very) famous.

sŏmun 서문 preface; foreword; introduction.

somyŏl 소멸. *somyŏrhada* 소멸하다 disappear; vanish; cease to exist.

sŏmyŏng 서명 signature; autograph. *sŏmyŏnghada* 서명하다 sign one's name.

sŏmyu 섬유 fiber. *injo sŏmyu* 인조 섬유 staple fiber.

son 손 hand. *orŭn[oen]son* 오른[왼]손 right[left] hand. *sone nŏt'a* 손에 넣다 get; obtain.

sŏn 선 line; route. *p'yŏnghaengsŏn* 평행선 parallel line. *kyŏngbusŏn* 경부선 kyŏngbu line.

sŏn 선 interview with a view to marriage.

sonagi 소나기 shower. *sonagirŭl mannada* 소나기를 만나다 be caught in a shower.

sonamu 소나무 pine(tree). → **sol** 솔.

sonarae 손아래. *sonaraeŭi* 손아래의 younger; junior. *sonaraet saram* 손아랫 사람 one's junior [inferiors, subordinates].

sŏnbae 선배 senior; elder; old-timer(*Am.*).

sŏnbak 선박 vessel; ship; shipping; marine. *sŏnbak hoesa* 선박 회사 shipping company.

sŏnbal 선발 selection; choice. *sŏnbarhada* 선발하다 select; choose.

sŏnban 선반 shelf; rack.

sŏnbul 선불 payment in advance. *sŏnburhada* 선불하다 pay in advance.

sonchit 손짓 gesture; signs; hand signal. *sonjit'ada* 손짓하다 (make a) gesture; beckon.

sŏnch'ul 선출 election. *sŏnch'urhada* 선출하다 elect; return (*Eng.*).

sondokki 손도끼 hand ax; hatchet.

sŏndong 선동 instigation; agitation. *sŏndonghada* 선동하다 instigate; agitate.

sŏndu 선두 head; top; lead. *sŏndu t'aja* 선두 타자 lead-off (batter); first batter.

sondŭlda 손들다 ① raise[hold up] one's hand ② yield[submit] (to).

sŏng 성 castle; fortress; citadel.

sŏng 성 family name; surname.

sŏng 성 gender; sex. *sŏngchŏk* 성적 sexual.

sŏng 성 anger; wrath; rage. *sŏngi nada* 성이 나다 grow angry.

sŏn-gaek 선객 passenger. *idŭng sŏn-gaek* 2등 선객 second-class passenger.

songaji 송아지 calf.

sŏngbun 성분 ingredient; component; constituent.

songbyŏl 송별 farewell; send-off. *songbyŏrhoe* 송별회 farewell party[meeting].

sŏngpyŏng 성병 venereal disease(V.D.); sexual disease; social disease(*Am.*).

songch'ungi 송충이 pine caterpillar.

sŏngdae 성대 vocal cords[bands].

sŏngdang 성당 church; catholic church; sanctuary.

songduritchae 송두리째 all; completely; thoroughly. *songduritchae kajyŏgada* 송두리째 가져가다 take away everything.

sŏnggashida 성가시다 (be)troublesome; annoying; bothersome.

sŏnggong 성공 success. *sŏnggonghada* 성공하다 succeed; be successful.

songgot 송곳 gimlet; drill; awl.

songgŭm 송금 remittance. *songgŭmhada* 송금하다 send money; remit money.

sŏnggyo 성교 sexual intercourse.

sŏnggyŏng 성경 (Holy) Bible; Scriptures.

songhwan 송환 sending back; repatriation. *songhwanhada* 송환하다 send back; repatriate.

songi 송이. *songibŏsŏt* 송이버섯 pine mushroom.

songi 송이 cluster; bunch; flake (of snow).

sŏngin 성인 sage; saint; holy man.

sŏngjang 성장 growth. *sŏngjanghada* 성장하다 grów (up). *sŏngjanghan* 성장한 grown-up.

sŏngjik 성직 holy orders; ministry. *sŏngjikcha* 성직자 churchman; clergyman.

sŏngjil 성질 nature; character.

songjogi 성조기 Stars and Stripes; Star-spangled Banner.

sŏngjŏk 성적 result; record; merit. *sŏngjŏkp'yo* 성적표 list of students' record; grade sheet.

sŏngkwa 성과 result; fruit; outcome.

sŏngkyŏk 성격 character; personality.

songmul 속물 vulgar person; snob; worldling.

sŏngmyo 성묘. *sŏngmyohada* 성묘하다 visit one's ancestor's grave.

sŏngmyŏng 성명 declaration; statement. *sŏng-*

myŏnghada 성명하다 declare; announce.

sŏngmyŏng 성명 (full) name.

sŏngnip 성립. *sŏngnip'ada* 성립하다 be formed [organized]; be effected.

songnunssŏp 속눈썹 eyelashes. *injo songnunssŏp* 인조 속눈썹 false eyelashes.

sŏngnyang 성냥 matches. *sŏngnyangkap* 성냥갑 match box. *sŏngnyang kaebi* 성냥 개비 match stick.

songnyo 송료 carriage; postage.

songnyŏk 속력 →**sokto** 속도. *chŏnsongnyŏgŭro* 전 속력으로 (at) full speed.

sŏn-go 선고 sentence; verdict. *sŏn-gohada* 선고하다 sentence; condemn.

sŏn-gŏ 선거 election. *sŏn-gŏhada* 선거하다 elect; vote for.

sonkŏul 손거울 hand mirror.

songp'ung 송풍 ventilation. *songp'unggi* 송풍기 ventilator; blower; fan.

sŏngshil 성실 sincerity; honesty. *sŏngshirhan* 성 실한 sincere; faithful.

sŏngsŏ 성서 (Holy) Bible; Scripture.

songsuhwagi 송수화기 hand set.

sŏngsuk 성숙. *sŏngsuk'ada* 성숙하다 ripen; get ripe. *sŏngsuk'an* 성숙한 ripe; mature.

sŏngt'anjŏl 성탄절 Christmas (day).

sŏngŭi 성의 sincerity; faith.

sŏn-guja 선구자 pioneer; forerunner.

sŏn-gŭm 선금 advance; prepayment. *sŏn-gŭmŭl ch'irŭda* 선금을 치르다 pay in advance.

sŏn-gyo 선교 missionary work. *sŏn-gyohada* 선교 하다 evangelize. *sŏn-gyosa* 선교사 missionary.

sŏngyok 성욕 sexual desire(s)[appetite].

songyu 송유 oil supply. *songyugwan* 송유관 (oil) pipeline.

sonhae 손해 damage; injury; loss. *sonhae paesang* 손해 배상 compensation for damages.

sŏninjang 선인장 cactus.

sŏnipkyŏn 선입견 preconception; preoccupation; prejudice; preconceived idea.

sonjabi 손잡이 handle; knob; gripe.

sŏnjang 선장 captain; skipper; master mariner.

sŏnjo 선조 ancestor; forefather.

sŏnjŏn 선전 propaganda; publicity; advertisement. *sŏnjŏnhada* 선전하다 propagandize; advertise.

sonkabang 손가방 briefcase (*Am*); brief bag (*Eng.*); handbag; gripsack (*Am.*).

sonkarak 손가락 finger. *ŏmjisonkarak* 엄지손가락 thumb. *chipke[kaundet, yak, saekki]sonkarak* 집게[가운뎃, 약, 새끼]손가락 index[middle, ring, little] finger.

sonkkopta 손꼽다 count on one's fingers. *sonkkomnŭn* 손꼽는 leading; prominent.

sŏnmul 선물 present; gift. *sŏnmurhada* 선물하다 give[send] a present.

sonnim 손님 ① guest; caller; visitor ② customer; client; audience ③ passenger.

sŏnmyŏng 선명. *sŏnmyŏnghada[hage]* 선명하다[하게] distinct(ly); clear(ly); vivid(ly).

sonnyŏ 손녀 granddaughter.

sŏnnyŏ 선녀 fairy; nymph.

sonppyŏkch'ida 손뼉치다 clap (one's) hands.

sŏnp'unggi 선풍기 fan; electric fan.

sonsaek 손색 inferiority. *sonsaegi ŏpta* 손색이 없다 bear[stand] comparison (with); be equal (to)

sŏnsaeng 선생 teacher; instructor; schoolmaster; schoolmistress(*Am.*).

sonshil 손실 loss; disadvantage; damage. *k'ŭn sonshil* 큰 손실 great[heavy, serious] loss.

sonsu 손수 with one's own hands; personally.

sŏnsu 선수 player; athlete(*Eng.*); champion.

sonsugŏn 손수건 handkerchief.

sŏnt'aek 선택 selection; choice; option. *sŏnt'aek'ada* 선택하다 select; choose.

sont'op 손톱 fingernail. *sont'op kkakki* 손톱 깎이 nail clipper.

sontŭng 손등 back of the hand.

sŏnttŭt 선뜻 lightly; readily; willingly; offhand.

sŏnŭi 선의 favo(u)rable sense; good faith. *sŏnŭiŭi* 선의의 well-intentioned.

sŏnŭrhada 서늘하다 (be) cool; refreshing; chilly.

sŏnŏn 선언 declaration; proclamation. *sŏnŏnhada* 선언하다 declare; proclaim.

sonwi 손위. *sonwiŭi* 손위의 older; elder; senior *sonwit saram* 손윗 사람 senior; superior.

sŏnwon 선원 seaman; crew; sailor.

sŏnyak 선약 previous engagement.

sonyŏ 소녀 (young) girl; lass; maid.

sonyŏn 소년 boy; lad. *sonyŏnŭi* 소년의 juvenile.

sŏnyul 선율 melody. *sŏnyulchŏk* 선율적 melodious.

sop'o 소포 parcel; package; packet.

sŏpsŏp'ada 섭섭하다 (be) sorry; sad; disappointed; regrettable; reproachful.

sŏpssi 섭씨 Celsius(C.); centigrade.

sop'ung 소풍 outing; excursion; picnic. *sop'ung kada* 소풍 가다 go on an excursion[a picnic].

sora 소라 top[wreath] shell.

soran 소란 disturbance; commotion. *soranhada* 소란하다 (be) noisy; disturbing.

sŏrap 서랍 drawer.

sori 소리 ① sound; noise ② voice; cry. *k'ŭn[chagŭn] soriro* 큰[작은] 소리로 in a loud[low] voice.

sŏri 서리 frost; white frost.

sorich'ida 소리치다 →**sorijirŭda** 소리지르다.

sŏrida 서리다 steam up; get steamed.

sorijirŭda 소리지르다 shout; cry[call] (out);scream; roar; yell.

sŏro 서로 mutually; each other; one another.

sŏron 서론 introduction; introductory remarks.

sŏrŭn 서른 thirty. *sŏrŭnsal* 서른살 thirty years of age.

soryang 소량 small quantity[amount]. *soryangŭi* 소량의 little; small·quantity[amount] of.

soryŏng 소령 major(*army*); lieutenant commander (*navy*); wing commander(*air*).

sŏryu 서류 documents; papers. *sŏryu kabang* 서류가방 briefcase(*Am.*); brief bag(*Eng.*).

sosaeng 소생 revival; reanimation. *sosaenghada* 소생하다 revive; come to oneself.

sosang 소상 earthen[clay] image.

soshik 소식 news; tidings; information.

sŏshik 서식 (fixed) form; formula. *sŏshige ttara* 서식에 따라 in due form.

sŏsŏhi 서서히 slowly. →**ch'ŏnch'ŏnhi** 천천히.

sosok 소속. *sosok'ada* 소속하다 belong to; be attached to. *sosogŭi* 소속의 attached[belonging] to.

sosŏl 소설 novel; story; fiction. *sosŏlga* 소설가 novelist.

sosong 소송 lawsuit; legal action. *sosonghada* 소

송하다 sue; bring a lawsuit.

sŏsŏnggŏrida 서성거리다 walk up and down restlessly; go back and forth uneasily.

sosu 소수 minority; few; small number. *sosu minjok*[*p'a*] 소수민족[파] minority race[faction].

sosu 소수 decimal. *sosuchŏm* 소수점 decimal point.

sot 솥 iron pot; kettle. *sottukkŏng* 솥뚜껑 lid of a kettle.

sotta 솟다 ① rise[soar, tower] high ② gush [spring] out; well out.

sŏttal 섣달 December. *sŏttal kŭmŭm* 섣달 그믐 New Year's Eve.

sŏt'urŭda 서투르다 (be) unfamiliar; (be) awkward; clumsy; unskil(l)ful; stiff; poor.

Sŏul 서울 Seoul (capital of Korea).

soŭm 소음 noise. *soŭm pangji* 소음 방지 arrest of noise. *soŭm konghae* 소음 공해 noise pollution.

sowi 소위 second lieutenant (*army*); ensign (*navy*); second sublieutenant (*Eng.*).

sowi 소위 what is called; so-called.

sŏyak 서약 oath; pledge. *sŏyak'ada* 서약하다 swear; vow; pledge.

sŏyang 서양 the West; the Occident. *sŏyangŭi* 서양의 Western; Occidental. *sŏyang saram* 서양 사람 Westerner; European.

soyongdori 소용돌이 whirlpool; swirl.

soyu 소유 possession. *soyuhada* 소유하다 have; possess; own; hold.

ssada 싸다 wrap up[in]; do up; bundle; pack up.

ssada 싸다 (be) inexpensive; cheap; low-priced. *ssage* 싸게 cheaply; at a low cost.

ssada 싸다 excrete (urine or feces); void; discharge.

ssaida 쌓이다 be piled up; be heaped.

ssak 싹 bud; sprout; shoot. *ssagi t'ŭda* 싹이 트다 bud; shoot; sprout.

ssal 쌀 (raw, uncooked) rice. *ssalkage* 쌀가게 rice store. *ssalt'ong* 쌀통 rice chest.

ssalssarhada 쌀쌀하다 ① (be) chilly; (rather) cold ② distant; coldhearted; indifferent.

ssangan-gyŏng 쌍안경 binoculars; field glasses.

ssangbang 쌍방 both parties[sides]; either party. *ssangbangŭi* 쌍방의 both; either; mutual.

ssangkŏp'ul 쌍거풀 double eyelid.

ssat'a 쌓다 ① pile[heap] (up); stack; lay ② accumulate; store up.

ssauda 싸우다 fight; make war; struggle; quarrel.

ssi 씨 seed; stone; kernel; pit; pip. *ssi ŏmnŭn* 씨 없는 seedless.

ssi 씨 Mr.; Miss; Mrs. *Kimssi* 김씨 Mr. Kim.

ssiat 씨앗 seed. →**ssi** 씨.

ssikssik'ada 씩씩하다 (be) manly; manful; brave.

ssipta 씹다 chew; masticate.

ssirŭm 씨름 wrestling; wrestling match. *ssirŭmhada* 씨름하다 wrestle.

ssitta 씻다 wash; wash away; cleanse.

ssoda 쏘다 shoot; fire; discharge.

ssŏk 썩 ① right away; at once ② very much; exceedingly.

ssŏkta 썩다 go bad; rot; decay; corrupt. *ssŏgŭn* 썩은 bad; rotten; stale.

ssollida 쏠리다 ① incline; lean ② be disposed to; tend to; get enthusiastic (about).

ssŏlmae 썰매 sled; sleigh; sledge.

ssotta 쏟다 ① pour out; spill; shed; drop ② concentrate; devote; effort.

ssŭda 쓰다 use; make use of; spend (money) on.

ssŭda 쓰다 write; scribe; describe; compose.

ssŭda 쓰다 put on; wear; cover.

ssŭdadŭmta 쓰다듬다 stroke; pat; smooth; caress.

ssŭiuda 씌우다 put on; cover.

ssuksŭrŏpta 쑥스럽다 (be) unbecoming; indecent.

ssŭlda 쓸다 sweep (up, away, off). *pangŭl ssŭlda* 방을 쓸다 sweep a room.

ssŭlssŭrhada 쓸쓸하다 (be) lonely; lonesome.

ssŭlteŏpta 쓸데없다 be of no use[value]; (be) useless; worthless.

ssŭnusŭm 쓴웃음 bitter[grim] smile.

ssŭrebatki 쓰레받기 dustpan.

ssŭregi 쓰레기 garbage; rubbish; trash(*Am.*). *ssŭregit'ong* 쓰레기통 garbage can; dustbin.

ssŭrida 쓰리다 smart; burn; ache; be tingling.

ssŭrŏjida 쓰러지다 ① collapse; fall down ② sink [break] down ③ fall dead ④ go bankrupt.

ssushida 쑤시다 ① pick; poke ② throb with pain; twinge; tingle; ache.

sswaegi 쐐기 wedge; chock.

su 수 embroidery. *sunot'a* 수놓다 embroider.

subae 수배 make[spread] (a) search (for). *subae inmul* 수배 인물 criminal wanted by the police.

subak 수박 watermelon.

subi 수비 defense. *subihada* 수비하다 defend; guard. *subidae* 수비대 garrison.

subu 수부 mariner. → **subyŏng** 수병.

subun 수분 moisture; juice; water. *subuni manŭn* 수분이 많은 watery; juicy.

subyŏng 수병 sailor; seaman; blue jacket.

such'aehwa 수채화 water colo(u)r (painting).

such'i 수치 shame; disgrace. *such'isŭrŏn* 수치스런 shameful; disgraceful.

sŭch'ida 스치다 graze; glance (off); go past by.

such'ul 수출 export; exportation. *such'urhada* 수출하다 export; ship abroad.

sudan 수단 means; way; measure; step.

sudang 수당 allowance; bonus. *kajok sudang* 가족 수당 family allowance.

sudasŭrŏpta 수다스럽다 (be) talkative; chatty.

sudo 수도 capital; metropolis. *sudoŭi* 수도의 metropolitan.

sudo 수도 waterworks; water service[supply].

sudo 수도 asceticism. *sudowon* 수도원 monastery; cloister. *sudosŭng* 수도승 monk.

sudong 수동 passivity. *sudongjŏk(ŭro)* 수동적(으로) passive(ly).

suduruk'ada 수두룩하다 (be) abundant; plentiful.

sugap 수갑 handcuffs; manacles.

sugi 수기 note; memoirs; memorandum.

sugo 수고 trouble; pains; efforts. *sugohada* 수고하다 take pains[trouble].

sugŏ 숙어 idiom; (idiomatic) phrase.

sugŏn 수건 towel. *sesu sugŏn* 세수 수건 face towel. *sugŏn kŏri* 수건 걸이 towel horse[rack].

sugong 수공 handicraft; manual work. *sugongŏp* 수공업 manual industry.

sugŭm 수금 bill collection. *sugŭmhada* 수금하다 collect bills[money].

sugun-gŏrida 수군거리다 talk in whispers; speak under one's breath.

sugŭrŏjida 수그러지다 ① droop; be bowed; hang (down) ② subside; abate; dwindle.

suhae 수해 damage by a flood; flood disaster.

suhak 수학 mathematics.

suhamul 수하물 luggage (*Eng.*); baggage (*Am.*).

suho 수호. *suhohada* 수호하다 protect; guard.

suhŏm 수험. *suhŏmhada* 수험하다 take[undergo, sit for] an examination.

suhwagi 수화기 (telephone) receiver; earphone.

suhwak 수확 harvest; crop. *suhwak'ada* 수확하다 harvest; reap; gather in.

suhyŏl 수혈 blood transfusion. *suhyŏrhada* 수혈하다 transfuse blood.

suil 수일 a few days; several days.

suip 수입 income; earnings. *suipkwa chich'ul* 수입과 지출 income and outgo.

suip 수입 importation; import. *suip'ada* 수입하다 import. *suipp'um* 수입품 imported articles[goods].

sujae 수재 genius; talented[brilliant] man.

suji 수지 income and outgo; revenue and expenditure. *suji mannŭn* 수지 맞는 profitable.

sujik 수직. *sujigŭi* 수직의 perpendicular; vertical. *sujiksŏn* 수직선 vertical line.

sujip 수집 collection. *sujip'ada* 수집하다 collect. *sujipka* 수집가 collector.

sujŏng 수정 crystal. *chasujŏng* 자수정 amethyst.

sujŏng 수정 amendment; modification. *sujŏnghada* 수정하다 amend; modify.

sujŏnno 수전노 miser; niggard.

sujun 수준 ① water level ② level; standard. *munhwa sujun* 문화 수준 cultural level.

sujupta 수줍다 (be) shy; bashful; timid.

sukche 숙제 homework; home task. *panghak sukche* 방학 숙제 holiday task.

sukchik 숙직 night duty[watch]. *sukchik'ada* 숙직하다 be on night duty; keep night watch.

sutkarak 숟가락 spoon. *papsutkarak* 밥숟가락 tablespoon. *ch'assutkarak* 찻숟가락 teaspoon.

sukpak 숙박. *sukpak'ada* 숙박하다 lodge; stay. *sukpangnyo* 숙박료 lodging charge; hotel charges.

sukpu 숙부 uncle.

sukso 숙소 place of abode; one's address.

sul 술 wine; rice wine; liquor. *surŭl mashida* 술을 마시다 have a drink. *sure ch'wihada* 술에 취하다 get drunk.

sulchan 술잔 wine cup; liquor glass; goblet.

sulchip 술집 bar (room); saloon (*Am.*); public house (*Eng.*); tavern.

sŭlgiropta 슬기롭다 (be) wise; prudent; sensible.

sŭlgŭmŏni 슬그머니 stealthily; secretly; furtively.

sulkkun 술꾼 (heavy) drinker; tippler.

sulpyŏng 술병 liquor bottle.

sŭlp'ŭda 슬프다 (be) sad; sorrowful; pathetic.

sŭlp'ŭm 슬픔 sorrow; sadness; grief.

sullaejapki 술래잡기 tag; blindman's buff.

sŭlsŭl 슬슬 slowly; gently; lightly.

sum 숨 breath; breathing. *sumŭl shwida* 숨을 쉬다 breathe; respire.

suman 수만 tens[scores] of thousands.

sumta 숨다 hide[conceal] oneself; take cover. *sumŭn* 숨은 hidden; unknown.

sumbakkokchil 숨바꼭질 hide-and-(go)-seek; I-spy; hy-spy.

sumch'ada 숨차다 pant; be out[short] of breath.

sumgida 숨기다 hide; conceal; shelter.

sŭmida 스미다 soak; permeate through; ooze out.

sumilto 수밀도 juicy peach.

sumok 수목 trees(and shrubs); arbors.

sumyŏng 수명 life; span of life; life expectancy.

sun 순 pure; genuine. *sunhan-gukshik* 순한국식 purely Korean style.

sunan 수난 suffering; ordeals; crucifixion.

sunbak 순박. *sunbak'an* 순박한 naive; unsophisticated; homely; simple and honest.

sunbŏn 순번 order; turn. →**ch'arye** 차례.

sun-gan 순간 moment; instant; second. *sun-ganjŏk* 순간적 momentary; instantaneous.

sungbae 숭배 worship; adoration. *sungbaehada* 숭배하다 worship; admire; adore.

sŭngbu 승부 victory or defeat; match; game; bout. *musŭngbu* 무승부 drawn[tie] game; draw.

sŭngch'a 승차. *sŭngch'ahada* 승차하다 take[board] a train; get on a car.

sŭnggaek 승객 passenger; fare.

sŭngin 승인 recognition; acknowledg(e)ment; approval. *sŭnginhada* 승인하다 recognize; approve.

sŭngjin 승진 promotion; advancement. *sŭngjinhada* 승진하다 rise (in rank); be promoted[advanced].

sŭngma 승마 riding; horse riding.

sŭngmuwon 승무원 trainman; carman; crew.

sungmyŏng 숙명 fate; destiny; fatality.

sŭngnak 승낙 consent; assent; approval. *sŭngnak'ada* 승낙하다 consent[agree, assent] to.

sŭngni 승리 victory; triumph. *sŭngnihada* 승리하다 win; win[gain] a victory.

sungnyŏ 숙녀 lady; gentlewoman. *sungnyŏdaun* 숙녀다운 ladylike.

sŭngnyŏ 승려 Buddhist monk; priest.

sungnyung 숭늉 scorched-rice tea.

sungnyŏn 숙련 skill; dexterity. *sungnyŏn-gong* 숙련공 skilled worker.

sŭngsan 승산 chance[prospect] of victory; chances of winning.

sun-gŭm 순금 pure gold; solid gold.

sun-gyŏl 순결 purity; chastity; virginity. *sun-gyŏrhan* 순결한 pure; chaste; clean; unspotted.

sunhwan 순환 circulation; rotation; cycle. *hyŏraek sunhwan* 혈액 순환 circulation of blood.

suniik 순이익 net profit[gain]; clear profit.

sŭnim 스님 Buddhist priest[monk]; bonze.

sunjik 순직. *sunjik'ada* 순직하다 die[be killed] at one's post of duty; die in harness.

sunjin 순진. *sunjinhan* 순진한 naive; pure; innocent; genuine.

sunjong 순종. *sunjonghada* 순종하다 obey; submit tamely.

sunmo 순모 pure wool. *sunmoŭi* 순모의 all-wool; pure-wool(en).

sunsŏ 순서 order; sequence. *sunsŏrŭl ttara* 순서를 따라 in proper sequence.

sunwi 순위 order; ranking; grade.

sunyŏ 수녀 nun; sister. *sunyŏwon* 수녀원 nunnery; convent. *sunyŏwonjang* 수녀원장 abbess.

sunyŏn 수년 several years; some[a few] years. *sunyŏn chŏn* 수년 전 some years ago.

sŭngyongch'a 승용차 passenger car; private car; motorcar for riding.

suŏp 수업 teaching; instruction; lesson. *suŏp'ada* 수업하다 teach; instruct.

sup 숲 wood; forest; grove.

sŭpchi 습지 swampy land; boggy ground; marsh.

sup'il 수필 essay. *sup'ilga* 수필가 essayist.

sŭpki 습기 moisture; dampness; humidity.

sŭpkwan 습관 habit; custom. *sŭpkwanjŏgin* 습관적인 habitual; customary. *sŭpkwanjŏgŭro* 습관적으로 habitually; from habit.

sŭpkyŏk 습격 attack; assault; raid. *sŭpkyŏk'ada* 습격하다 attack; raid; charge.

sup'ok 수폭, **suso p'okt'an** 수소 폭탄 hydrogen bomb; H-bomb.

supŏp 수법 technique; style; way; trick.

sup'yo 수표 check (*Am.*); cheque (*Eng.*). *pojŭng sup'yo* 보증 수표 certified check. *pudo sup'yo* 부도 수표 dishonored check.

sup'yŏng 수평 water level; horizon. *sup'yŏngsŏn* 수평선 sea line; horizon.

surak 수락 acceptance; agreement. *surak'ada* 수락하다 accept; agree to.

sure 수레 wagon; cart. *surebak'wi* 수레바퀴 wheel.

suri 수리 repair; mending. *surihada* 수리하다 repair; mend; have (a thing) mended. *surigong* 수리공 repairman.

surip 수립 establishment. *surip'ada* 수립하다 establish; found; set up.

suro 수로 waterway; watercourse.

suryang 수량 quantity; volume.

suryo 수료 completion. *suryohada* 수료하다 complete; finish (course).

suryŏk 수력 water power; hydraulic power. *su-*

ryŏk palchŏnso 수력 발전소 hydraulic plant.

suryŏn 수련 training; practice. *suryŏnhada* 수련하다 train; practice. *suryŏnŭi* 수련의 intern; apprentice doctor.

suryŏng 수령 leader; head; chief; boss.

suryŏp 수렵 shooting (*Eng.*); hunting (*Am.*). *suryŏp'ada* 수렵하다 hunt.

suryut'an 수류탄 hand grenade; pineapple (*mil.*).

susa 수사 criminal investigation; search. *susahada* 수사하다 investigate; search.

susaek 수색 search; investigation. *susaek'ada* 수색하다 look[hunt, search] for.

susan 수산. *susanmul* 수산물 marine products. *susan taehak* 수산 대학 fisheries college. *susanŏp* 수산업 fisheries.

susang 수상 prime minister; premier.

susang 수상. *susanghan* 수상한 suspicious(-looking); doubtful; questionable.

suse 수세. *suseshik pyŏnso* 수세식 변소 flush toilet; water closet.

sushin 수신 receipt of message. *sushinhada* 수신하다 receive a message. *sushin-gi* 수신기 receiver. *sushinin* 수신인 addressee.

susok 수속 →**chŏlch'a** 절차.

susŏk 수석 head; chief; top[head] seat.

susŏn 수선 repair; mending. *susŏnhada* 수선하다 repair; mend; have (a shoe) mended.

susong 수송 transportation. *susonghada* 수송하다 transport; convey.

susŏnhwa 수선화 daffodil; narcissus.

susukkekki 수수께끼 riddle; puzzle; mystery. *susukkekki kat'ŭn* 수수께끼 같은 enigmatic; mysterious; riddling.

susul 수술 (surgical) operation. *susurhada* 수술하다 operate on; perform a surgical operation. *susulshil* 수술실 operating room.

sŭsŭng 스승 teacher; master; mistress.

sŭsŭro 스스로 (for) oneself; in person. *sŭsŭroŭi* 스스로의 one's own; personal.

susuryo 수수료 commission; fee; service charge.

sut 숯 charcoal. *sutpul* 숯불 charcoal fire.

sucha 수자 figure; numeral.

sut'ong 수통 water flask; canteen.

suu 수우 (water) buffalo. →**mulso** 물소.

suŭn 수은 mercury; quicksilver. *suŭnju* 수은주 mercurial thermometer.

suwan 수완 ability; talent; capacity. *suwan-ga* 수완가 man of capacity; go-getter(*Am.*).

suwi 수위 guard; doorkeeper; gatekeeper.

Sŭwisŭ 스위스 Switzerland, Swiss Confederation.

suworhada 수월하다 (be) easy; be no trouble. *suworhage* 수월하게 easily; with ease.

suyo 수요 demand. *suyo konggŭp* 수요 공급 demand and supply. *suyoja* 수요자 user.

suyoil 수요일 Wednesday.

suyong 수용 accommodation. *suyonghada* 수용하다 accommodate; receive. *suyongso* 수용소 asylum; camp.

suyŏng 수영 swimming; swim. *suyŏnghada* 수영하다 swim; have a swim. *suyŏngbok* 수영복 swimming suit.

syassŭ 샤쓰 shirts; undershirts; vest (*Eng.*).

syawo 샤워 shower. *syaworŭl hada* 샤워를 하다 have[take] a shower.

◄◄◄ **T** ►►►

ta 다 ① all; everything; everybody ② utterly; completely. *tahaesŏ* 다해서 in all; all told. *tagach'i* 다같이 together.

tabang 다방 tearoom; teahouse; coffee house; coffee shop (of hotel).

tach'ida 다치다 be[get, become] wounded[hurt, injured, damaged]; bruised.

tadari 다달이 every month; monthly.

tadŭmta 다듬다 ① make beautiful; embellish; adorn; trim up ② prune.

tae 대 bamboo. *taebaguni* 대바구니 bamboo basket.

taebi 대비 provision; preparation. *taebihada* 대비하다 be ready for.

taebŏbwon 대법원 Supreme Court. *taebŏbwonjang* 대법원장 Chief Justice.

taebu 대부 loan(ing). *taebuhada* 대부하다 lend; loan; (make an) advance.

taebubun 대부분 most; major part (of); mostly; largely; for the most part.

taebyŏn 대변 excrement; feces. *taebyŏnŭl poda* 대변을 보다 go to stool; evacuate.

taech'aek 대책 countermeasure. *taech'aegŭl seuda* 대책을 세우다 work out a countermeasure.

taech'e 대체. *taech'ejŏgin* 대체적인 general; main; rough. *taech'ero* 대체로 generally; as a whole.

taech'ung 대충 almost; nearly; about; roughly.

taedae 대대 battalion. *taedaejang* 대대장 battalion commander.

taedae 대대. *taedaero* 대대로 from generation to

generation; for generations.

taedaejŏk 대대적. *taedaejŏgin* 대대적인 great; grand; wholesale. *taedaejŏgŭro* 대대적으로 extensively; on a large scale.

taedam 대담. *taedamhan* 대담한 bold; daring. *taedamhage* 대담하게 boldly; daringly.

taedanhada 대단하다 (be) enormous; severe; intense; grave. *taedanhi* 대단히 very; seriously; exceedingly; awfully.

taedap 대답 answer; reply. *taedap'ada* 대답하다 answer; reply; respond (to); give an answer.

taedasu 대다수 large majority; greater part.

taedongmaek 대동맥 main artery.

taegada 대가다 arrive on time; be in time (for).

taegae 대개 mostly; for the most part; in general.

taegang 대강 ① general principles; outline; general features. ② generally; roughly.

taegŏmch'alch'ŏng 대검찰청 Supreme Public Prosecutor's Office.

taegŭm 대금 price; charge; money. *taegŭm ch'ŏnggusŏ* 대금 청구서 bill; check (*Am.*).

taegyumo 대규모 large scale. *taegyumoro* 대규모로 on large scale.

taehak 대학 university; college. *taehaksaeng* 대학생 university student. *taehagwon* 대학원 graduate school; (post) graduate course; *taehak pyŏngwon* 대학 병원 university hospital.

Taehan 대한 Korea. *Taehanmin-guk* 대한민국 Republic of Korea.

taehang 대항 opposition; rivalry. *taehanghada* 대항하다 oppose; cope with.

taehapshil 대합실 waiting room.

taehoe 대회 great[grand] meeting; mass meeting; rally; convention. *taehoerŭl yŏlda* 대회를 열다 hold a mass meeting.

taehwa 대화 conversation; dialogue. *taehwahada* 대화하다 talk[converse] with. 「success.

taeinki 대인기 great popularity; big hit; great

taejang 대장 general (*army, air*); admiral (*navy*).

taejang 대장 ledger; register.

taejangbu 대장부 (brave) man; manly[great] man.

taejangjangi 대장장이 smith; blacksmith.

taejangkan 대장간 blacksmith's shop; smithy.

taeji 대지 site; lot; plot. *kŏnch'uk taeji* 건축 대지 building[housing] site[lot, land].

taejo 대조 contrast; collation. *taejohada* 대조하다 contrast; check; collate.

taejŏn 대전 great war; the World War. *cheich'a segye taejŏn* 제2차 세계 대전 World War Ⅱ.

taejŏp 대접 treatment; entertainment; reception. *taejŏp'ada* 대접하다 treat; entertain; receive.

taejugyo 대주교 archbishop.

taejung 대중 masses; populace; multitude. *kŭllo taejung* 근로 대중 working masses.

taek 댁 ① (your, his, her) house; residence ② you ③ the wife of (a person); Mrs ….

taemaech'ul 대매출 special bargain; great sale.

taemŏri 대머리 bald head; bald-headed person.

taemuncha 대문자 capital letter.

taenggi 댕기 pigtail ribbon.

taep'o 대포 gun; cannon; artillery. *taep'orŭl ssoda* 대포를 쏘다 fire a gun.

taep'yo 대표 representation; representative. *taep'yohada* 대표하다 represent; stand[act] for.

taeri 대리 procuration; representation; agency. *taeriin* 대리인 proxy; substitute; deputy; agent. *taerijŏm* 대리점 agency.

taerip 대립 opposition; rivalry; confrontation;antagonism. *taerip'ada* 대립하다 be opposed to.

taerisŏk 대리석 marble.

taeryang 대량 large quantity. *taeryang saengsan* 대량 생산 mass production.

taeryŏng 대령 colonel (*army*); captain (*navy*); flight colonel (*air*).

taeryuk 대륙 continent. *taeryukkan t'andot'an* 대륙간 탄도탄 intercontinental ballistic missile.

taesa 대사 ambassador. *chumi〔chuil, chuyŏng〕 taesa* 주미〔주일, 주영〕 대사 ambassador to the United States〔Japan, Great Britain〕.

taesagwan 대사관 embassy. *Miguk taesagwan* 미국 대사관 American Embassy.

taesang 대상 object; target.

taeshin 대신 (Cabinet) minister. →**changgwan** 장관.

taesŏyang 대서양 the Atlantic (Ocean).

taet'ongnyŏng 대통령 president. *taet'ongnyŏngŭi* 대통령의 presidential. *taet'ongnyŏng sŏn-gŏ* 대통령 선거 presidential election. *taet'ongnyŏng yŏngbuin* 대통령 영부인 first lady.

taettŭm 대뜸 at once; immediately; outright.

taeu 대우 treatment; reception; pay; service. *taeuhada* 대우하다 treat; receive; pay. *nomuja taeu kaesŏn* 노무자 대우 개선 improvement of labor condition.

taewi 대위 captain(*army*, *air*); lieutenant (*navy*).

taeyong 대용 substitution. *taeyongp'um* 대용품 substitute article.

taeyŏsŏt 대여섯 about five or six.

tagalsaek 다갈색 (yellowish) brown; liver-color.

tagaoda 다가오다 approach; draw[come] near; draw close.

tagŭp'ada 다급하다 (be) imminent; urgent; pressing.

tagwa 다과 tea and cake; light refreshments.

tahaeng 다행 good fortune[luck]. *tahaenghada* 다행하다 (be) happy; lucky; fortunate. *tahaenghi* 다행히 happily; fortunately; luckily.

tajida 다지다 ① ram; harden (the ground) ② mince; chop (up) ③ make sure of; press (a person) for a definite answer.

tajim 다짐 promise; pledge; assurance. *tajimhada* 다짐하다 assure; pledge; (make a) vow.

tak 닭 hen; cock[rooster]. *takkogi* 닭고기 chicken. *takchang* 닭장 coop; henhouse.

takch'ida 닥치다 approach; draw[come] near; be at hand.

takta 닦다 ① polish; shine; burnish; brush; wipe; scrub ② improve; cultivate; train.

tal 달 ① moon. *porŭmtal* 보름달 full moon ② month. *k'ŭn[chagŭn]dal* 큰[작은]달 odd[even] month. *chinandal* 지난달 last month.

talda 달다 weigh. *chŏullo talda* 저울로 달다 weigh (a thing) in the balance.

talda 달다 (be) sweet; sugary.

talda 달다 ① attach; affix; fasten ② fix; set up ③ put on; wear ④ register ⑤ burn.

talguji 달구지 cart; ox-cart.

talk'omhada 달콤하다 (be) sweet; sugary; honeyed.

tallaeda 달래다 appease; soothe; coax; beguile; calm; amuse; pacify; dandle.

tallajida 달라지다 change; undergo a change; alter; vary.

tallida 달리다 run; dash; gallop.

tallyŏdŭlda 달려들다 pounce on; fly at; jump[leap, spring] at[on].

tallyŏk 달력 calendar; almanac.

tallyŏn 단련 ① temper; forging ② training; drilling; discipline. *tallyŏnhada* 단련하다 ① temper; forge ② train; drill; discipline.

talp'aengi 달팽이 snail.

talsŏng 달성 achievement. *talsŏnghada* 달성하다 accomplish; achieve; attain.

talt'a 닳다 ① be worn out[down]; be rubbed off [down]; wear threadbare ② be boiled down ③ lose (one's) modesty.

tam 담 wall; fence. *toldam* 돌담 stone[brick] wall. *hŭktam* 흙담 mud[earthen] wall.

tam 담 phlegm; sputum.

taman 다만 ① only; merely; simply ② but; however; and yet; still.

tambae 담배 tobacco; cigaret(te). *tambaerŭl p'iuda* 담배를 피우다 smoke (tobacco). *tambae kage* 담배 가게 cigar store.

tambo 담보 security; mortgage; guarantee; warrant. *tamborŭl chapta* 담보를 잡다 take security.

tamdang 담당 charge. *tamdanghada* 담당하다 take charge (of); be in charge of.

tamgŭda 담그다 ① soak[steep, dip, immerse] (in water) ② pickle; brew.

tamhwa 담화 talk; conversation; statement. *tamhwamun* 담화문 official statement.

tamjaengi 담쟁이 ivy. *tamjaengi tŏnggul* 담쟁이 덩굴 ivy vines.

tamta 담다 put in; fill. *kwangjurie tamta* 광주리
에 담다 put into a basket.

tamulda 다물다 shut; close (one's lips). *ibǔl tamulda* 입을 다물다 hold one's tongue.

tan 단 bundle; bunch; sheaf; faggot.

tanbal 단발 bob; bobbed hair. *tanbarhada* 단발하
다 bob one's hair.

tanch'e 단체 group; organization. *tanch'e haengdong* united action. *tanch'e yǒhaeng* 단체 여행
group trip.

tanchǒm 단점 weak point; shortcoming; defect;
fault.

tanch'u 단추 button; stud. *tanch'urǔl ch'aeuda*
단추를 채우다 button up; fasten a button. *tanch'urǔl kkǔrǔda* 단추를 끄르다 unbutton (a coat).

tanch'uk 단축 reduction; shortening. *tanch'uk'ada*
단축하다 reduct; shorten; curtail.

tandanhada 단단하다 (be) hard; solid; strong; firm.
tandanhi 단단히 hard; solidly; firmly.

tando 단도 dagger; short sword.

tandok 단독. *tandogǔro* 단독으로 independently;
separately; individually; alone; singly.

tangch'ǒm 당첨 prize winning. *tangch'ǒmhada* 당
첨하다 win a prize; draw a lucky number.

tangdanghada 당당하다 (be) grand; imposing; fair.
tangdanghi 당당히 stately; fairly.

tanggida 당기다 pull; draw; tug; haul.

tanggu 당구 billiards. *tanggurǔl ch'ida* 당구를 치
다 play at billiards.

tangguk 당국 authorities (concerned). *hakkyo tangguk* 학교 당국 school authorities.

tanghwang 당황. *tanghwanghada* 당황하다 be confused[upset]; lose one's head.

tan-gi 단기 short term[time]. *tan-giŭi* 단기의 short
(-term) ; short-dated.

tangjik 당직 being on duty[watch]. *tangjik'ada*
당직하다 be on duty[watch].

tangmil 당밀 molasses.

tan-gol 단골 custom; connection; patronage. *tan-gol
sonnim* 단골 손님 customer; client; patron; regular visitor.

tangshi 당시 then; that time; those days. *tang-
shiŭi* 당시의 of those days; then.

tangsŏn 당선. *tangsŏnhada* 당선하다 be elected;
win the election.

tangwon 당원 member of a party; party man.

tan-gyŏl 단결 union; combination; cooperation. *tan-
gyŏrhada* 단결하다 unite[hold, get] (together) ;
combine[cooperate] (with a person).

tangyŏn 당연. *tangyŏnhan* 당연한 reasonable;
right; proper; natural. *tangyŏnhi* 당연히 justly; naturally; deservedly.

tanhwa 단화 shoes. →**kudu** 구두.

tanida 다니다 ① go to and from (a place) ; go[walk]
about[around] ② ply (between) ③ commute.

tanji 단지 housing development[estate (*Eng.*)];
collective[public] housing area. *kongŏp tanji* 공
업 단지 industrial complex.

tanjo 단조 monotony; dullness. *tanjoropta* 단조롭다
monotonous; flat; dull.

tanmat 단맛 sweetness; sweet taste. *tanmashi
nada* 단맛이 나다 be[taste] sweet; have a sweet
taste.

tanŏ 단어 word; vocabulary. *kibon tanŏjip* 기본 단

어집 collection of basic words; basic wordbook.

tanp'a 단파 short wave. *tanp'a sushin-gi* 단파 수신기 short wave receiver.

tanp'ung 단풍 maple. *tanp'ung tŭlda* 단풍 들다 turn red[crimson, yellow]. *tanp'ungnip* 단풍잎 maple leaves.

tanp'yŏn 단편 short piece; sketch. *tanp'yŏn sosŏl* 단편 소설 short story.

tanshik 단식 fast; fasting. *tanshik'ada* 단식하다 fast; abstain from food.

tansŏ 단서 ① beginning; start; first step ② clue; key. *tansŏrŭl chapta* 단서를 잡다 have[get, find] a clue (to, for).

tansok 단속 control; regulation; management; supervision. *tansok'ada* 단속하다 control; supervise; oversee; keep order.

tansume 단숨에 at a stretch[stroke]; at[in] a breath; at one effort.

tansun 단순. *tansunhada* 단순하다 (be) simple; simple-minded. *tansunhi* 단순히 simply; merely.

tanwi 단위 unit; denomination.

tanyŏn 다년 many years. *tanyŏn-gan* 다년간 for many years.

tap 답 answer; reply; solution. *tap'ada* 답하다 answer; reply; give an answer; respond.

tapchang 답장 written reply; reply letter.

tapsa 답사 survey; exploration; field investigation. *tapsahada* 답사하다 explore; survey.

taptap'ada 답답하다 be stifling; suffocating; stuffy. *kasŭmi taptap'ada* 가슴이 답답하다 feel heavy in the chest.

tarak 다락 loft; garret.

taramjwi 다람쥐 squirrel; chipmunk.

taranada 달아나다 run away; flee; escape; take to flight; break[get] loose; fly away.

tari 다리 bridge. *tarirŭl kŏnnŏda* 다리를 건너다 cross a bridge.

tari 다리 leg; limb.

tarida 달이다 boil down; decoct; infuse. *yagrŭl tarida* 약을 달이다 make a medical decoction.

tarimi 다리미 iron; flatiron. *chŏn-gi tarimi* 전기 다리미 electric iron.

taruda 다루다 handle; manage; deal with; treat.

tarŭda 다르다 differ (from, with); be different (from, with); vary; unlike.

tashi 다시 again; overagain; once more[again]; again and again.

tasŏt 다섯 five. *tasŏtchae* 다섯째 the fifth *tasŏt pae(ŭi)* 다섯 배(의) fivefold.

tasu 다수 large[great] number; many; majority. *tasuŭi* 다수의 many; large number of; numerous.

tat 닻 anchor. *tatchul* 닻줄 cable; hawser.

tat'uda 다투다 ① brawl; quarrel; have words (with) ② contend; compete; struggle.

taŭm 다음 next; following; second. *taŭmnal* 다음 날 next[following] day.

tchada 짜다 wring; squeeze. *sugŏnŭl tchada* 수건을 짜다 wring a towel.

tchada 짜다 (be) salty; briny.

tchajŭng 짜증 fret; irritation; vexation.

tchak 짝 pair; couple; partner.

tchaksarang 짝사랑 one-sided love; unrequited love. *tchaksaranghada* 짝사랑하다 love in vain [without return].

tchaksu 짝수 even number.

tchalta 짧다 (be) short; brief. *tchalke* 짧게 short; briefly.

tchaptcharhada 잡짤하다 ① (be) nice and salty; saltish ② suitable.

tchetchehada 쩨쩨하다 ① (be) miserly; stingy; niggardly ② commonplace; dull; foolish.

tchinggŭrida 찡그리다 frown; scowl; (make a) grimace[wry face].

tchikta 찍다 ① stamp; seal; impress ② stab; stick ③ (take a) photograph.

tchip'urida 찌푸리다 ① grimace; frown[scowl] ② cloud over; get cloudy.

tchirŭda 찌르다 pierce; stab; thrust; prick.

tchit'a 찧다 pound (rice); hull; ram (against).

tchitta 찢다 tear; split; cleave; rip.

tchodŭllida 쪼들리다 be troubled[annoyed]; be hard pressed; importune.

tchoeda 쬐다 ① shine on[over] ② bask in the sun.

tchogaeda 쪼개다 split; chop; crack.

tchok 쪽 direction; side; way. *orŭn*[*oen*]*tchok* 오른[왼]쪽 right[left] side.

tcholttak 쫄딱 totally; completely; utterly.

tchotta 쫓다 ① drive away ② chase; pursue.

tchugŭrŏttŭrida 쭈그러뜨리다 press[squeeze] out of shape; crush.

teda 데다 get burnt; have a burn; scald oneself.

teryŏgada 데려가다 take (a person) with.

teryŏoda 데려오다 bring (a person) along.

teuda 데우다 warm; heat (up); mull.

tŏ 더 more(*quantity*); longer(*time*); farther(*distance*). *tŏ mani* 더 많이 much more. *tŏhan-*

ch'ŭng 더한층 more and more; still more.

toan 도안 design; sketch. *toan-ga* 도안가 designer.

tobak 도박 gambling; gaming. *tobak'ada* 도박하다 gamble; play for money.

tobal 도발. *tobarhada* 도발하다 provoke; arouse; incite. *tobalchŏk* 도발적 provocative.

tobo 도보 walking. *toboro* 도보로 on foot. *tobo yŏhaeng* 도보 여행 walking tour.

tŏburŏ 더불어 together; with; together with.

tŏburuk'ada 더부룩하다 (be) tufty; bushy; shaggy.

toch'ak 도착 arrival. *toch'ak'ada* 도착하다 arrive (in, at, on); reach; get to.

toch'ŏ 도처. *toch'ŏe* 도처에 everywhere; all over; throughout.

todaech'e 도대체 on earth; in the world.

todal 도달 arrival. *todarhada* 도달하다 arrive in [at]; reach; get to.

todŏk 도덕 morality; virtue; morals. *todŏkchŏk* 도덕적 moral; ethical. *todŏksang* 도덕상 morally.

toduk 도둑 thief; burglar; robber; sneak. *toduk matta* 도둑 맞다 be stolen; be robbed (of).

tŏdŭmta 더듬다 feel[grope] for; grope about[around] for; fumble for.

tŏdŭmgŏrida, ttŏdŭmgŏrida 더듬거리다, 떠듬거리다 stammer; stutter; falter.

toeda 되다 ① become; get; grow ② turn[change] into; develop ③ be realized; be accomplished ④ turn out; result; prove ⑤ come to; reach.

toeda 되다 (be) thick; tough; hard. *toenchuk* 된죽 thick gruel.

toeda 되다 measure.

toenjang 된장 soybean paste.

toenŭndaero 되는대로 at random; roughly; slovenly; suitably; adequately.

toep'uri 되풀이 repetition; reiteration. *toep'urihada* 되풀이하다 repeat.

toesaegida 되새기다 chew over and over again.

togi 도기 china(ware); earthenware; pottery.

Togil 독일 Germany. *Togirŏ* 독일어 German (language). *Togirin* 독일인 German; the Germans.

togu 도구 tool; implement; utensil; instrument.

togŭm 도금 gilding; plating. *togŭmhada* 도금하다 plate (with gold); gild.

tŏgundana 더군다나 besides; moreover; furthermore; in addition.

togyak 독약 poison; poisonous drug[medicine].

tŏhada 더하다 ① add (up); sum up ② get worse; grow harder.

tohap 도합 (grand, sum) total; in all; all told; altogether; in the aggregate.

tojang 도장 seal; stamp. *tojangŭl tchikta* 도장을 찍다 seal; put one's seal to.

tojisa 도지사 provincial governor.

tojung 도중 on the way; on one's way.

tok 독 poison; venom. *togi innŭn* 독이 있는 poisonous; venomous; harmful.

tok 독 jar; jug; pot.

tok'ak 독학 self-education; self-study. *tok'ak'ada* teach oneself; study[learn] by oneself.

tokcha 독자 reader; subscriber.

tokch'ang 독창 (vocal) solo. *tokch'anghada* 독창하다 sing a solo. *tokch'anghoe* 독창회 (vocal)

tokchik 독직 corruption; bribery; graft. [recital.

tokch'ok 독촉 demand. *tokch'ok'ada* 독촉하다 press

〔urge〕 (a person to do).

tokchŏm 독점 monopoly; exclusive possession. *tokchŏmhada* 독점하다 monopolize.

tokkaebi 도깨비 bogy; ghost; spectre.

tokkam 독감 influenza; bad cold; flu.

tokki 도끼 ax; hatchet.

tokpack 독백 monolog(ue); soliloquy. *tokpaek'ada* 독백하다 talk〔speak〕to oneself.

tokpon 독본 reader. *Yŏngŏ tokpon* 영어 독본 English reader.

toksal 독살 poisoning. *toksarhada* 독살하다 poison; kill by poison.

tokshin 독신. *tokshinŭi* 독신의 single; unmarried. *tokshinja* 독신자 bachelor; spinster (*female*).

toksŏ 독서 reading. *toksŏhada* 독서하다 read (books). *toksŏ chugan* 독서 주간 book week.

tŏkt'aek 덕택 *tŏkt'aegŭro* 덕택으로 due to; thanks to; by (a person's) favor〔help, aid〕.

tol 돌 stone; pebble. *rait'ŏ tol* 라이터 돌 flint for the lighter.

tolboda 돌보다 take care of; care for; look after; attend to; back up; assist; protect.

tolda 돌다 ① turn round; rotate; revolve.

tŏlda 덜다 ① diminish; reduce; mitigate; lighten ② subtract; deduct; take off.

tolgyŏk 돌격 charge; dash; rush. *tolgyŏk'ada* 돌격하다 charge; dash; rush.

tollida 돌리다 ① turn; revolve; roll; spin ② pass (round); hand round. *sulchanŭl tollida* 술잔을 돌리다 pass a glass round.

tolp'a 돌파 *tolp'ahada* 돌파하다 break through; pass (an exam).

tolp'ari 돌팔이. *tolp'ari ŭisa* 돌팔이 의사 quack (doctor); charlatan.

toltchŏgwi 돌쩌귀 hinge.

tomae 도매 wholesale. *tomaehada* 도매하다 sell wholesale. *tomaesang* 도매상 wholesale dealer.

tomang 도망 escape; flight; desertion. *tomangch'ida*[*hada*] 도망치다[하다] run away; flee; fly; desert. *tomangja* 도망자 fugitive.

tŏmbul 덤불 thicket; bush. *kashi tŏmbul* 가시 덤불 thorny bush.

tŏmi 더미 heap; pile; stack. *ssŭregi tŏmi* 쓰레기 더미 rubbish[trash] heap.

ton 돈 money; cash; coin. *tonŭl pŏlda* 돈을 벌다 make[earn] money; make a fortune.

tonan 도난. *tonandanghada* 도난당하다 be robbed; have (one's money) stolen; be stolen.

tong 동 copper. *tongp'an* 동판 sheet copper.

tongan 동안 ① period; span; interval ② time; space ③ for; during; while.

tongbaek 동백 camellia.

tongbok 동복 winter clothes; winter wear[suit].

tongch'ang 동창 classmate; school fellow; fellow student. *tongch'anghoe* 동창회 old boys' association (*Eng.*); alumni[almunae] association (*Am.*).

tongch'imi 동치미 turnips pickled in salt water.

tongdŭng 동등 equality; parity. *tongdŭnghada* 동등하다 (be) equal.

tonggam 동감 same opinion; sympathy. *tonggamida* 동감이다 agree; be of the same opinion.

tonggap 동갑 same age. *tonggabida* 동갑이다 be (of) the same age.

tonggi 동기 motive; incentive; motivation.

tonggi 동기 same class. *tonggisaeng* 동기생 classmate; graduates of the same year.

tonggul 동굴 cavern; cave; grotto.

tŏnggul 덩굴 vine; tendril.

tonggŭrami 동그라미 circle; ring; loop. *tonggŭramip'yo* 동그라미표 circle symbol.

tonghoe 동회 village assembly. *tonghoe samuso* 동회 사무소 village office.

tonghwa 동화 fairy tale; nursery story[tale].

tongjak 동작 action; movement(s); manners.

tongjang 동장 town-block headman; village headman.

tongji 동지 the winter solstice.

tongji 동지 comrades; friend.

tŏnjida 던지다 throw; hurl; fling; cast.

tongjŏn 동전 copper coin.

tongjŏng 동정 sympathy; compassion. *tongjŏnghada* 동정하다 sympathize; have compassion (on).

tongmaek 동맥 artery. *taedongmaek* 대동맥 main artery.

tongmaeng 동맹 alliance; union; league. *tongmaenghada* 동맹하다 ally with; be allied[leagued] with; combine. *tongmaengguk* 동맹국 allied power. *tongmaeng p'aŏp* 동맹 파업 strike.

tongmin 동민 villager; village folk.

tongmu 동무 friend; companion; comrade. *yŏja tongmu* 여자 동무 girl friend.

tongmul 동물 animal; beast. *tongmurwon* 동물원 zoological garden; zoo.

tongmyŏn 동면 hibernation; winter sleep. *tongmyŏnhada* 동면하다 hibernate.

tongnan 동란 disturbance; upheaval; riot; war.

Han-guk tongnan 한국 동란 the Korean War.

tongnip 독립 independence; self-reliance; self-support. *tongnip'ada* 독립하다 become independent (of); stand alone. *tongnibŭi* 독립의 independent.

tongnyo 동료 associate; colleague; comrade; fellow; co-worker; companion. worker.

tongnyŏk 동력 (motive) power. *tongnyŏksŏn* 동력선 power vessel. *tongnyŏk chawonbu* 동력 자원부 Ministry of Energy and Resources.

tŏngŏri 덩어리 lump; mass; clod.

tongp'o 동포 brethren; one's fellow countryman.

tongsa 동사 death from cold. *tongsahada* 동사하다 be frozen to death.

tongsang 동상 frostbite; chilblains. *tongsange kŏllida* 동상에 걸리다 be[get] frostbitten.

tongsang 동상 bronze statue; copper image.

tongshi 동시 the same time. *tongshiŭi* 동시의 simultaneous; concurrent. *tongshie* 동시에 at the same time; simultaneously with.

tongshingmul 동식물 animal and plants; fauna and flora.

tongtchok 동쪽 east. *tongtchogŭi* 동쪽의 east; eastern; easterly. *tongtchogŭro* 동쪽으로 to[in, on] the east.

tongŭi 동의 consent; assent; agreement. *tongŭihada* 동의하다 consent[assent, agree] (to).

tongwon 동원 mobilization. *tongwonhada* 동원하다 mobilize. *tongwon haeje* 동원 해제 demobilization.

tongyang 동양 the Orient; the East. *tongyangin* 동양인 Oriental; the Orientals.

tongyo 동요 shake; quake; tremble. *tongyohada* 동요하다 shake; quake; stir; tremble.

tongyo 동요 children's song; nursery rhyme.

top'i 도피 escape; flight. *top'ihada* 도피하다 escape; flee.

tŏpkae 덮개 covers; coverlet; lid. →**ttukkŏng** 뚜껑

topta 돕다 ① help; aid; assist ② relieve; give relief to ③ promote.

top'yo 도표 chart; diagram; graph.

toraboda 돌아보다 look back; turn one's head; turn round.

toradanida 돌아다니다 wander[roam] about; walk [go] about; make a round.

toragada 돌아가다 go back; return; turn back.

toraji 도라지 (Chinese) balloon flower; Chinese bellflower.

torang 도랑 ditch; gutter; drain; dike.

toriŏ 도리어 on the contrary; instead; rather; all the more.

toro 도로 road; street; highway.

tŏrŏpta 더럽다 (be) unclean; dirty; filthy; foul; soiled.

tŭryŏbonaeda 들여보내다 send (a person) into; let (a person) in.

toryŏn 돌연 suddenly; on[all of] a sudden; all at once. *toryŏnhan* 돌연한 sudden; abrupt; unexpected; unlooked-for.

toryŏnaeda 도려내다 scrape out; cut off[out, away], cleave.

tosaek 도색 pink; rose colo(u)r. *tosaek yŏnghwa* 도색 영화 sex film; blue movies. *tosaek chapchi* 도색 잡지 yellow journal.

toshi 도시 cities; towns.

toshirak 도시락 lunch box; lunch.

tosŏ 도서 books. *tosŏgwan* 도서관 library.

tot 돛 sail; canvas.

tŏt 덫 trap; snare.

tŏnni 덧니 double[side] tooth.

totpogi 돋보기 long-distance glasses.

tŏuk 더욱 more; more and more; still more.

towajuda 도와주다 help; assist[aid]; relieve; give relief to; support.

tŏwi 더위 heat; hot weather.

ttabunhada 따분하다 ① (be) languid; dull ② (be) boring; tedious; wearisome.

ttada 따다 ① pick; pluck; nip ② open; cut out ③ get; take; obtain.

ttadollida 따돌리다 leave (a person) out (in the cold); cut (a person) out.

ttae 때 ① time; hour; moment ② case; occasion ③ chance; opportunity.

ttae 때 dirt; filth; grime.

ttaemun 때문. *ttaemune* 때문에 on account of; because of; owing to.

ttaerida 때리다 strike; beat; hit; slap.

ttaettaero 때때로 occasionally; now and then; at times; from time to time.

ttajida 따지다 ① distinguish (between right and wrong); demand an explanation of ② calculate.

ttak 딱 ① accurately; exactly; just ② firmly; stiffly ③ flatly; positively.

ttak'ada 딱하다 ① (be) annoying; embarrassing ② (be) pitiable; pitiful; sorry; regrettable.

ttakchi 딱지 ① stamp; sticker; label; tag ② picture card. *up'yo ttakchi* 우표 딱지 postage stamp.

ttakchi 딱지 ① scab ② shell; carapace ③ case.

ttakkŭmhada 따끔하다 smart; prick; bite.

ttakttak'ada 딱딱하다 ① (be) hard; solid; stiff; tough ② strict; rigid ③ (be) stiff; bookish.

ttalgi 딸기 strawberry.

ttalkkukchil 딸꾹질 hiccup; hiccough.

ttam 땀 sweat; perspiration. *ttamŭl hŭllida* 땀을 흘리다 sweat; perspire.

ttan 딴 another; other; different. *ttande[got]* 딴 데[곳] another place. *ttansaram* 딴사람 another person; someone else.

ttang 땅 ① earth; ground ② land; territory; soil.

ttangk'ong 땅콩 peanut; groundnut.

ttanim 따님 your[his] (esteemed) daughter.

ttaogi 따오기 sacred[crested] ibis.

ttaragada 따라가다 go with; accompany; follow (a person).

ttarasŏ 따라서 ① accordingly; therefore ② in accordance with; according to.

ttaro 따로 apart; separately; besides; in addition; additionally.

ttarŭda 따르다 ① accompany; follow; go along with ② model (after) ③ obey; yield to.

ttattŭt'ada 따뜻하다 ① (be) mild; warm; genial ② (be) kindly; cordial; heart-warming.

ttawi 따위 ① and such like; such (a thing) like [as]… ② and so on[forth]; and[or] the like.

tte 떼 group; crowd; throng; herd; flock. *tterŭl chiŏsŏ* 떼를 지어서 in crowds[flocks].

tteda 떼다 ① take off[away]; remove ② part; pull apart; pluck[tear] off ③ break[open] the seal; cut (a letter) open.

ttemilda 메밀다 push; thrust; elbow (a person)

out.

tti 띠 belt; sash; girdle; band.

tto 또 ① again; once more; repeatedly ② too; also; as well ③ and; moreover.

ttǒdǔlda 떠들다 make a noise; clamo(u)r; make a fuss[disturbance].

ttoeyakpyǒt 뙤약볕 scorching[broiling, burning] sunshine.

ttǒk 떡 rice cake. *ttǒkkuk* 떡국 rice-cake soup.

ttǒkkalnamu 떡갈나무 oak (tree).

ttokparo 똑바로 straight; in a straight line; erect; upright.

ttokttok'ada 똑똑하다 ① (be) clever; sharp; bright ② (be) distinctive; vivid; plain.

ttǒlda 떨다 shake; tremble; shiver; quake; shudder.

ttǒmatta 떠맡다 undertake; assume; take (a thing) upon oneself.

ttǒnada 떠나다 ① leave; start from; set out; depart ② quit; resign (from); part from[with].

ttong 똥 feces; stool; excrement; dung.

ttǒrǒjida 떨어지다 ① fall; drop; come down ② come[fall] off ③ go down; decline.

ttǒrǒttǔrida 떨어뜨리다 ① drop; throw down; let fall ② lose; miss.

ttǔda 뜨다 ① float (on the water, in the air) ② rise; come up.

ttǔda 뜨다 open (one's eyes); wake up; awake.

ttǔgǒpta 뜨겁다 (be) hot; heated; burning.

ttǔiuda 띄우다 fly; let fly; make fly. *yǒnǔl ttǔiuda* 연을 띄우다 fly a kite.

ttujangi 뚜장이 pimp; pander.

ttukkǒng 뚜껑 lid; cover; cap; shield; case. *ttu-*

kkŏngŭl yŏlda 뚜껑을 열다 lift[take off] a lid; uncover. *ttukkŏngŭl tatta* 뚜껑을 닫다 put on the lid.

ttult'a 뚫다 bore; punch; make[drill] a hole.

ttungttungbo 뚱뚱보 fatty[plump] person.

tturŏjige poda 뚫어지게 보다 stare (at); look hard (at); gaze (at, into).

tturyŏshi 뚜렷이 clearly; distinctly; evidently.

tturyŏt'ada 뚜렷하다 (be) clear; vivid; evident; obvious.

ttŭt 뜻 ① intention; intent ② meaning; sense.

ttŭtpak 뜻밖. *ttŭtpakkŭi* 뜻밖의 unexpected; surprising; accidental. *ttŭtpakke* 뜻밖에 unexpectedly; all of a sudden.

ttŭtta 뜯다 ① take down; tear apart ② pluck; pick ③ play; perform on ④ bite[gnaw] off ⑤ clamor for; importune.

ttwida 뛰다 ① run; dash ② jump; leap; skip.

ttwiŏgada 뛰어가다 run; rush; dash; dart.

ttwiŏnada 뛰어나다 (be) superior (to); excel (in).

tubu 두부 bean-curd. *tubu changsu* 두부 장수 bean-curd seller[dealer].

tuda 두다 put; place; lay; set.

tŭdiŏ 드디어 finally; at last; eventually; at length.

tudŏlgŏrida, t'udŏlgŏrida 두덜거리다, 투덜거리다 grumble; mutter; complain.

tudŭrida, ttudŭrida 두드리다, 뚜드리다 strike; beat; hit; knock.

tudŭrŏgi 두드러기 nettle rash.

tugŭn-gŏrida 두근거리다 palpitate; throb.

tuk 둑 bank; dike; embankment.

tŭkchŏm 득점 marks; point; score. *tŭkchŏmhada*

득점하다 score (a point).

tukkŏpta 두껍다 (be) thick; thick and heavy. *tukkŏpke* 두껍게 thickly; heavily. *tukkŏun ch'aek* 두꺼운 책 thick book.

tul 둘 two. *tulssik* 둘씩 by[in] twos.

tŭl 들 field; plain; green.

tŭlda 들다 take[have, carry] in one's hand; hold.

tŭlda 들다 clear (up); stop (raining).

tŭlkŏt 들것 litter; stretcher.

tŭlguk'wa 들국화 wild chrysanthemum.

tulle 둘레 circumference; girth. *tullee* 둘레에 round; around; about.

tŭllil 들일 farm work; field labor.

tŭllori 들놀이 picnic; outing. *tŭllori kada* 들놀이 가다 go on a picnic.

tŭllŭda 들르다 drop[look] in at; stop by[in] (*Am.*); visit; stop over

tultchae 둘째 the second; number two (No. 2). *tultchaero* 둘째로 second(ly); in the second place.

tŭltchuknaltchuk'ada 들쭉날쭉하다 (be) uneven; rugged; indented.

tumok 두목 chief; head; leader; boss; ringleader.

tŭmulda 드물다 (be) rare; scarce; unusual; uncommon. *tŭmulge* 드물게 rarely; seldom.

tŭmundŭmun 드문드문 occasionally; once in a while; at (rare, long) intervals.

tŭng 등 ① back ② ridge.

tŭngdae 등대 lighthouse; beacon.

tŭndŭnhada 든든하다 ① (be) strong; firm; stout; solid ② heartening; feel safe[secure].

tunggŭlda 둥글다 (be) round; circular; globular.

tŭngjang 등장. *tŭngjanghada* 등장하다 enter[appear] on the stage. *tŭngjang inmul* 등장 인물 dramatis personae; characters; cast.

tungji 둥지 nest.

tŭnggi 등기 registration; registry. *tŭnggi up'yŏn* 등기 우편 registered mail.

tŭngkol 등골 spine; line of the backbone.

tŭngnamu 등나무 wisteria.

tŭngnok 등록 registration; entry. *tŭngnok'ada* 등록하다 register; enroll.

tŭngpul 등불 lamplight; lamp. *tŭngpurŭl k'yŏda* 등불을 켜다 light a lamp.

tŭngsa 등사 copy; transcription. *tŭngsahada* 등사하다 copy; make a copy; reproduce; mimeograph. *tŭngsap'an* 등사판 mimeograph (machine).

tŭngsan 등산 mountain climbing; mountaineering. *tŭngsanhada* 등산하다 climb a mountain.

tunguri 둥우리 (square) basket; cage.

tunhada 둔하다 (be) dull; slow; slow-witted; stupid; thick-headed; dumb (*Am.*).

tunoe 두뇌 head; brains. *chŏnja tunoe* 전자 두뇌 electronic brain.

turebak 두레박 well-bucket.

tŭribatta 들이받다 run[bump] (a thing) into; butt; knock (a thing) against.

turibŏn-gŏrida 두리번거리다 look about[round].

tŭrida 드리다 give; offer up; present; dedicate.

tŭrik'ida 들이키다 drink up; drain; swallow.

tŭrŏgada 들어가다 ① enter; go[get, walk, step] in[into] ② join; enter.

turŏng 두렁 levee; bank of a rice-paddy.

tŭrŏnupta 드러눕다 lie down; lay oneself down; lie oneself down; lie on one's back.

turŭda 두르다 enclose; encircle; surround.

turumari 두루마리 roll (of paper); scroll.

turumi 두루미 (white) crane; sacred crane.

tŭryŏdaboda 들여다보다 ① peep [look, peek] into; see through[into] ② gaze[stare] (at); observe; watch.

turyŏwohada 두려워하다 fear; be afraid of; dread.

tusŏnŏ, tusŏnŏt 두서너, 두서넛 two or three; a few.

tut'ong 두통 headache. *tut'ongi nada* 두통이 나다 have a (bad, slight) headache.

tŭtta 듣다 ① hear; listen (to); lend an ear to ② obey; accede to ③ be good[effective] (for).

twaeji 돼지 pig; swine; hog. *twaejigogi* 돼지고기 pork. *twaejigirŭm* 돼지기름 lard.

twi 뒤 back; rear; next; after; future; tail; reverse. *twie* 뒤에 afterwards; later.

twiboda 뒤보다 go to stool; ease[relieve] oneself.

twich'uk 뒤축 heel. *twich'ugi nop'ŭn[najŭn]* 뒤축이 높은[낮은] high[low]-heeled.

twidŏpta 뒤덮다 cover; overspread; veil; hang over; wrap; muffle. 「out; turn upside down.

twijipta 뒤집다 turn over; turn (a coat) inside

twinggulda 뒹굴다 roll (about); tumble about.

twiŏpta 뒤엎다 upset; overturn; overthrow.

twisŏkta 뒤섞다 mix up; mingle together.

twisungsunghada 뒤숭숭하다 ① (be) confused; disturbed ② be[feel] restless; uneasy.

twitchim 뒷짐. *twitchimjida* 뒷짐지다 fold one's hands behind one's back.

twitchotta 뒤쫓다 follow; go after; pursue; chase.

twitkolmok 뒷골목 back alley[lane, street].

twittari 뒷다리 hind leg.

twittŏlmi 뒷덜미 nape; back[scruff] of the neck.

twittŏrŏjida 뒤떨어지다 ① fall[drop] behind; be backward ② stay behind.

twit'ŭlda 뒤틀다 twist; wrench.

T'

t'ada 타다 burn; blaze.

t'ada 타다 ride; take; take[have] a ride in; get in[on]; go[get] aboard; embark in[on].

t'ada 타다 play (on); perform on.

t'aea 태아 embryo; unborn child.

t'aedo 태도 attitude; manner; behavior; bearing.

t'aegŭkki 태극기 national flag of Korea.

t'aek'ada 택하다 choose; make choice (of); select.

t'aeman 태만 negligence; neglect. *t'aemanhan* 태만한 neglectful; negligent.

t'aeŏnada 태어나다 be born; come into the world.

t'aep'yŏngnyang 태평양 Pacific (Ocean).

t'aesaeng 태생 ① viviparity ② birth; origin; lineage. *oeguk t'aesaengŭi* 외국 태생의 foreign-born.

t'aeuda 태우다 carry; let ride; take on board.

t'aeuda 태우다 burn; kindle. *hyangŭl t'aeuda* 향을 태우다 burn incense.

t'aeyang 태양 sun. *t'aeyangŭi* 태양의 solar. *t'aeyangnyŏl* 태양열 solar heat. *t'aeyangnyŏl chut'aek* 태양열 주택 solar house.

t'agaso 탁아소 day[public] nursery.

t'agonada 타고나다 be born[gifted] (with)

t'agyŏk 타격 blow; hit; shock. *t'agyŏgŭl chuda* 타격을 주다 strike a blow.

t'ahyang 타향 strange[foreign] land.

t'ain 타인 another person; stranger.

t'airŭda 타이르다 reason; admonish; advise.

t'aja 타자 batter; batman.

t'ajagi 타자기 typewriter. *yŏngmun t'ajagi* 영문 타자기 English character typewriter.

t'ajasu 타자수 typist.

t'akcha 탁자 table; desk.

t'akchu 탁주 →**makkŏlli** 막걸리.

t'akku 탁구 ping-pong; table tennis.

t'al 탈 mask. *t'arŭl ssŭda* 탈을 쓰다 wear a mask.

t'alchimyŏn 탈지면 absorbent[sanitary] cotton.

t'alse 탈세 evasion of taxes. *t'alsehada* 탈세하다 evade[dodge] a tax.

t'alsŏn 탈선 ① derailment ② digression. *t'alsŏnhada* 탈선하다 (be) derailed; make a digression.

t'alt'oe 탈퇴 secession; withdrawal. *t'alt'oehada* 탈퇴하다 secede; withdraw; leave.

t'amgu 탐구 search; investigation. *t'amguhada* 탐구하다 search for; seek for.

t'amhŏm 탐험 exploration; expedition. *t'amhŏmhada* 탐험하다 explore.

t'amnaeda 탐내다 want; wish; covet; be greedy [hanker] for (money).

t'anap 탄압 oppression; suppression. *t'anap'ada* 탄압하다 suppress; oppress; bring pressure upon.

t'anhaek 탄핵 impeachment; denunciation.

t'anhwan 탄환 shot; bullet; shell.

t'ansaeng 탄생 birth; nativity. *t'ansaenghada* 탄생하다 be born; come into the world.

t'anshik 탄식 sigh; lamentation. *t'anshik'ada* 탄식하다 (heave[draw] a) sigh; lament; deplore.

t'anso 탄소 carbon. *t'ansoŭi* 탄소의 carbonic.

t'anyak 탄약 (a round of) ammunition. *t'anyakko* 탄약고 (powder) magazine.

t'ap 탑 tower; pagoda; steeple.

t'apsŭng 탑승. *t'apsŭnghada* 탑승하다 board[get on] (a plane). *t'apsŭnggaek* 탑승객 passenger.

t'arae 타래 bunch; skein; coil. *shil han t'arae* 실 한 타래 a skein of thread.

t'arak 타락 degradation; corruption. *t'arak'ada* 타락하다 be corrupted; degenerate. *t'arak'an* 타락한 corrupt; fallen; depraved.

t'arŭi 탈의. *t'arŭishil* 탈의실 dressing[changing] room. *t'arŭijang* 탈의장 bathing booth.

t'awon 타원 oval; elliptic. *t'awonhyŏng* 타원형 oval; ellipticity.

t'e 테 ① hoop; band; stripe ② rim; brim; frame.

t'ikkŭl 티끌 dust; mote.

t'ŏ 터 site; place; ground; lot. *chipt'ŏ* 집터 building lot[site, land].

t'ŏbŏkt'ŏbŏk 터벅터벅 ploddingly; trudgingly.

t'odae 토대 foundation; base; groundwork.

t'odam 토담 earthen wall; mud wall; dirt wall.

t'oegŭn 퇴근. *t'oegŭnhada* 퇴근하다 leave one's office; go home from work.

t'oehak 퇴학. *t'oehak'ada* 퇴학하다 leave[give up, quit] school (halfway).

t'oejik 퇴직 retirement; resignation. *t'oejik'ada* 퇴직하다 retire from office.

t'oewon 퇴원. *t'oewonhada* 퇴원하다 leave (the) hospital.

t'ogŏnŏp 토건업 civil engineering and construction.

t'ogul 토굴 cavern; cave; den; grotto.

t'ohada 토하다 vomit; spit; throw[fetch] up.

t'oji 토지 land; soil; earth.

t'ŏjida 터지다 explode; burst; erupt; blowup; break-out; rip; tear; collapse; disclosed; be struck; split.

t'ŏk 턱 jaw; chin. *t'ŏkppyŏ* 턱뼈 jawbone. *araet'ŏk* 아래턱 lower jaw.

t'okki 토끼 rabbit; hare.

t'okkip'ul 토끼풀 clover.

t'okt'ok'i 톡톡히 much; lot; great deal. *t'okt'ok'i pŏlda* 톡톡히 벌다 make quite a lot of money.

t'ŏl 털 hair. *t'ŏri manŭn* 털이 많은 hairy; haired.

t'ŏlbo 털보 hairy[shaggy] man.

t'ŏlda 털다 shake off; throw off; dust; brush up.

t'ŏljanggap 털장갑 fur[woolen] gloves.

t'ŏlshil 털실 wool(l)en yarn; knitting wool.

t'ŏlt'ŏrhada 털털하다 (be) unaffected; free and easy.

t'omak 토막 piece; bit; block. *t'omangnaeda* 토막 내다 sever; cut in pieces.

t'omnibak'wi 톱니바퀴 toothed wheel; cogwheel.

t'omok 토목 engineering works. *t'omok kongsa* 토목 공사 public (engineering) works.

t'ŏmuniŏpta 터무니없다 (be) groundless; unreasonable; absurd.

t'ong 통 tub; barrel; pail; bucket. *mult'ong* 물통 water bucket. *sult'ong* 술통 wine-barrel.

t'ongch'i 통치 rule; government. *t'ongch'ihada* 통치하다 rule; reign over.

t'ongdak 통닭. *t'ongdakkui* 통닭구이 roast chicken; chicken roasted whole.

t'onggam 통감. *t'onggamhada* 통감하다 feel keenly.

t'onggŭn 통근. *t'onggŭnhada* 통근하다 attend of-

fice; commute. *t'onggŭn pŏsŭ*[*yŏlch'a*] 통근 버
스[열차] commuters' bus[train].

t'onggwa 통과 passage; passing. *t'onggwahada*
통과하다 pass; pass by[through].

t'onggwan 통관. *t'onggwanhada* 통관하다 pass the
customs. *t'onggwan chŏlch'a* 통관 절차 customs
formalities; clearance.

t'onggye 통계 statistics. *t'onggye*(*sang*)*ŭi* 통계 (상)
의 statistic(al).

t'onghada 통하다 ① run[lead] to ② be understood
③ be familiar (with).

t'onghaeng 통행 passing; traffic. *t'onghaenghada*
통행하다 pass (by); go along.

t'onghak 통학. *t'onghak'ada* 통학하다 attend[go
to] school.

t'onghwa 통화 currency; current coins[money].

t'onghwa 통화 (telephone) call. *t'onghwajung* 통
화중 The line is busy.

t'ongil 통일 unity; unification. *t'ongirhada* 통일
하다 unify. *nambuk t'ongil* 남북 통일 unification
of North and South (Korea).

t'ongjang 통장 passbook. *yegŭm t'ongjang* 예금 통
장 bankbook; deposit passbook.

t'ongji 통지 notice; report; notification; information. *t'ongjihada* 통지하다 inform; notify.

t'ongjorim 통조림 canned goods. *t'ongjorimhan*
통조림한 canned; tinned. *soegogi t'ongjorim* 쇠고
기 통조림 canned[tinned] beef.

t'ongk'wae 통쾌. *t'ongk'waehan* 통쾌한 extremely
delightful; thrilling; very exciting.

t'ongnamu 통나무 log. *t'ongnamu tari* 통나무 다리
log bridge. *t'ongnamujip* 통나무집 log cabin.

t'ongno 통로 passage; passageway; way; path; aisle.

tongsang 통상 commerce; trade; commercial relations. *t'ongsanghada* 통상하다 trade with. *t'ongsang choyak* 통상 조약 commercial treaty.

t'ongshin correspondence; communication. *t'ongshinhada* 통신하다 correspond (with).

t'ungso 퉁소 bamboo flute.

t'ongsol 통솔 command; leadership. *t'ongsorhada* 통솔하다 command; control; lead.

t'ongtchae(ro) 통째(로) whole; wholly; bodily. *t'ongtchaero mŏkta* 통째로 먹다 eat (something) whole.

t'ongt'onghada 통통하다 (be) plump; chubby.

t'ongyŏk 통역 interpretation. *t'ongyŏk'ada* 통역하다 interpret. *t'ongyŏkcha* 통역자 interpreter.

t'op 톱 saw; handsaw. *t'oppap* 톱밥 sawdust.

t'ŏpsuruk'ada 텁수룩하다 (be) unkempt; untrimmed; shaggy; bushy.

t'orajida 토라지다 pout; sulk; get sulky[cross].

t'oron 토론 discussion; debate. *t'oronhada* 토론하다 debate (on); discuss (with). *t'oronhoe* 토론회 forum; debate.

t'ŏrot 털옷 fur[woolen] garment.

t'osanmul 토산물 local products; native produce.

t'oshilt'oshil 토실토실. *t'oshilt'oshirhan* 토실토실한 plump; chubby; puffy.

t'ŏttŭrida 터뜨리다 explode; burst; break.

t'oŭi 토의 discussion; debate. *t'oŭihada* 토의하다 discuss; debate[deliberate] upon.

t'oyoil 토요일 Saturday.

t'ubak'ada 투박하다 ① (be) crude; vulgar ② (be)

coarse; unseemly; unshapely.

t'uch'ang 투창 javelin throw(ing). *t'uch'ang sŏnsu* 투창 선수 javelin thrower.

t'ŭda 트다 ① sprout; bud out ② be chapped.

t'udŏlgŏrida 투덜거리다 grumble (at, about, over); complain (of); murmur.

t'ŭgi 트기 hybrid; half-breed[blood]; mulatto.

t'ŭgyakchŏm 특약점 special agent; agency.

t'uja 투자 investment. *t'ujahada* 투자하다 invest; put[sink] in; lay out.

t'ujaeng 투쟁 fight;strife; struggle. *t'ujaenghada* 투쟁하다 fight; struggle.

t'ŭjip chapta 트집 잡다 find fault with; pick flaws [holes] in.

t'ŭkching 특징 characteristic; special feature. *tŭkching innŭn* 특징 있는 characteristic; peculiar.

t'ŭkchŏn 특전 privilege; special favo(u)r.

t'ŭkkongdae 특공대 commando; ranger corps(*Am.*).

t'ŭkkŭp 특급 limitted[special] express. *tŭkkŭp yŏlch'a* 특급 열차 special express (train).

t'ŭkkwon 특권 privilege. *t'ŭkkwon gyegŭp* 특권 계급 privileged class(es).

t'ŭk'ŏ 특허 patent. *t'ŭk'ŏkwon* 특허권 patent right. *tŭk'ŏp'um* 특허품 patented article.

t'ŭkpyŏl 특별. *tŭkpyŏrhan* 특별한 special; particular. *tŭkpyŏrhi* 특별히 particularly; specially.

t'ŭksa 특사 amnesty; special pardon. *t'ŭksahada* 특사하다 grant an amnesty.

t'ŭksaek 특색 →**t'ŭkching** 특징.

t'ŭksang 특상 special prize[reward].　　　[ciality.

t'ŭksanmul 특산물 special product; (local) spe-

t'ŭksu 특수. *t'uksuhan* 특수한 special; particular;

specific; peculiar.

t'ŭkt'ŭng 특등 special class[grade]; top grade.

t'ŭl 틀 ① frame; framework ② mold.

t'ŭllida 틀리다 go wrong[amiss]; be mistaken[erroneous]. *t'ŭllin* 틀린 mistaken; wrong; false.

t'ŭm 틈 crevice; crack; gap; opening.

t'umyŏng 투명. *t'umyŏnghan* 투명한 transparent; lucid; limpid; clear.

t'ŭnt'ŭnhada 튼튼하다 ① (be) robust; sturdy; stout ② solid; firm; strong.

t'up'yo 투표 vote. *t'up'yohada* 투표하다 vote; ballot (for); give[cast] a vote[ballot].

t'ŭrim 트림 belch. *t'ŭrimhada* 트림하다 belch; burp.

t'ŭrŏmakta 틀어막다 ① stop up; stuff; plug ② muzzle; gag ③ obstruct; disturb; binder.

t'usŏ 투서 anonymous letter. *t'usŏhada* 투서하다 send (a note) anonymously.

t'usu 투수 pitcher.

t'uu 투우 bullfight. *t'uusa* 투우사 bullfighter; matador. *t'uujang* 투우장 bull ring.

t'wida 튀다 ① spring; bound; hop; bounce ② run away; flee; sneak away.

t'wigida 튀기다 ① flip; snap ② splash; spatter.

t'wigim 튀김 (batter) fried food; fried dish; fry.

⟨⟨ U ⟩⟩

ua 우아 elegance. *uahan* 우아한 elegant; graceful.

ubang 우방 friendly nation; ally; allied nation.

uch'e 우체. *uch'eguk* 우체국 post office; *uch'et'ong* 우체통 post; mailbox (*Am.*).

uch'ŭk 우측 right side. *uch'ŭk t'onghaeng* 우측 통행 "keep to the right."

udae 우대 special[warm] treatment. *udaehada* 우대하다 treat warmly[cordially]. *udaekwon* 우대권 complimentary ticket.

udu 우두 cowpox; vaccinia.

uduk'ŏni 우두커니 absent-mindedly; vacantly; blankly; idly.

udumŏri 우두머리 top; head; boss; chief.

udŭng 우등 top[superior] grade; excellency. *udŭng-ŭi* 우등의 excellent; superior. *udŭngsang* 우등상 honor prize.

ugida 우기다 demand one's own way; force; persist in; assert; stick to; be obstinate.

ugŏjida 우거지다 be[grow] thick; dense; luxuriant; be overgrown with.

ugŏjisang 우거지상 frown[wry] face; scowl.

ugŭlgŏrida 우글거리다 swarm; be crowded; be alive with.

ugŭrŏjida 우그러지다 be crushed out of shape; be dented; hollowed; depressed.

uhwa 우화 fable; allegory.

ŭibok 의복 clothes; garments; clothing.

ŭich'i 의치 false[artificial] tooth; denture.

ŭido 의도 intention; design; aim. *ŭidohada* 의도하다 intend (to do); aim at.

ŭigi yangyang 의기 양양. *ŭigi yangyanghada* 의기 양양하다 (be) triumphant; be in high spirits.

ŭigyŏn 의견 opinion; view; idea. *ŭigyŏnŭi taerip [ch'ungdol]* 의견의 대립[충돌] disagree[opposition, conflict, split, clash] of opinion.

ŭihak 의학 medical science; medicine.

ŭihoe 의회 National Assembly (*Korea*); Parliament (*Eng.*); Congress (*Am.*); Diet (*Jap.* • *Den.* • *Swed*).

ŭija 의자 chair; bench. *kin ŭija* 긴의자 sofa; couch.

ŭijang 의장 chairman; Speaker.

ŭiji 의지 will; volition.

ŭiji 의지 leaning; trust; reliance. *ŭijihada* 의지하다 lean on; depend [rely] on [upon].

uik 우익 right wing [flank, column]; rightists. *uiksu* 우익수 right fielder.

ŭikwa 의과 medical department. *ŭikwadaehak* 의과 대학 medical college.

ŭimi 의미 meaning; sense; significance. *ŭimihada* 의미하다 mean; imply; signify.

ŭimu 의무 duty; obligation. *ŭimujŏk* 의무적 obligatory; compulsory.

ŭimun 의문 question; doubt. *ŭimunŭi* 의문의 doubtful; questionable.

ŭinon 의논 consultation; conference. *ŭinonhada* 의논하다 consult (with); counsel (with).

ŭioe 의외. *ŭioeŭi* 의외의 unexpected; unforeseen. *ŭioero* 의외로 unexpectedly.

ŭiri 의리 duty; obligation; justice.

ŭiroe 의뢰 request; trust. *ŭiroehada* 의뢰하다 request; ask; entrust; commission.

ŭiryo 의료 medical treatment. *ŭiryo pohŏm* 의료 보험 medical (care) insurance. *ŭiryobi* 의료비 medical expenses [fee].

ŭisa 의사 doctor; physician; surgeon. *ŭisa chindansŏ* 의사 진단서 medical certificate.

ŭisa 의사 intention; mind; purpose.

ŭisang 의상 clothes; dresses; garments; costume.

ŭishik 의식 consciousness; senses. *ŭishik'ada* 의

식하다 be conscious[aware] of.

ŭishikchu 의식주 food, clothing[clothes] and shelter [housing].

ŭishim 의심 doubt; question. *ŭishimhada* 의심하 다 doubt; be doubtful of; suspect.

ŭiwon 의원 member of the Assembly; assemblyman; Congressman; Senator (*Am.*); member of Parliament (M.P.).

ŭiyak 의약 medicine; physic. *ŭiyakp'um* 의약품 medical supplies.

ŭiyok 의욕 volition; will; desire. *ŭiyokchŏgin* 의 욕적인 ambitious; aspiring.

ujŏng 우정 friendship; fellowship. *ujŏngi innŭn* 우정이 있는 amicable; friendly.

uju 우주 universe; cosmos; aero space. *ujuŭi* 우 주의 universal; cosmic. *uju yŏhaeng* 우주 여행 space travel[flight].

ulda 울다 cry; weep.

ult'ari 울타리 fence; hedge.

ŭm 음 sound; note; tone.

ŭmak 음악 music. *ŭmakchŏk* 음악적 musical. melodious. *ŭmakka* 음악가 musician.

ŭmban 음반 phonograph record.

umch'ŭrida 움츠리다 shrink; hang back; recoil.

ŭmdok 음독. *ŭmdok chasal* 음독 자살 (commit) suicide by taking poison.

ŭmhyang 음향 sound; noise. *ŭmhyang hyokwa* 음 향 효과 sound effect.

umjigida 움직이다 ① move; stir; shift ② work; operate; run ③ be moved[touched, affected].

ŭmjŏl 음절 syllable. *taŭmjŏrŏ* 다음절어 polysyllable.

ŭmju 음주 drinking. *ŭmju unjŏn* 음주 운전 drunken

driving.

umk'yŏ chapta umk'yŏ chwida 움켜 잡다 움켜 쥐
다 seize; grab; clench; grasp; grip; hold.

ummak 움막 hut; dugout; hovel; shack.

ŭmmo 음모 plot; conspiracy. *ŭmmohada* 음모하다
plot; intrigue. *ŭmmoga* 음모가 conspirator; schemer.

ŭmnyo 음료 beverage; drink. *ŭmnyosu* 음료수 drink

ŭmnyŏk 음력 lunar calendar. ⌊ing water.

ŭmshik 음식 food; foodstuff; diet.

ŭmsŏng 음성 voice. →**moksori** 목소리.

ŭmt'ang 음탕. *ŭmt'anghan* 음탕한 dissipated; lewd;
obscene; wanton.

umul 우물 well. *umulmul* 우물물 well-water.

umulgŏrida 우물거리다 mumble; mump.

umultchumul 우물쭈물 hesitantly; hesitatingly.
umultchumurhada 우물쭈물하다 hesitate; waver.

un 운 fortune; luck. *uni chok'e* 운이 좋게 fortunately; luckily; by good luck. *uni nappŭge* 운이
나쁘게 unluckily; unfortunately; by ill luck.

ŭn 은 silver. *un-gŭrŭt* 은그릇 silverware.

unban 운반 conveyance; transportation. *unbanhada* 운반하다 carry; convey; transport.

ŭnban 은반 ① silver plate ② skating rink.

ŭnch'ong 은총 favo(u)r; grace. *ŭnch'ongŭl ipta*
은총을 입다 be in favor with.

undong 운동 ① motion; movement ② sports;
exercise. *undonghada* 운동하다 take exercise;
move. *undonghoe* 운동회 athletic meet.

undonghwa 운동화 sports shoes; sneakers(*Am.*).

ungbyŏn 웅변 eloquence; fluency. *ungbyŏn-ga* 웅
변가 eloquent speaker.

ŭnggŭp 응급 emergency. *ŭnggŭp ch'iryŏ* 응급 치료 first aid; first-aid treatment.

ungjang 웅장. *ungjanghan* 웅장한 grand; magnificent; sublime; majestic.

ŭngjŏp 응접 reception; interview. *ŭngjŏp'ada* 응접 하다 receive (a visitor).

ŭngmo 응모 subscription; application. *ŭngmohada* 응모하다 apply for; make an application.

ungŏlgŏrida 옹얼거리다 mutter; murmur.

ŭngŏri 응어리 knot[cramp] in a muscle.

ŭngshi 응시. *ŭngshihada* 응시하다 apply for an examination.

ŭngsŏkpurida 응석부리다 play the baby; presume upon another's love.

ŭn-gŭp 은급 →*yŏn-gŭm* 연금.

ŭngwon 응원 aid; help; support. *ŭngwonhada* 응 원하다 aid; assist; support.

ŭngyong 응용 (practical) application. *ŭngyonghada* 응용하다 apply. *ŭngyong munje* 응용 문제 applied question.

unha 운하 canal; waterway (*Am.*).

ŭnhaeng 은행 bank. *ŭnhaengkwon* 은행권 bank bill[note]. *ŭnhaengju* 은행주 bank stock.

ŭnhonshik 은혼식 silver wedding (anniversary).

ŭnhye 은혜 favor; benefit; grace.

unim 운임 ① fare ② freight rates (*Am.*); goods rates; freightage; shipping charge[expenses].

ŭnin 은인 benefactor; patron.

unjŏn 운전. *unjŏnhada* 운전하다 drive; operate. *unjŏn kisa* 운전 기사 driver; chauffeur.

ŭnmak 은막 (silver) screen; filmdom.

unmyŏng 운명 fate; destiny; fortune; one's lot.

ŭnŏ 은어 secret language; jargon; argot; cant.

ŭnpit 은빛 silver (color). *ŭnpich'ŭi* 은빛의 silver-colored; silvery.

ŭnsa 은사 hermit; recluse.

ŭnsa 은사 one's (respected) teacher; one's former teacher.

ŭnt'oe 은퇴 retirement. *ŭnt'oehada* 은퇴하다 retire.

unyŏng 운영 operation; management. *unyŏnghada* 운영하다 manage; run; operate.

up'yo 우표 postage-stamp; stamp.

up'yŏn 우편 post(*Eng.*);mail(*Am.*). *up'yŏn paedalbu* 우편 배달부 mailman.

uri 우리 we. *uriŭi* 우리의 our. *uriege* 우리에게 us. *urirŭl* 우리를 us.

uri 우리 cage; pen; fold; corral.

ŭriŭrihada 으리으리하다 (be) magnificent; majestic; stately; be overawed (by); gorgeously.

uroe 우뢰 thunder. *uroe kat'ŭn* 우뢰 같은 thunderous.

urŏnada 우러나다 soak out; come off; draw.

urong 우롱 mockery; derision. *uronghada* 우롱하다 mock (at); fool; make fun[a fool] of.

urŏngch'ada 우렁차다 (be) resounding; resonant.

urŏrŏboda 우러러보다 look up (at); look upward.

ŭrŭda 으르다 threaten; menace; intimidate.

urŭm 울음 crying; weeping. *urŭmŭl t'ŏttŭrida* 울음을 터뜨리다 burst out crying.

ŭrŭrŏnggŏrida 으르렁거리다 roar; growl; howl.

ŭrye 으레 habitually; usually; all the time.

uryŏ 우려 worry; anxiety; fear. *uryŏhada* 우려하다 worry over; be anxious about.

usan 우산 umbrella. *usanŭl ssŭda* 우산을 쓰다 put up[raise] an umbrella.

usang 우상 idol; image. *usanghwahada* 우상화하다 idolize. *usang sungbae* 우상 숭배 idol worship.

use 우세 superiority; predominance. *usehada* 우세 하다 (be) superior; predominant.

usŏn 우선 first (of all); in the first place.

usu 우수. *usuhan* 우수한 good; excellent; superior.

usŭgae 우스개 jocularity. *usŭgaessori* 우스갯소리 joke; jest; fun; pleasantry.

usŭm 웃음 laugh; laughter; smile; ridicule.

usŭng 우승 victory; championship. *usŭnghada* 우 승하다 win the championship.

usŭpta 우습다 (be) funny; amusing; laughable.

ŭsŭsŭ 으스스. *ŭsŭsŭhan* 으스스한 chilly; chill; be thrilled.

utta 웃다 ① laugh; smile; chuckle; grim ② laugh 〔sneer〕 at; ridicule; jeer at.

uttuk 우뚝 high; aloft. *uttuk'ada* 우뚝하다 (be) high; lofty; towering.

ŭttŭm 으뜸 first; top; head. *ŭttŭmganŭn* 으뜸가 는 the first; the best; top; leading.

uul 우울. *uurhan* 우울한 melancholy; gloomy.

uyŏl 우열 superiority and inferiority. *uyŏrŭl ta- t'uda* 우열을 다투다 vie for superiority.

uyŏn 우연 chance; accident. *uyŏnhan* 우연한 cas- ual; accidental; unexpected. *uyŏnhi* 우연히 acci- dentally; by chance〔accident〕; incidental.

uyu 우유 (cow's) milk. *punmal uyu* 분말 우유 milk powder.

⸻◈⸻ W ⸻◈⸻

wae 왜 why; how; for what reason.

waejŏng 왜정 Japanese rule. *waejŏng shidae* 왜정 시대 Japanese administration period.

waeshik 왜식 Japanese food. *waeshikchip* 왜식집 Japanese restaurant.

wagŭlgŏrida 와글거리다 ① throng; swarm; crowd ② be clamorous; noisy.

wanch'i 완치. *wanch'idoeda* 완치되다 be completely cured〔recovered〕.

wandu 완두 pea. *p'udwandu* 풋완두 green pea.

wang 왕 king; monarch. *wangŭi* 왕의 royal.

wangbok 왕복 going and returning; round trip. *wangbok'ada* 왕복하다 go and return. *wangbok ch'ap'yo* 왕복 차표 return ticket.

wangbi 왕비 queen; empress.

wanggung 왕궁 king's〔royal〕 palace.

wanggwan 왕관 crown.

wangja 왕자 (Royal, Imperial) prince.

wangjin 왕진 doctor's visit (to a patient). *wangjinhada* 왕진하다 call on one's patient.

wangjo 왕조 dynasty. *wangjoŭi* 왕조의 dynastic.

wan-go 완고 obstinacy; stubbornness. *wan-gohan* 완고한 stubborn; obstinate.

wangshil 왕실 royal family〔household〕.

wanjang 완장 armband; brassard.

wanjŏn 완전 perfection; completeness. *wanjŏnhan* 〔*hi*〕 완전한〔히〕 perfect〔ly〕; complete〔ly〕.

wannap 완납 full payment. *wannap'ada* 완납하다 pay in full.

wansŏng 완성 completion; perfection; accomplishment. *wansŏnghada* 완성하다 complete; accomplish; finish.

wennil 웬일 what matter; what business. *wenni-*

rinya 웬일이냐? what is the matter?

wi 위 stomach.

wi 위 upside; upper part. *wiŭi* 위의 upper; upward. *wie* 위에 above; over; on; upon.

wiban 위반 violation. *wibanhada* 위반하다 violate; disobey; break; be against.

wibŏp 위법 violation of law. *wibŏbŭi* 위법의 illegal; unlawful.

wich'i 위치 situation; location; position; place; site. *wich'ihada* 위치하다 be situated[located].

wich'uk 위축 withering. *wich'uk'ada* 위축하다 ① wither (away); shrink; dwindle ② be daunted.

widae 위대 greatness; mightiness. *widaehan* 위대한 great; mighty; grand.

wido 위도 latitude. *widoŭi* 위도의 latitudinal.

widok 위독. *widok'ada* 위독하다 (be) serious; critical; be seriously ill.

wigi 위기 crisis; critical moment.

wihada 위하다 do for the sake of; respect; value. *wihayŏ* 위하여 for; for the sake of.

wihŏm 위험 danger; peril; risk. *wihŏmhan* 위험한 dangerous; perilous.

wihyŏp 위협 menace; threat; intimidation. *wihyŏp'ada* 위협하다 menace; threaten; frighten.

wiim 위임 trust; commission; charge. *wiimhada* 위임하다 entrust; delegate to.

wiin 위인 great man; hero; mastermind.

wijang 위장 stomach and intestines.

wijo 위조 forgery; fabrication. *wijohada* 위조하다 forge; counterfeit. *wijochoe* 위조죄 forgery.

wimun 위문 consolation; consolatory visit. *wimunhada* 위문하다 console.

wiro 위로 consolation; solace; comfort. *wirohada* 위로하다 console; comfort.

wiryŏk 위력 great power; mighty force.

wisaeng 위생 hygiene; sanitation. *wisaengjŏk* 위생적 sanitary; hygienic.

wishin 위신 prestige; dignity; authority.

wisŏn 위선 hypocrisy. *wisŏnja* 위선자 hypocrite.

wisŏng 위성 satellite. *wisŏngguk* 위성국 satellite state. *wisŏng chungge* 위성 중계 satellite telecast.

wiwon 위원 member of a committee. *wiwonhoe* 위원회 committee; commission.

wolbu 월부 monthly instalment[payment].

wolbuk 월북. *wolbuk'ada* 월북하다 go to North Korea.

wolgan 월간 monthly publication. *wolganŭi* 월간의 monthly. *wolgan chapchi* 월간 잡지 monthly (magazine.).

wolgŭp 월급 monthly salary[pay].

wolgyŏng 월경 menstruation; menses[flowers].

wollam 월남. *wollamhada* 월남하다 come down to South Korea.

wolli 원리 principle; theory. [timer.

wollo 원로 elder statesman; senior (member); old-

wollyŏ 원료 raw material; materials.

wolmal 월말. *wolmare[kkaji]* 월말에[까지] at[by] the end of the month.

wolse 월세 monthly rent.

wolsegye 월세계 lunar world; moon.

won 원 desire; wish. *wonhada* 원하다 desire; wish.

wonbon 원본 original(work; copy; text; document).

wonch'ik 원칙 principle; fundamental rule[law]; general rule.

wondongnyŏk 원동력 motive power[force].

won-gi 원기 vigo(u)r; energy; vitality; spirits.

won-go 원고 manuscript (MS.); copy; draft. *wongoryo* 원고료 copy money; contribution fee.

won-go 원고 accuser; plaintiff.

won-gŭm 원금 capital; principal.

wonhan 원한 grudge; bitter feeling; spite.

wonhyŏng 원형 archetype; prototype; model.

wonin 원인 cause; origin. *wonin-gwa kyŏlgwa* 원인과 결과 cause and effect.

wonja 원자 atom. *wonjaryŏk* 원자력 atomic energy. *wonja p'okt'an* 원자 폭탄 atom(ic) bomb; A-bomb.

wonjang 원장 director[president; superintendent] (of a hospital; an institution).

wonjo 원조 help; support; assistance; aid. *wonjohada* 원조하다 assist; help; support.

wonjŏng 원정 playing tour; expedition; visit.

wonka 원가 (prime) cost; cost price.

wonman 원만. *wonmanhan* 원만한 amicable; smooth; peaceful. *wonmanhi* 원만히 amicably; harmoniously; smoothly.

wonmang 원망 grudge; resentment. *wonmanghada* 원망하다 reproach; bear a grudge against.

wonŏ 원어 original language[word].

wonsaek 원색 primary color; original color(s).

wonshi 원시. *wonshijŏgin* 원시적인 primitive. *wonshi shidae* 원시 시대 primitive times.

wonsŏ 원서 (written) application; application form.

wonsu 원수 chief of state; sovereign; ruler.

wonsu 원수 general of the army; fleet admiral (*Am.*); (field) marshal; admiral of the fleet (*Eng.*).

wonsungi 원숭이 monkey; ape.
woryoil 월요일 Monday.

～⋘ **Y** ⋙～

ya 야 Oh, dear!; O my!; Hey (you)!; Hi; Hello.
yabi 야비. yabihan 야비한 vulgar; mean; coarse.
yach'ae 야채 vegetables; greens. *yach'ae kage* 야채 가게 greengrocery.
yadam 야담 unofficial historical romance[story].
yadang 야당 opposition party.
yagan 야간 night; night time. *yaganŭi* 야간의 night; nocturnal. *yagane* 야간에 at night.
yagollida 약올리다 make (a person) angry; fret; irritate; provoke.
yagu 야구 baseball. *yagu kyŏnggi* 야구 경기 baseball game. *yakujang* 야구장 baseball ground; ball park.
yagŭn 야근 night duty; night work. *yagŭnhada* 야근하다 take night duty; be on night work.
yahoe 야회 evening party. *yahoebok* 야회복 evening dress[suit].
yak 약 medicine; remedy; drug. *yakpang* 약방 drugstore; pharmacy.
yak 약 about; some; nearly; around (*Am.*).
yak'ada 약하다 (be) weak; frail; delicate; faint. *yak'age* 약하게 weakly; feebly; faintly.
yak'ada 약하다. →**saengnyak'ada** 생략하다.
yakcha 약자 the weak; weak person.
yakcha 약자 simplified character.
yakche 약제 drugs; medicine. *yakchesa* 약제사 druggist; pharmacist (*Am.*); chemist (*Eng.*).

yakch'o 약초 medical herbs[plants].

yakchŏm 약점 weak point; disadvantage; one's blind side; weakness.

yakchu 약주 ① rice wine ② medicinal liquor.

yakkap 약값 charge for medicine; medical[drug] fee; pharmacy's bill.

yakkan 약간 some; little; bit; few; somewhat.

yakkuk 약국 pharmacy; drugstore (*Am.*); chemist's shop (*Eng.*).

yak'on 약혼 engagment; betrothal. *yak'onhada* 약혼하다 engage oneself to; getengaged. *yak'on panji* 약혼반지 engagement ring.

yakpang 약방. → **yakkuk** 약국.

yakp'um 약품 medicines; drugs; chemicals.

yakso 약소. *yaksohan* 약소한 small and weak. *yakso kukka* 약소 국가 lesser[minor] power.

yaksok 약속 promise; engagement. *yaksok'ada* 약속하다 promise. *yaksogŭl chik'ida* 약속을 지키다 keep one's promise.

yaksom 약솜 sanitary cotton. →**t'alchimyŏn** 탈지면.

yakt'al 약탈 plunder; pillage. *yakt'arhada* 약탈하다 plunder; loot; sack; strip.

yakto 약도 rough sketch; sketch map.

yalgutta 얄궂다 (be) perverse; eccentric; queer. *yalgujŭn saram* 얄궂은 사람 queer[odd] fish.

yalmipta 얄밉다 (be) offensive; hateful; detestable.

yaman 야만. *yamanjŏk* 야만적 savage; barbarous. *yamanin* 야만인 barbarian; savage.

yamang 야망 personal ambition; aspiration.

yamjŏnhada 얌전하다 (be) gentle; well-behaved; modest. *yamjŏnhi* 얌전히 gently; modestly.

yamujida 야무지다 (be) stout; sturdy; staunch.

yamujige 야무지게 firmly; steadily.

yang 양 sheep; lamb. *yanggajuk* 양가죽 sheepskin. *yanggogi* 양고기 mutton. *yangt'ŏl* 양털 wool.

yang 양 quantity; amount; volume.

yangban 양반 nobility; nobleman. *chuin yangban* 주인 양반 master (of a house).

yangbo 양보 concession; compromise. *yangbohada* 양보하다 concede (to); make a concession.

yangbok 양복 Western[European] clothes. *yangbok-chŏm* 양복점 tailor; tailor's (shop); slopshop.

yangbuin 양부인 →**yanggalbo** 양갈보.

yangbun 양분 nourishment; nutriment.

yangch'in 양친 parents. *yangch'inŭi* 양친의 parents.

yangch'o 양초 candle; taper.

yangch'ŏl 양철 galvanized iron; tin plate. *yang-ch'ŏl chibung* 양철 지붕 tin roof.

yangdo 양도 transfer; conveyance. *yangdohada* 양도하다 transfer (to); convey.

yangdon 양돈 hog[pig]-farming. *yangdonhada* 양돈하다 raise[rear] hogs.

yanggalbo 양갈보 foreigners' whore.

yanggok 양곡 corn; grain; cereals; provisions. *yanggoksang* 양곡상 grainmerchant.

yanggung 양궁 western-style archery.

yanggwaja 양과자 Western confectionary[cakes].

yanggye 양계 poultry farming; chicken raising. *yanggyehada* 양계하다 raise poultry.

yanghae 양해 understanding; comprehension. *yang-haehada* 양해하다 understand; comprehend.

yanghwa 양화 →**kudu** 구두. *yanghwajŏm* 양화점 shoe store.

yangja 양자 foster child; adopted son.

yangjae 양재 dressmaking. *yangjaesa* 양재사 dressmaker.

yangjang 양장 foreign[Western] style of dress. *yangjanghada* 양장하다 be dressed in Western style. *yangjangjŏm* 양장점 dressmaker's (shop).

yangjo 양조 brewing; brewage; distillation. *yangjohada* 양조하다 brew; distill.

yangju 양주 foreign wine[liquors].

yangmal 양말 socks; stockings.

yangmo 양모 wool. *yangmoŭi* 양모의 woolen.

yangmul 약물 drugstuffs; medicines. *yangmul chungdok* 약물 중독 medical poisoning.

yangmyŏn 양면 both faces[sides]. *yangmyŏnŭi* 양면의 double[both]-sided.

yangnyŏ 양녀 foster daughter; adopted daughter.

yangnyŏm 양념 spices; flavo(u)r; seasoning; condiments.

yangnyŏk 양력 solar calendar.

yangnyŏk 약력 brief (personal) history[record].

yangok 양옥 Western-style house.

yangp'um 양품 foreign articles[goods]. *yangp'umjŏm* 양품점 fancy(-goods) store.

yangsan 양산 parasol. *yangsanŭl p'yŏda[chŏpta, ssŭda]* 양산을 펴다[접다, 쓰다] open[close, put-up] a parasol.

yangshik 양식 form; style; mode. *saenghwal yangshik* 생활 양식 style[mode] of living.

yangshik 양식 Western[European] style.

yangshik 양식 Western food; foreign dishes; foreign cookery. *yangshikchŏm* 양식점 foreign-style[Western] restaurant.

yangshik 양식 provisions; food. *yangshigŭl taeda*

양식을 대다 provide (a person) with food.

yangshim 양심 conscience. *yangshimŭi kach'aek*
양심의 가책 pangs[pricks] of conscience.

yangsŏ 양서 foreign[Western] book.

yangsŏ 양서 good book; valuable work.

yangt'anja 양탄자 carpet; rug. *yangt'anjarŭl kkalda* 양탄자를 깔다 spread a carpet[rug].

yangtchok 양쪽 both sides; either side. *yangtchogŭi* 양쪽의 both; either.

yaoe 야외 field; open air. *yaoeŭi* 야외의 outdoor; open air. *yaoe-esŏ* 야외에서 in the open air.

yarŭt'ada 야릇하다 (be) queer; odd; curious.

yashim 야심 ambition; designs; treason; treachery. *yashimjŏk* 야심적 ambitious.

yasu 야수 wild beast. *yasu kat'ŭn* 야수 같은 beastly; brutal.

yatchapta 얕잡다. →**yatpoda** 얕보다.

yatpoda 얕보다 look down on[upon]; make light of; despise; neglect; hold in contempt.

yatta 얕다 (be) shallow. *yat'ŭn kaeul[kŭrŭt, mot]* 얕은 개울[그릇, 못] shallow stream[dish, pond].

yawida 야위다 →**yŏwida** 여위다.

yayŏng 야영 camp; camping. *yayŏnghada* 야영하다 camp (out); encamp.

yayu 야유 picnic; outing. *yayuhoe* 야유회 picnic party.

yayu 야유 banter; jeer. *yayuhada* 야유하다 banter; make fun of; tease; chaff; rally. 「dent.

ye 예 instance; example; practice; custom; prece-

yebae 예배 worship; church service. *yebaedang* 예배당 chapel. *yebaeja* 예배자 worshipper.

yebang 예방 prevention; protection. *yebanghada*

예방하다 prevent; keep off; protect. *yebang chusa* 예방 주사 preventive injection.

yebi 예비 preparation; reserve. *yebihada* 예비하다 prepare[provide] for.

yebo 예보 forecast(ing). *yebohada* 예보하다 forecast; predict. *ilgi yebo* 일기 예보 weather forecast.

yebok 예복 full-dress; ceremonial dress.

yegam 예감 premonition; presentiment. *yegami tŭlda* 예감이 들다 have a presentiment (of).

yego 예고 advance[previous] notice. *yegohada* 예고하다 announce[inform] beforehand.

yegŭm 예금 deposit; bank account. *yegŭmhada* 예금하다 deposit money.

yejŏng 예정 plan; program; schedule. *yejŏngdaero* 예정대로 according to program.

yekwa 예과 preparatory course. *taehak yekwa* 대학 예과 preparatory course of a college.

yemae 예매 advance sale. *yemaehada* 예매하다 sell (ticket) in advance.

yennal 옛날 ancient times; old days. *yennare* 옛날에 once upon a time.

yennil 옛일 things of the past; bygones; past event.

yeoe 예외 exception. *yeoeŭi* 예외의 exceptional.

yeŏn 예언 prophecy; prediction.

yeppŭda 예쁘다 (be) pretty; lovely; shapely; nice.

yeri 예리. *yerihan* 예리한 sharp; acute; keen.

yesan 예산 estimate; budget.

yesang 예상 expectation; forecast; anticipation. *yesanghada* 예상하다 expect; foresee. *yesang oero* 예상 외로 beyond all expectations.

yesŏn 예선 ① previsional elect; pre-election ② preliminary (contest); tryout (*Am.*).

yŏltŭng 열등 inferiority. *yŏltŭnggam* 열등감 inferiority complex.

yŏmbul 염불 Buddhist invocation[prayer].

yŏmch'i 염치 sense of honor[shame]. *yŏmch'iga ŏpta* 염치가 없다 be shameless.

yŏmju 염주 rosary. *yŏmjual* 염주알 bead.

yŏmmosŭp 옆모습 profile; side face.

yŏmnyŏ 염려 anxiety; worry; care. *yŏmnyŏhada* 염려하다 be[feel] anxious about; worry.

yŏmsaek 염색 dyeing. *yŏmsaek'ada* 염색하다 dye.

yŏmso 염소 goat.

yŏnae 연애 love; amour. *yŏnaehada* 연애하다 be [fall] in love with; lose one's heart to.

yŏnan 연안 coast; shore. *yŏnane* 연안에 on[along] the coast. *yŏnanŭi* 연안의 coastal.

yŏnbang 연방 federal state; union; confederation; commonwealth.

yŏnbong 연봉 annual[yearly] salary.

yŏnch'ak 연착 late arrival; delay. *yŏnch'ak'ada* 연착하다 arrive late; be delayed[overdue].

yŏnch'ul 연출 production. *yŏnch'urhada* 연출하다 produce; perform; represent.

yŏndae 연대 regiment. *yŏndaejang* 연대장 regimental commander.

yŏndae 연대 age; epoch; era. *yŏndaep'yo* 연대표 chronological table.

yŏndan 연단 platform; rostrum.

yŏndara 연달아 one after another; successively.

yŏndusaek 연두색 yellow green.

yŏng 영 zero; nought. *iltae yŏngŭro* 1 대 0 으로 by score of one to zero.

yŏng 영 spirit; soul. *yŏngtchŏgin* 영적인 spiritual.

yŏn-gam 연감 yearbook; annual.

yŏngcha 영자 English letter. *yŏngcha shinmun* 영자 신문 English newspaper.

yongdo 용도 use; service. *yongdoga mant'a* 용도가 많다 have various[many] uses.

yonggam 용감 bravery. *yonggamhan[hi]* 용감한 [히] brave[ly]; heroic[ally].

yŏnggam 영감 inspiration; brain wave.

yonggi 용기 courage; bravery. *yonggi innŭn* 용기 있는 courageous; brave.

yonggi 용기 instrument; tool.

yonggu 용구 tool; instrument; appliance.

yŏnggu 영구 coffin; hearse; casket. *yŏngguch'a* 영구차 funeral car; (motor) hearse.

yŏnggu 영구. *yŏngguhi* 영구히 eternally; forever; permanently.

yŏngguk 영국 England; (Great) Britain; United Kingdom. *yŏnggugŭi* 영국의 English; British. *yŏnggugin* 영국인 Englishman; the English.

yŏnggwang 영광 hono(u)r; glory. *yŏnggwang-sŭrŏun* 영광스러운 glorious; honorable.

yŏngha 영하 below zero; sub-zero.

yŏnghan 영한 English-Korean. *yonghan sajŏn* 영한 사전 English-Korean dictionary.

yŏnghon 영혼 soul; spirit.

yŏnghwa 영화 movie; (motion) picture; film. *yŏnghwa paeu* 영화 배우 movie actor[actress]. *yŏnghwagwan* 영화관 movie theatre; cinema.

yŏnghwa 영화 glory. *yŏnghwaropta* 영화롭다 be glorious; pompous.

yŏnghyang 영향 influence; effect. *yŏnghyangŭl mich'ida* 영향을 미치다 influence; affect.

yongi 용이. *yongihan* 용이한 easy; simple. *yongihage* 용이하게 easily; readily; with ease.

yon-gi 연기 smoke. *yŏn-giga nanŭn* 연기가 나는 smoky; smoking.

yŏn-gi 연기 performance; acting; playing. *yŏn-gija* 연기자 performer; actor.

yŏn-gi 연기 postponement; deferment. *yŏn-gihada* 연기하다 postpone; put off; adjourn; suspend.

yongji 용지 paper (to use); (blank) form; printed form; blank (*Am.*).

yŏngjŏn 영전 promotion. *yŏngjŏnhada* 영전하다 be promoted to; be transferred[raised] to.

yŏngju 영주 permanent residence. *yŏngjuhada* 영주하다 reside permanently; settle down.

yongmang 욕망 desire; ambition; wants.

yŏngmi 영미 Britain and America. *yŏngmiŭi* 영미의 English and American; Anglo-American.

yongmo 용모 face; looks; features.

yongmu 용무 business; matter of business.

yŏngmun 영문 English (writing); English sentence.

yŏngni 영리. *yŏngnihan* 영리한 wise; clever; smart; bright.

yongnyang 용량 capacity; volume.

yongŏ 용어 term; terminology. *chŏnmun yongŏ* 전문 용어 technical terms.

yŏngŏ 영어 English; English language. *yŏngŏŭi* 영어의 English. *yŏngŏro* 영어로 in English.

yŏngŏp 영업 business; trade. *yŏngŏp'ada* 영업하다 do[carry on] business.

yŏn-gŏp'u 연거푸 continuously; successively.

yongpŏp 용법 way to use; usage; direction for use.

yongp'um 용품 supplies; article. *kajŏng yongp'um*

가정 용품 household goods.

yongsa 용사 brave man; warrior; hero.

yŏngsa 영사 consul. *yŏngsagwan* 영사관 consulate.

yŏngshi 영시 English poetry; English poem.

yongsŏ 용서 pardon; forgiveness. *yŏngsŏhada* 용서하다 pardon; forgive; excuse.

yŏngsu 영수 receipt. *yŏngsuhada* 영수하다 receive. *yŏngsujŭng* 영수증 receipt.

yŏngchang 영장 warrant; writ. *kusok yŏngchang* 구속 영장 warrant of arrest.

yŏngt'o 영토 territory; domain.

yongton 용돈 pocket money; spending money.

yŏn-gu 연구 study; research. *yŏn-guhada* 연구하다 (make a) study; investigate.

yŏn-gŭk 연극 play; drama. *yŏn-gŭgŭl hada* 연극을 하다 play; act (a play).

yŏn-gŭm 연금 annuity; pension.

yŏngung 영웅 hero. *yŏngungjŏgin* 영웅적인 heroic.

yŏngwon 영원 eternity; permanence. *yŏngwonhan* [*hi*] 영원한[히] eternal[ly].

yŏngyang 영양 nourishment; nutrition.

yŏn-gyŏl 연결 connection. *yŏn-gyŏrhada* 연결하다 connect; attach; join.

yŏnha 연하. *yŏnhachang* 연하장 New Year's card.

yŏnhada 연하다 ① (be) tender; soft ② (be) light. *yŏnhan pitkkal* 연한 빛깔 light color.

yŏnhap 연합 combination; incorporation; alliance. *yŏnhap'ada* 연합하다 combine; join; union.

yŏnhoe 연회 feast; banquet; dinner party.

yŏnin 연인 sweetheart; lover.

yŏnjang 연장 tool; inplement; utensil.

yŏnjang 연장 extension. *yŏnjanghada* 연장하다

extend; lengthen; prolong; continue.

yŏnju 연주 musical performance. *yŏnjuhada* 연주 하다 perform; play. *yŏnjuhoe* 연주회 concert.

yŏnmaeng 연맹 league; federation; union.

yŏnmal 연말 end of the year; year-end.

yŏnmibok 연미복 tail coat; evening coat.

yŏnmot 연못 lotus pond; pond.

yŏnp'il 연필 (lead) pencil. *yŏnp'ilkkakki* 연필깎이 pencil sharpener.

yŏnsa 연사 speaker; orator.

yŏnsang 연상 association (of ideas). *yŏnsanghada* 연상하다 asssociate; be reminded (of).

yŏnsok 연속 continuity; continuation. *yŏnsok'ada* 연속하다 continue; last.

yŏnsŏl 연설 (public) speech; address. *yŏnsŏrhada* 연설하다 make a speech.

yŏnsŭp 연습 practice; exercise; training. *yŏnsŭp'ada* 연습하다 practice; exercise.

yŏnt'an 연탄 briquet. *yŏnt'an kasŭ chungdok* 연탄 가스 중독 briquet gas poisoning.

yŏp 옆 side; flank. *yŏp'ŭi* 옆의 side; next; adjoining. *yŏp'esŏ* 옆에서 by the side (of); by. *yŏp'ŭro* 옆으로 on[to] one side; aside.

yŏpchip 옆집 next door[house]; neighboring house. *yŏpchip saram* 옆집 사람 neighbor.

yŏpch'ong 엽총 hunting gun; shotgun.

yŏpkil 옆길 byroad; sideway.

yŏpkuri 옆구리 flank; side (of the chest).

yopŏp 요법 remedy; cure. *min-gan yopŏp* 민간 요법 folk remedy.

yŏpsŏ 엽서 postcard; postal card.

yoram 요람 survey; outline; handbook; manual.

yori 요리 ① cooking; cookery ② dish; food; fare.
yorisa 요리사 cook. *yorichip* 요리집 restaurant.
yŏrŏ 여러 many; several; various.
yŏrŏbŏn 여러번 often; several[many] times; repeatedly; over and over again.
yŏrŏkaji 여러 가지 various; all kinds of; several.
yorŏn 요런 such; this; like this.
yŏron 여론 public[general] opinion. *yŏron chosa*
여론 조사 public opinion poll[survey].
yŏrŭm 여름 summer; summertime.
yoryŏng 요령 (main) point; essentials. *yoryŏng*
innŭn 요령 있는 sensible; pointed. *yoryŏng ŏmnŭn*
요령 없는 pointless; vague.
yŏryu 여류 lady; woman; female. *yŏryu shiin* 여
류 시인[작가] poetess[authoress]. *yŏryu pihaengsa*
여류 비행사 woman aviator.
yŏsa 여사 Lady; Madame; Mrs.; Miss. *Kim yŏsa*
김여사 Mrs.[Miss] Kim; Madame Kim.
yosae 요새 fortress; stronghold; fortification.
yosae 요새 recently; lately; these days.
yŏsaeng 여생 rest[remainder] of one's life.
yŏsamuwon 여사무원 office girl; female clerk.
yoso 요소 element; factor; essential part.
yŏsŏng 여성 womanhood; women. *yŏsŏngŭi* 여성
의 female. *yŏsŏngyongŭi* 여성용의 for ladies' use.
yŏsŏt 여섯 six. *yŏsŏtchae* 여섯째 the sixth.
yosul 요술 magic; witchcraft; sorcery. *yosul-*
jangi 요술장이 magician; sorcerer.
yŏt'aekkaji 여태까지 till[until] now; up to the
present; by this time; hitherto.
yŏtpoda 엿보다 watch[look] for; spy on; steal a
glance at.

yŏttŭtta 엿듣다 overhear; eavesdrop; listen secretly.

yŏŭida 여의다 lose [be bereaved of] one's parents [husband, wife, etc.].

yŏwang 여왕 queen. *sagyogyeŭi yŏwang* 사교계의 여왕 queen of society.

yŏwida 여위다 grow thin[lean]. *yŏwin* 여윈 thin; lean; skinny; slender.

yŏu 여우 fox. *yŏu kat'ŭn* 여우 같은 foxy; sly.

yoyak 요약. summary; digest. *yoyak'ada* 요약하다 summarize; epitomize; abridge.

yoyang 요양 recuperation. *yoyanghada* 요양하다 recuperate; receive medical treatment. *yoyangso* 요양소 sanatorium; sanitarium (*Am.*).

yŏyu 여유 surplus; room. *yŏyuga itta* 여유가 있다 have in reserve; have time[money] to spare.

yua 유아 baby; infant; child[children].

yubang 유방 (woman's) breast(s).

yuch'ang 유창. *yuch'anghan* 유창한 fluent; flowing; smooth; eloquent. *yuch'anghage* 유창하게 fluently; smoothly.

yuch'i 유치. *yuch'ihan* 유치한 infantile; childish; crude; immature. *yuch'iwŏn* 유치원 kindergarten.

yudo 유도 judo.

yuga 육아 childcare; nursing; child-rearing.

yugajok 유가족 bereaved family.

yugam 유감 regret; pity. *yugamsŭrŏun* 유감스러운 regrettable; deplorable; pitiful.

yugi 유기 abandonment; desertion. *yugihada* 유기하다 abandon; desert; leave.

yugoe 유괴 kidnap(p)ing; abduction. *yugoehada* 유괴하다 abduct; kidnap; carry off.

yugyo 유교 Confucianism.

yuhae 유해 remains of the dead.

yuhaeng 유행 fashion; vogue. *yuhaenghada* 유행 하다 be in fashion[vogue]; prevail; be prevalent.

yuhak 유학 studying abroad. *yuhak'ada* 유학하다 study abroad; go abroad to study.

yuhok 유혹 temptation; lure. *yuhok'ada* 유혹하다 tempt; allure; entice; seduce.

yuhwa 유화 oil painting[color].

yuhyo 유효 validity; efficiency. *yuhyohada* 유효하 다 be effective; hold good; remain valid. *yuhyohage* 유효하게 effectively; efficiently.

yuik 유익. *yuik'an* 유익한 profitable; beneficial. *yuik'age* 유익하게 usefully; profitably.

yuim 유임 remaining in office. *yuimhada* 유임하 다 remain[continue] in office.

yuin 유인 temptation; allurement. *yuinhada* 유인 하다 tempt; induce; invite; attract.

yujok 유족 →**yugajok** 유가족.

yujŏk 유적 remains; relics; ruins; historic spots.

yujŏn 유전 oil field.

yujŏn 유전 heredity. *yujŏnhada* 유전하다 be inherited; run in the blood.

yuk 육 six; *che yuk* 제6 the sixth.

yuk'aegonggun 육해공군 army[land], navy[sea], and air force; armed forces.

yukch'e 육체 flesh; body. *yukch'eŭi[jŏk]* 육체의 [적] bodily; physical.

yukchi 육지 land; shore.

yukkak 육각 sexangle; hexagon.

yukkam 육감 the sixth sense.

yukkun 육군 army; miltary service. *yukkunŭi* 육

군의 military.

yuksang 육상 land; ground. *yuksang kyŏnggi* 육상 경기 athletic sports. 「sixtieth.

yukship 육십〔60〕 sixty. *che yukship* 제 60 the

yuk'wae 유쾌. *yuk'waehan* 유쾌한 pleasant; joyful; cheerful; jolly.

yukwonja 유권자 voter; elector.

yul 율 rate; ratio; proportion. *t'up'yo〔samang, ch'ulsan〕yul* 투표 〔사망, 출산〕율 voting〔death, birth〕 rate.

yulli 윤리 ethics; morals. *yullijŏk* 윤리적 ethical; moral.

yultong 율동 rhythm; rhythmic movement.

yumang 유망. *yumanghan* 유망한 promising; hopeful.

yumul 유물 relic; remains.

yumyŏng 유명. *yumyŏnghan* 유명한 famous; noted; renowned; notorious.

yundal 윤달 leap〔intercalary〕 month.

yungdan 융단 carpet; rug.

yungno 육로 overland〔land〕 route. *yungnoro* 육로로 by land; overland.

yungt'ongsŏng 융통성. *yungt'ongsŏng innŭn* 융통성 있는 adaptable; versatile; flexible.

yun-gwak 윤곽 outline; contour; general idea.

yunhwa 윤화 traffic〔car〕 accident.

yunŭng 유능. *yunŭnghan* 유능한 able; capable; competent; talented.

yuŏn 유언 will; testament; last words. *yuŏnhada* 유언하다 make〔leave〕 a will.

yup'a 유파 school; sect.

yurae 유래 origin; history; source. *yuraehada* 유

래하다 originate (in).

yuram 유람 sightseeing; excursion. *yuramhada* 유람하다 go sightseeing.

yurang 유랑 vagrancy; roaming. *yuranghada* 유랑하다 roam[wander, rove] about.

yuri 유리. *yurihan* 유리한 profitable; advantageous. *yurihage* 유리하게 profitably.

yurin 유린. *yurinhada* 유린하다 violate; infringe upon; trample; overrun; devastate.

yuryŏk 유력. *yuryŏk'an* 유력한 powerful; influential; strong; leading.

yuryŏng 유령 ghost; specter; apparition.

yusa 유사 similarity; resemblance; likeness; analogy. *yusahada* 유사하다 be similar (to).

yusan 유산 abortion. *yusanhada* 유산하다 miscarry; abort; produce abortion.

yusan 유산 inheritance; legacy; bequest.

yuse 유세 canvassing; stump-speaking (*Am.*). *yusehada* 유세하다 go canvassing; stump.

yushik 유식. *yushik'an* 유식한 learned; educated; well-informed.

yusŏ 유서 (written) will; testament; suicide note.

yut 윷 Four-Stick Game; Yut.

yut'an 유탄 stray bullet[shot].

yuŭi 유의. *yuŭihada* 유의하다 bear[keep] in mind; care about; be mindful of; take care[notice].

yuwol 유월 June.

yuwonji 유원지 amusement park; resort.

yuyong 유용. *yuyonghan* 유용한 useful; valuable; serviceable.

yuyong 유용 diversion. *yuyonghada* 유용하다 divert; misappropriate; apply to.

HANGŬL WRITING MODELS

Perpendicular strokes are written from top to bottom; horizontals from left to right. (Read these charts left and down.)

ㄱ k(g)	ㅌ t'	아 a	애 yae
ㄴ n	ㅍ p'	야 ya	에 e
ㄷ t(d)	ㅎ h	어 ŏ	예 ye
ㄹ r(l)	ㄲ kk	여 yŏ	외 oe
ㅁ m	ㄸ tt	오 o	위 wi
ㅂ p(b)	ㅃ pp	요 yo	의 ŭi
ㅅ s(sh)	ㅆ ss	우 u	와 wa
ㅇ -ng	ㅉ tch	유 yu	워 wo
ㅈ ch(j)		으 ŭ	왜 wae
ㅊ ch'		이 i	웨 we
ㅋ k'		애 ae	